A Companion to
MEDIEVAL ENGLAND
1066—1485

A Companion to
MEDIEVAL ENGLAND
1066—1485

NIGEL SAUL

TEMPUS

This edition first published 2005

Tempus Publishing Limited
The Mill, Brimscombe Port,
Stroud, Gloucestershire, GL5 2QG
www.tempus-publishing.com

British Library Cataloguing in Publication Data.
A catalogue record for this book is available from the British Library.

ISBN 0 7524 2969 8

Typesetting and origination by Tempus Publishing Limited
Printed and bound in Great Britain

CONTENTS

PREFACE

I am grateful to Jonathan Reeve of Tempus Publishing for making possible the reissue of this work. In its original imprint, the Companion had all the hallmarks of a young man's book. While primarily conceived as a compendium of factual material it was yet replete with overly bold youthful judgements. This new edition is a more sober work. The judgements are more measured, and the tone more reflective; the writing is more assured. Most of the entries have been substantially or totally revised. Many have been enlarged, and new ones have been included. Bibliographical references have been revised or extended. There are many more illustrations. I hope that the expanded and revised book will be one of some lasting value.

I am grateful to Caroline Barron for checking some of the entries. I am also grateful to Christopher Dyer for assistance with the illustrations. But my greatest debt is to my wife and family who allowed me the opportunity to revise the book at weekends and in the evenings when I should have been giving my time to them.

Nigel Saul
Royal Holloway, University of London
May 2000

ABOUT THE AUTHOR

Nigel Saul is Professor of Medieval History at Royal Holloway, University of London. He is widely recognised as a leading authority on the history of medieval England. His other books include *The Three Richards*, *The Oxford Illustrated History of Medieval England* and *Richard II*. He lives in Egham, Surrey.

ADVOWSON

The right of a patron to fill a vacant benefice was known as the right of advowson. English law regarded an advowson as a piece of property which, like any other property, could be bought or sold or inherited. If a lord had built a church on his estates, it followed that he and his descendants should enjoy the right of nominating the parson. By the twelfth century, however, the canon lawyers had arrived at a different view. They claimed that a church belonged to the saint to whom it was dedicated, and that cases of disputed patronage should, in the words of Pope Alexander III, 'only be decided by judgement of the Church and settled before an ecclesiastical judge.' In England Henry II (q.v.) rejected this novel interpretation and in the Constitutions of Clarendon restated the older view that disputes over advowsons should be heard in the royal courts. Neither side was ever formally to abandon its position. But in the late 1170s, after Becket's (q.v.) murder, Henry issued a writ prohibiting the hearing in church courts of pleas relating to advowsons, and thereafter the clergy seem tacitly to have accepted that they could do little to stop the king dealing with such cases if he insisted. The Church was less successful in recovering jurisdiction over the filling of benefices in England than it was in other parts of Europe.

AGINCOURT

Agincourt was one of the great English victories of the Hundred Years War. In August 1415 Henry V led an expedition to France in pursuit of his claim to the crown of France. He spent over a month besieging the port of Harfleur and, after capturing it on 22 September, had to consider what to do. He settled on a dash across northern France to Calais – a bold decision in view of his loss of men, but one justified by the knowledge that France was bitterly divided between the Burgundians and the Armagnacs. He hoped the two factions would never unite to challenge him. In the event, however, they did, and near Agincourt on 25 October they forced him to offer battle. The French fielded an army of perhaps 20,000 men, against Henry's 6,000. But their overwhelming numerical superiority was of little assistance to them because they were confined by the surrounding woods to advancing along a narrow front, and then only at a speed that left them an easy prey for the English archers. Agincourt was perhaps the greatest English victory of the Hundred Years War (q.v.), yet strategically it was insignificant. It enabled Henry to return in triumph, but it brought him no nearer to winning the French crown. To do that he had to embark on the systematic conquest of Normandy (q.v.) two years later.

AGRICULTURE

Medieval England, despite growing commercialization, was a predominantly agrarian society. Most of its people lived in the countryside and gained their living from the soil. Patterns of settlement varied from one part of the country to another. The densely settled lowlands of the Midlands and south were characterized by the compact nucleated vill, and the hills and moors of the north and west by dispersed homesteads and farms. It was the classic nucleated vill of the Midland Plain which lay at the centre of the well-known 'open-field' system of cultivation. Evidence relating to the early history of the open fields is sparse and the question of their origins is probably unanswerable. The most that can be said is that charter evidence suggests that the main characteristics of the 'open-field' system were in existence in some parts of England as early as the tenth century. The main characteristics of the 'open-field' system may be described as follows. The arable land of the village was divided into two or three large fields, on which a scheme of crop rotation would be operated. One field would be given over to winter-sown crops, a second to spring-sown crops, and the third left uncultivated, to allow it to recover fertility for the next year's sowing. Each of the fields would be divided into furlongs, and each of the furlongs into strips known as selions. Within each field some of the strips would be held by the tenants of the village and some held 'in demesne' (q.v.) by the manorial lord. Whether the demesne lands were usually scattered indiscriminately through the fields or concentrated in one locality is hard to say in the absence of any number of early maps or surveys. At Cuxham (Oxon), however, a policy of purchase and exchange had succeeded in bringing the demesne arable together into two compact blocks of land. The system of cooperative agriculture that applied to the crop-growing fields applied also to the meadowland, which would similarly be divided into strips.

Like all generalized pictures, this image of open-field agriculture needs to be qualified somewhat. To start with, as we have seen, it applies largely to Midland and southern England. Secondly, the number of fields varied from village to village and from one part of the country to another. There is reason to believe that, under pressure of growing population, in many villages there was a movement from a two- to a three-field system in the thirteenth century: the point being that only a third and not a half of the available arable would then be left fallow each year. Finally, and again possibly as a response to growing population pressure, additional fields were created and brought under cultivation on the edge of the village. These were known as the 'outfields', as opposed to the 'infields' or long-established arable fields nearer the centre of the settlement. It should not be supposed that the outfields necessarily formed a permanent feature of the scene. On the contrary, a possible model would be to visualize a shifting line of cultivation at the margin, as land was brought under the plough whenever it was needed.

What sort of crops were grown on the fields of a medieval village? It used to be thought that the three-field organization of the arable necessarily implied a three-course rotation of crops. In many cases it did. Thus one field would be sown in winter with wheat, another in spring with rye or barley; and the third would be left fallow. But a three-course rotation could be practised on a two-field system, and similarly a four-course one on a three-field system. Cropping schemes could be based on the unit of the furlong rather than of the field, in this way allowing, for example, winter wheat to be sown in one field and a combination of legumes and barley in the next. By the procedure known as 'inhoking', legumes could also be planted in the field which under previous arrangements would be left fallow. Schemes of crop rotation could therefore become quite complex. Indeed, they had to be, if the village were to grow all the crops that it needed – wheat for sale on the open market, barley for brewing, oats for fodder and so on. Crop yields in the Middle Ages, however, were low; indeed, by comparison with modern expectations they were very low. For wheat a likely yield was eight or nine bushels an acre, or little more than a quarter of the expected yield today. Medieval agriculture simply did not have the manures and the technical resources available to the modern farmer to raise productivity, and the soil became exhausted in consequence.

The century which best illustrates the agrarian system described here is the thirteenth. This was the age of so-called 'high farming'. A long period of high prices and low wages, encouraged by the rise in population (q.v.), acted as an inducement to lords to run their demesnes at full capacity. After the Black Death, however, conditions changed. The labour shortage led to a rise in wages. And in the 1370s prices began to fall, and to fall sharply. The movement of prices and wages, in other words, spelled the end of large-scale demesne husbandry as it had been practised in the thirteenth century. Lords who had once been active entrepreneurs now preferred to lease their demesnes, usually in parcels to the tenants of the village. The implications for agrarian society were far-reaching. In the late Middle Ages the market was supplied not by big producers like the Benedictine monasteries but by smaller proprietors who added to their holdings by acquiring parcels of the demesne. By running smaller estates than those of the great landlords they were able to cut overheads, and by preventing their estates from becoming too big they were able to economize on labour. Late medieval agriculture was almost certainly run on more efficient lines than its 'high' medieval predecessor. Land use was probably becoming more varied too. Now

that cereal prices were lower than they had been a century earlier, landowners began to look for other ways of making a profit. Many of them turned to livestock. John Brome of Baddesley Clinton (Warks) specialized in fattening cattle for sale to local butchers and on occasion to London dealers as well. If Brome made his money supplying the meat trade, other landowners made theirs supplying principally the wool and cloth merchants. They turned their lands over to sheep. They did so less because they envisaged large profits – the price of wool was by and large depressed in the late Middle Ages – than because sheep grazing carried fewer hazards than cereal growing. In particular, it was economical on labour at a time when labour was scarce. So sheep, as contemporaries complained, took the place of people. Whole villages disappeared. If any one part of England suffered worse than others from depopulation in the early sixteenth century, it was probably the East Midlands. At Charwelton and Fawsley in Northamptonshire, for example, the existence of a former settlement is testified by the sight of the parish church standing alone in the fields. Striking though the transformation in parts of the Midland landscape may have been, the hardship it caused scarcely justified the complaint that the sheep were eating up the people. The villages that disappeared were ones that were already on the wane. Depopulation was an act of desperation, not of oppression, on the part of landlords.

Studies of Field Systems in the British Isles, ed. A.R.H. Baker and R. Butlin, Cambridge, 1973; *A New Historical Geography of England*, ed. H.C. Darby, Cambridge, 1973; *An Agrarian History of England. II, 1042-1350*, ed. H.E. Hallam, Cambridge, 1988; *An Agrarian History of England. III, 1350-1500*, ed. H.P.R. Finberg, Cambridge, 1991; B.M.S. Campbell, *English Seigniorial Agriculture, 1250-1450*, Cambridge, 2000.

AILRED OF RIEVAULX

The coming of the first Cistercian monks (q.v.) opened a new chapter in the history of northern England. Their simplicity and austerity, their uncompromising rejection of the values of material life, found an ideal setting in the rugged contours of northern society. Among those who responded to the Cistercians' challenge was Ailred, a young man of about twenty-five when in 1134 he encountered the White Monk community recently established by Walter l'Espec, lord of Helmsley, on a site in the Rye valley later to become famous as Rievaulx. Within twenty-four hours Ailred had joined the monks in their life of solitude. The new recruit had spent his younger years at the Scottish court, where he had been a close friend of King David I (q.v. SCOTLAND). In 1143 he was appointed abbot of Revesby (Lincs), a dependent cell of Rievaulx, but four years later he was recalled to become abbot of the mother house itself. He remained in that office until his death on 11 January 1167. Ailred's saintly personality left its mark on the life of the community at Rievaulx. As David Knowles once wrote, gentleness, radiance of affection and wide sympathy are not the qualities one normally associates with the early Cistercians, but they are the ones that Ailred possessed to the full. He has been described as the St Bernard of the North. Like Bernard he was the intimate friend of kings and princes. But unlike Bernard he was never a controversialist. He was an active writer, indeed a prolific one considering the busy life he led and the physical pain he suffered during his later years. But the strength of his compositions lies in their warmth and sincerity, not in the compelling force of their arguments. Ailred lived by setting an example. That he did not labour in vain is evidenced by the loving tribute paid by the monk Walter Daniel in his biographical *Life of Ailred of Rievaulx*.

Walter Daniel's Life of Ailred Abbot of Rievaulx, ed. F. M. Powicke, Nelson's Medieval Classics, 1950.

AMERCEMENT

In the Middle Ages a fine incurred in a court was known as an amercement, because an offender had to purchase the mercy of the lord whose peace he had broken. By the twelfth century an unsuccessful litigant in the courts would also be amerced for bringing what turned out to be a false plea (q.v. JUSTICE).

ANSELM

One of the most gentle and saintly men ever to have occupied the see of Canterbury, Anselm was first and foremost a thinker and only on the insistence of others an ecclesiastical administrator.

Anselm was born at the Alpine town of Aosta in 1033, the son of genteel parents who had come down in the world. In 1056, after the death of his mother, he abandoned the town of his birth in favour of the life of a wandering scholar. Why he chose to go to France rather than south into Italy is hard to say. One possibility is that he was attracted by the fame of Lanfranc (q.v.), for he traced a path to Normandy. In 1060 he was admitted to Lanfranc's abbey of Bec. Three years later he succeeded Lanfranc as prior of the house, and in 1078 he became abbot. Intellectually he owed a lot to Lanfranc, with whom he continued to correspond after the latter's departure to England on appointment as Archbishop of Canterbury. When Lanfranc died in 1089 Anselm was considered by many his natural successor. King William Rufus (q.v.), however, was not interested in making an early appointment as during the vacancy he could himself enjoy the revenues of the archdiocese, and it was not until 1093 that he was brought to accept Anselm's election.

Rufus, however, was not the only man who viewed the appointment with dismay. Anselm himself did. Anselm was an innocent in the world of high politics. And Rufus was the very last man to appreciate the qualities of his saintly and unworldly archbishop. 'You are yoking an untamed bull and a weak old sheep', was the way that Anselm described their relationship. He was entirely right. One dispute cropped up after another. By the summer of 1097 Anselm had had enough. He went into exile. Three years later, after Rufus's premature death, he returned to England. From that time on, the dispute took a different course. The new king, Henry I (q.v.), asked Anselm to do homage for the lands which he held as a tenant-in-chief. Anselm refused, because at the Easter Council he had attended at Rome in 1099 the clergy were forbidden by the Pope both to do homage for ecclesiastical honors (q.v. FEUDALISM) and to accept investiture from laymen. These were the measures of independence for which the Church was fighting in what was to become known as the 'Investiture Contest'. But Anselm was hardly interested in arguing the merits of the case. In his view it was a matter of obedience to the Pope. Accordingly he resumed his exile. Messengers went to and fro, and embassies were sent to Rome, but not until 1105 was there any sign of movement. Frightened by the excommunication of some bishops who had received investiture from his hands, Henry went to meet Anselm at Laigle in Normandy. Rather surprisingly, agreement was reached. The terms were that the king would retain homage, but forego investiture. It may not have been a settlement to Anselm's liking, but once it had received the Pope's blessing, there was little he could do but accept. He returned to England in September 1106.

Though he was able to devote the last few years of his life (he died on 21 April 1109) to tackling abuses that he found in the English Church, he was not a practical reformer in the mould of Lanfranc. He had made his reputation as a philosopher and theologian. His first two important works were the *Monologion* and *Proslogion*, written in 1077 and 1078 respectively. It is in the latter work that he gives his famous argument for the existence of God. He begins by defining God as a being than whom no greater can exist. According to the fool in the Psalms (13, 1) however, there is no God. But in order to say that, the fool must have an idea in his own mind of what God is. For a Platonist like Anselm it was impossible to conceive of something in one's mind if it did not exist in reality. Therefore a being than whom no greater can exist, must exist. In that case we could think of a being greater than God. That would be logically impossible. Therefore God must exist. It is a tribute to the power of Anselm's argument that philosophers can still argue about his proof to this day.

R.W. Southern, *St Anselm. A Portrait in a Landscape*, Cambridge, 1990.

APPEAL

Until the fifteenth century the common law offered two main ways of bringing a malefactor to justice — appeal or indictment by jury. Appeal was the older procedure, requiring the appellant to pursue his charge against the appellee by personal appearance in the county court, and to justify it, if need be, by judicial combat. However, so many procedural pitfalls lay in the path of the unsuspecting appellant that few appeals terminated in resort to arms.

The process of appeal was also employed to bring charges of treason in parliament. It was used apparently for the first time in the Good Parliament of 1376 by Sir John Annesley. It was taken up again in 1388 when Richard II's (q.v.) opponents were seeking a way to indict the king's favourites after the judges had declared in the previous year that the newly forged weapon of impeachment (q.v.) could not be used against ministers without royal permission. The 'Appellant' lords therefore brought appeals of treason against de Vere and Richard's other favourites which were heard in the Merciless Parliament of 1388, regardless of the absence of four of the accused.

APPROPRIATION

An ecclesiastical benefice was said to have been appropriated when it passed into the ownership of a community such as a monastery, which became the corporate rector and entrusted the cure of souls to a stipendiary known as a vicar (q.v. TITHES).

ARCHITECTURE, ECCLESIASTICAL

For much of the Middle Ages English architecture developed in response to trends which had their origins on the continent. The great churches of late Anglo-Saxon England, for example, owed much to those of Ottonian Germany, while the earliest Gothic churches were heavily indebted to those of France. At all times in the Middle Ages, however, English masons reinterpreted continental ideas in the light of their own distinctive tastes and the liturgical practices of their native land.

At the time of the Norman Conquest, the prevailing architectural style in Europe was Romanesque. Churches were solidly built and their interiors only dimly lit by small, round-headed windows. Many of the late Anglo-Saxon cathedrals had been built on a very grand scale, Winchester being one of the biggest churches of its day. Yet in the generation or two after the Conquest, these churches were all rebuilt. The Normans, coming as conquerors, wanted to impress through the strength and size of their buildings. Norman architecture was the architecture of imperialism. Some of the highest-status churches built by the Normans in England were of immense

length. The nave of Peterborough Abbey, for example, was ten bays long, those of Ely and St Albans thirteen, and that at Norwich no less than fourteen. The sensation of length conveyed by these immense Norman naves was emphasized by the strongly horizontal division of their interior elevations. Above the main arcade which separates the nave from the aisles on each side was the triforium (or tribune) and above it in turn, the clerestory. Thus the view eastwards along the nave of a great monastic church like Ely conveyed an impression of slow and regular rhythm, arch upon arch, shaft upon shaft, until at last the eye reached the pulpitum screen and, beyond it, the east end.

The cathedrals of Peterborough, Ely and Gloucester and the abbey of Tewkesbury are all excellent examples of Norman architecture. But the finest Norman 'great church' of all is Durham. Durham is the supreme masterpiece of English Romanesque art. Here, between 1093 and 1133 was raised up a church without equal in its day for dignity, nobility and architectural sophistication. For the interior elevation the master mason employed pairs of bays, in which a pillar of multiple shafts alternates with a mighty cylinder ornamented with patterns. The proportions of Durham are more satisfying than those of most Norman cathedrals. The triforium is smaller, and the horizontal emphasis yields to the vertical in a way which foreshadows the Gothic age. Where Durham most strikingly anticipates the later designs, however, is in its conception of a stone rib-vault, using the pointed arch, to cover the central vessel of the church (plate 112).

Suggestive though Durham was in its vocabulary and engineering, its example was not followed. It remained an isolated masterpiece. Some fifty years later when new ideas were again explored in English church building, it was in response to architectural currents coming from France. In the early 1140s in the Ile de France a group of masons had begun constructing churches with much thinner walls, bigger windows and higher roofs – in other words, the first Gothic churches. A number of technical innovations had made the development of the new style possible. One was the pointed arch, an architectural feature probably imported from the Islamic East, while another was the flying buttress, a bridge of stone which carried the weight of a high roof across an aisle and down to the ground. But Gothic was much more than an architecture of technology. It was an architecture of space. It was an architecture of light. It involved an entirely new way of approaching and understanding the world.

The earliest pure Gothic churches in France were the abbey of St Denis (c.1135–44) and the cathedral of Sens (c.1140–1200). It was the architectural vocabulary developed in these two churches which the mason, William of Sens, brought to England in 1174 when he was commissioned to design a new choir for Canterbury Cathedral. William's choir was a free adaptation of the style with which he was familiar at Sens. It made use of a high main arcade, a triforium with grouped openings, a clerestory with interior wall passage and six-part rib vault (plate 113). The design encountered a mixed reception in England. Its direct influence was to be confined to the retro-choir at Chichester (1187–99) and St Hugh's choir at Lincoln (1192–1200). But in its extensive use of Purbeck marble shafts set against a light coloured stone it set a fashion which was to be immensely popular in England in the thirteenth century.

It seems likely that the new choir at Canterbury was too alien in spirit to gain immediate acceptance in England. In the south-western counties and the Severn valley, however, a school of masons were experimenting with a version of Gothic better suited to English taste. In the west bays of the nave at Worcester and in the nave and choir at Wells they developed a style that drew on the English liking for thick walls and strong linear patterns. The Wells programme, although almost contemporary with that at Canterbury, was unlike it in every respect. Multi-shafted piers took the place of alternating circular and octagonal ones. Horizontal divisions took the place of vertical. Stiff leaf foliage took the place of acanthus leaves. In almost every respect, Wells rejected French influence. Even the great sculpture gallery on the west front was handled differently. Where the French masons placed their figure sculpture on the entrance portals, the Wells masons draped it across the vast flat expanses of the façade. The doors, humble by French standards, are dwarfed by the statuary around them.

The diversity of early Gothic development in England attests the importance of regionalism and local style in English architecture. No one paradigm gained a general acceptance. It is important to bear this in mind when considering the most familiar monument of early Gothic in England – Salisbury Cathedral. Salisbury is often considered the archtype of Early English Gothic. It brought together a rich variety of features previously used elsewhere – Purbeck marble shafts derived from Canterbury and Lincoln, four-part vaulting and horizontal layering from Wells, the slimmed down Lady Chapel from Lambeth, and so on. But it brought together these features in a building of unprecedented harmony and homogeneity. Salisbury was a summative statement of the new style. But it was also in some ways a highly untypical building. In Salisbury there was none of the visual opulence and rich surface texture of contemporary Lincoln. Salisbury was a relatively austere building. Its design owed much to the influence of Richard Poore (1217–28), the bishop under whom the cathedral was begun. Richard was a liturgical reformer and an enthusiast for the Use of Sarum. The new cathedral was the architectural embodiment of his ideas of well ordered worship.

Before Salisbury was completed, England was exposed to a fresh wave of French influence in the form of the newly rebuilt Westminster Abbey. The great rebuilding of Westminster Abbey was begun by Henry III in 1245. Henry's ambition was to give the English monarchy a coronation church comparable in splendour with that of the French kings at Rheims. The design of the new church owed a great deal to French exemplars and the master mason may, indeed, have been a Frenchman. The traditional English square east end, for example, was rejected in favour of the semicircular or 'apsidal' scheme. There was a French-style emphasis on verticality made possible by the heavy use of flying buttresses – Westminster had the highest internal elevation in England. And the so-called 'bar tracery' of the choir windows was derived directly from that at Rheims. Westminster set new standards of richness in English church architecture (plate 115).

But the English reaction to Westminster, like that to Canterbury three-quarters of a century earlier, was mixed. The Westminster design was too alien to be accepted in its entirety. Its legacy was to be found rather in the area of detail than overall design. The apsidal layout of the east end was never popular with English masons, who preferred the square end. On the other hand, the striking triangular windows of the aisles were adopted in the cathedrals of Hereford and Lichfield, and the beautiful angels high up in the transepts may have provided the inspiration for the Angel Choir at Lincoln (1256–80). Equally influential was the new window tracery. Before this time, English windows had taken the form of single or paired lancets. The new 'bar tracery', by joining a couple of lancets together, placing an oculus above them, and putting them all in a single frame, opened the way to much bigger windows. By the end of the thirteenth century massive east windows were being punched into the end walls of many English churches and cathedrals.

The lavish rebuilding of Westminster inaugurated a new style in English architecture – the style known since the nineteenth century as 'Decorated'. The name is a highly appropriate one. Decorated was concerned principally with breaking up and dissolving the lines of a composition.* Several devices were called on to achieve this end. In the West Country the masons were fond of 'ball-flower' ornament. This was a small rose bud form of decoration used with profusion on the central tower of Hereford and around the windows of Leominster Priory. Another popular device was the ogee arch, the double curved arch which was extensively employed in wood on choir stalls and in stone on window tracery and wall niches. In the Lady Chapel of Ely in the 1330s the creative ability of the sculptors reached new heights with the invention of the 'nodding ogee': in this the double curved ogee arches which form an arcade around the wall reach outwards as well as upwards, so as to give a lovely wavy effect to the composition. If the Lady Chapel is the most luxuriant creation of the Decorated period, the great central Octagon in the same church was the most adventurous. When the Norman central tower collapsed in 1322, it was decided to cover the crossing not with another conventional tower but with an octagonal lantern, thus giving Ely a silhouette unique in English cathedral architecture. It has rightly been said that seen from afar the long outline of Ely, with its tall western tower at one end and the octagon in the middle resembles nothing so much as a ship in full sail on the seas.

Sooner or later there was bound to be a reaction against all this Baroque frivolity. It came in the 1340s and 1350s, when the Decorated style gave way to Perpendicular (c.1350–c.1500). The traditional English liking for linear effect reasserted itself to produce

* G. Webb, *Architecture in Britain: The Middle Ages*, p.124

buildings marked by a simple emphasis on the straight line. The earliest surviving large-scale work in the new style is found in the choir and transepts at Gloucester. The remodelling of Gloucester took place from the 1340s. The masons, instead of replacing the old structure, pared down the surfaces and covered them with a network of transoms and mullions to produce a simple grid design. The strong vertical emphasis which characterizes Perpendicular was present right from the start. And so too was another element – a feeling for spatial unity. In the choir of Gloucester the traditional plan which conceived of a church as divided into three parallel aisles was abandoned in favour of altogether excluding the aisles from sight behind the stone panelling. Thus the interior of Gloucester strikingly anticipates King's College Chapel, Cambridge, where spatial unity was attained within the structure of a single aisleless hall.

Although the eastern parts of Gloucester afford the earliest extant evidence of the new style, a number of its features were anticipated in buildings long since destroyed. The most important of these structures was St Stephen's Chapel, Westminster, which, except for the crypt, was consumed in the fire of 1834. St Stephen's was begun in 1292, and not finished until three-quarters of a century later. From antiquarian drawings we know that its upper chapel was an aisleless hall illuminated on each side by tall windows. Between the window heads the stonework was decorated with the kind of panelling later taken up at Gloucester and elsewhere. Gloucester Perpendicular was a court style exported to the provinces. Unlike Early English and Decorated, it was to remain a distinctively English style which found no counterpart across the Channel. France moved on to the aptly named Flamboyant style, exuberant and over-florid. England opted for an art of line. Perpendicular is as appropriate a name for it as any.

By the time that the Gloucester choir was nearing completion, two other large-scale works were under way – the naves of Winchester (1360–c.1450) and Canterbury (1379-1405), both of which rank among the great achievements of English Gothic. By the middle of the fifteenth century, when the Winchester project was finished, most of the greater churches stood complete, and there was little more to be done. Bath Abbey was the only top-flight church built in the half-century to the Reformation. Some of the best Perpendicular architecture, therefore, is to be found not in the cathedrals, but in royal chapels like King's College, Cambridge, and St George's Chapel, Windsor, and of course in the parish churches. During the fifteenth century few English parish churches escaped at least some rebuilding or enlargement. Clothiers in East Anglia, wool merchants in the Cotswolds, burgesses in the towns and captains returning from the battlefields of France all stored up treasure in heaven by improving God's houses on earth.

The parish churches of fifteenth-century England were much influenced by mendicant architecture. The friars' churches were essentially big preaching halls, with vast naves. So likewise in late medieval parish churches it is the nave which dominates: the chancels were tiny by comparison. The archetypal church skyline was stepped: there was a tall tower at the west end, next to it a big nave, and at the east a lower chancel. In parish church architecture, as in that of 'great churches', there was much regional variation. Schools of masons with distinctive styles can be found operating in Yorkshire, the Cotswolds and East Anglia. The churches of Chipping Campden, Northleach, Chipping Norton and Cirencester, all in the Cotswolds, are the work of a school of masons who probably relied for patronage on the great abbeys of the Severn valley. Their style differed markedly, for example, from that of the masons of Devon and Cornwall, whose churches generally had three aisles of equal height and dispensed with the traditional clerestory altogether.

It needs to be remembered that, although by the sixteenth century, our churches and cathedrals had assumed the architectural form in which we see them today, internally they presented a very different aspect. A medieval church would have been ablaze with colour. Its windows would have been filled with stained glass (q.v.), its roof bosses and other architectural details picked out in bright reds and golds, its chapels and aisles divided by brightly coloured screens; in Romanesque churches expanses of blank walling would have been covered with fresco. Such brightness would today perhaps be regarded as vulgar, but it was integral to the medieval aesthetic. A medieval interior was designed to evoke an image of the heavenly kingdom. It had to move the faithful to greater devotion. Colour conveyed richness. As Abbot Suger of St Denis wrote, 'the multi-coloured reliquaries made me think of the diversity of sacred virtues... I was transported mystically to a higher realm.' The most admired interiors were the most jewel-like. In these exuberant interiors medieval man could savour his vision of the world to come.

See also BUILDING; WYNFORD, WILLIAM; YEVELE, HENRY

G.F. Webb, *Architecture in Britain: the Middle Ages*, Harmondsworth, 1956; *The Age of Chivalry: Art in Plantagenet England, 1200-1400*, ed. J. Alexander and P. Binski, London, 1987; C. Wilson, *The Gothic Cathedral. The Architecture of the Great Church, 1130-1530*, London, 1990; N. Coldstream, *The Decorated Style. Architecture and Ornament, 1240-1360*, London, 1994; J. Harvey, *The Perpendicular Style*, London, 1978.

ARCHITECTURE, VERNACULAR

Medieval vernacular architecture covers a range of housing types (even if castles (q.v.) are excluded) from the manor houses of the gentry down to the cottages of the peasantry. Within the genre there are naturally wide variations of size and status. However, it is possible to identify a number of shared architectural characteristics which embrace the dwellings of the affluent and the less affluent alike. By the late Middle Ages it is also possible to trace the emergence of local style in vernacular architecture, for example in the distinctive Wealden houses erected by the prosperous yeomen of Sussex and Kent.

Architectural styles in any society are influenced by the building materials available for use, and English medieval peasant housing was no exception. On the eve of the Conquest, and for several centuries after, in lowland England the peasant house would have consisted of a light timber frame cut from the local woodlands, filled with clay or wattle and daub and roofed with thatch. In highland England, on sites such as those excavated at Hound Tor and Hutholes in Devon, stone took the place of the timber frame. What evidence there is, mainly collected from deserted village sites,' suggests that the insubstantial timber dwelling would have needed rebuilding every generation or so. It was this consideration perhaps, rather than improved living standards, that led to peasant houses in many parts of the country being rebuilt in the thirteenth century. The kind of dwelling that has been uncovered in excavations is known from its shape as the 'long-house'. Extending to anything up to 100ft from end to end, it incorporated under a single roof the peasant's living area, a storage room and a byre for the livestock. The stone-built long-house survived to enjoy a long post-medieval history in the north and west of England, and good examples from the sixteenth and seventeenth centuries are still to be seen in the Pennines and parts of Devon.

Down in the south-east, however, a region with ample supplies of timber, a very different sort of house made its appearance by the fifteenth century. In the late Middle Ages the rise in wages and fall in prices that followed the demographic collapse favoured the advancement of lesser yeomen proprietors who could run a small estate of 100 acres or more with a minimum of overheads. These were the sort of men for whom the Wealden houses of Kent and Sussex were built. In ground plan the timber-framed Wealden house followed the long-established pattern of gentry manor houses. In the centre lay a lofty, open hall, flanked at each end by a two-storied service wing, the upper floor jettied, and the whole dwelling under a single hipped roof. The Pilgrim's Rest Cafe at Battle is a good example of this style.

In the Midlands in the same period and earlier, the cruck cottage became a common form of construction. The crucks were two big end-timbers, inclined towards each other so as to meet at the crown of the roof. The crucks, in other words, supported the roof, as opposed to the lateral walls in any other kind of house. Noakes's Court at Defford (Worcs) is an example of a house of such construction which, to judge from its name, must have been built for a lord of the manor. By the mid-fifteenth century, however, yeomen and gentlemen were building houses that offered more commodious accommodation, and cruck cottages became associated with their dependent tenantry.

As the discussion of Wealden houses has already indicated, across a broad spectrum of medieval housing there was remarkable consistency in the arrangement of the main living accommodation. Generally, three main elements were involved: firstly, the hall, or principal living room; secondly, at one end of the hall, the cross passage and service area; and finally, at the other end of the hall, the lord's retiring room, or solar. These units were as commonly found in well-to-do peasant dwellings as in the houses of the gentry.

From the earliest times the main room of any substantial house had been the hall. The seventh-century Northumbrian royal palace at Yeavering had consisted simply of one enormous timber hall. Both in the Saxon period and later the hall had served not only as a banqueting chamber for the lord and his tenants but also as a meeting place for the manorial court or, in Norman times, the honorial court. Some of the servants might even have slept there. By the twelfth century, in castles and big manor houses the hall had become a very grand apartment and was usually built of stone. One of the best surviving examples is the hall of Oakham Castle (Rutland). This structure is notable for having aisles.

By the twelfth century it was becoming fairly common for other units to be built alongside the hall. In knightly dwellings the most substantial of these was the chamber block, containing the lord's private rooms. This was usually built at the end of, and at right angles to, the hall. One of the best examples of such a block is that at Boothby Pagnell (Lincs). This was a two-storey structure with a couple of chambers on each floor, placed end to end. The larger chamber upstairs, which contained the only fireplace, appears to have served as a combined reception room and bedroom, and the smaller one as the owner's own bedroom. The two downstairs rooms probably served as storage or service rooms. It used to be thought that the block at Boothby Pagnell represented the whole of the twelfth-century house, and that the upper room was the hall. This notion, however, is now rejected. It is generally accepted that it is in fact only the chamber block. Excavation has recently uncovered the footings of a conventional hall at right angles to it.

By the thirteenth century the L-shaped ground plan was the most common layout for manor houses. The main feature of the house would typically have been the hall, rising to the full height of the house, with, at right angles to it at one end, a two-storied block, separately roofed, containing the solar and other rooms. This is the arrangement found at Little Wenham (Suffolk), interestingly a brick-built dwelling, and at Old Soar (Kent). In most cases the kitchen or service area, the last of the three units mentioned above, would have been placed at the opposite end of the hall, across a screens passage. This is the arrangement found at the Vernons' house, Haddon Hall (Derbyshire), and in Oxford colleges today. Sometimes, as at Stokesay (Shropshire) (c.1285), the area in front of the hall block was enclosed by a wall, creating a courtyard house (plate 119). By the fifteenth century it was usual for the courtyard space to be used for servants' or retainers' accommodation.

Few medieval furnishings have survived to indicate what comforts there might have been in a house like Stokesay or Old Soar. Today the interior walls are bare. In their heyday, however, they would have been decorated with wall paintings, like those commissioned at Longthorpe by Robert de Thorpe, steward of Peterborough Abbey, or hung with tapestries, suspended from mounts a few inches off the wall so as to prevent damage from the damp. Sanitation by modern standards was primitive – however, not so primitive as sometimes made out. The solar at thirteenth-century Old Soar had a garderobe or latrine, which emptied into a pit. Windows in lower status dwellings were unglazed and closed with wooden shutters. In higher status dwellings glass was used from the thirteenth century. At Stokesay in the 1280s Laurence de Ludlow had glazing in the upper lights of his hall windows, but in the lower lights only shutters; Laurence probably also had glass in the windows of the solar. As for heating, the only source of warmth in eleventh- and twelfth-century manor houses, to judge from Boothby Pagnell, was the fireplace in the hall. In many large halls, even that built as late as 1340 by Sir John de Pulteney at Penshurst, the fire took the form of a central hearth from which the smoke would escape through a vent or louvre in the roof. At one time cooking might well have been done at such a hearth, but later on it became usual to erect a kitchen at one end of the hall, behind the screens passage.

In the towns domestic housing took on its own characteristics. The late medieval street scene, which can be recaptured by walking along The Shambles or Petergate at York, owed what is now regarded as its picturesqueness to the limitations imposed by urban geography. Space was limited. So the plan of a house followed that of the tenement plot on which it was built. In other words, it combined a narrow frontage with a depth of anything up to 400ft back from the front. As often as not the owner would conduct his business from the house, in which case the ground floor would probably serve as a shop. The main living rooms would be upstairs, and the servants' or employees' accommodation right at the top. The constraints of space meant that expansion had to be upwards. Each time a new storey was added to a standard timber-framed building, it would be 'jettied', or projected forwards, to obtain a few more square feet of floor space, until in due course a person leaning forward from the top window on one side of the street could shake hands with someone leaning out of the top window opposite. How the medieval urban working class lived is very hard to say, as their dwellings have not survived; but it is a reasonable guess that their surroundings would have been neither spacious nor salubrious.

E. Mercer, *English Vernacular Houses: A Study of Traditional Farmhouses and Cottages*, London, 1975; A. Emery, *Great Medieval Houses of England and Wales, 1300-1500, 1: Northern England*, Cambridge, 1996; A. Emery, *Greater Medieval Houses of England and Wales, 1300-1500, 2: East Anglia, Central England and Wales*, Cambridge, 2000.

ARMOUR and ARMS

Although the earliest extant medieval armour dates from the fourteenth century – the first major finds are those of the battle of Wisby in Sweden in 1361 – a great deal can be learned about early armour from illuminated manuscripts, tombs and brasses (q.v.).

From the Bayeux Tapestry's depiction of the battle of Hastings it is evident that the main body armour in the eleventh century was the haubergeon of chain mail. Both English and Normans are shown wearing it. The Normans' leg mail was of full length, but that of the English knee-length, reflecting the fact that the former fought on horseback and the latter on foot. Under the haubergeon a coat known as the gambeson was worn, to prevent the mail from chafing the skin.

From the mid-twelfth century a loose flowing surcoat was generally worn over the haubergeon. This may have been adopted to deflect the rays of the sun, but no less importantly it could be used to display heraldic insignia – or, in the East, crusading crosses.

By the late thirteenth century, measures were being taken to strengthen the body defences. On the legs, quilted 'cuisses' were worn as thigh defences. To the bottom of the cuisses were attached the poleyns, small plates of metal or boiled leather which defended the kneecaps. Parallel developments took place on the arms. Over the elbows were worn disc-shaped pieces known as 'couters', shown for the first time on the tomb in Salisbury Cathedral of the younger William Longespee, earl of Salisbury, dated c.1260. Later, the arms received additional defences in the form of 'vambraces' over the forearms, 'rerebraces' over the upper arms, and small circular 'besagews' over the armpits. The surcoat became shorter, and by the second quarter of the fourteenth century it was cut away in front to reveal underneath the coat of plates, a garment of cloth or leather lined with metal plates.

Armour of the early to mid-fourteenth century is well represented on the two brasses at Stoke d'Abernon (Surrey) of Sir John d'Abernon the elder, c.1330, and his son Sir John II, c.1345. The elder John is shown wearing a full haubergeon, loose surcoat and poleyns, and his son a shorter haubergeon, the coat of plates, and plate defences on the arms and legs. In the course of the period 1340-60, however, a series of major changes occurred. Firstly, the linen surcoat was superseded by the leather jupon, a close-fitting garment which covered the chest and stomach; this can be seen to advantage on the effigy of the Black Prince at Canterbury. And, secondly, there was a proliferation in the plate defences to the point where almost the whole body was covered. The arm defences were strengthened, and so too were those of the lower leg. The head was protected by a pointed helmet or 'bascinet', and the feet by 'sollerets' of laminated plates. Across the hips was slung the baldric, or belt, from which hung on one side the sword and on the other the misericord dagger – the latter so called because it was used to put an end to the misery of an opponent mortally wounded.

The one substantial piece of mail left exposed by 1400 was the aventail, which hung from the bascinet and protected the shoulders. This survived until the early years of the fifteenth century, when it was replaced by the steel gorget. At the same time a number of other changes occurred. The jupon was superseded by a steel breastplate over the chest and a 'fauld', or skirt of steel hoops, over the lower stomach; and the sword belt was now slung diagonally across the body. These features were introduced by the Italian armourers, notably the Missaglia family of Milan, whose workshop was perhaps the most renowned of its day. Also highly regarded for their work were the armourers of south Germany, in particular of Augsburg. The chronicler Froissart tells us that it was to the armourers of Augsburg that Thomas Mowbray, duke of Norfolk, turned for his equipment when preparing for his duel against Bolingbroke in 1397. German armour tended to be characterized by its symmetry and simplicity. It is well illustrated on the brass of Sir Hugh Halsham at West Grinstead (Sussex), 1441 (plate 38).

From the middle of the century armour styles tended to become more exaggerated. The couters on the elbows became much bigger, and massive pauldrons were worn on the shoulders. The fauld became shorter. These changes are clearly represented on the brass of Robert Ingleton at Thornton (Bucks), 1472 (plate 125).

By the fifteenth century, for our knowledge of armour we are no longer dependent entirely on the evidence of tombs and brasses. Examples of complete harnesses survive. After the mid-fifteenth century, then, it is possible to say something about the weight of armour. It is often maintained that late medieval armour was very heavy: so heavy as to be cumbersome. However, this is only partially true. Some suits, admittedly, were weighty. A complete Italian armour of about 1450, now at Glasgow, weighs just over four stones. One of the heaviest harnesses, a jousting suit made at Augsburg in about 1500, weighs six stones. These examples, however, are exceptional. Most armour would have weighed less. Stories of knights having to be lifted onto the backs of their horses by cranes are much exaggerated.

The notion that a knight was likely to be bankrupted by the cost of his armour is also somewhat fanciful. In the 1370s, when the Datini were acting as agents for the sale of Italian armour in Spain and France, a complete harness of bascinet, aventail, hauberk, breastplate, fauld and leg armour cost roughly 45 livres, or £10-£12 in English money of the time. Considering that a knight would have enjoyed a minimum income of £40 per annum, and most knights much more, this was not exorbitant. It needs to be remembered too that the price quoted was for a complete harness. An esquire or hard-up knight who would not see more than a season or two's service could settle, if he wanted, for just hauberk and bascinet. Armour, moreover, unlike modern motorcars, did not suffer from built-in obsolescence. It could be passed on

from father to son. Only the wealthiest knight would trouble to turn up on the battlefield (or in the lists) sporting an up-to-date Milanese suit. The further down the social scale a wearer was, the simpler and cheaper armour became. Henry II's (q.v.) Assize of Arms (1181) prescribed that the holder of a knight's fee should wear a mail shirt, helmet, shield and lance, and a burgess or freeman a quilted jacket, iron cap and lance. The quilted jacket worn by the infantryman can still be seen in manuscript illustrations of three centuries later. Infantry attire was slow to change. In fact, the only item worn by the footman that assumed a novel and distinctive form of its own was the kettle-hat, or *chapeau de fer* to give it its contemporary title, a wide-brimmed head-piece remarkably similar to the tin hats issued in the two World Wars. Although most commonly associated with the foot-soldiers, it was sometimes worn by members of the nobility, like Aymer de St Amand, who is shown sporting one on the brass of Sir Hugh Hastings at Elsing (Norfolk).

C. Blair, *European Armour*, London, 1958.

ARTHURIAN LEGENDS

The man responsible for launching King Arthur on his medieval career was Geoffrey of Monmouth (q.v.), who made this hitherto obscure British king the hero of his *History of the Kings of Britain*. Most of Geoffrey's so-called history, completed in about 1138, is pure fantasy; but the existence in the fifth or sixth century of someone called Arthur is attested by a ninth-century writer called Nennius, who credits him with defeating the Saxons in a series of battles culminating in Mount Badon. Just how shadowy Arthur's existence was, however, is indicated by the fact that Gildas attributed the victory to someone else, Ambrosius Aurelianus. What Geoffrey of Monmouth did was to take the figure of Arthur, and use his considerable powers of artistry to transform him into a hero figure, a patriot king. Arthur, he wrote, was the son of Uther Pendragon and Ygerna, duchess of Cornwall. Crowned king of Britain at Silchester at the age of fifteen, he defeated the Saxons at Lincoln and Bath, and then crossed the Channel to subdue France. He was about to set out for Rome, when news reached him that his nephew, Mordred, had seized the crown. Returning to Britain, he defeated Mordred at the battle of Camblan, but was himself mortally wounded and had to be carried away to Avalon. After his mysterious death the crown passed in 542 to his cousin, Constantine.

Such, in its bare outline, is the career invented for Arthur by Geoffrey. There was enough in it to appeal to the imagination – his obscure death, for example, and the exploits of the four knights, Cador, Gawain, Bedevere and Kay; and enough, too, for later writers to build on. For example, in the *Mort Artu*, part of a thirteenth-century Arthurian cycle, the story of the king's death was worked up to a magnificent romantic climax. After a fierce battle, we are told, both Arthur and Mordred were mortally wounded, and Arthur ordered Gifflet to hurl the sword Excalibur into the lake. A hand rose from the waters, and grasped the weapon. A boat then drifted along, carrying Morgan and her ladies, who took Arthur on board and sailed off again into the distance.

Although the *History* was fiercely criticized a generation later by the chronicler William of Newburgh, Geoffrey's Arthurian yarns were quickly taken up by other writers, both in England and in France. Indeed, the popularization of Arthur in the twelfth and thirteenth centuries owed less to English than to French poets, not least among them Chretien de Troyes, who between 1160 and 1180 wrote at least five romances with an Arthurian setting. In England Arthur made an appearance in Layamon's alliterative English *Brut* of

c.1200–20 and in later Brut chronicles. But from the literary point of view the two most accomplished treatments of the Arthurian legend in English in the Middle Ages were the anonymous *Sir Gawain and the Green Knight* of 1360–70 and Malory's (q.v.) *Morte d'Arthur*, written in 1469 and printed by Caxton (q.v.) sixteen years later.

The literary Arthur quickly became a European figure, the common property of aristocracies in countries as far apart as England and Cyprus. He became the object of an international cult. The English kings from Stephen to Henry III (q.v.), like their peers elsewhere, subscribed to that cult, but it was Edward I (q.v.) at the end of the thirteenth century who first seized on the political advantages to be derived from identifying the English crown more closely with the memory of the early British king. He and Queen Eleanor were present at Glastonbury in Easter 1278 when the reputed remains of Arthur and Guinevere were transferred to a magnificent new tomb of black marble. Round Tables – a kind of festive tournament – were celebrated on at least three occasions in Edward's reign, at Kenilworth in 1279, Nefyn in Wales in 1284 and at Falkirk in 1302. The advantage of harnessing the Arthurian cult to the national cause was not lost on Edward's successors. Edward III (q.v.) evidently had in mind founding a chivalric order on the Arthurian model, before settling instead for the Garter, because he had a circular house built at Windsor suitable for holding a Round Table. This is very likely the one, dating from about the 1330s, that now hangs on the wall of Winchester Castle. Henry VIII significantly took the Emperor Charles V to Winchester to see this table on the occasion of his visit to England in 1522. Arthurianism was always good propaganda.

Geoffrey of Monmouth, *The History of the Kings of Britain*, ed. L. Thorpe, Harmondsworth,

1966; S. Knight, *Arthurian Literature and Society*, London, 1983.

ASSARTING

The process of reclaiming land from the wild was known as assarting (Latin, *ex* – out, *sarrire* – to hoe). As population grew in the twelfth and thirteenth centuries, so it became necessary to extend the margin of cultivation into areas of marsh and moorland that had lain waste. The pace of assarting varied from one part of the country to another. In some areas, like the Felden of south Warwickshire, the limits of cultivation had been reached by the time that Domesday Book was compiled in 1086. In other, more inhospitable localities, like the Fens, the frontier was still being pushed back in the thirteenth century. The Fenland included much potentially good farmland, but the bare expanses of moorland known to have been assarted at the same time were too poor to have repaid anything but the most intermittent husbandry, and were abandoned a century later.

ATTAINDER

In the early fourteenth century the verb 'to attaint' could describe any process by which judgement was given and the accused found guilty. A century and a half later attainder had become the most solemn penalty known to the common law, incurred usually on conviction for treason, and entailing forfeiture of all possessions and the corruption of blood passing to all direct descendants. During the Wars of the Roses (q.v.), when governments came and went with unnerving rapidity, Acts of Attainder were regularly used by one side to liquidate the other. But in fact their effects were not as bad as the simple figures would suggest: out of the 397 people attainted between 1453 and 1504 no fewer than 256 had the good fortune to see their sentences reversed.

AUGUSTINIAN CANONS

The Augustinian canons were one of the new orders which came into existence in the twelfth century. The canons' model was the set of rules which St Augustine of Hippo (354-430) had drawn up for a community of women who wanted to live a life in common. Following a decree of the Lateran Council of 1059 Augustine's rules were modified and updated to form a regularized code for clerks outside the cloister who wished to follow a semi-monastic way of life.

The canons were distinguished from the monks by the relative looseness of their lifestyle. Unlike the monks, they were allowed to go into the world, to undertake pastoral work, and to hold cure of souls. Many communities of canons were established in the towns, where they ran hospitals and schools, provided help for the poor and sang soul-masses for the rich. From the very beginning, the canons were a popular order. The main reason for this was that their houses were cheap to endow. The canons had low material expectations; they asked little of their founders. The greater part of their endowment came from appropriated churches given to them by laymen under pressure to divest themselves of ecclesiastical sources of revenue.

By 1350 there were over 200 Augustinian houses in England. Many of these were humble establishments, surviving on a shoestring budget, and the number had declined slightly by the Reformation. But some were substantially endowed, and whatever the original intentions of the canonical way of life, had become for all intents and purposes indistinguishable from regular monastic foundations. The Augustinians were never pre-eminent for their way of life or for the intellectual activity of their number, but they produced some men of note, like John Mirk of Lilleshall, a sermon-writer and author of tracts for parish priests.

The surviving buildings of the Augustinian canons are almost indistinguishable from those of the regular monks. From the early twelfth century there survive the roofless nave of St Botolph's, Colchester, and the choir of St Bartholomew's Smithfield, and from the reign of Henry II the impressive late Romanesque work at St Frideswide's, Oxford (now Christ Church Cathedral). Of the conventual buildings of the Augustinians, which conformed to the normal monastic plan, those at Lilleshall (Salop) and Christ Church, Oxford, provide the best examples.

See also MONASTICISM, SERMONS

J.C. Dickinson, *The Origin of the Austin Canons and their Introduction into England*, London, 1950.

AULNAGE

First imposed in 1353, the aulnage was a tax levied on all cloths that were intended for sale, whether at home or abroad. Its administration lay in the hands of officials known as aulnagers who were appointed by the crown not only to collect the tax but to inspect the cloths for size and quality. From the fifteenth century there is ample evidence to show that they were succumbing to the corrupt practices that proved an irresistible temptation to all but the most scrupulous medieval officials. For example, they would seize a cloth under some pretext, and then sell it themselves for private gain. As a cover they rendered spurious accounts to the exchequer. For all the notoriety that the aulnage returns have earned, there is, however, little reason to doubt that the earlier accounts, surviving from the fourteenth century, give a reasonably accurate picture of cloth sales for their time.

B

BACON, ROGER

Of the English scientific writers of the Middle Ages Bacon is the most well known, though not necessarily the most important. A member of an East Anglian knightly family, he studied at Oxford under the great Robert Grosseteste (q.v.), and then lectured at Paris, before returning to Oxford in about 1247 to resume his theological studies. Some ten years later he joined the Franciscans (q.v.). By this time he had given himself over almost wholly to scientific investigations, which he was to write up in the *Opus Maius*, the *Opus Minor* and the *Opus Tertium*. Whether for the alleged 'suspected novelties' his work contained or, more likely, for the hostility aroused by his relentless criticism of many of the greatest churchmen of his day, he found himself placed in confinement by 1278. When he was released we do not know. All we can say is that he was at large again in Oxford shortly before his death in 1292.

Bacon's modern reputation should not hide from us the fact that as a thinker he stood firmly within the time-honoured Augustinian tradition that saw intellectual illumination as coming only from God. It was quite understandable of him, therefore, to say that 'theology is the mistress of all the other sciences', and to believe that the purpose of studying science was to attain a deeper knowledge of the truths of theology. As a pupil of Grosseteste, Bacon favoured the study of mathematics as the best way of demonstrating connections between events. Mathematics, he wrote, is 'the door and the key' 'of the sciences and things of this world'. But, as we know, he was not one to accept blindly the increasing separation between pure thought and experience that was to prove the fatal flaw in medieval scholasticism. He was a great believer in the value of experimenting. In this he was not new. He was merely following the lead given by the Frenchman, Peter de Mauricourt, who had worked on magnetism. But he does seem to have been possessed of an inventive and speculative mind. He dabbled in alchemy, astronomy, astrology and optics. All the same, his importance lay not so much in his own discoveries and achievements as in the experimental method by which he reached them. One phenomenon, for example, that he like Grosseteste sought to explain was the rainbow. He tells us how he had examined prisms, crystals and the spray thrown up by mill-wheels to collect instances of colours similar to those seen in the rainbow, so that he could relate the latter to the general phenomenon of spectral colours. Why these advances in experimental method nevertheless failed to emancipate medieval science from its Aristotelian framework raises questions that are better dealt with in a more general discussion of medieval science (q.v.).

D. Knowles, *The Evolution of Medieval Thought*, London, 1962.

BANNOCKBURN

When Robert Bruce, King of Scots, destroyed Edward II's army at Bannockburn, he effectively ended any possibility that Scotland (q.v.) might be conquered by the English. The battle was the outcome of the English king's attempt to relieve his beleaguered garrison in Stirling Castle. The English force arrived at the Bannock burn, a stream a few miles south of Stirling, on 23 June 1314. Although numbering some 15,000 men, as against a Scots force of 6–10,000, they were an ill-led and ill-coordinated force. Bruce arranged his men in four 'schiltroms', or well-armed brigades of infantry, against which, when battle was joined on 24 June, the English cavalry could make little headway. Too late Edward thought of deploying the archers. Bruce replied by throwing in his cavalry, and the English broke up in disorderly retreat. Among the noble casualties on the English side was the earl of Gloucester, and among the prisoners the earl of Hereford, Sir Maurice de Berkeley and Sir Anthony de Lucy. For Edward II the political consequences were scarcely less serious than the military. Deprived of any moral authority at home, he had to acquiesce in the demands of Thomas, earl of Lancaster, for the enforcement of the Ordinances (q.v.), the programme of reforms imposed on him three years before.

BASTARD FEUDALISM

The term 'bastard feudalism' describes the structure of relationships between lords and retainers in late medieval England. The phrase implies that the phenomenon was a debased form of 'pure' feudalism (q.v.). This may be true in the very limited sense that the tenurial link between lord and vassal was replaced by a monetary one between lord and man. However, this aspect apart, there are no grounds for privileging one system of retaining over another. Both were equally valid according to their own terms, and both were shaped by the conditions of their day. In the feudal conditions of the twelfth century the relationship was created by the oath of homage and the granting of land. In the bastard feudal late-medieval period it was created by a document – the indenture of retinue.

A good example of bastard feudal retaining is provided by the indenture which John of Gaunt, duke of Lancaster (q.v.) made with Sir Maurice de Berkeley of Uley in 1391. Maurice was retained to stay with the duke for life in peace and war. When summoned, he would attend the duke, from whom he would receive food and drink in common with the other knights of his rank. In return he would receive annually a retaining fee of £20 assigned on Gaunt's lordship of Monmouth, the first instalment to be paid at Easter, the second at Michaelmas.

The origins of bastard feudalism are much debated. The view used to be held that the system had its origins in the dissolution of the feudal host and the king's need to find some other way of recruiting knights. By Edward I's reign, the argument went, it had become common for the crown to supplement its feudal resources of manpower by hiring knights and esquires whose terms of service came to be written down in indentures. And where the king led, his magnates followed. To provide themselves with the nucleus of a force that could be called upon when needed, the magnates formed their own retinues – which were again raised by indenture.

The view that military imperatives explain the transition from feudalism to bastard feudalism, however, is one that is no longer accepted. Recent archival research has uncovered extensive evidence of retaining by money fees at an earlier stage in the thirteenth century, indeed back into the twelfth century, well before the dissolution of the feudal host. Other reasons for the transition have to be found. One suggestion that has been made is that the assize of novel disseisin of 1166 accounts for the change. What the assize did was give new protection to tenants against their lords. From this time, a lord could not expel a tenant without showing good cause. In consequence, lords chose to reward their servants with money instead of land. There may well be something in the theory. However, it is possible that a more general explanation is to be preferred. Quite simply, from the middle of the twelfth century it was more convenient for lords to reward men with money than with land. Money was a more flexible medium. In the generation after the Conquest it had suited lords to offer land because land was plentiful; the new Norman aristocracy could draw on the confiscated lands of the English. But by the twelfth century, after a generation or two of enfeoffment, land was in short supply. Lords had to find another form of reward – money.

Discussions of bastard feudalism have tended to focus on the life retainers – the men formally retained by indenture: the knights and the richer esquires. These were indeed the key figures in the structure. But they represent only one section of the whole. The world of bastard feudalism is better seen as a series of concentric circles. In the centre were the knights and rich esquires – the men who were generally retained to serve for life in peace and war. Outside and surrounding them were the lesser servants and estate officials. And outside them in turn were the men linked in a looser relationship, the 'well wishers' as they were known to contemporaries. The life retainers were generally given a collar or robe as a mark of their affiliation, and the lesser folk a badge. The most familiar late medieval collar was the Lancastrian collar of SS. Examples of badges are Richard II's badge of the white hart, the Bohuns' swan, and the Beauchamps' bear and ragged staff.

Since the late nineteenth century, when Charles Plummer first coined the term, bastard feudalism has had a bad press. Historians have blamed it for the widespread collapse of public order in the mid-fifteenth century. The proliferation of retaining, it is argued, led to the build-up of large gangs of baronial hangers-on, who provided the mainstay of the armies that fought in the Wars of the Roses (q.v.). Yet at the same time, and quite inconsistently, historians have pointed to the shifting and unstable nature of the ties between lord and retainer, one consequence of which was that bastard feudalism could not provide the same degree of cohesiveness as 'pure' feudalism had in the twelfth century. If in fact a lord could not fully rely on the loyalty of his feed men, then it is hard to see how he could count on them to follow him into battle. The case against bastard feudalism is certainly not proven. Nonetheless, concern was voiced at the time about the unruliness of some retainers. From the early 1380s it was alleged in parliamentary petitions that the magnates were failing adequately to discipline their dependants, and that folk of lesser status were usurping the privileges of the magnates by distributing badges or other forms of attachment themselves. These complaints form the background to the first comprehensive medieval legislation on retaining, the so-called Statute of Livery and Maintenance of 1390. The statute enshrined the hierarchical principle of retaining. It forbade any but lords to retain men, and any but esquires and above to be retained. The statute was subsequently reissued but hardly ever enforced. Further legislation was issued in 1468 by Edward IV (q.v.) and in 1504 by Henry VII. Its purpose was less to curb retaining than to regulate it.

To focus unduly on the malign aspects of bastard feudalism, however, is to distort our appreciation of its workings. Retinues were formed not principally for military purposes but for social or political ones. A lord surrounded himself with an indentured following for two reasons – to attest his importance in society and to strengthen and extend his links with the local gentry. A few late medieval retinues were very large. John of Gaunt, for example, had nearly 100 knights and 200 esquires in his pay. But Gaunt's retinue was exceptional; most were far more modest in size. There is no evidence of the nobility bankrupting themselves by inordinate spending on fees. While gentry would often compete with one another for a place in the retinue, lords would refuse them if their lists were full. Those fairly numerous gentry who were unattached, however, would still be touched by lordship. The influence of a great lord stretched far beyond the ranks of his immediate dependants. It reached out through the circles of life retainers and annuitants and the penumbra of well wishers into the middling and lesser gentry of the shire. Lordship was by far the most important informal institution in society.

K.B. McFarlane, *England in the Fifteenth Century*, London, 1981; M. Hicks, *Bastard Feudalism*, Harlow, 1995.

BAYEUX TAPESTRY

The Bayeux Tapestry is a major record of the Norman Conquest of England. Although called a tapestry, it is in fact an embroidery, executed in woollen threads on a ribbon of linen 230ft long and 20in wide. It traces the story of Duke William's great exploit in over seventy consecutive scenes (plates 75-7).

The tale as narrated gives the Normans' viewpoint on events. Its purpose is to present a moral case by tracing the fall of a man, King Harold, who had dared to break a solemn oath. In the early scenes of the Tapestry Harold, still earl of Wessex, is shown leaving England to make a journey across the Channel, the purpose of which is not stated. On landing on the French coast, he is taken into custody by Guy, count of Ponthieu, by whom he is transferred, again for reasons unstated, to William, duke of Normandy. William takes Harold with him on a campaign against the Bretons in the course of which he enters into a relationship of feudal dependence on the duke. On the company's return to Bayeux he is shown swearing the famous oath to William, the terms of which, we are told by the Norman chroniclers, were to uphold William's succession to the English throne. Ignoring his commitment, however, on Edward's death on 5 January 1066 Harold seized the crown for himself. The dire consequences that God was to lay in store for the perjurer are indicated in the Tapestry by the appearance after the coronation of Halley's Comet – an event interpreted as a bad omen. The focus of events then switches to Normandy, where we are shown the duke's men building the ships that were to carry them across the Channel to England. After disembarking on Pevensey beach, they march to Hastings, where we are shown a simple motte and bailey castle (q.v.) being thrown up. A messenger brings news of the approach of Harold's army, and after a pep talk from their leader, the Normans prepare for battle. The remaining scenes portray with great vigour the events of 14 October 1066 that led to Harold's death and William's victory.

It would be wrong to regard the Tapestry as a source of historically accurate or verifiable information. To interpret it thus would be to misunderstand its purpose. The Tapestry is an *ex parte* statement: it is arguing a case. It was conceived as a justification for Duke William's action in invading England. The narrative of the Tapestry is consistent with the narratives of the Norman chroniclers. They all argue much the same case and place emphasis on much the same events. It accordingly follows from this that the Tapestry's witness is at many points at variance with that of the English writers. No English source so much as mentions Harold's journey across the Channel. Whether the Tapestry invented this episode is hard to say. In any event, there is little point in trying to reconcile the conflicting accounts. The two are simply irreconcilable.

A proper understanding of the Tapestry would be greatly assisted by fuller knowledge of its provenance and origins. It has long been accepted that the Tapestry was made in England because stylistically it has close affinities with late Anglo-Saxon manuscript illumination. The suggestion has been made that it was embroidered at Canterbury. But in that case who could have commissioned it? A powerful case has been made for the patronage of Odo, bishop of Bayeux, Duke William's half brother. Bishop Odo figures prominently in the narrative. It is Odo who blesses the dinner at Hastings, and it is Odo who rallies the troops in the heat of battle. Moreover, it is with Odo's cathedral city of Bayeux that the Tapestry has always been associated. Interestingly, at the one point where the Tapestry is at variance with other sources – the place where Harold swore his oath to Duke William – its authority is to the advantage of Bayeux. The case for Odo's patronage is strengthened by the bishop's English associations. After the Conquest Odo was given the English earldom of Kent, and the chief city of Kent is Canterbury. But the case for Odo's responsibility is not entirely convincing. If Odo were indeed the patron, one would imagine the Tapestry to have been displayed in a church or a cathedral. But cathedrals do not offer the expanses of uncluttered wall space in which to unfold so lengthy an object. It is much easier to visualize it being hung around the walls of a castle. Now there was one major castle in Kent in which it is conceivable that it was hung, and that is Dover. The lord of Dover was Robert of Mortain, another of the Conqueror's half brothers. The possibility of Robert's patronage of the work cannot be ruled out.

The overall design of the Tapestry was probably the work of a single artist, and one moreover who was familiar with the world of manuscripts. The needlework was then executed, in wool on a linen background, by a group of embroiderers who presumably operated in a single workshop. How exactly they went about their job is unclear, but close examination of the Tapestry shows that they made it in eight separate pieces of uneven length which were then joined together. Bearing in mind its antiquity and the vicissitudes through which it has passed, the Tapestry is in remarkably good condition. Twice during the French Revolution it had to be saved from destruction. Yet it has come down to us complete, apart from the loss of a few feet at the end. If it survived the threats of the revolutionaries, the Tapestry did not escape the attention of nineteenth-century restorers who rewove several parts which were faded. The work was in fact accomplished very well, but it does mean that one or two of the most famous scenes – the death of King Harold for example – are largely modern restorations.

The Tapestry is a unique source for the history of the Norman Conquest; and as a work of art it has no parallel in the early Middle Ages. Within the limits set by the stylized form of portrayal with which he was familiar, the designer showed himself to be a genius. His horses were superb. He could portray the rough and tumble of battle brilliantly. His border scenes excite, tease and amuse. It would be nice to know his name; but unfortunately that is probably beyond recovery.

The Bayeux Tapestry. A Comprehensive Survey, ed. F.M. Stenton, 2nd ed., London, 1965; *The Bayeux Tapestry. The Complete Tapestry in Colour*, ed. D.M. Wilson, London, 1985.

BEAUFORT, HENRY

The Beauforts were the illegitimate offspring of John of Gaunt, duke of Lancaster (q.v.) by Catherine Swynford, his mistress and later his third wife. Their high birth, and their kinship with the Lancastrian house, guaranteed them a position of political eminence in the fifteenth century. The most distinguished of Gaunt's three illegitimate sons was Henry, the clerical member of the family. Born in about 1376 at the castle of Beaufort, whence the family derived their surname, he was educated at Aachen and Queen's College, Oxford. Ecclesiastical preferment soon followed. In 1398 he became bishop of Lincoln, and in 1404, while still only in his twenties, he was translated to Winchester, the richest diocese in England.

On the accession of Henry V (q.v.) in 1413 Beaufort, who had already served on the council, was appointed chancellor, but his ambitions were by no means confined to the politics of his native land. He had been influential in healing the schism in the Church by promoting the election of Martin V as Pope. When Martin offered him the reward of a cardinal's hat in 1417, he eagerly accepted. However, he had unwisely neglected to obtain the king's permission beforehand. Henry V was not a man to take such presumption lightly. Henry blocked Beaufort's acceptance of the red hat, and it was not until 1426 in Henry VI's (q.v.) reign that he was able to accept the honour.

It was during Henry VI's long minority that Beaufort exercised his greatest influence in English affairs. He was one of the key figures on the minority council. However, his advice did not always pass unchallenged. He had a rival in the king's uncle, Humphrey, duke of Gloucester (q.v.). The two men adopted sharply differing foreign policies. Duke Humphrey advocated vigorous prosecution of the French war, including action in the Low Countries, while Beaufort, appreciating the importance of diplomacy to maintaining the English position in France, sought to preserve the English conquests by a long truce. In the next generation Humphrey's arguments were to be taken up by Richard, duke of York, and Beaufort's by his relative the duke of Somerset. To that extent, the factional divisions of the 1430s anticipate the line-up of forces later to be found in the Wars of the Roses (q.v.).

If Beaufort enjoyed an advantage over his opponents, it was an advantage conferred by money. His name became a by-word for immense wealth. The source of his fortune is hard to identify: some of it perhaps came from his father, and some from the wealthy see of Winchester. However, what he did with it is much clearer. He lent it to the crown. His dealings were not usurious, because generally interest was not paid on loans to the crown. Nevertheless, his position as the crown's biggest creditor gave him leverage which he might not otherwise have enjoyed. The scene at his deathbed in 1447, which made its way into Shakespeare's *Henry VI, Part II*, suggests that he felt remorse as he looked back over his career. But however humbly he faced his Maker, the magnificent tomb and chantry chapel which he commissioned in Winchester Cathedral suggest that humility was never among the qualities with which he had faced his fellow men.

G.L. Harriss, *Cardinal Beaufort. A Study in Lancastrian Ascendancy and Decline*, Oxford, 1988.

BECKET, THOMAS

The quarrel between Henry II (q.v.) and Becket, involving a clash of both personality and principle, is one of the epic struggles of the Middle Ages. Less than three years after his being done to death at Canterbury, Becket was canonized and his shrine in the cathedral became one of the great pilgrimage centres of Europe.

Thomas Becket was born in 1118, the son of Norman parents who had settled in London. He was educated at Merton Priory (Surrey), and joined the household of Archbishop Theobald, where he was soon marked out for promotion. In 1154 he was appointed archdeacon of Canterbury, and later in the same year, on Theobald's recommendation, chancellor of England. During the eight years that he served as chancellor he conducted himself, whether at home or abroad, with a panache that gave little indication of the asceticism that he was later to show at Canterbury. He enjoyed hunting, gaming and feasting. However, his biographers say that he resisted the temptations of the flesh, and there is no evidence of his public extravagance being matched by immorality in private.

In 1162 he was appointed to the see of Canterbury on Theobald's death. His lifestyle changed immediately. Gone were the days of high living. A regime of study and prayer took the place of that of hunting and feasting. His lavish extravagance became lavish charity, and his household of courtiers became one of scholars and lawyers. In an act calculated to annoy Henry he resigned as chancellor. Henry took offence because the very reason he had wanted Becket archbishop in the first place was to have a minister of his heading the Church. Within months the two men were at loggerheads. At a council at Westminster in October 1163 Henry demanded that criminous clerks found guilty in church courts should be handed over to the secular arm for punishment. Swayed by Becket, the bishops refused, and when Henry followed up his proposal with the demand that they should swear to maintain the ancient customs of the kingdom, they annoyed him still further by agreeing only if the words 'saving their order' were added. Henry might still have obtained verbal agreement to his proposals had he used gentle persuasion, but at the next meeting, at Clarendon in January 1164, he committed the mistake of codifying them in a written document, known as the Constitutions of Clarendon. The bishops felt unable to set their seals to such a document but, as soon as they had become firm in their resolve, Becket caved in. He gave his consent, and urged them to do likewise. Whatever pressure had led him to capitulate at the council, once he had left Clarendon he repented of his oath, and twice unsuccessfully attempted to leave the country. By now Henry was bent on the final destruction of his opponent. The chance was given to him in October 1164 at Northampton, when John FitzGilbert, marshal of the royal household, appealed to the king over a case that he had lost in the archbishop's court. Becket had failed to attend an earlier meeting at Westminster, enabling Henry to accuse him of contempt of court. Henry intensified the pressure by also accusing him of embezzlement while chancellor. On the final day of the meeting (12 October), king and archbishop met in different rooms, with intermediaries passing between them. The bishops told Henry that Becket had appealed to the Pope against the judgement they had passed on him in the FitzGilbert case – a clear breach of the Constitutions of Clarendon. When they agreed among themselves to appeal to Rome against Becket, Henry released them from the obligation of sentencing him in the embezzlement case. That pleasure was now left for the barons. But as they descended to the lower room, where the clergy were assembled, Becket stormed out. A few days later he left the country.

Becket's destination was Sens, where Pope Alexander III was living in exile under French protection. With a characteristic sense of the theatrical he threw himself at the Pope's feet. For the next six years he lived at Pontigny Abbey nearby, waging a war of words that went largely unheeded by Henry II and his advisers. Henry knew perfectly well that Becket could do little without the authority of Alexander III and that Alexander would do nothing for fear of driving the king into the obedience of his rival, the antipope Paschal III, who was sponsored by Frederick Barbarossa.

Despite several attempts at mediation by Louis VII of France, the dispute showed no signs of coming to a conclusion, until a crisis was provoked by the coronation of Henry's son and heir on 14 June 1170. The crowning of a ruler's heir during his father's lifetime was an Angevin practice, and the right of performing this, as of performing all coronation ceremonies, lay with the Archbishop of Canterbury. Since Becket was abroad, Henry asked the Archbishop of York to act in his place. Henry was well aware of the offence that the invitation would give to Becket; and, to defuse the situation, he offered to meet his adversary and make peace. Thus negotiations between the two sides were reopened, and resulted on 2 July 1170 at Freteval in an agreement for Becket's return. The reason for the breakthrough was quite simply that the great issues in question – appeals and criminous clerks, notably – were ignored. It was agreed that Becket should come back, and that the property of the see of Canterbury should be restored: that was all.

The settlement was much too superficial to assuage the bitter feelings that had been aroused over the previous six years, and when Becket landed at Sandwich on 1 December he was given a hostile reception by Gervase de Cornhill, Sheriff of Kent, and other well known supporters of the king. For his part, Becket hardly helped matters by excommunicating the Archbishop of York and the bishops of London and Salisbury. When news of these events reached Henry in Normandy, he flew into a rage so terrible that four of his knights taking, as they saw it, the hint, made their way to Canterbury. On 29 December Becket was murdered in his cathedral. His cult spread rapidly throughout Europe, and on 21 February 1173 he was canonized.

Henry managed to escape the Pope's wrath by going to Ireland for a year. Although an interdict was imposed on his French lands by the Archbishop of Sens, he was never excommunicated, only prohibited from entering a church. In May 1172 at a meeting with papal envoys at Avranches he was formally reconciled to the Church. The terms negotiated were ones personal to himself. Henry agreed to go on crusade; to restore the lands of the Church of Canterbury; and to abolish customs prejudicial to the Church. The difficult issues that had divided him from his archbishop were conspicuously ignored. At no point was any reference made to the matter of criminous clerks. For this reason Becket's supporters claimed that he had died in vain. However, the position was not as simple as this. Even though the issue of criminous clerks was omitted from the Avranches settlement, Henry quietly abandoned his earlier position. He gave up his attempt to bring criminous clerks before the secular arm. The principle was thus implicitly established of 'benefit of clergy', which entitled an indicted clerk to trial in the court Christian.

The problem which the quarrel between king and archbishop had so clearly highlighted was that of reconciling the jurisdiction of the reformed Church, as expressed in canon law, with the jurisdiction of the secular monarchy, as expressed in the ancient customs of the realm written down at Clarendon. In different times, and with different men, these issues might have been resolved in less dramatic fashion. But Henry and Becket found their respective lines of thought becoming increasingly divergent. As D. Knowles has written, it was only when he became archbishop that Becket's personality, hitherto concealed under a veil of worldliness, stood revealed. He had found a cause to fight for. He was neither a scholar nor a philosopher; and unlike Anselm (q.v.) or Francis of Assisi, he was not by nature a saint. But he did have the makings of a martyr.

F. Barlow, *Thomas Becket*, London, 1986.

BENEDICTINES

The Rule of St Benedict provided the foundation of monastic life in the medieval West. Composed by St Benedict of Nursia around 526, it was a simple and straightforward code. The monastic day, it said, was to be divided into three parts – four hours prayer, four hours reading and six hours labour, while the affairs of the community were to be looked after by an abbot and subordinate officials. The Rule was introduced into England by the keen Romanist, St Wilfrid (d.709) for his monasteries at Hexham and Ripon. Adoption of the Rule was entirely voluntary, however, and many monasteries, cherishing their autonomy, followed their own rules. The first attempt to bring a measure of uniformity to English monasticism was made in about 970, when a code known as the *Regularis Concordia* was adopted. The association of this code with the fallen Wessex monarchy ensured that it would be put aside after the Norman Conquest. To take its place Lanfranc (q.v.), the new Norman archbishop, issued his own Monastic Constitutions, addressed solely to the monks of his cathedral of Canterbury (q.v.) but widely imitated all the same in other houses. Until the end of the eleventh century all monks had regarded themselves as Benedictine. But at the beginning of the new century the Benedictine monopoly was shattered by the rise of the new orders – the Cluniacs (q.v.), the Cistercians (q.v.) and the Augustinian canons (q.v.). One effect of this revolution was to make the Black Monks (as they were known from the colour of their habit) organize themselves more formally than they had done hitherto. The Fourth Lateran Council in 1215 created a legislative body for the order in the form of the General Chapter. And later in the thirteenth century the system of episcopal visitation, from which the Benedictines had previously been exempt, was introduced to correct abuses and maintain standards of religious life.

The Benedictines numbered among their houses some of the oldest and most distinguished foundations in England – Glastonbury, Bury St Edmund's, Peterborough and the cathedral priories of Canterbury (q.v.), Winchester, Worcester and Ely. After the Conquest they were joined by important new houses like Selby and Tewkesbury. Unlike those of the Cistercians, the Benedictines' houses were fully integrated into the fabric of feudal society. Most of their abbots held as tenants-in-chief of the crown and were responsible for the provision of a quota of knights in the feudal host. As large-scale landowners, the Benedictines did much to shape the economic and social life of medieval England. They were usually conservative proprietors. In the thirteenth century, the age of 'high farming', when their manors were organized for production for the market, they made extensive use of the labour services of their villeins (q.v.) to cultivate the demesnes (q.v.), and after the Black Death (q.v.) in the following century they tried to keep up these services when more flexible landlords were abandoning demesne cultivation altogether. It was the Benedictines' economic conservatism that made some of their biggest monasteries, like St Albans, the objects of vehement hostility in the Peasants Revolt (q.v.) of 1381.

Within the cloister the life of the Black Monks was governed by the Benedictine Rule as amended and reinterpreted over the centuries. The house would be ruled by an abbot, or in the case of a priory by a prior. Beneath him the officials known as 'obedientiaries' looked after the administration and handled the money. The manner of recruitment to the cloister varied over the centuries. According to the Rule admission could be by 'oblation' as a child or by free choice as an adult. One such child recruit in Norman England was the future chronicler, Orderic Vitalis, who tells us that at the age of ten he was given by his father to a monk who was charged with admitting him to a monastery overseas. The young Orderic was received into the house of St Evroult in Normandy, and there he was to spend the rest of his days. Towards the end of the twelfth century, however, childhood oblation came to be regarded with disapproval. It was no longer felt that a child should be committed to a life in the cloister by a decision not of its making. The steady flow of mature recruits in the twelfth century enabled this change of policy to be accomplished without any diminution in the numbers admitted. But in the late Middle Ages, when a wider range of careers opened up, in administration, in the universities, in magnate service, the numbers in the houses of the Benedictines as of the other orders began to decline.

D. Knowles, *The Monastic Order in England*, 2nd ed., Cambridge, 1966, and *The Religious Orders in England*, 3 vols, Cambridge, 1948-59.

BLACK DEATH

To our great grief the plague carried off so vast a multitude of people of both sexes that nobody could be found who would bear the corpses to the graveyard. Men and women carried their own children on their shoulders to the church and threw them into the common pit. From these pits such an appalling stench was given off that scarcely anyone dared even to walk beside the cemeteries.*

The scene described here by William de Dene, a monk of Rochester, would have been an unpleasantly familiar one in England and western Europe in 1348 and 1349. The Black Death had arrived in England in early June 1348 when two ships from Gascony unloaded at Melcombe Regis in Dorset. From there it spread within weeks to London and the South-East and then to every part of England. Its symptoms were vividly described by the Italian poet Boccaccio:

In men and women alike it first betrayed itself by the emergence of certain tumours in the

groin or the arm-pits, some of which grew as large as an apple… which the common folk call gavocciolo. From the two said parts of the body this deadly gavocciolo soon began to propagate itself in all directions… after which the form of the malady began to change, black spots making their appearance in many cases on the arm or the thigh… And as the gavocciolo had been and still was an infallible token of approaching death, so also were these spots on whomsoever they showed themselves.*

What Boccaccio was describing here was the symptoms of bubonic plague. The virus was carried by a flea which lived on mice and rats. In the crowded and unhygienic conditions of mid-fourteenth century England it was virtually impossible to stop it spreading. The effects of the plague were devastating. It has been estimated that between 30% and 45% of the population were carried off. The incidence of mortality, however, varied sharply between one social class and another. The clergy saw their ranks decimated because the nature of their work brought them into daily contact with the afflicted. The gentry and the nobility, on the other hand, almost certainly suffered much less. The more hygienic surroundings in which they lived presumably enabled them to escape affliction.

After the fifteen months of the visitation life returned to normal remarkably quickly. The economy recovered and vacant tenements were filled. Wages rose rapidly, leading to the Statute of Labourers in 1351, but so too did prices: which allowed landowners to maintain their profit levels. In 1361, however, the pestilence returned. This time the death rate overall was lower, but the upper classes suffered proportionately worse. The suggestion has been made that this second outbreak took the form of pneumonic plague: in other words, the infection was spread through the air. Many more outbreaks were to follow – in

* P. Ziegler, *The Black Death*, p. 168

* Ibid., pp. 18-19

1368, 1375, 1390 and at intervals in the fifteenth century.

In the 1980s a large plague cemetery, almost certainly dating from the Black Death, was excavated at East Smithfield in London. The mass burials were all made in neat rows, indicating that the catastrophe, though terrifying, did not lead to a breakdown in orderly and decent disposal of the remains.

See also POPULATION

The Black Death, ed. R. Horrox, Manchester, 1994; C. Platt, *King Death. The Black Death and its Aftermath in Late Medieval England*, London, 1996.

BOSWORTH, BATTLE OF

The death of Richard III (q.v.) at Bosworth in 1485 brought the Yorkist line to an end and put the pretender Henry Tudor on the throne. King Richard had been in Nottinghamshire when he heard that his rival had landed near Milford Haven on 7 August. Richard had been taken by surprise. Henry had crossed Wales unopposed and had by now advanced well into the Midlands. The two forces met at Market Bosworth, near Hinckley, on 22 August. Henry's force numbered about 5,000 and the king's about 8,000. The engagement was closely fought. A key factor in the outcome was the earl of Northumberland's failure to deploy his men on Richard's behalf. It used to be thought that the earl's failure was the result of treachery. However, it is now considered more likely to have been a consequence of geographical problems. Richard had staked out a strong position for himself on Ambien Hill. From this vantage point he was able to survey the surrounding landscape. However, the hilltop site left him with a shortage of space, which prevented him from deploying his men along a wide front. He had no alternative but to draw them up in a column, one division behind another. Northumberland, who was in the rear, thus failed to engage because he was unable to do so. It was the duke of Norfolk's men at the front

who bore the brunt of the struggle. Observing the difficulties that Norfolk was in, Richard led a charge himself, but in the heat of the battle was cut down. Henry Tudor emerged victorious, and Richard III acquired the unenviable distinction of being the only king since the Norman Conquest to die on an English battlefield.

M.J. Bennett, *The Battle of Bosworth*, Gloucester, 1985; M.K. Jones, *Bosworth 1485: Psychology of a Battle*, Stroud, 2002.

BRACTON, HENRY

The most important legal treatise to have survived from medieval England is the one commonly known as Bracton's *De legibus et consuetidinibus Anglie* (*The Laws and Customs of England*). A large work, this is the first comprehensive exposition of English law, written apparently in the mid-thirteenth century by a judge drawing on many years' experience on the bench. He had at his disposal the court rolls of his predecessors from which he extracted cases to compile the other volume perpetuating his name, known as *Bracton's Note Book* (ed. F.W. Maitland, 3 vols, 1887). Of Bracton himself relatively little is known. Bratton Fleming and Bratton Clovelly in Devon both claim him as one of their sons. By the 1230s he was a clerk in the service of the king's justice, William de Ralegh, and from 1244 was himself a justice in eyre (q.v.). He died in 1268, and was probably buried in Exeter Cathedral, of which he had been appointed chancellor in May 1264.

The famous treatise on the laws of England has long been associated with Henry Bracton because it is his name which occurs at the front of the manuscript which is the archetype of all manuscripts of the work. But, as S.E. Thorne has shown, its textual history is more complicated than might be supposed. A prototype *De legibus* had been written before 1236 by someone connected with Martin de Pateshull, a distinguished judge of Henry III's early years. It was then subjected to a number of revisions, one of them by a clerk of William de Ralegh who may or may not have been Henry Bracton. Over the next twenty years it was subjected to further revisions, in the course of which the name of the original author was lost and that of Bracton substituted. Soon after 1256 another editor reduced this, by now, swollen text into the archetype of *De legibus*. If Thorne's reconstruction is correct, then the treatise probably reflects the thinking more of Ralegh or Pateshull than of the man whose name it now bears.

See also JUSTICE

Bracton on the Laws and Customs of England, ed. G.E. Woodbine, trans. S.E. Thorne, Selden Soc., 1977.

BRASSES

A brass is a flat metal plate, engraved with a figure or inscription or both, and laid in a church as a memorial.

The origins of brass engraving are to be found in northern and eastern Europe in the twelfth and thirteenth centuries. The earliest brass effigies to have survived are to be found in Germany. The oldest of all is a plate covering the grave of St Ulrich at Augsburg and dating from 1187; after this comes the brass of Bishop Yso von Wolpe, 1231, at Verden. A great many brasses are known to have been laid in thirteenth-century France, although these are all now lost. A third cluster of brasses was laid *c.*1290–1300 on the edge of the Germanic world, in Silesia. The stylistic variety and wide geographical range of these early brasses makes it unlikely that they were of common origin. The examples in Germany probably originated as two-dimensional versions of the low relief bronze effigies produced there since the eleventh century. West of the Rhine, brasses appear to have emerged as a by-product of stone incised slabs. Incised slabs were a very popular form of memorial in the thirteenth

century. At some stage the idea developed of inlaying these with alabasters or resins to give a richer effect. Increasingly, the inlay used was 'latten' – brass: an alloy chosen for its durability. Bodily features such as the head or hands might first be inlaid; eventually the entire composition was. When that stage had been reached, the brass may be said to have arrived.

The making of the first brasses in England is closely associated with the production of incised slabs. The earliest surviving brasses – those dating from *c.*1290–1300 – are very similar in design to the products of the London incised slab workshops. Evidently the engraving of brasses was developed in these ateliers as a sideline. As the popularity of brasses caught on, however, the engraving of brasses became a business in its own right. A wide variety of brass memorial types was produced. On the one hand, there were the magnificent full-length figures, like those of Joan de Cobham, *c.*1305, at Cobham (Kent), Sir John d'Abernon, *c.*1330, at Stoke d'Abernon (Surrey) (plate 45) and Sir Robert de Bures, d.1331, at Acton (Suffolk), which rank among the finest memorials of the age; while, on the other, there were smaller figures or busts in floriated cross compositions, like those at Merton College, Oxford, which were very popular with the clergy.

The majority of surviving medieval brasses were engraved in workshops in London. The products of these workshops can be identified by certain stylistic conventions which they have in common. Most medieval effigies, whether tombs (q.v.), incised slabs or brasses, were not portraits; they were stylized representations of the deceased. A client could ask to be shown in an up-to-date suit of armour, and he could, and often did, request that his tomb be modelled on another that he had seen. But he did not expect his effigy to be a physical resemblance. For this reason each workshop could develop its own standard designs which the master would pass on to the apprentices he trained; and, even when these designs had to be updated to accommodate changes in fashion, stylistic continuity survived in the way that small details were portrayed. It is through observation of these details – these trademarks – that the main schools of engraving in London in the period from the Black Death to the Reformation can be identified. Following the conventional classification used by scholars, these are:

Style A (c.1360–1410): a very active workshop which produced brasses of varying quality, some, such as the priest at Edlesborough (Bucks) very good but others rather clumsy; style A's trademark is the profile nose.

Style B (c.1360–c.1470): a prolific workshop, which produced graceful though rather monotonous brasses identifiable by such motifs as a rose with four petals and four spines (e.g. in a canopy) and the criss-cross pattern for depicting grass below the feet. A good example is the brass of Sir Hugh Halsham at West Grinstead (Sussex), 1441.

Style C (c.1390–c.1408): a minority workshop which produced richly detailed brasses recognizable, in the case of military figures, by the criss-cross pattern on the sword hilt.

Style D (c.1410–c.1485): a workshop which may have taken over the business run by A, D's brasses are more elaborate than those of B, and identifiable by the use of rose windows in canopies and flowery bases at the feet of figures. The style is well represented by the brasses of Thomas Brounflete at Wymington (Beds), 1430, and Robert Ingleton at Thornton (Bucks), 1472.

Style E (c.1415–c.1440): another minority workshop, whose output is distinguishable by the staring eyes of the figure.

Style F (c.1475 onwards): perhaps the successor to B; the brasses of this series can be iden-

tified by the bubbly, stalkless plants on the base and by the downward sloping horizontal bars of the capital H on inscriptions.

These were the main London workshops in the post-Black Death period. Before the Black Death there were workshops in a host of provincial centres – York, Lincoln, Carlisle, Exeter and perhaps even Shrewsbury. In the middle of the fourteenth century, however, most of these centres ceased production. The reasons for their extinction were several. One was almost certainly the effect of the Black Death in disrupting production. The second, and perhaps the more important, was the sheer prestige and authority of the London-made brasses. These offered assured standards of workmanship and design.

Much later, in the fifteenth century, however, the regional centres experienced a revival of fortune. New or revived ateliers were established at Norwich, Cambridge and Bury, while much higher production levels were recorded at York. The growing affluence of the lesser proprietors probably sustained a buoyant local demand. But the ability of local producers to undercut transport costs from London may also have been a factor.

The men who engraved English medieval brasses were known as 'marblers'. The reason for this was that London-made brasses were set in slabs of marble – Purbeck marble from Dorset. The connection between brass and marble had been forged in the thirteenth century, when the fashion developed of inlaying marble slabs with separate-letter inscriptions. By a happy coincidence the brass of one such 'marbler' is still extant. At Sudborough (Northants) is the brass of William West, his wife and their eleven children, one of whom, another William, is described as a 'marbler'. This man is to be identified with the William West known to have been a marbler in London in the 1430s, about the time that this brass, a standard style-B product, was engraved. If, as is almost certain, West was responsible for placing the brass as a memorial to his parents, then there are grounds here for associating West with B. How long he remained in charge of the workshop is not clear, but there is evidence that by 1454 it was under new management. In that year John Essex, marbler, William Austen, founder, and Thomas Stevyns, coppersmith, contracted to make an inscription for the tomb of Richard Beauchamp, earl of Warwick, at St Mary's, Warwick. The lettering of this inscription is of the style found on B's brasses. In other words, it is likely that Essex and Stevyns took over the workshop on the retirement of West. Before the Black Death it is more difficult to identify the men who engraved the brasses, but one figure stands out. This is Adam of Corfe (the Dorset name is significant), who dominated the 'marbling' trade in London between c.1305 and 1331, when he died. It is almost certainly Adam who was responsible for the great early brasses such as those at Stoke d'Abernon and Acton.

A little can be said about the process of manufacture of brasses. What is referred to as 'brass' was in fact an alloy of copper (75%-80% in the early fourteenth century), zinc (15%-20%), lead and tin, known by the term 'latten' and imported into England from the continent. The plain metal was cut into plates up to 3ft in length, which at some stage would be butted together and, in the case of the larger brasses, joined by a rectangular backing plate to make a life-size effigy. Next, the design was sketched lightly on the surface, and the lines engraved to the required pattern using chasing tools and a burin. Cross-hatching was employed to show areas of shade. Like most medieval monuments, brasses were originally coloured. The lines were filled with black mastic, and the surface enamelled or gilded. When the brass was ready, it was fixed into the slab. The big, early brasses were heavy enough to be held down on a bed of pitch in the indent simply by the force of their own weight. Smaller brasses, however, needed to be

secured by rivets driven into lead-filled sockets in the slab. The finished monument, slab and all, was then ready to be taken to its destination, along water routes wherever possible for reasons of both economy and convenience. Not surprisingly, when it is recalled how bulky the finished product would be, the expense of carriage added considerably to final cost. A really big brass, like that ordered by Sir John de St Quintin in 1397 for Brandsburton church (Yorks), could cost as much as twenty marks (£13 6s 8d). St Quintin's brass still remains and is clearly the product of a workshop at York: he saved on transport by ordering locally.

English medieval brasses differed greatly from the majority of those made on the continent. Most continental brasses took the form of big rectangular plates engraved all over. English brasses, however, were products of the separate-inlay technique: that is to say, they were made of separate pieces, all laid individually in the stone. Continental brasses were grand and expensive: virtuoso displays of the engraver's art. English brasses were generally more modest. Precisely because they were made up of separate pieces, they could be assembled in different ways. A rich patron could order a grand canopied brass with accessories, a middling patron a more modest one with a figure and an inscription, and a humble tenant farmer an inscription and perhaps an emblem. If the grandest brasses cost the equivalent of many months' income, the smaller brasses were much cheaper. A coat of arms and inscription could be got for a couple of pounds.

In the late Middle Ages brasses became a domesticated phenomenon. They were a very popular form of memorial, particularly in the south and the east. Over to the west and in the Midlands, alabaster incised slabs were also favoured. Some 7,500 brasses survive in England, more than in any other part of Europe, but many more were originally laid. Brasses tell us a great deal about the ambitions and aspirations of those they commemorate. Inscriptions can supply biographical details, while the selection of saints represented as weepers and in canopies can open a window onto piety. The rich heraldic display on knightly tombs attests the competitiveness of the knightly class, while the merchants' marks on the brasses of the Cotswold woolmen attest the confidence and self-consciousness of the trader elite. But brasses should not be interpreted in isolation. They were only one of a range of types of memorial used in the Middle Ages. In the thirteenth century Purbeck marble cross slabs were popular with the clergy. Later, relief effigies in marble, free-stone and alabaster, generally more expensive than brasses, gained a following among the gentry, nobility and higher clergy.

See also TOMBS

M. Norris, *Monumental Brasses. The Memorials*, 2 vols, London, 1977; M. Norris, *Monumental Brasses. The Craft*, London, 1978; *Monumental Brasses as Art and History*, ed. J. Bertram, Stroud, 1996.

BRÉTIGNY, TREATY OF
See HUNDRED YEARS WAR

BRISTOL
Bristol was one of the two or three leading cities of medieval England and the most important centre of population in the West Country. The first evidence of the city's economic life is provided by the chance survival of a couple of early eleventh-century silver pennies, which indicate that it had a mint in Ethelred II's reign. From Domesday Book (q.v.) seventy or eighty years later it is evident that it had become a place of some importance, although unfortunately the information provided by the survey is too incomplete to give any idea of the size of the population or the trades engaged in.

The town of Bristol was located in one corner of the royal manor of Barton Regis, near the junction of the Avon and Frome rivers. Across the Avon, on the Somerset side, lay the suburb of Redcliffe, which was held by the Berkeleys of Berkeley Castle. Redcliffe had geographical advantages over Bristol itself, which enabled it in the thirteenth century to prosper at the expense of the older port. The burgesses of Bristol were resentful of this competition, and rivalry between the two communities culminated in attempts made by each to build harbour facilities to attract trade from the other. There were also disputes between the Bristol folk and the Berkeley lords of Redcliffe, which culminated in 1305 in attacks on the Berkeleys' property. In the late Middle Ages, when a number of other English towns experienced decline, Bristol appears to have prospered. The town's merchants throve on the long-established English tie with Gascony (q.v.). Further afield, traders went to Spain, Portugal, and even to Madeira. Among the many products which they exported was cloth from the near-by cloth-making villages (q.v. INDUSTRY). At the end of the fifteenth century Bristol was involved in the new voyages to the west: it was from Bristol that John Cabot embarked on his voyage in the *Matthew* in 1497.

Like their contemporaries elsewhere, the burgesses of Bristol invested some of their wealth in rebuilding or enlarging the local churches. The town had no cathedral of its own until 1542, when St Augustine's Abbey became the centre of a new diocese carved out of that of Worcester. But across the Avon at Redcliffe it had in St Mary's a church of such magnificence that it was to be described by Queen Elizabeth as 'the fairest, goodliest and most famous parish Church in England'. The architectural history of St Mary's is ill documented but it seems that the rebuilding process began in the later fourteenth century and that the design owed much to work on the east end of Wells Cathedral.

B. Little, *The City and County of Bristol*, 2nd ed., 1967; *'Almost the Richest City'. Bristol in the Middle Ages*, ed. L. Keen, *British Archaeological Assoc. Transactions*, xix, 1997.

BUILDING

A great deal is known about methods of building and construction in the Middle Ages, partly because the documentary sources are rich and partly because the buildings themselves provide evidence of their construction.

For sake of example, let us consider how the planning and building of a great church was undertaken. The motives that led a bishop or a cathedral chapter to embark on a lengthy programme of reconstruction were various. At Canterbury it was a disastrous fire that caused the choir to be rebuilt after 1174. At Ely it was the collapse of the central tower. On other occasions it was the desire to create larger and more dignified surroundings for a saint's shrine.

Once the decision had been taken, money had to be raised. For this purpose a fabric fund would be opened. Churches like Canterbury fortunate enough to possess the relics of a popular saint were assured of a regular income from the offerings of pilgrims. Others had to supplement their ordinary revenues, just as we do today, by launching an appeal. Bishops organized preaching tours to create an enthusiasm for the project, and local landowners were persuaded to dig into their pockets.

As soon as the money started flowing in, the clergy were free to think about possible designs. So often in guide books we read statements attributing rebuilding operations to this or that bishop that we gain the impression that the clergy themselves were responsible for the execution of all the plans. Almost certainly this view is mistaken. Just occasionally the evidence points to the guiding hand of a clerk or monastic official, like Alan of Walsingham, the sacrist at Ely, who is usually credited with conceiving the Octagon; but more often the responsibility for architectural planning rested with the master mason. Here we must notice an important difference between medieval and modern building organization. Today it is the professional architect who draws the plans and the builder who supervises construction. In the Middle Ages, however, this distinction did not exist, and the master mason who had overall direction of the works and responsibility for the design would have begun his career years before as a trainee in the stonemason's yard.

Although responsibility for conceiving a design would be his, the master mason would need to take into account the wishes of those who were paying him. On the continent the mason was often asked to construct a model to enable his clients to see what the completed building would look like. In England this does not seem to have been done, although we can hardly suppose that a cathedral chapter would authorize an ambitious scheme without first inspecting the plans. Whatever happened, we can assume that drawings would have been made at some stage, whether in a sketch book, like the one kept by an early thirteenth century Frenchman, Villard de Honnecourt, or on a plaster tracing floor, like the ones that have survived in upstairs chambers at York Minster and Wells Cathedral.

As soon as the designs had been agreed, work could begin on laying the foundations. Sometimes, as at Westminster Abbey in 1245, the old walls had to be demolished before erection of the new could begin. Elsewhere, particularly if it was an eastwards extension that was contemplated, the new foundations could be laid out around and beyond the old work. Orientation was at first rather rough and ready, but the rediscovery of geometry in the twelfth century enabled builders to be more precise in working out the lines and angles, and accumulated experience no doubt counted for still more. Trenches were then dug – to a depth of as much as 31ft for the tower of St Stephen's, Bristol – and filled with rubble as a footing for the walls. If the ground was marshy, it would be necessary first to reinforce the base by ramming in timber piles; the dangers that arose if this precaution was not taken were shown in 985 at Ramsey Abbey, where a newly built tower gave way and had to be dismantled.

By the time the foundations were being set, arrangements would have been made for stone to be quarried. A few important churches enjoyed rights over a particular quarry, but others less favoured had to hire a quarry as needed, or simply buy stone on the open market. The celebrated quarry at Caen in Normandy was even used as a source by English builders after the Conquest. For churches like Canterbury it was probably cheaper to buy stone in France and ship it across the Channel than to cart it overland from some English quarry. The most celebrated English quarries used in the Middle Ages were those at Barnack, which supplied stone for Norwich, Ely and Cambridge, Doulting, which supplied Wells, Chilmark, which supplied Salisbury, and Reigate, which supplied London.

When the stone had arrived, work could start on erecting the walls. The manner of construction varied according to time and place. Some walls would be composed of rubble, roughly hewn blocks of stone cemented by mortar, others, at least in part, of 'ashlar', regularly shaped pieces of stone so placed as to give a smooth surface. In Norman times the surfaces would usually be rough before being plastered to receive frescoes, but later, as tools became more sophisticated, it became common, even if most of the wall was rubble, to give it a smooth ashlar finish. Once the walls started rising, scaffolding would be needed. There are plenty of illustrations in contemporary manuscripts showing the various forms of scaffold known to medieval man. One of the most ingenious was spiral scaffolding, probably devised to facilitate the construction of the circular towers that are a feature of military architecture in the thirteenth and fourteenth centuries. On most sites, however, the scaffolding would probably have looked little different from that in use today, except that it was constructed of wood instead of steel, and instead of planks, the walkways were made of wattled hurdles. When the walls had reached their full height, a wooden roof would be built, so that the job of erecting the stone vault could be carried out underneath in the dry.

One of the most difficult and dangerous operations must have been raising the stone up to the dizzy heights attained by some medieval towers. Large blocks like roof bosses, which had to be placed at the intersection of vaulting ribs, were fashioned either at the quarry or on the site, using a hammer and chisel. They would then have to be hoisted up by some sort of device, of which the simplest and earliest was a great hempen cable passed over a pivot. In the thirteenth century the treadwheel came into use, and the one that survives today in the tower of Salisbury Cathedral was very likely used in its construction in the fourteenth century. By the end of the Middle Ages another advance was made when cranes, for long in use on the quayside, were adopted for building purposes and erected on roof-lines to hoist up stones and roof timbers.

How quickly was a building finished in the Middle Ages? There is no end of examples to show that construction of a cathedral nave could take the best part of half a century. By the 1180s, when the nave at Peterborough was completed, the Romanesque style in which it had been started was looking decidedly outmoded. On the other hand, work proceeded quite quickly at Salisbury, where the present cathedral (except the spire) was finished in thirty-eight years (q.v. ARCHITECTURE, ECCLESIASTICAL). Certainly as far as ecclesiastical buildings were concerned what slowed down the pace of building was the irregular supply of funds: at St Albans shortage of money brought work on the west front to a halt in the early thirteenth century and the hard-pressed abbot had to organize preaching tours to raise cash. In some of the greater churches as soon as construction finished at one end of the building, it was time to start again at the other. At York, for example, the commencement of work on a new nave in 1290 inaugurated a long and intermittent era of building that was not to end until the central tower was completed in 1472.

Looking at the cathedrals, the grandest creations of the Middle Ages, we can easily come away with the impression that most medieval building was done in stone. Nothing could be further from the truth. For most domestic, and even some ecclesiastical, architecture timber-frame construction was the rule. Wood was more widely available than stone, and in those parts of England where quarries were few there was bound to be a forest that could provide supplies of oak. Carpenters never had to seek far for their raw material. But once they had obtained it, they rarely allowed it time to season. The result inevitably was that it warped, producing the rakish lines that today characterize so many timber-framed houses constructed in this period.

While the carpenters were cutting the timber to size, preparation of the foundations could go ahead. If the timber-frame were to be rested directly on the ground, the soil would be levelled and rammed down firm. But it made better sense, for avoiding rot, to erect the frame on a low stone wall to the height of about three or four feet. On the more substantial properties, this precaution would almost certainly be taken. When the groundworks were ready, the end-frames would be erected. Sometimes these frames were assembled on the site and sometimes at a distant yard, whence they were dragged to their destination and lifted into position. It was possible to use this prefabricated technique because of the construction method, based on the mortice and tenon, which enabled one timber to be locked into another. Once all the framing was in position, work could begin on filling the spaces between the timbers. This was usually done by the well-known method of 'wattle and daub', by which interwoven reeds or twigs were covered with plaster. The inside walls, as in a church, would very probably have been whitewashed and painted. As for roofing, thatch would probably have been employed most often in the earlier part of our period and tiles or lead later on, by those who could afford it.

L. F. Salzman, *Building in England down to 1540*, 2nd ed., Oxford, 1967; J.H. Harvey, *English Medieval Architects. A Biographical Dictionary down to 1550*, 2nd ed., Gloucester, 1984.

CADE'S REBELLION

Jack Cade was a Kentishman who gave his name to a rebellion against Henry VI's government in 1450. His background and parentage are obscure (which is puzzling because he could hardly have drawn the support he did from gentry as well as commoners had he been an upstart). The course of the rebellion was not dissimilar to that of the Peasants' Revolt (q.v.) of 1381. Towards the end of May the rebels gathered in Kent and then took over the capital. There they behaved so badly that the citizens, aided by the garrison of the Tower, fought to regain control of London Bridge. A few days later a free pardon was offered and the rebels withdrew. Jack Cade's rebellion, however, much more than the Peasants' Revolt, was a product of mainly political grievances arising from corruption at home and defeat abroad. The dominance at Henry VI's court in the 1440s of a clique around the duke of Suffolk had given rise to widespread resentment, which boiled over after the duke's murder on 3 May 1450. All the predictable complaints found expression in Cade's manifesto, a document embodying familiar ideas that had been the stock-in-trade of reform movements for the previous two centuries. It blamed the evils of the realm on the 'false counsel' that the king had received from Suffolk and his progeny who, it said, should be dismissed and replaced by lords of the blood royal like the duke of York. Although the manifesto was considered by the council at the end of May, it passed into oblivion once the rebels had been dispersed and Cade himself captured and killed. But, if it achieved nothing else, the rebellion did have the important consequence of encouraging York to hurry back from Ireland to claim the position in national politics sought for him by the commoners of Kent.

I.M.W. Harvey, *Jack Cade's Rebellion of 1450*, Oxford, 1991.

CALAIS

The town of Calais was England's bridgehead to the continent in the late Middle Ages. In proportion to its size it was the most costly to win of Edward III's many prizes in the Hundred Years War (q.v.), but it was also, as it turned out, the most important and the most long-lasting. Edward had defeated the French at Crécy (q.v.) on 26 August 1346. After the battle he marched to Calais and surrounded the town. The siege which then began was to last for eleven months. English losses were heavy, and when the town eventually surrendered on 4 August 1347 the king was in no mood to be merciful to the burghers. According to the famous story he spared them only after the pleading of his queen.

They were shortly expelled, and the town was repopulated by the English.

The strategic advantages which the English gained from their possession of Calais were obvious. They won control of both sides of the Channel and they obtained a continental foothold from which to undertake future campaigns against France. The town was defended by a permanent garrison, which in the fifteenth century became a force to reckon with in domestic politics. Whoever won the captaincy of Calais had at his call a private army that he could use in the struggle for power in England. Warwick (q.v.) got the post in 1455, when the Yorkists were temporarily ascendant, and it was from Calais five years later that he launched the invasion which culminated in his victory at Northampton on 10 July 1460 (q.v. WARS OF THE ROSES).

A difficulty faced by the English crown was that of paying the Calais garrison. Calais was dependent on exchequer subsidies to the tune of some £1,500 per annum in peacetime and £3,000–£4,000 in wartime. The soldiers' wages were often in arrears. A solution to the problem of payment was offered by the establishment in 1363 of the Calais 'staple' through which nearly all of England's wool exports to the continent would pass. The creation of the staple brought to an end the long and often bitter argument over the exporting of wool and the taxes to be paid on it. On the one hand, the king wanted to restrict the right of exporting to a group of merchants assured of making sufficient profit to enable them to lend to the crown on the security of the subsidy levied on wool; on the other, the growers favoured a larger consortium of merchants with whom they could bargain for the best price they could get. The Calais staple was a compromise – a mart run by a broadly based company of some 200 merchants whose monopoly position would nonetheless enable them to make loans, repayable later from the customs. The exchequer still retained responsibility for paying the garrison, but they could anticipate income by contracting loans with the Staplers. It was to be another century before what was to be the ultimate solution was conceived. This was the Act of Retainer, 1466, by which the Company of the Staple itself assumed responsibility for collecting the customs and subsidy on wool, out of the proceeds of which they would meet the cost of the garrison.

The arms of the Company can be seen on brasses to Staplers at Thame (Oxon) and Northleach (Glos). These brasses (q.v.) constitute some of the few visible survivals of the English occupation of Calais. There is little to see at the town itself.

CAMBRIDGE

Long before the scholars arrived, there had been a settlement of sorts at Cambridge. A number of roads converged here. Moreover, it was the northernmost point at which passage from East Anglia to the Midlands was practicable before the Fens made communications impossible. The Romans had built an enclosure north of the Cam in the Chesterton Lane area, but by the twelfth century the centre of life in Cambridge, as indicated by church building, had shifted south to where the modern town centre is. The first evidence for the existence of a community of scholars in Cambridge comes in 1209, when tension between town and gown in Oxford (q.v.) led to the migration eastwards of a group of masters. Why they chose Cambridge is not clear. It may have been because it was near to the rich and populous East Anglian counties.

In their organization and constitutional development the Cambridge schools closely followed those of Oxford. The Chancellor of the University is first mentioned in 1230 within a year or two of the appearance of the same official in Oxford. In both universities the undergraduates lived in houses around the town rented by Principals which in Oxford were known as halls and in

Cambridge as hostels. The colleges which characterize the two cities today were called into being to cater for the needs of graduates undertaking the long courses of study that would carry them to a doctorate. The first college in Cambridge was Peterhouse, founded in 1280 by Hugh de Balsham, bishop of Ely, for 'studious scholars living according to the rule of the scholars of Oxford called of Merton'. In the first half of the fourteenth century there followed King's Hall (before 1316), Michaelhouse (1324), University or Clare Hall (1326), Pembroke (1347), Gonville (1348), Trinity Hall (1350) and Corpus Christi (1352). Of these the most remarkable were King's Hall, originating as its name suggests in an endowment from the king, and Corpus, the only college in either university to be founded by the town guilds. For the next century there were no more colleges until the foundation of God's House in 1439 and King's College by Henry VI (q.v.) in 1441. The early history of King's was chequered, for the collapse of the Lancastrian monarchy in 1461 brought work on its great chapel to a halt for sixteen years until it was resumed by Edward IV in 1477 and then carried to completion by Henry VIII in 1515. At 94ft high and nearly 300ft in length this great building of cathedralesque proportions must have towered even more than it does today over the country town at its feet. It needs to be remembered that for the first century and a half of its existence Cambridge was a much smaller university than Oxford, probably less than half its size in terms of total numbers. Only in the fifteenth century did it start to catch up.

See also UNIVERSITIES

D.R. Leader, *A History of the University of Cambridge. I. The University to 1546*, Cambridge, 1989.

CANTERBURY

The origins of Canterbury are to be found in the Roman settlement of Durovernum Cantiacorum, which occupied the site. In Saxon times Canterbury was the seat of the Jutish kings who ruled Kent. When Augustine and his missionaries landed at Ebbsfleet in 597, they were assured of a sympathetic reception at the Kentish court because Bertha, Ethelbert's queen, was a Christian from the royal house of France. Bede tells us that she used a church on the eastern side of the city dedicated to St Martin of Tours, which had been built by the Christians in Roman times. St Martin's is still standing today, and claims with some justice to be the oldest church in England. A couple of hundred yards to its west Augustine established the abbey of St Peter and St Paul, later known as St Augustine's, because it received the missionary's body when he died in 605. Bede also tells us that Augustine took over the site of another former Romano–British place of worship for the church, dedicated to Christ, which was destined to become Canterbury Cathedral. Later in the Middle Ages its archbishop, by virtue of his lineal descent from Augustine, claimed the title of 'Primate of All England'. Constitutionally Canterbury was a cathedral monastery. In other words, its services were sung by a community of Benedictine (q.v.) monks. The monastic precincts, rightly described as one of the best architectural mazes in England, survive on the northern side of the cathedral, partly hidden under the later buildings of King's School.

The story of the present fabric of the cathedral begins with Lanfranc (q.v.), the first Norman archbishop, who rebuilt the church after his appointment in 1070. Barely a generation later, however, the eastern half was rebuilt again, the crypt in the time of Prior Ernulf and the choir in the time of Prior Conrad. Ernulf's crypt is the largest and most luxurious Romanesque crypt in England. Conrad's choir was destroyed by a fire in

1174, and shortly replaced by the present choir and Trinity Chapel, each a seminal study in early Gothic owing much to the cathedrals of Sens and Laon in France. The first master mason of the choir was one William of Sens, which helps to explain the similarity to Sens, but the indebtedness to that cathedral probably owed something, too, to the fact that Becket had spent part of his exile there; the design was an indirect form of homage. The cathedral was partly rebuilt in the fourteenth and fifteenth centuries, when the present nave and transepts were constructed to a design by Henry Yevele (q.v.) and the great central tower, 'Bell Harry', to a design by John Wastell. Visually, Canterbury offers one of the most remarkable interiors in England. The view eastwards along the nave ends abruptly at the crossing. The strainer arches under the tower and the huge flight of steps up to the screen deny any glimpse into the choir. Everything further east is hidden; it is mysterious. In the eastern arm there are more steps, creating a sense of expectancy on the approach to Becket's shrine. The steps were necessitated by the need to raise the choir over the crypt. The crypt was not a crypt in the strict sense; rather it was an undercroft built at ground level; so the choir had to be raised up. The Canterbury crypt is the largest in England. This was because it housed so many saints' relics. The most important of these were of course the bones of 'the holy, blissful, martyr', Becket (q.v.). Murdered in his own cathedral in December 1170, he was canonized three years later, and his cult soon made Canterbury the one pilgrimage centre in England of European importance (plates 63 and 64). In 1220 the bones were translated to a new shrine in the Trinity Chapel behind the high altar where they were to remain until their destruction at the Reformation. They attracted countless pilgrims (q.v. PILGRIMAGES). Then, as now, Canterbury prospered on the tourist trade.

A History of Canterbury Cathedral, ed. P. Collinson, N. Ramsay, M. Sparks, Oxford, 1995; F. Woodman, *The Architectural History of Canterbury Cathedral*, London, 1981.

CARTHUSIANS

In 1084 Bruno, a canon of Rheims, abandoned a brilliant career as a teacher to found a religious community at La Chartreuse near Grenoble. Instead of opting for the traditional monastic life, he re-created the eremetical life of the desert fathers. He and his brethren did not eat and sleep in common; they lived in separate cells around the cloister. They followed St Benedict in dividing the day between work, reading and prayer; but they assembled in the church for only a few of the services, the rest being recited in private in the cell. What Bruno did at Chartreuse was to graft the ancient tradition of the hermits onto the communal tradition of orthodox Benedictine monasticism. Yet his achievement might have died with him, had not Guigo, the fifth prior, put his usage into writing, and encouraged the foundation of more Charterhouses in France.

The first English Charterhouse was established in 1178 at Witham (Somerset) as one of the monasteries founded by Henry II in atonement for the murder of Becket (q.v.). But it was only much later, in the fourteenth and fifteenth centuries, that the Carthusian ideal, still pure and austere, began to exercise a strong appeal over potential founders. Seven of the nine Carthusian houses in England were founded between 1370 and 1420. Remarkably, the men responsible for this late flowering of the order were members of the military aristocracy, like Sir Walter Mauny, who founded the London Charterhouse, Thomas Mowbray, earl of Nottingham, who founded Epworth, Thomas Holland, duke of Surrey, who founded Mount Grace, and King Henry V (q.v.) himself, who endowed Sheen in 1415. The Carthusians were among the beneficiaries of that growth of lay piety which characterized the late Middle Ages. What appealed to their high-born patrons was the order's preservation of a life of poverty and solitude to a degree remarkable for the period. This they were able to do by remaining a small and select band and by adopting the Cistercian practice of annual chapters or meetings to legislate for the order.

The manner in which the distinctive quality of Carthusian life influenced the layout of their priories can be appreciated by looking at the ruins of Mount Grace in Yorkshire. Around the main cloister were ranged the church and the cells of the monks, fifteen in number and each with its own garden. To the south another and smaller cloister was built early in the fifteenth century to provide accommodation for six more monks. It says much for the popularity of the Carthusians that Mount Grace should have had to cater for rising numbers at a time when most houses did well to prevent them from falling.

See also MONASTICISM

CASTLES

The effective history of the castle as the private fortified residence of a lord begins with the Norman Conquest. In the Anglo-Saxon period some of the Wessex kings had built communal fortifications – burhs – to protect traders, and there is evidence that by the eleventh century earls and thegns were living in private fortified dwellings. But castle-building after the French model begins with the Conquest. The reasons for this were essentially twofold. The first was the experience of military occupation. The Normans, coming to England as they did as invaders, needed a series of strongpoints with which to hold down the country, and castles provided them with these. The second was the need to proclaim the establishment of a new lordship. In the eleventh century the castle was the pre-eminent symbol of lordship, its battlemented walls a witness to lay power. The castle thus from the earliest times had a duality of function: it was both a fortress and a strongpoint; but it was also a residence and administrative centre. The history of the castle is the history of the changing balance between these functions.

The earliest Norman castles, whether built by the king or his barons, were generally simple affairs, laid out on the motte and bailey plan. The motte was a large mound of earth, crowned by a wooden palisade, at the foot of which lay an enclosure known as the bailey. The entire fortification would be surrounded by a ditch, and in most cases the bailey would itself be separated by another ditch from the motte, which was regarded as a strongpoint of last resort, capable of holding out after the rest of the castle had fallen. These simple fortifications could be erected both cheaply and quickly because earth and timber were the only raw materials required. The Bayeux Tapestry (q.v.) shows the Normans heaping up a motte at Hastings before they went out to meet Harold in battle. According to the chronicler Orderic Vitalis, in 1068 William the Conqueror (q.v.) had castles built at Warwick, Nottingham, York, Lincoln, Huntingdon and Cambridge, all in the course of a campaign lasting only a few months. Almost certainly the Conqueror made use of conscript labour. Very few of these early castles, possibly only the great keeps of Colchester and the Tower of London, were built of stone right from the start. Most would have been built of timber, and then rebuilt in stone as soon as time allowed, or not rebuilt at all.

If any feature is popularly identified with the Norman castles, it is surely the keep. Yet the great stone keeps often referred to as 'Norman' usually date from the twelfth century, not eleventh, and are the creation of the Angevin kings, not their predecessors. As we have seen, the keeps of Colchester and the Tower of London are probably the only ones dating from the reign of the Conqueror himself. It was the lengthy periods of peace in the reigns of Henry I and Henry II that gave both king and barons the chance to modernize and strengthen their old motte and bailey fortifications. By dint of marshalling huge resources, the two Henrys built the mighty keeps of Norwich, Rochester and Dover. And as was so often to be the case, where the king led, the nobility followed. The equally mighty keeps of William d'Albini at Castle Rising, Aubrey de Vere at Hedingham and Geoffrey de Clinton at Kenilworth matched in splendour any that the king could build. The keep was conceived principally as a strongpoint and power symbol, but it also served a functional purpose, containing the domestic quarters: the hall, solar, garrison rooms, cellars and so on. This helps to explain the size of these structures, which were sometimes so large that the motte had to be flattened to make way for them. In many cases, however, the wooden palisade crowning the motte was replaced not by a square keep but by the circular structure known as the shell keep. In this design the domestic apartments were ranged against the inside wall of the 'shell'.

The castles of the twelfth century were powerful enough for considerable ingenuity to be applied to the business of reducing them – in other words, to the science of siege warfare. From a strategic perspective, the castle's function was to provide a defensive strongpoint which had to be taken by the opposing force if it was to be free from attack in the rear. Much of the military history of the period thus turns not on battles in the field but on sieges of castles. A classic instance is the civil war of King Stephen's reign (1135–54). Battles in this long-drawn-out struggle were very few, but sieges were undertaken all the time. According to the chronicler Henry of Huntingdon, the fall of Faringdon Castle to Stephen in 1147 tipped the strategic balance emphatically in the latter's favour. The weapons at the disposal of twelfth-century besiegers were stone-throwing machines, like mangonels, and battering rams that could be used to breach a hole in the wall. If all else failed, the garrison could be starved into submission.

The value of the Norman castle was found principally in its defensive strength. But by the end of the twelfth century military architects were looking for ways by which the besieged could turn the attack back onto the besiegers. They achieved this by two main advances. Firstly, they erected projecting battlements, or machicolations, on top of the walls so that the defenders could fire down on the men attacking below – and not just fire down but pour boiling water as well. Secondly, they placed towers at regular intervals along the walls to provide cover for the wall's exposed outer face. Since the keep was deemed strong enough already, these towers were usually placed along the much weaker perimeter of the bailey. An enemy attacking any part of the wall would then be exposed to fire from a flanking tower on each side of him. Mural towers of this kind, which were ultimately of Roman origin, first made their appearance at Dover (c.1179–91), and were then taken up at Framlingham (c.1200), where their implications for the future were made apparent. In this castle, the keep was dispensed with altogether, leaving only the bailey. The castle had become a simple walled enclosure defended by the flanking towers. The old dichotomy of motte and bailey was abandoned in favour of an integrated fortification in which the defence was no longer concentrated on a single strongpoint but disposed equally around the walls.

The new concept of military architecture found its fullest expression in the castles which Edward I (q.v.) built in north Wales (q.v.) to encircle Snowdonia. Thus Conway (1283–87), for example, is planned as a rectangle, irregularly shaped so as to exploit the contours of the rocky prominence on which it was built, and fortified by massive drum towers which punctuate the circuit of the walls. More sophisticated still, and the logical culmination of this line of architectural development, was the concentric castle. The principles upon which this was founded can be appreciated by looking at Beaumaris Castle in Anglesey. One ring of fortifications encloses another, and the approaches to north and south are commanded by matching gatehouses. The idea of the concentric castle almost certainly came from the Middle East, where the majestic Crusader castles were constructed on this principle. The earliest concentric works in England to which a definite date can be assigned are those at the Tower of London undertaken by Edward after he had returned from Palestine in 1274. No sooner had Edward set his masons to work than one of his greatest subjects, Gilbert de Clare, earl of Gloucester, began building a completely new castle at Caerphilly (Glamorgan), which by the time of its completion was to become the purest concentric fortress of its day, and very likely a model for Beaumaris. Although patrons like Edward I and Gilbert de Clare commissioned these great castles, they did not of course design them. The principal architect, or master mason, responsible for the Edwardian castles was James of St George, a Savoyard who settled in England and developed the science of military architecture to a level of sophistication never to be surpassed in the Middle Ages.

The history of military architecture in the late Middle Ages is often presented in terms of decline. But this is a slightly misleading view. While it is true that fortifications on the scale of those in north Wales were never to be built again, to put the whole emphasis on 'decline' is to focus on only one aspect of the complex phenomenon of the castle. A castle was not only a fortress or strongpoint. It was also a residence and power house; it proclaimed the prestige and status of its owner. It is these showy aspects of the castle which were to see further development in the late medieval period. In many ways, the quintes-

sential late medieval castle is Bodiam (Sussex), built by Sir Edward Dallingridge in the 1380s. Externally the castle looks formidable. It is surrounded by a broad moat, and bristles with machicolations, towers and gun loops. But all this is for show. The castle is low-lying and could never properly be defended. Bodiam is a status symbol. Dallingridge, a largely self-made man, wanted to proclaim his arrival. His ambition was to live in the manner appropriate to a great lord.

Castellated forms remained popular right into the Tudor period. They were part of the established language of power; they provided owners with the legitimizing imagery of chivalry. In the fifteenth century there was a remarkable revival of interest in the keep. The earl of Northumberland built a massive tower-house, or keep, at Warkworth Castle (Northumberland). A little later, Lord Cromwell built one at Tattershall (Lincs), and Lord Hastings one at Kirby Muxloe (Leics.). These were classic power houses. Internally, they were luxuriously appointed. Tattershall was even built of brick, not stone – useless defensively, but highly impressive for show. By comparison with most continental states, England was a peaceful realm. Owners could afford to downplay the defensive aspect; their properties would never be subjected to a serious siege. The castle form looked grand and boastful from without. Inside, however, the transition to the stately home had begun.

N.J.G. Pounds, *The Medieval Castle in England and Wales. A Social and Political History*, London, 1990.

CAXTON, WILLIAM

William Caxton's achievement was to introduce the new technology of printing to England. Caxton was uniquely qualified to do this. He had spent the greater part of his life as a merchant in the Low Countries. For some of his time there he had probably worked in a printing house. However, to his mastery of technical process Caxton was able to bring, in addition, a keen interest in literature. He had translated the 'Recuyell of the Historyes of Troye', a work which he and a partner later printed at Bruges in the 1470s. When he returned to England, he established a printing press in the precincts of Westminster Abbey, and in 1477 the first book was printed there. The books that Caxton printed included romances; perhaps the most famous of these was Malory's (q.v.) *Morte D'Arthur*, published in 1485, the year of Bosworth. But nearly half of the works which he published up to his death in 1491 were manuals of piety and devotion, like Jacob of Voragine's *Golden Legend*. Caxton's output merely reflected the tastes of the reading public of the day. Caxton's introduction of printing mightily contributed to the development of the English language. It assisted in the emergence of an accepted written standard. At the risk of exaggeration, printing did for written English in the late fifteenth century what the BBC is supposed to have done for spoken English in our own time.

N.F. Blake, *Caxton and his World*, London, 1969.

CHAMBER
See GOVERNMENT

CHANCERY
See GOVERNMENT

CHANTRIES
A chantry was a privately endowed mass celebrated regularly for the repose of the souls of the founder and any others named by him. In the late Middle Ages it was widely believed that regular performance of the mass would induce the Almighty to shorten the sufferings of the soul in Purgatory (q.v. LITURGY). Chantry foundations, in consequence of this belief, became a popular form of endowment, particularly among the gentry and mercantile elites, whose members wished to make spiritual provision for themselves but lacked the means to found a monastery.

Chantries could take a variety of forms. The humblest kind of foundation was the anniversary, or obit – a mass celebrated each year on the anniversary of the beneficiary's death. Tombs and brasses (q.v.) were often the focus of such celebrations. Another form of chantry was the fixed-term chantry – one that existed for only a specified number of years, usually until the income from the endowment ran out. The grandest form of foundation was the perpetual chantry, one supported by a landed endowment that would provide for a priest to celebrate masses at a side altar as far ahead as could be seen. It was to provide adequate surroundings for these altars that chantry chapels were built. Splendid examples of such chapels can be seen in the aisles of Tewkesbury Abbey and Winchester Cathedral. The men who paid for these chapels, and were remembered in them, were the wealthy – the great figures of Church and state, like Cardinal Beaufort (q.v.) or Richard, earl of Warwick. But it is important to remember that these grander foundations represented only a tiny proportion of the total number founded. By the time of the Reformation, there were probably some 3,000 or more chantries in England, the majority of them humble or poorly endowed. In the towns, where many of the chantries were established, a whole community of chantry priests was called into being. The presence of these priests contributed substantially to the work of the parish, and the chantries as a whole enriched the musical and liturgical life of the medieval Church.

G. H. Cook, *Medieval Chantries and Chantry Chapels*, London, 1968; C.R. Burgess, "'For the Increase of Divine Service": Chantries in the Parish in Late Medieval Bristol', *Journal of Ecclesiastical History*, 36 (1985); J.A.A. Goodall, *God's House at Ewelme*, Aldershot, 2001.

CHAUCER, GEOFFREY

Medieval England's two greatest poets – William Langland (q.v.) and Geoffrey Chaucer – were contemporaries, and lived and worked within a short distance of each other in London. Yet for all that they had in common, they could have lived worlds apart. Langland was a humble chantry priest, a sympathizer with the sufferings of the poor. Chaucer was a king's esquire, someone who mingled with the rich and the powerful.

But Chaucer was a man of many parts. Although a frequenter of the court, he was in fact born into the burgess class. His father was a London vintner. As young man he gained a position in the household of Elizabeth de Burgh, countess of Ulster. From Elizabeth's household, in the 1360s, he moved to the court as a king's esquire. In 1359–60 he joined Edward III (q.v.) on his expedition to France, but had the misfortune to be captured; the king paid £16 for his ransom. His activities in the decade after his return are obscure. However, he made a number of journeys on the king's business abroad: to France, apparently, on several occasions, and to Italy in 1372–3 and 1378. The journeys to Italy were of great importance to his poetic development because they brought him into direct contact with the work of Dante and Boccaccio. The latter's *Il Filostrato*, for example, forms the basis of Chaucer's *Troilus and Criseyde*, and *Teseide* the basis of *The Knight's Tale*. It is difficult to be certain of the dating of all of Chaucer's works but other poems likely to have been written in his early or middle years are the *Boke of the Duchesse* (*c*.1368–69), the *House of Fame* (*c*.1380) and the *Parlement of Foules* (*c*.1382). By the time that he embarked on *The Canterbury Tales* in about 1387, Chaucer was both more

independent in his approach to poetry and also more mature in his outlook on life. His retention at court continued to involve him in various employments. He was a clerk of the king's works and, for a time, a customs officer in London. In October 1385 he was appointed a JP in Kent, and twelve months later served in parliament as an MP for the same county. After the 1380s he figures much less in the public records than before. In 1391 he was replaced as clerk of the king's works and compensated with the office, largely a sinecure, of subforester of North Petherton (Somerset).

Almost certainly, a factor in his gradual withdrawal from public life was a desire to press on with the great work for which he is chiefly remembered, *The Canterbury Tales*. On the suggestion of the Host, Harry Bailly, the pilgrims assembling at the Tabard Inn at Southwark agree to tell a couple of tales each on the outward journey to Canterbury and a couple on the return. This scheme, as it turned out, was overly ambitious. Chaucer never produced the necessary number of tales, and there are other signs in the work that the project was left uncompleted. Nonetheless, the *Tales* remains an undoubted masterpiece. The prologue with which it opens contains the most memorable portrait gallery in English literature. In the *Tales* themselves, Chaucer is found at his most versatile, equally skilful whether handling the story of Palamon and Arcite, as in *The Knight's Tale*, adapting a Breton lay, as in *The Franklin's Tale*, or just telling a good dirty yarn, as in *The Miller's Tale*. Chaucer was a born storyteller. But he was never superficial. He was a man of the world, acute, ironic and perceptive in his observations. Although close to the court, he always steered clear of direct involvement in politics, preferring instead to stand on the sidelines watching how others acted in the great drama of human experience. Unlike his contemporary Langland, however, Chaucer does not seem to have been a deeply religious man. In fact he is the first great English poet whose work is not religious in purpose or content. He is the first 'courtly maker', father of a long line of poets stretching down to Wyatt and Surrey in the sixteenth century.

Chaucer died on 25 October 1400. Because he had lived his last years in the precincts of Westminster Abbey, he was buried in the Abbey's south transept, the area later to become famous as Poets' Corner. His genius was recognized in his own lifetime, and lesser poets who followed, like Hoccleve and Lydgate, acknowledged him as their master. Chaucer's record of employment in royal service was matched by that of his son, Thomas, who made himself an indispensable counsellor of the Lancastrian kings. Marriage to the heiress Maud Burghersh brought Thomas extensive lands in Oxfordshire and the south Midlands, and his only daughter and heiress, Alice (d.1475), rose still higher to marry, as her second husband, William de la Pole, duke of Suffolk.

D. Pearsall, *The Life of Geoffrey Chaucer*, Oxford, 1992; *The Riverside Chaucer*, ed. L.D. Benson, Oxford, 1987.

CHICHELE, HENRY

Henry Chichele (born *c.*1362), unusually for a late medieval primate, was not a scion of a noble family but the son of a merchant of Higham Ferrers (Northants). Perhaps through the good offices of John of Gaunt, duke of Lancaster (q.v.), the lord of the manor, he was given an education at Winchester and New College, Oxford. This gave him a thorough grounding in canon law, which he was to put to good use in the service of Richard Medford, bishop of Salisbury, from about 1396 to 1406. Chichele's ability and his connections with the Lancastrian house also brought him employment at governmental level, first on an embassy to France and later in conciliar diplomacy. When in 1409 it was decided to hold a council at Pisa in an attempt to heal the schism in the Church, Chichele was one of the two principal English delegates.

In the later years of Henry IV's reign, as relations between the king and his eldest son, the Prince of Wales, worsened, Chichele identified with the latter. In 1410 he was admitted a member of the council, doubtless on the prince's initiative. Two years earlier he had entered the episcopate as bishop of St David's. In 1414, on the death of Archbishop Arundel, he was translated to Canterbury. His period as primate saw the English Church pass through some difficult times. In 1417 the schism was brought to an end with the election of Martin V, who quickly set about recovering for the papacy the power that it had lost to the secular arm in the previous generation. The unfortunate Chichele was charged with securing the repeal of the Statutes of Provisors and Praemunire – something to which he knew the English parliament would never agree. In politics at home he also had to tread carefully, most notably on Henry V's death in 1422, when the crown passed to a child. Chichele had to guard against the machinations of his rival, Bishop Beaufort (q.v.), who in 1426 finally procured the cardinal's hat that had been denied him in the previous reign. He also had to steer a middle path in the minority council between the rivalries of Beaufort and Humphrey, duke of Gloucester (q.v.).

Today, however, it is as a patron of learning that Chichele is chiefly remembered. At Oxford he founded two colleges, St Bernard's (1438) for the Cistercians (q.v.) and All Souls (1438) for graduates in the arts and law. The former was dissolved at the Reformation and incorporated in what is now St John's, but the latter survives to perpetuate its founder's memory. Chichele died at Lambeth on 12 April 1443 and is buried in Canterbury Cathedral. His tomb, on the north side of the choir, shows him in vestments above and as a naked corpse below.

E.F. Jacob, *Henry Chichele*, London, 1967.

CHRONICLES

In the Middle Ages events were recorded, and commented on, in narratives called chronicles. The chronicler was a kind of historian, but his outlook and approach were very different from those of the historian today.

Chronicles were essentially annals: a year by year record of events considered noteworthy enough to be written down. In origin, they were a by-product of the Easter tables compiled in the Dark Ages. Easter being a moveable festival, it was useful to have a table or calendar that would give its date for years ahead. Before long this purely liturgical data was accompanied by short notices of events, whether of national or local importance, which occurred in the world outside the cloister. In due course these annals acquired an existence, almost a momentum, of their own, but as late as the eleventh and twelfth centuries the nature of their origins can be detected in the kind of material that was included. For example, the Worcester chronicle commissioned by Bishop Wulfstan (1062–95) opens with an account of the early history of the diocese, and then gives the familiar Easter tables and lists of consuls, kings and bishops before launching into a universal history that interpreted English preoccupations in the light of God's general scheme for mankind.

The liturgical origins of chronicles overlap with the theological framework within which the events noted were interpreted. Medieval chroniclers believed in the theory of the Seven Ages of the World. As set out in St Augustine's City of God, these were:

1. From the Creation to the Flood
2. From the Flood to Abraham
3. From Abraham to David
4. From David to the Babylonian Captivity
5. From the Captivity to the birth of Christ
6. From the birth of Christ till the Second Coming
7. The Eternal Sabbath.

Medieval chroniclers, writing as they saw it in the Sixth Age, would begin their narratives with the birth of Christ or, if they were ambitious, with the Creation, drawing on the works of their predecessors for the early part of the story. Bartholomew Cotton, for example, the early fourteenth-century chronicler at Norwich, used an earlier Norwich chronicle for the period from the Creation to 1290, from which point he drew on his own experience to bring the story down to his own day. It is apparent, then, that medieval explanations were not so much historical as theological. History studied the gradual unfolding of God's scheme for the world. If men were faithful, God would reward them; if they were sinful, he would chastize them. Inexplicable phenomena, natural disasters and the like could be seen as the expressions of God's anger, and the reigns of bad kings as punishments for an errant people.

Artless and disjointed though it may appear, medieval chronicle writing was at least inspired by a way of looking at the past. It sought to reconcile the evident chaos of temporal affairs with the presumed coherence of the divinely created order. The chronicler could allow his story simply to unfold. He himself need do no more than commend the good and condemn the evil for the guidance of those readers who sought to lead a better life. Most writers, therefore, were content to hide behind the anonymity of their work. Only a few emerge as men of some ability and insight, deserving we might say of the title of historian. In early medieval England there was pre-eminently Bede (672–735), whose *Ecclesiastical History* was to be a source of inspiration for the rest of the Middle Ages. In the twelfth century there was William of Malmesbury, like Bede a polymath and one who could turn his hand equally to biography, hagiography, topography and history. And in the thirteenth century there was Matthew Paris (q.v.), the fiercely patriotic chronicler of St Albans from 1236 to 1259.

William of Malmesbury is worthy of further attention because he was the most distinguished product of the revival of historical studies that followed the Norman Conquest. Intelligent observers could see that Hastings (q.v.) had effected a clean break with the past, and that things were never going to be the same again. The coming of the Normans bred a nostalgic renewal of interest in the Old English past; but it also stimulated solid research. Churches had to protect their lands from the encroachments of predatory Norman landowners and the reputations of their saints from the contempt of sceptical Norman clerics. Writers therefore had to start digging into the past to look after their ancient inheritance. Thus William of Malmesbury wrote the *De Antiquitate Glastoniensis Ecclesiae* to provide a cloak of historical justification for the mythical origins of Glastonbury Abbey, and the *Gesta Pontificum* to recall the memories of those Saxon bishops whose saintliness was being challenged. William travelled, looked at buildings and transcribed documents. In other words, he engaged in research. But he was not alone in so doing. Writers at Canterbury, Worcester, Evesham and Durham were also busy compiling cartularies (collections of charters) and writing chronicles and biographies in the cause of propaganda and self-justification.

The twelfth century saw medieval historical writing in England reach its peak. The reign of Henry II (q.v.) produced some excellent writers, such as Robert of Torigni, William of Newburgh and Ralph of Diceto, not to mention all the biographers who recorded Becket's every word and deed. Most of these men were monks, but a few, like Ralph of Diceto, dean of St Paul's, were secular clergy. By the thirteenth century almost every monastery of any consequence was keeping its chronicle. The most voluminous compilation was that of St Albans, started by Roger Wendover or an anonymous predecessor in the reign of King John (q.v.), and kept up by Matthew Paris and a succession of writers until as late as 1440. By the later Middle Ages, however, the position of the monks was being challenged not only by secular clerks like Diceto but by friars and members of the laity. Not all of this work can match the best twelfth-century writing in terms of quality, but for modern historians the value of such a wide range of sources is beyond question. In the fourteenth century, of particular note were the *Scalacronica*, written by Sir Thomas Grey, a Northumberland knight, and the *Life of the Black Prince*, by the herald of one of the prince's companions, Sir John Chandos. Many of these chronicles are, however, for reasons already mentioned, of anonymous authorship. The *Gesta Henrici Quinti* (*Deeds of Henry V*) was obviously written by a chaplain who was with the English army at Agincourt in 1415, but alas we do not know his name. Finally, mention ought to be made of the various town chronicles compiled in the late Middle Ages, of which the most important are the succession of London chronicles that give such a valuable insight into the capital's often turbulent political struggles.

A. Gransden, *Historical Writing in England, c.550–c.1307*, London, 1974; A. Gransden, *Historical Writing in England, II. c.1307 to the Early Sixteenth Century*, London, 1982; C. Given-Wilson, *Chronicles*, London, 2004.

CISTERCIANS

In the decades around 1100, when a process of spiritual renewal was sweeping across European society, there was a move to recapture the original purity of the Rule of St Benedict. In 1098 Robert, a monk of Molesme, led a small group of brethren in search of a stricter life in the Burgundian forests at Cîteaux. From this modest beginning grew one of the great orders of medieval

Europe. By 1115 Cîteaux had four daughter houses, including Clairvaux, of which the celebrated propagandist St Bernard became abbot; in 1153, by the time of Bernard's death, Cistercian houses numbered over 300.

The Cistercians were the most radical of the reformed orders of the twelfth century. They challenged not merely existing Benedictine monasticism but the entire basis of feudal society. Unlike the Benedictines (q.v.), whose abbeys lay in the towns, the Cistercians chose rural sites. Unlike the Benedictines, whose estates were integrated within the manorial system, the Cistercians rejected feudal sources of income in favour of tilling land reclaimed from the wild. Unlike the Cluniacs (q.v.), who elaborated the liturgy (q.v.), the Cistercians opted for a simple form of worship. The Cistercians responded to the aspirations of those who viewed with concern the growing wealth and materialism of twelfth-century society.

In the time given to them by the shortening of the liturgy the Cistercian monks were charged with engaging in manual work, reading and private prayer. It was never the founders' intention that they should be solely responsible for tilling the soil, for theirs was a life of prayer. The task of cultivating the lands furthest from the house was given to a group of associates known as the lay brothers. The lay brothers were a Cistercian innovation. They were men attached to the monastery and bound to a life of near total silence, whose only reward lay in contributing to the needs of a pioneering religious community. The idea of lay brothers was quickly taken up by the Gilbertines (q.v.) and the Carthusians (q.v.).

Hardly less radical than the alterations made to the internal economy of their houses were the measures which the Cistercians took to secure the continued observance of the Rule. There was an understandable worry that, unless uniformity were maintained in the order's houses, laxity would set in. Thus the arrangement was made that all the order's abbots would meet yearly at Cîteaux to legislate for the order and provide for an annual visitation of each abbey by the abbot of the house from which it had sprung. Never before had such elaborate machinery been established to unite the houses of an international order.

The first Cistercian house to be established in England was Waverley (Surrey), founded in 1138. But it was in the north that the order was to make its greatest impact, and characteristically in a manner that makes a good story. The first Cistercian abbey in the north was that of Rievaulx (Yorks), founded in 1132 by Walter Espec, lord of Helmsley. Among its earliest monks were some of the Yorkshiremen who had been with Bernard at Clairvaux, and as they proceeded north they passed through York (q.v.), unconsciously provoking a crisis in the Benedictine abbey of St Mary. The example of the Cistercians from Clairvaux encouraged a group of dissident monks, led by Prior Richard, to protest to the abbot that laxity was setting in. After initial hesitation the abbot resisted the demands of the prior and his supporters, and they turned for help to Archbishop Thurstan, who decided to visit the abbey on 17 October 1133. The prospect of a visitation was not well received by the abbot and his friends, and when the archbishop arrived he encountered such opposition that he was obliged to flee accompanied by the thirteen dissidents. To provide them with shelter he gave them a site near Ripon, later to be distinguished by the name of Fountains.

The early Cistercians attracted men of distinction, and set for themselves rigorous standards of discipline. But for how long did they succeed in living up to them? In the first century of the order's existence Cistercian abbeys would certainly have struck the visitor as different from those of the Benedictines. Their churches would have seemed bare, devoid of ornamentation, and colourless. The layout of the buildings would have been different because of the need to accommodate the lay brothers in quarters of their own on the west of the cloister. By the fourteenth century, however, these differences would have seemed less pronounced. The prohibition on learning was soon relaxed, and in the thirteenth century the Cistercians even followed the other orders in founding a house for their monks in the University of Oxford (q.v.). The beautiful choir of Rievaulx Abbey, rebuilt in the thirteenth century, suggests that they were also succumbing to the temptation to replace their earlier buildings with grander structures characteristic of the Gothic age. At the same time the Cistercians had little option but to adjust their methods of economic organization. Faced as they were by the increasing reluctance of any but a few to contemplate a life so arduous, they had to abandon the use of lay brothers. Instead they took on hired labour. The change did little to affect the prosperity of the Cistercians, however, because they relied far less for their income on arable farming, which was labour intensive, than on sheep breeding, which was not. The sheep runs brought to the Cistercian abbeys of the Yorkshire dales those trappings of worldly wealth from which the founding fathers of the order had done their best to escape.

D. Knowles, *The Monastic Order in England*, 2nd ed., Cambridge, 1966; P.J. Ferguson, *Architecture of Solitude: Cistercian Abbeys in Twelfth-Century England*, Princeton, 1984.

CLOSE ROLLS
See GOVERNMENT

CLUNIACS
The Cluniac Order was more important in the history of European monasticism (q.v.) than their modest numbers in medieval England might suggest. The Cluniacs took their name from the Burgundian abbey of Cluny, founded in 910. Under the rule of two able and long-lived abbots, Odilo (994–1049) and Hugh (1049–1109), Cluny achieved a position of such eminence that she became a source of inspiration and assistance to religious houses in many lands. In the tenth century the working of Cluny's influence had been mainly through informal ties between the abbey and those who went from its walls to reform a house that had appealed for help. The formation of the Cluniac Order followed in the eleventh century from the insistence that monasteries that adopted the customs of Cluny should enter into a relationship of dependence on the abbey. Thus the Cluniacs were not so much an order as such as a family owing allegiance to a mother house. In this way was reconciled the desire of each Cluniac community to be self-governing with the need for supervision by the abbot of Cluny himself.

The chief characteristic of the Cluniac way of life was its elaborate liturgy (q.v.). The simple horarium of St Benedict, which had struck a balance between the demands of public worship, private study and manual labour, gave way at Cluny to an unceasing round of services in the church. This luxuriant ritual had its admirers; but it also produced a reaction in favour of simplicity from which the Cistercians (q.v.) were to profit.

In their heyday the Cluniacs were remarkable for the large number of friends they had in high places. In England they had the support of William the Conqueror himself and members of his aristocracy. The first Cluniac house in England, St Pancras' at Lewes, was founded in 1077 by one of the Conqueror's principal lieutenants, William de Warenne, and his wife. From Lewes sprang a family of daughter houses, including Castle Acre and Thetford in Norfolk. Even in the twelfth century, when their way of life was coming under attack, the Cluniacs still enjoyed the support of rulers like Henry I (q.v.), who founded Reading, and Stephen (q.v.), who founded

Faversham, both staffed by Cluniac monks. Indeed, the success of the order in England lay not so much in the size or number of its houses, in each case small, as in the prominence attained by some of its monks. Two of the most distinguished bishops in the twelfth century had been monks at Cluny itself – King Stephen's brother Henry of Blois, bishop of Winchester, and Gilbert Foliot (q.v.), bishop of London and a long-standing opponent of Becket (q.v.). The prominence attained in the corridors of power by Cluniac sympathizers led the leaders of the order to develop some ideas of their own about Church/state relations. They believed that the Church was less likely to be liberated from unwelcome secular interference by the aggressive tactics of the Gregorian reformers than by opening the lines of communications, as Bishop Henry hoped to do with his brother, King Stephen. Few Cluniac houses in England have left extensive remains. The ruins of Lewes Priory suffered badly when the railway was driven across them in the nineteenth century. In Norfolk, however, there are extensive ruins at Castle Acre and at Thetford, where the complete ground plan of the buildings can be traced.

H.E.J. Cowdrey, *The Cluniacs and the Gregorian Reform*, Oxford, 1970.

COINAGE

A major achievement of the pre-Conquest kings was the creation of a sound and stable system of coinage based on a metallic standard. With the recovery of trade in the seventh and eighth centuries, there was a growing need for an acceptable medium of exchange, satisfied in the case of England by the minting of both gold and silver coins. The gold coin was to be quickly phased out, leaving the silver penny the only coin in circulation, but for 600 years this coinage served the needs of the English economy.

On the eve of the Conquest the English coinage was to be numbered among the strongest in Europe. The main reason for this was the centralized system of control maintained by the crown over the supply of coin. By Edward the Confessor's reign coins were struck at some sixty or seventy mints, mostly in central and southern England; however, the dies from which the coins were struck could only be obtained from a limited number of die-cutting workshops controlled by the king. The monopoly thus given to the king over the supply of dies enabled him to reconcile the easy availability of coins with overall direction of the currency. Royal authority was demonstrated equally dramatically by the regularity with which these dies were changed. The purpose of the changes appears to have been to exact profit, because each time a change was effected the moneyers had to pay the king before receiving the new dies to take back to their mints. Methods of coin production changed little in the course of the Middle Ages. The coins were cut by hand from a pound weight of silver, and flattened and moulded to shape by the use of a hammer and anvil. Although they were supposed to be as nearly as possible of equal weight and size, no standard weight was set for individual coins until the reign of James I, and so long as the correct number was cut from a pound of metal small variations in weight from one coin to another were disregarded.

From the reigns of the first two Norman kings there survive thirteen types of coin, all of them inscribed 'WILLEM' without indicating either father or son, allowing us to guess on a roughly proportionate basis that perhaps the first eight belong to the Conqueror and the remaining five to Rufus. The gradual deterioration in the quality of the coinage under Rufus (plate 23) and Henry I (q.v.) provides the background to the action which Bishop Roger, the justiciar, took in 1125 in summoning all the moneyers to Winchester and sentencing them to mutilation for flooding the land with false money. After the accession of Henry II (q.v.) the regular changing of dies which had been carried out in the past was abandoned, and the first type, introduced in 1158, lasted until the reform of 1180, which inaugurated the so-called 'short-cross' issue. The remarkable thing about the coins of this type is that although they were in circulation under Richard I, John and in the early years of Henry III they all bear the name HENRICUS. By 1247, however, clipping had become such a problem that a new coinage was issued, known as the 'long-cross' issue from the cross on the reverse which continued right to the edge of the coin. Any pennies on which the four ends of the cross were not visible would not be considered legal tender.

As we have seen, the only coin in circulation since the reign of the Saxon king Edgar had been the silver penny. Pounds, shillings and marks existed only as units of account. It was therefore a new departure when in 1279 Edward I (q.v.) introduced further denominations in the form of the groat (4d) and the farthing. At the same time, the weight of the silver penny was reduced from 22½ to 22¼ grains. In appearance the penny differed little from Henry II's issue. On the obverse side was the crowned head of the king and on the reverse a long cross with three round pellets in each of the angles. Allowing for various permutations, this remained the standard design for silver pennies for the rest of the Middle Ages (plate 24).

The striking of new denominations suggests that by the thirteenth century the mints were meeting a demand for a more flexible system of currency. If small change had been wanted in the past, it had been obtained by cutting a penny into halves or quarters. In the countryside petty transactions had usually been settled by resort to barter – a coin worth a penny represented a lot of money given that in the thirteenth century a labourer's daily wage was unlikely to be much more than that

amount. On the other hand, as the pace of trade quickened, a coin of higher value was needed for international transactions. In Italy the city of Florence responded to the new conditions in 1252 by minting a golden florin, the first golden coin to appear in western Europe since the Dark Ages. English merchants had no wish to be dependent on foreign coins for trade, so in 1257 Henry III (q.v.) put an English gold currency into circulation, in the form of a penny which would exchange for 20 silver pence. This coin met with a bad reception because it was undervalued. It was shortly revalued at 24 pence, but even so lack of confidence led to its withdrawal in about 1270.

A second and more successful attempt to introduce a gold coin was made in 1344 in the reign of Edward III (q.v.). In the 1330s complaints had been made in parliament about the shortage of good coin. The background to the problem lay in Edward III's heavy expenditure on foreign war. From 1337 Edward was spending huge sums of money in his struggle against the French, both on wages for his soldiers and on subsidies for his allies in the Low Countries. This spending had the effect of reducing the amount of coin in circulation from about £1 million in the 1290s to half that amount in the 1340s. Gold, on the other hand, was commanding a high price. This encouraged people to import it, so making the production of a domestic gold currency almost inevitable. The initial gold issue of January 1344 consisted of three coins – a florin worth 6s, for use in international transactions, and a half and a quarter, known from the designs on their reverse sides as the 'leopard' and the 'helm' respectively. The currency had a chequered history, however. It seems that the gold was too highly valued in relation to silver. Eight months after the initial issue the florin and its smaller denomination were withdrawn and replaced with the 'noble', worth 6s 8d, and its half and quarter. These early gold coins of Edward III rank among the most beautiful ever minted in England. The obverse of the florin showed the king seated in majesty. On the noble this was replaced by the king standing in ship holding his shield and sword, perhaps an allusion to the naval victory of Sluys (1340) a few years earlier (plate 25). The reverse of the florin, as of its successor, the noble, had a floriated cross as its main feature with a scriptural motto round the border.

The reign of Edward III also saw the introduction in 1351 of a multiple of the silver penny, known as the groat and worth 4d, along with a half groat worth 2d. After these initiatives, few changes of any importance were made to the coinage until the reign of Edward IV, when two new gold coins were issued in 1465, one known from the design on its reverse as the 'rose noble or ryal', worth 10s, and the other known from the design on its obverse as the 'angel', worth 6s 8d and replacing the noble (plate 26). One more denomination was added to the list in the reign of Henry VII, to complete the picture. This was the famous gold 'sovereign', a large coin worth 20s featuring on the obverse the king in majesty and on the reverse a shield set against a luxuriant rose.

If the English coinage suffered from any problem in the Middle Ages, it was paradoxically that it was too good. It was because of this that complaints were so often made in the fourteenth century about poor quality coins, known variously as lusshebournes or crockards and pollards, entering the country from abroad and, on the operation of what was later to be known as Gresham's Law, driving out of circulation the better-quality English coins. The French kings frequently resorted to debasing their country's coinage. The English kings, by and large, refrained from doing so before the sixteenth century. Consequently their problem was how to ensure an adequate supply of high-value coins.

G.C. Brooke, *English Coins*, 2nd ed., London, 1950; C.H.V. Sutherland, *English Coinage, 600-1900*, London, 1973; P. Grierson and M. Blackburn, *Medieval European Coinage, I: The Early Middle Ages*, Cambridge, 1986.

CORONER

After the sheriff (q.v.), the coroner is the oldest of the local offices to have come down to us from the Middle Ages. The office was established in September 1194 when the eyre justices were told to have three knights and a clerk elected in each county 'to keep the pleas of the crown'. Coroners were authorized in the boroughs for the first time a few years later in 1200. It was the coroner's duty to hear appeals (q.v.), hold inquests on dead bodies, receive confessions from felons in sanctuary who wanted to leave the realm, and record outlawries that were pronounced at sessions of the county court. Unlike his colleague the sheriff, who was appointed by the exchequer and held office for a year at a time, the coroner was elected and held office for life. According to the order of 1194, coroners were to be drawn from the ranks of the knightly class, but before too long much humbler people were accepted. Like all local officials coroners were unpaid, but they had ample chance to profit from bribery and corruption.

R.F. Hunnisett, *The Medieval Coroner*, Cambridge, 1961.

CORRODY

A corrody (Latin, *corredium*, provision for maintenance) was a form of pension or annuity given by monasteries. It might entitle the corrodian either to residence with the monks or to a ration distributed each day at the abbey gates. Corrodies were awarded not so much as an act of charity as on a strict calculation of financial gain. They could be given, for example, to the vicar of an impropriated (i.e., acquired) church instead of a money salary. Alternatively, they could be awarded to layfolk in exchange for property. In 1392, for instance, Robert Aleyn and Matilda, his wife, received from the monks of Westminster a corrody of fourteen loaves and fourteen gallons of ale per week and £6 13s 4d per annum in return for granting to the abbey their mill at Stratford, Essex. On other occasions the sale of a corrody, very likely to someone wanting to provide for his old age, was a straight means of raising cash. The price would be pitched according to the means of the corrodian and perhaps, too, according to his life expectancy. Failure in these circumstances to make sound actuarial calculations could land a house with unwelcome financial burdens, as Merton Priory, Surrey, found when it sold a corrody to a man for the modest sum of 20s, hardly expecting him to survive, as it turned out, for another twenty-nine years.

CRÉCY

Like the engagements at Poitiers (q.v.) in 1356 and Agincourt (q.v.) in 1415, Crécy was a battle in which an inferior English army took on and defeated a much larger French one. The English triumph arose in large part from a change in Edward III's strategy. Instead of invading France in force from the Low Countries, as he had done between 1338 and 1340, Edward put two armies in the field – one in the south-west under Henry of Lancaster and the other in the north under his own command. He landed in Normandy on 12 July 1346. His intention, it seems, was to march east to Flanders, creating as much havoc as possible, but near the village of Crécy in Ponthieu on 26 August he found his passage blocked by the presence of a French force under King Philip VI. The enthusiasm of the French overcame their tactical sense, and they launched an attack on the English position that afternoon when their vision was blinded by the setting sun. The French

knights charged forward, only to be mown down by a storm of arrows from the English longbowmen. Among the casualties on the French side were the count of Flanders and the blind king of Bohemia. The English owed their success to the tactic which they had developed during the previous half-century of Scottish wars of combining archers with dismounted men-at-arms – a ploy which was to bring them victory again at Poitiers in 1356. The sequel to the battle of Crécy was the siege of Calais (q.v.), which began on 4 September. The town was taken by the English just under a year later.

See also HUNDRED YEARS WAR

J. Sumption, *The Hundred Years War. Trial by Battle*, London, 1990.

CRUSADES

On 27 November 1095 Pope Urban II preached the First Crusade at Clermont in central France. The pope's unprecedented offer of a plenary indulgence for military service to liberate the Holy Land evoked an enthusiastic response from his audience. In the following year a massive force set out on a journey to the East. Among the commanders were Raymond, count of Toulouse, Godfrey of Bouillon, duke of Lower Lorraine, and his brother Baldwin, Bohemund, son of Robert Guiscard, the Norman count of Sicily, and his nephew Tancred and Robert, duke of Normandy, son of William the Conqueror (q.v.). William Rufus (q.v.), King of England, was the most notable absentee. The crusaders were inspired by a variety of motives. Some, perhaps, were driven by the lure of profit and adventure. Many more, however, appear to have acted from genuine spiritual zeal. The intense spirituality of the age, which also found expression in the monastic movement, was something to which the Popes appealed in their crusading propaganda. As Cardinal Odo of

Châteauroux said in 1145, when preaching a new crusade from France:

> It is a clear sign that a man burns with love of God and zeal for God when he leaves country, possessions, house, children and wife, to go overseas in the service of Jesus Christ... Whoever wishes to take and to have Christ ought to follow him; to follow him to Death.★

The love of God, to which Odo referred, had to be made comprehensible to the men of a feudal age. Accordingly, it was presented as family love: Christ had been robbed of his patrimony by the infidel, and it was a responsibility incumbent on his children to recover it for him. The crusades were not envisaged as wars of conversion. Rather, they were wars authorized by the Pope for the recovery of Christian lands from the infidel. In the late Middle Ages, admittedly, the definition of crusading was widened: from the thirteenth century crusades were directed against heretics and schismatics like the Albigensians in southern France, who were held to constitute as much of a threat to Christendom as the Muslims in the east. The redefinition was controversial but valid according to its own terms.

The immediate background to Urban's appeal at Clermont was to be found in developments in the East. In the late eleventh century the Byzantine empire was coming under renewed pressure from the Turks. In 1071 a major Byzantine army had suffered defeat at Manzikert. The Emperor Alexius Comnenus had sent an urgent appeal to the Pope for assistance. The crusade which the Pope sent in response to the appeal was envisaged principally as a relief force; however, it quickly developed a momentum of its own. In 1098 the crusaders took the Syrian town of

Antioch, after a long siege. In the following year, on 15 July, they took Jerusalem itself. The native population were expelled, and a feudal state was set up.

The fledgling feudal kingdom was never self-sufficient. Many of the First Crusaders decided to stay in the east, but their numbers were never adequate to satisfy the needs of defence. Whenever a crisis arose (which was often), a new relief force – a crusade – had to be sent out to assist. In 1144 the important Syrian city of Edessa was taken by the Muslims; a Second Crusade was preached at Vezelay by the great reformer St Bernard. The crusade ended two years later in failure. In the third quarter of the century the great Turkish commander Nur-ad-Din extended his power into Egypt and completely surrounded the Latin state. In July 1187 his successor, the famous Saladin, defeated the crusaders at the battle of Hattin, and in October entered Jerusalem. In response to this terrible disaster, the Third Crusade was preached. Armies set out from Germany under Frederick Barbarossa, who died on the way, from France under King Philip, and from England and the Angevin lands under King Richard (q.v.). The crusaders took Acre and Jaffa in 1191 and came within sight of Jerusalem but that was all. Philip and Richard quarrelled with each other, and the crusade collapsed in the face of internal dissent. Philip returned home in October 1191 and Richard in the following year. Early in the next century Pope Innocent III preached a fresh crusade. This set sail in 1202 but never reached the Holy Land. The prospect of plundering Constantinople proved too attractive. In 1204 the crusaders stormed the city, deposed the emperor, and put Baldwin of Flanders in his place. The Byzantines did not recover possession until 1261.

In the meantime the western crusaders had adopted a new strategy for recovering Jerusalem. Instead of launching a direct attack on Palestine, they chose to invade Egypt,

★ Quoted by J. Riley-Smith, 'Crusading as an Act of Love', *History*, 65 (1980), p.180

which was the power base of Saladin's empire. A Fifth Crusade set off in 1218 and captured Damietta on the Nile delta. The strategy very nearly succeeded. The sultan offered Jerusalem in return for Damietta but the crusaders unwisely rejected his terms. They held out for too much, and in the end got nothing. St Louis, however, adopted the same strategy when he set sail for the East in 1219. He recaptured Damietta and marched up the Nile. But at Mansurah his army was surrounded by the enemy, and in the ensuing retreat the king was captured. After his release, Louis sailed for Acre (May 1250) and spent the next four years in Palestine.

It was Acre which was the Lord Edward's destination when he led an English force to the East in August 1270. This was an expedition composed largely of royalists who used the pretext of the crusade to obtain the Church's protection for the lands which they had grabbed from their opponents in the baronial wars of the 1260s. There was little for them to do when they reached their destination. The states of Tyre and Acre were at loggerheads with each other. Edward settled their differences as best he could, made a truce with the sultan and then sailed for

home in 1272. Some nineteen years later, on 18 May 1291, Acre fell, and what was left of the Latin Kingdom ceased to exist. Crusading fervour, however, lived on. Late medieval Popes constantly promoted the unity of Christendom as the essential precondition for the liberation of the East. At the same time, they argued that it was pointless confronting external foes until internal ones had been eliminated. This was a justification for the suppression of heresy. In the late Middle Ages this redefinition of crusading attracted the ire of critics such as John Wycliffe (q.v.).

Although England was never so fertile a recruiting ground for crusaders as France, English crusaders were found on all the main passagia to the east. In the fourteenth century men such as Sir Stephen Scrope, Sir Richard Waldegrave and the esquire Nicholas Sabraham had distinguished crusading records. In the 1390s Henry of Derby, the future Henry IV (q.v.), made two visits to the Baltic theatre.

J. Riley-Smith, *The Crusades. A Short History*, London, 1987; C. Tyerman, *England and the Crusades, 1095-1588*, Chicago, 1988; J.P Phillips, *The Crusades*, 1095-1197, London, 2002.

D

DECORATED

See ARCHITECTURE, ECCLESIASTICAL

DEMESNE

When a text says that X held his lands in demesne (Latin, *in dominico*), it means that he held them himself and not from anyone else. Thus the royal demesne consisted of those manors held directly by the king, the revenues from which went to support the estate and dignity of the crown. Similarly, the demesne manors of a great estate or feudal honor were those which the lord had not subinfeudated to any of his vassals.

If we turn to the internal organization of the manor, the land which the lord himself cultivated was known as the demesne, to distinguish it from the land held and cultivated by the tenants. The demesne in this sense was a home farm, worked either by the *famuli* (paid estate labourers) or by the labour services owed by the unfree tenants, the villeins. By the early fifteenth century, when high costs and low prices caused most landlords to abandon large-scale cultivation, manorial demesnes were usually put out to lease.

DIET

A wide range of sources shed light on the medieval diet. Cookery books describe the ideal dishes – the often elaborate meals which were served to guests. Archaeological finds illuminate what was actually served or, to be more precise, what was thrown away afterwards. Corrodies (q.v.), monastic maintenance agreements, tell us what religious houses considered appropriate for their dependants. Cookery books, of course, mainly pandered to the rich, but archaeological evidence illuminates the dietary habits of rich and poor alike.

The nobility generally entertained on a lavish scale. The quantities of food which were served at feasts may appear shocking today, but conspicuous consumption was what was expected of them and conspicuous consumption was what was offered. The feast prepared to celebrate the enthronement of George Neville as Archbishop of York in 1465 is a good example. The larders were stocked up with 300 quarters of wheat, 300 tuns of ale, 100 tuns of wine, 6 bulls, 1,000 sheep, 304 calves, 400 swans, 2,000 geese, 2,000 pigs, 13,500 birds, 1,500 hot pasties of venison, not to mention countless spices, custards and jellies. However large the guests' appetites – and there were several thousands of them – they could hardly have made more than limited inroads into such quantities.

If it is argued that this was hardly a typical banquet, the less pretentious but still lavish standards set at the table of Chaucer's Franklin may be considered:

His bread, his ale were finest of the fine
And no one had a better stock of wine.
His house was never short of bake-meat pies,
Of fish and flesh, and these in such supplies
It positively snowed with meat and drink
And all the dainties that a man could think.*

To judge from these and other descriptions of meals, the pre-modern palate evidently delighted in very different tastes from the modern. To some extent the limited range of eating utensils known in medieval England imposed restrictions on the kind of food that could be served. Forks were unknown here before the seventeenth century. For that reason meats had to be chopped up beforehand into small, easily digestible portions that could be lifted to the mouth by hand, and grain and other foods pounded into a soft mess that could be sipped from a spoon. In the Middle Ages, when so much of the diet, particularly for the lower classes, was grain-based, eating could have been painful had not the roughness been moderated.

Yet these considerations, however important, hardly prepare us for the extraordinary combinations of food we find recommended in the recipe books. Today the aim is to bring sympathetic and complementary tastes together on a dish. In the Middle Ages, on the other hand, they mixed together ingredients without any apparent consideration for incongruity. Today, again, we try to cook our food in such a way as to preserve its taste, while in the Middle Ages they apparently prepared it in such a way as to destroy whatever taste it once had. The following recipe, given in a fifteenth-century cookery book, can stand for innumerable other concoctions that would seem bizarre to modern taste:

Take some apples, stew them, let them cool, pass them through a hair sieve. Put them in a pot,

* Chaucer, *The Canterbury Tales*, ed. N. Coghill, Penguin, 1951, p.28

and on a flesh day add good fat beef broth, white grease, sugar and saffron. Boil it, mess it out, sprinkle on good spices and serve.

Alternatively we might contemplate the 'sop-in-wine', so 'well-loved' by Chaucer's Franklin. This was made by cutting up pieces of bread or cake and pouring over them a sauce of wine, almond milk, saffron, ginger, sugar, cinnamon and cloves.

It is generally agreed by nutritionists that the upper-class diet in the Middle Ages suffered from serious deficiencies in the intake of vitamins. It appears to have been particularly low in the intake of vitamins A and C because of the shortage of fruit. On the other hand, if the diet of the Westminster community is typical, it was very strong on the intake of vitamin D. The Westminster monks ate many milky dishes, such as cheese flans and 'charlet' – the last made with chopped meat, eggs and milk – which were rich in vitamin D. The diet of the Westminster monks also had a remarkably high protein content. While this was not in itself a bad thing, it may have contributed to kidney malfunctioning.

In affluent secular households in the Middle Ages there were two principal meals of the day. The first was dinner, which was taken at 10 or 11 in the morning, and the second supper which was taken at about 4 in the afternoon. The diet of the lower orders was, of course, very different from that of the aristocracy. What the peasants ate, and in what quantities, depended largely on the level of income they enjoyed – and to some extent on where they lived. One dish apparently popular in peasant households was 'pease pottage', a name which survives as that of a Sussex hamlet. This consisted of old pea soup left to solidify. As an alternative, there was pease pudding, which was made of soaked dried peas cooked together in a cloth with salted pork. By and large the bulk of the rural peasantry, certainly in the thirteenth century, must have lived on a diet which was weighted heavily towards carbohydrates. Of the cereals which they grew, wheat would have been sold to raise cash, and barley and oats kept for making into bread. According to Sir William Ashley in his study *Bread of our Forefathers*, it was not until the eighteenth century that the rural population was regularly eating a wheaten loaf. In earlier times they would have relied heavily on grains like barley, rye or even oats for making flour. It is worth mentioning that on the tables of the polite, bread was served without its crust, for reasons that are unclear. Perhaps the crust was too hard. Or possibly it was thought too dirty.

In the post–Black Death period, when peasant living standards improved, meat figured more prominently in the diet. Sheep and cattle would be kept in varying proportions in every medieval village. The sheep were slaughtered for their mutton when they were too old to be worth keeping for their wool. Bone deposits unearthed at Wharram Percy (Yorks), a village deserted in the late Middle Ages, suggest that its inhabitants had enjoyed a meat diet that was 60% mutton, 30% beef and 8% pork. Their heavy consumption of mutton is hardly surprising in view of the predominantly pastoral economy of east Yorkshire.

How did people wash down the often strange combinations of food that they ate? Water was generally out of the question because it was undrinkable. For the rich there were many varieties of wine to choose from, imported mostly from Gascony (q.v.), France and the Rhine. For the great mass of the population, however, ale would have been the standard beverage, brewed usually from barley or oat malt. The normal reckoning, in upper class households at least, was that sixty gallons of ale could be made from a quarter of malt. In the admittedly affluent monastic community of Westminster large quantities of ale were drunk; remarkably, this beverage accounted for 19% of the whole energy value of the diet on a normal day.

In the fourteenth century brewing was a sideline undertaken by many tenants in the countryside, quite a proportion of them women, but in the fifteenth growing specialization encouraged the emergence of professional brewers who ran their own alehouses or pubs, as we would call them today. Beer was unknown in England before the sixteenth century, when hops were introduced from the Netherlands 'to the detryment of many Englysshe men', as Andrew Boorde put it in 1542 in his *Dyetary of Helth*. It was presumably the more bitter taste of the new beverage that incurred his disapproval.

C. Dyer, 'English Diet in the Later Middle Ages', in *Social Relations and Ideas. Essays in Honour of R. H. Hilton*, ed. T. Aston, P. Coss, C, Dyer and J. Thirsk, Cambridge, 1983; B. Harvey, *Living and Dying in England, 1100–1540*, Oxford, 1993.

DISTRAINT

Medieval governments were lacking in coercive power. The English government had no police force, no band of officers in its pay whose duty it was to enforce the law. Thus if an indicted malefactor failed to turn up in court when summoned, some other means had to be found of compelling him. The common law did this by the process of 'distraint', or seizure of his lands and chattels. If an accused was absent from a hearing, the sheriff would order the hundred (q.v.) bailiff to take possession of his lands and goods until such time as his attendance had been secured. Distraint was, and still is, used to effect the collection of debts. The term was also employed in a more specialized sense to describe the policy of compulsory knighthood which was practised from the thirteenth century onwards. Writs of distraint were sent to the sheriffs asking them to return the names of those eligible for knighthood who had not yet taken it up. By the early fourteenth century the qualification had become more or less fixed at an annual income of £40. Since these writs were commonly issued when the king was planning a military expedition, it seems likely that their purpose was to swell the number of knights in the English army. From those who persisted in declining to take up the honour of knighthood the king was still able to reap some financial advantage by imposing fines for exemption.

DOMESDAY BOOK

This is the name given to the great survey of England undertaken in the last years of William the Conqueror's (q.v.) reign. It became such an indispensable reference book that by the 1170s it had acquired the nickname 'Domesday', because like the Day of Judgement (*doom* = judgement), its sentence could not be quashed or set aside. Domesday Book survives in two volumes, now preserved in the Public Record Office, which are the oldest of our public records.

The compilation of Domesday Book was ordered by William the Conqueror at his Christmas court in 1085. According to the Old English chronicler, the king 'held deep discussions with his council about this country, how it was peopled, and with what sorts of men'. It is possible that earlier and more limited enquiries had been made into the size and taxable wealth of the country. Then, when these were found to be unsatisfactory, William embarked on a larger and more searching enquiry: Domesday Book. According to the same chronicler, 'so thoroughly did William have the kingdom investigated that there was not a single (piece of land)... or even (it is shameful to record but it did not seem shameful to him to do), one ox or one cow or one pig that was omitted from his record; and all these records were afterwards brought to him.'

The manner in which the information was collected carries a surprisingly modern ring. England was divided into seven circuits, each

covering about five counties. To each of these circuits a group of commissioners was assigned. These men went from county to county, collecting the information they wanted from juries that came before them in a session of the county court. These enquiries provided the commissioners with a vast amount of information, but if the resulting survey were not to be unwieldy, this had to be reduced to a manageable size. Moreover, it had to be decided whether the information was to be assembled on a geographical basis, county by county, village by village, or on a feudal basis, landowner by landowner. In the event, an uneasy compromise was reached. The arrangement was by counties, but within each county it was by landowner. In other words, the survey was converted from a gazetteer into a directory of feudal tenants. The returns for most of England were condensed in this manner to produce the main volume of Domesday Book, which may well have been complete by the time of the Conqueror's death in 1087, but those for the eastern circuit (Norfolk, Suffolk, Essex) remained separate and unabbreviated in volume two.

Once the evidence was written down in the form in which it survives today, it did not lie idle. It was kept in the treasury at Winchester, where it may well have been used to increase the yield from taxation, for a contemporary tells us that at that time 'the land was vexed with many calamities arising from the collection of the royal money'. But Domesday Book was not merely an elaborate tax return. The arrangement of the material within counties on a feudal basis suggests that it may also have been William's intention to take stock of the territorial revolution which had been a prime consequence of the Conquest. In any dispute about the ownership of land this great survey could be cited as a source of unimpeachable authority, not lightly to be set aside.

A great deal can be learned from Domesday Book about William the Conqueror's England. Yet it is a source which has to be interpreted with care. As H.R. Loyn has written, 'it tells much, but it does not always tell what is wanted'. Because of the internal arrangement by landowner, a searcher has to cast around for the details concerning a single village. If, for example, he or she is looking for the description of the village of Harpswell (Lincs), which was divided into three manors, then a search is needed for the appropriate entry under each of its three lords – the king, the Archbishop of York and Jocelyn FitzLambert. However, once the practical difficulties of using it are mastered, Domesday Book becomes an invaluable guide to the social and economic conditions of its day. For example, the commissioners in most cases attempted to trace changes in the value of manors by recording their worth in 1066, at the end of Edward the Confessor's reign, and in 1086. From these figures it can be appreciated how the new Norman lords increased the value of their landed estates by exploiting them more intensively, and also how the taxable capacity of Yorkshire declined in this interval as a result of William's harrying of the north in 1069–70. But Domesday Book tells us more than anything else about the nature of the government which created it. It is a document without parallel in eleventh-century Europe. Its compilation is a tribute to the ability and ambitions of the new Norman kings and to the efficiency of the administrative machine they had at their disposal.

F.W. Maitland, *Domesday Book and Beyond*, Cambridge, 1897, reprinted 1987; *Domesday Studies*, ed. J.C. Holt, Woodbridge, 1987.

DOMINICANS

Although the two orders of friars, the Dominicans and the Franciscans (q.v.), came into existence simultaneously, the initial aspirations and ideas of their founders were very different. Francis of Assisi was a man of deep spirituality who believed in teaching by example rather than argument; Dominic of Caleruega, on the other hand, wanted to create an order of intellectuals, trained theologians who could combat heresy. Each order, in the event, influenced the shape and growth of the other. The most obvious way in which the Dominicans were influenced by the Franciscans was in their adoption of the Franciscan idea of poverty. Dominic had originally intended to base the institutions of his order on those of the Augustinian Canons (q.v.). In 1220, however, reputedly after a meeting with Francis, he dropped the idea in favour of adopting the corporate poverty of the Franciscans; his followers, like those of Francis, were to become mendicants, dependent on the charity of others. In respect of constitutional organization, however, it was the Franciscans who followed the Dominicans. The arrangements which Dominic conceived for his order were complex, but at the same time effective. He divided Europe into provinces, each headed by a prior. Once a year the provincial chapter, composed of representatives from all of the constituent houses, would meet to elect a diffinitor, or representative, for the general chapter and four diffinitores to whom the business of the chapter would be delegated. The general chapter, which likewise met annually, ran in cycles of three years, for two of which it was composed of the diffinitores and for the third, of the provincial priors. At the summit of this organization was the master-general, who served for life and was elected by an ad hoc general chapter. The Franciscan constitution was much slower to evolve than its counterpart, but when it did, in the 1240s, it owed much to the Dominican model.

The Dominicans were a popular order in England. Within half a century of their arrival in 1221 they had established some forty-six houses here, and their final tally of fifty-three was only five short of that of the Franciscans. However, in terms of overall influence and distinction the Dominicans lost out to the Franciscans. The sheer popularity of the latter inspired so many of the brightest men of the time to don their grey habit that in the process the order was transformed from one of simple apostles into one of scholars and intellectuals. In other words, the Franciscans took over the role that the Dominicans had originally envisaged for themselves. Where the Dominicans were most successful was in serving as confessors to royalty and nobility. Virtually all of the late-medieval kings were served by Dominican confessors, Richard II by no fewer than five. Dominican teaching probably played a large role in shaping their view of the world. In the towns the Dominicans were evidently successful in attracting large congregations if the lengthy naves which they built for their churches are any guide. The nave of the Dominican church at Norwich (St Andrew's Hall) is a good example. Extensive remains of other Dominican friaries, particularly of their domestic buildings, can be seen at Bristol and Gloucester.

R.B. Brooke, *The Coming of the Friars*, London, 1975; *Dominican Painting in East Anglia*, ed. C. Norton, D. Park and P. Binski, Woodbridge, 1987.

EARLY ENGLISH
See ARCHITECTURE, ECCLESIASTICAL

EDMUND OF ABINGDON
Many of the materials for the life of Edmund of Abingdon arise from the proceedings for canonization instituted after he died in 1240. For that reason they verge on the hagiographical, and it is not always easy to distinguish fact from fiction.

Edmund was the son of an Abingdon burgess, Reginald, known as the Rich, and his wife Mabel. He and his brother were sent to the schools at Paris to read the Arts, and after he had incepted as a Master he returned to spend another six years studying the Arts at Oxford (q.v.). He then transferred, as was the custom, from the Arts to the higher faculty of Theology. He spent another four years at Paris before coming back to join the Oxford theology faculty, probably around 1214. It is unfortunate that so little is known about his Oxford years, not just because he was an influential teacher at a crucial period in the early history of the university but also because of the association of his name with the site in the parish of St Peter-in-the-East later occupied by St Edmund Hall.

In 1222 he became treasurer of Salisbury Cathedral and in September 1233 was elected Archbishop of Canterbury. Even before he was consecrated in April the following year he found himself drawn into the maelstrom of national politics. Angered by the prominence of Poitevin favourites at court, Richard the Earl Marshal had led an uprising against Henry III's (q.v.) government. Edmund used all his powers of conciliation to reconcile king and rebels, a task facilitated by the news of Richard's death in Ireland in February 1234. In the years to come, Edmund's relations with the king were to be far from harmonious. And it was to be much the same with the monastic chapter at Canterbury Cathedral. Edmund was keen to revive an old plan to found a college at Maidstone to provide for the numerous secular clerks in his service. The monks, however, saw this as a threat to their rights as the archiepiscopal electoral body, and neither side seemed ready to give way.

There are two conflicting accounts of the final months of Edward's life. According to the narratives submitted for the canonization proceedings, Edmund withdrew into voluntary exile at Pontigny, already famous as the refuge of his predecessors, Becket (q.v.) and Langton (q.v.). Allegedly to escape from the heat, he moved to Soisy, where he died on 16 November 1240. The reliability of this traditional hagiographical account has been called into question by Edmund's biographer, who points out that no contemporary sources mention that the archbishop chose to go into exile. On the contrary, one of the chronicles says that his purpose in leaving was to visit Rome. He had been summoned to a general council due to be held at Easter 1241 and was setting out early to enlist papal support in his dispute with the chapter at Canterbury. On the way he fell ill and died. Although depriving Edmund of his claim to a martyr's crown, this explanation does carry a ring of plausibility.

The archbishop was an attractive man whose reputation for fairness and purity of life enabled him to set an example to contemporaries. However, his years as archbishop were marred by a succession of disputes, not always of his own making, which meant that the expectations aroused by his appointment were never fulfilled.

C.H. Lawrence, *St Edmund of Abingdon*, Oxford, 1960.

EDUCATION
See SCHOOLS; UNIVERSITIES

EDWARD I

Edward I's reign witnessed major achievements in legislative and administrative reform. However, the wars of the king's later years in Scotland and France proved overambitious. Edward's legacy to his son was a mixed one.

Edward was born on 17 June 1239, the eldest son of Henry III and his wife Eleanor of Provence. In 1254, at the age of fifteen, he was married to Eleanor, half-sister of Alfonso X, king of Castile. Like all marriages at this level of society in the Middle Ages, the match cemented a diplomatic alliance: its aim was to secure the southern frontier of Gascony. But Edward and Eleanor seem to have been particularly devoted to each other, and when the queen died in 1290, Edward erected in her

memory a series of crosses – the Eleanor Crosses – marking the places where her body rested on its journey from Lincoln, where she died, to Westminster. Edward remained a widower for nine years, until in 1299 he took Margaret, sister of King Philip IV of France, as his second wife. The chroniclers say that he had long fancied a French princess; but, as they were probably referring to Margaret's sister, it seems that diplomatic considerations again explain the match.

Edward succeeded to the throne in 1272. His youth had offered little promise for the future. He had revealed himself a rather shifty individual. In 1258 the attraction of Simon de Montfort's (q.v.) personality seems to have drawn him to the baronial reform movement but he repented of his early enthusiasms and by 1264 was fully committed to restoring his father's authority. In the civil war that broke out in spring 1264 he was captured at Lewes, but escaped and led the royalists to victory at Evesham in 1265.

Edward was on crusade in the Holy Land when news reached him in December 1272 of his father's death. By the time he returned to England in 1274 he had been away for four years, and a host of allegations awaited him that local officials, both royal and baronial, had taken advantage of his absence to line their pockets and usurp royal lands. Edward reacted by launching a thorough investigation into local government, the records of which are known as the Hundred Rolls (q.v.). It was largely in response to the evidence uncovered in these enquiries that he published the first Statute of Westminster, 1275, remedying many long-standing abuses, and the Statute of Gloucester, 1278, initiating the *quo warranto* proceedings which questioned the warrant whereby baronial franchise holders exercised their rights. These were but two of the many important statutes that Edward issued in the 1270s and 1280s. The king was seeking both to reassert his authority and to remove the grievances which had fuelled the baronial reform movement in the reign of his father.

These early years of the reign also saw Edward complete the conquest of Wales (q.v.). In two short campaigns, in 1277 and 1282, he defeated Prince Llewellyn and took possession of his principality of Gwynedd. Edward consolidated his conquest by an ambitious programme of castle-building. His castles (q.v.) at Conway and Caernarfon represent the peak of the castle-builder's art in medieval Britain.

Encouraged by his easy triumph in Wales, Edward embarked on similar intervention in Scotland (q.v.). When the direct line of the Scottish kings came to an end in 1290, Edward awarded the Scottish crown to a vassal, John Balliol, and immediately attempted establishing an English ascendancy over the kingdom. His intervention proved ill judged. The English presence provoked a nationalist backlash, and Edward found himself fighting a war that he could never win. Balliol was expelled in 1296 and William Wallace, a charismatic personality, took up the cause of resisting the invader. The long wars against the Scots, which dragged on into the 1330s, formed the backcloth to English politics for the next three generations. The problems of heavy taxation and military service to which they gave rise contributed to a serious political crisis in 1297, when dissident barons led by the earls of Hereford and Norfolk formed an alliance with Robert Winchelsey, Archbishop of Canterbury, to resist the king's demands. Edward was embarking on yet another campaign in the North when he died at Burgh-on-the-Sands on 7 July 1307.

Edward was a forceful man and his reign illustrates English medieval kingship at its most dynamic. For all the undoubted opposition which he aroused in his later years, it is significant that his opponents never shackled him with a constitution as humiliating as the one which had been imposed on his father in 1258 in the Provisions of Oxford (q.v.).

M. Prestwich, *Edward I*, 2nd ed., New Haven and London, 1998.

EDWARD II

Edward II was the first English king to be deposed since the Norman Conquest. His reign was one of the most calamitous in the Middle Ages.

Edward was born on 25 April 1284 at Caernarfon, the eldest surviving son of Edward I (q.v.) and Eleanor of Castile. In 1301 he was created the first Prince of Wales. His early years revealed little in his character to inspire confidence, and already he was infatuated with a young Gascon, Piers Gaveston, whom his father was obliged to send into exile in February 1307. When Edward became king in July 1307 he immediately recalled Gaveston from exile and created him earl of Cornwall. The first signs of opposition to the king came at Boulogne in January 1308, when a group of barons swore to redress 'the oppressions which have been done and are still being done' against the people. This oath foreshadowed the additional clause which was to be inserted into the coronation oath in February 1308 requiring Edward to keep the laws and customs 'which the community of your realm' shall have chosen. This clause was almost certainly inserted to prevent Edward from going back on any future agreement in the way that his father had done. Indeed it was invoked only two months later to secure the exile of Gaveston.

Although the barons had got rid of Gaveston, they could not indefinitely prevent his return, and by 1309 he was back at the king's side. Dissatisfaction with Edward and his cronies continued to mount until in March 1310 the committee of Lords Ordainers was appointed in parliament to reform the state of the realm (q.v. ORDINANCES). The Ordainers' programme included the removal of Gaveston and the other favourites whose greed had impoverished the crown and the return (or 'resumption') of royal lands which had been granted away. Early in 1312, in defiance of the Ordinances, Gaveston returned to the king's side. He was captured at Scarborough, and executed by the earl of Lancaster a month later (19 June 1312).

The presence of avaricious favourites injected a note of bitterness into the politics of Edward II's reign, but as in his father's last years it was the continuing war in Scotland that cast the darkest shadow over English life. Edward would neither abandon the war nor pursue it with sufficient energy to achieve victory. When in 1314 he did finally lead a large force across the border, his initiative ended in disaster. He was heavily defeated by the Scots at Bannockburn (q.v.) near Stirling on 24 June 1314. As so often in history, external defeat led to reform at home. Edward had no alternative but to acquiesce in Lancaster's demands for the enforcement of the Ordinances. However, the timing was unfortunate for Lancaster, for his reforming efforts were thwarted by the terrible famines that followed the harvest failures of 1315 and 1316. At the same time, his position at court was being undermined by the rise of new favourites, the two Despensers, father and son. Lancaster withdrew from court, and did his best to frustrate Edward's and his friends' policies from the isolation of his estates in the north. A party of bishops strove tirelessly to reconcile the king and the earl but with only partial success. The Treaty of Leake (August 1318), which resulted from their efforts, met Lancaster's demand for the establishment of a standing council. However, with the earl himself bribed into dropping his claim to membership, the influence it exerted over the king amounted to little.

Although the bishop of Worcester commented on an improvement in the king's conduct in 1320 – he was getting up earlier in the morning – in the long run his optimism proved to be unfounded. Edward fell increasingly under the influence of the Despensers,

the younger of whom took advantage of his position to extend the lands he held in Glamorgan into a vast territorial lordship. His aggressive behaviour provoked almost the entire baronage into resistance, and in July 1321 Edward was forced to send him and his father into exile. The younger Hugh, however, like Gaveston before him, was soon back. Edward now acted quickly. He had the judgement against his favourites reversed in parliament and set about crushing his opponents. The Welsh marcher lords appealed to Lancaster for help. Characteristically, the earl was too preoccupied with a quarrel of his own to come to their aid. Edward scattered the opposition in the west and then marched northwards against Lancaster himself. The earl was heavily defeated at Boroughbridge (17 March 1322) and subsequently executed.

For the next four years Edward and the Despensers ruled almost without challenge. Since the king and his favourites had seized their opponents' lands, they were awash with money and had no need of parliament. There was no opportunity for dissent. The end, however, came suddenly. In September 1326 a party of exiles, led by the queen and her lover, Roger Mortimer, landed at Orwell (Suffolk). With them they brought the king's young son, Edward. Edward II's government collapsed and the king himself was captured near Neath in November. In January 1327 Isabella hastily summoned a parliament, and a delegation was sent to Edward to induce him to abdicate in favour of his son. He bowed to the inevitable and was led to confinement first at Kenilworth then at Berkeley. According to the traditional accounts, he was murdered at Berkeley on Mortimer's orders on 21 September 1327. However, in recent years some credence has been lent to a document known as the 'confession' of Edward II. This purports to be a narrative dictated to Manuel Fieschi, a clerk of Pope John XXII, in which the deposed king tells how he escaped from Berkeley and travelled through

France and Germany to eventual residence in an Italian hermitage. It is difficult to know what to make of this document, and no adequate explanation of it has yet been offered. For the moment, it is probably safer to accept that Edward did after all meet his end in Berkeley in September 1327.

M. Prestwich, *The Three Edwards*, London, 1980; R.M. Haines, *King Edward II: Edward of Caernarfon: His Life, His Reign and its Aftermath*, Montreal, 2003.

EDWARD III

Edward III was highly esteemed in his lifetime and has since enjoyed an enviable reputation with posterity. His two main achievements were to restore the authority of the crown and to win a series of brilliant victories on the continent.

Edward was born in November 1312, the son of Edward II and his queen Isabella of France. After her husband's triumph at Boroughbridge, Isabella left the country for France and took her son with her. In September 1326, in association with her lover Mortimer, she invaded England, removed her husband from the throne and installed her son in his place (25 January 1327). Edward endured his mother's tutelage for three years. In a surprise coup in 1330, however, he ordered her and her lover to be arrested – the former being despatched to comfortable retirement at Castle Rising. Edward began to rule in fact as well as in name.

Edward gained his military apprenticeship in the Scottish wars. In 1328 Isabella and Mortimer had signed the Treaty of Northampton which effectively granted the Scots their independence. After Robert Bruce's death, however, Edward saw a chance to reopen the struggle. In 1332 he backed an invasion by Bruce's rival, Edward Balliol, and a group of fellow exiles. The exiles scored an unexpected success at Dupplin Moor on 11

August; however, they were driven out in the following year. Edward then intervened in person and after a sweeping victory at Halidon Hill near Berwick (19 July 1333) installed Balliol on the throne. The tactic which Edward employed at Halidon Hill of combining archers with dismounted men-at-arms was one which he was to use again to great effect in France. After the onset of the continental war in 1338, Scotland received less of his attention. Nonetheless, in 1346 while he was fighting in France, his lieutenants scored another notable victory at Neville's Cross, where King David II was taken prisoner.

Edward's continental interests developed in the 1330s when arguments about the status of Gascony (q.v.) came to the fore again. In 1337 King Philip of France had confiscated the duchy of Gascony on the grounds of Edward's defiance of a summons. Edward responded to the challenge by laying claim to the crown of France himself. His claim was a good one. As the son of Isabella, sister of the last Capetian king, he was closer in blood to the Capetians than Philip VI, who was only the last king's cousin. However, the main attraction of staking the claim was diplomatic. It offered the disaffected French nobility a respectable means by which they could rally to his banner. In a sense, Edward was championing those who, for one reason or another, had a grievance against the French king.

In the opening years of the war, Edward attacked France in the same way that his grandfather had – by crossing to Flanders and assembling a coalition of supporters in the Low Countries. However, this proved to be an expensive and ultimately ineffectual strategy. In November 1340, when he returned to England after an absence of two years, he had nothing to show for his efforts but a naval victory at Sluys. In the next decade he changed his strategy. Abandoning the idea of an attack through the Low Countries, he launched a series of hit-and-run raids – *chevauchées* – from bases on the periphery, such as Brittany and Gascony. The new strategy was exceptionally successful. The French had no response to it. In 1342 Edward led a swashbuckling *chevauchée* across southern Brittany. In 1346 he led a much larger force in a raid across Normandy. On this occasion the French trailed him, and he was obliged to give battle near Crécy (q.v.). Using the tactics he had learned in Scotland, he scored a notable victory. The coming of the Black Death (q.v.) in 1348 brought a temporary lull in hostilities, but they were resumed in the next decade. In 1356 the king's son, the Black Prince (q.v.), leading a *chevauchée* across south-west France, scored a spectacular victory over the French at Poitiers (q.v.), even capturing the French king. The prince's victory transformed Edward's prospects. The French crown now appeared within his grasp. In 1359 he launched what he thought would be the *coup de grâce* – an assault on the city of Rheims, where the French kings were crowned. The outcome of the campaign, however, was disappointing and at Brétigny, near Chartres, negotiations were opened for peace. By a settlement subsequently ratified at Calais, Edward abandoned his claim to the crown in return for an enlarged Gascony in full sovereignty.

Edward spent the 1360s enjoying the fruits of his victories. A major project was the rebuilding of Windsor Castle (q.v.). In 1369, however, Charles V, the new French king, reopened the war and began recovering the lands ceded to the English. Edward by now was too old to challenge the French in person, and his son the Black Prince was dying of dysentery. The English response to the French recovery was inadequate and ineffectual. Criticism of the court was increasingly voiced in parliament. In June 1376, in the 'Good Parliament', there was a major crisis in the course of which a number of the king's ministers were impeached (q.v.). In his last years Edward fell under the influence of his rapacious mistress Alice Perrers. As he lay dying in June 1377 Alice was stealing the rings from his fingers.

Although the last years of his reign were unhappy, Edward was remembered by contemporaries for the achievements of his heyday. Even by his critics he was esteemed a great warrior. He had raised the English crown to unprecedented levels of renown. His court was famed for its companionship and honour. He had snatched the political leadership of Europe from the French. A major element in Edward's success was the harnessing of chivalric ritual. He was a keen sponsor of tournaments (q.v.) and Round Tables; indeed, he often took part in tournament jousts himself. In 1348, in a novel initiative, he established the first chivalric order, the Order of the Garter. The order was an exclusive brotherhood of twenty-six knights, each of whom had a stall in St George's Chapel in Windsor Castle. Election to the order was an honour much sought after by knights. Edward's chivalric kingship became the touchstone against which later medieval kings were to be judged.

Edward's character is hard to discern. It is clear that he was generous and forgiving, but he could also be harsh and quick-tempered. He was conventionally pious. He made pilgrimages to shrines before and after campaigns, and he gave money to churches connected with the English monarchy. His marriage to his queen, Philippa of Hainault, appears to have been a happy one.

Edward was buried in Westminster Abbey where he is commemorated by a bronze tomb effigy showing him in old age.

See also HUNDRED YEARS WAR

W.M. Ormrod, *The Reign of Edward III*, 2nd ed., Stroud, 2000.

EDWARD IV

Edward IV was the longest lived of the three Yorkist kings. He successfully restored stability after the strife of the Wars of the Roses (q.v.), but the very policies he pursued contributed to the breakdown of order after his death.

Edward was born on 28 April 1442, the eldest son of Richard, duke of York, and his wife, Cecily Neville. His father's opposition to the policies of Henry VI (q.v.) and his ministers led at the end of the 1450s to the outbreak of intermittent political disorder. In 1459 he and his son were obliged to flee the realm for fear of being seized and executed as traitors. In the following year the tables were turned. The Yorkists returned to crush their opponents at the battle of Northampton on 10 July 1460 and York himself was recalled and made heir to the throne. Yet only five months later, on 30 December, York was defeated and killed at Wakefield. The mantle of leadership now passed to his eldest son. Paradoxically it was another defeat that was soon to make this man king of England. In February 1461 Queen Margaret defeated the Yorkists at the second battle of St Albans and freed her husband, who had been little more than a prisoner for the previous six months. Having lost control of their puppet king, the Yorkists could only cling onto power by creating a king of their own. So they put the new duke of York on the throne as Edward IV.

Edward's was a shaky start, but on Palm Sunday, 29 April 1461, he made an effective job of disposing of Queen Margaret's army at the battle of Towton: the Lancastrian threat was henceforth as good as over. In southern England the Yorkists had for some time enjoyed the edge over their opponents in popular favour. In the north, however, a residual Lancastrianism lived on, but even this died the death after Edward's victory over the Beauforts at Hedgeley Moor in 1464. The main threat to political stability in England in the 1460s came less from any lingering Lancastrianism than from divisions within the Yorkist camp itself fostered by the king's own errors. Prime among these was the Woodville marriage. In October 1464 Edward made known that a few months earlier he had secretly married Elizabeth Woodville, widow of Sir John Grey. The consequences of his action would not have been so far-reaching had not Elizabeth brought with her to court a coterie of ambitious relatives, including no less than half a dozen sisters who all had to be found suitable marriages. Few nobles were more upset than Edward's most powerful supporter, Richard Neville, earl of Warwick (q.v.), who found it harder now to find appropriate husbands for his own two daughters. It must have become apparent to him as the years went by that Edward IV was not to be the pliable instrument in his hands for which he had hoped. In July 1469, in desperation, he risked an armed throw. With the support of the king's untrustworthy brother Clarence, he invaded England from Calais (q.v.), captured Edward and executed allies of his like Richard Woodville, Earl Rivers. But it was one thing to capture the king; quite another to try ruling the country in his name. Edward soon escaped, and Warwick fled to France, where he defected to Queen Margaret and the Lancastrians. On 13 September 1470 Warwick returned and put Henry VI back on the throne. For the moment Edward had to flee the realm but time was on his side. The mere sight of Henry VI again was enough to convince most people that the 'readeption' would never last. From his refuge in the Low Countries Edward planned a landing in the West Country which would lead in the following year to Warwick's death at Barnet (14 April 1471) and Queen Margaret's defeat at Tewkesbury three weeks later (4 May 1471).

Edward IV, like Charles II, was determined never to go on his travels again. After 1471, accordingly, he avoided the kind of errors that had cost him so dearly in his first reign. But the success which he enjoyed in restoring peace and prosperity did not extend to reconciling the opposing factions at court. The biggest problem he faced in the 1470s was the quarrel between his two brothers, George of Clarence and Richard of Gloucester, the future Richard III (q.v.), over the disposal of the Warwick inheritance, equal shares of which they laid claim to by virtue of their marriages to Warwick's daughters. The dispute over the inheritance was, however, merely the ground on which Clarence chose to pick his fight between 1471 and 1475. He had been a source of trouble to Edward in the past, and now he was jealous of the lands and offices that had been granted to his younger brother in the north. In 1477 charges of treason were brought against some of Clarence's servants, and Edward took the opportunity to encompass the downfall of the duke himself, who was executed – whether in a butt of Malmsey wine or not – in February 1478. 'False, fleeting perjur'd Clarence' is surely an unworthy recipient of our sympathy, but what Edward IV did was, in the words of his latest biographer, 'judicial fratricide', and a sad exception to his record of generosity and magnanimity towards fallen opponents. Time and again Edward had pardoned enemies like Henry Beaufort, duke of Somerset, who then showed their gratitude by simply rebelling once more as soon as the opportunity allowed.

Edward died on 9 April 1483 – peacefully in his deathbed, which was unusual for a fifteenth-century English king. So where, if at all, had he gone wrong? He was successful enough in his own lifetime, and in our own day he has won praise from historians for restoring order to royal finances after a period of insolvency. However, he was unable to ensure the peaceful succession of his thirteen-year-old son, Edward V (q.v.). The reason for this is that he had failed to resolve the long-standing antagonisms between his wife's Woodville relatives and their enemies in the Yorkist affinity. The confusion that surrounded even his testamentary wishes was an invitation to renewed bloodletting. Although he had apparently named Richard of Gloucester

as Protector in codicils added to his will, he left his elder son firmly under the control of the Woodvilles at Ludlow. In view of the distrust with which the Woodvilles regarded Richard (and vice versa), it is hardly surprising that a struggle for power should have followed. The Lancastrian family usually managed to stick together; the Yorkists had a habit of tearing themselves apart.

C.D. Ross, *Edward IV*, 2nd ed., New Haven and London, 1997.

EDWARD V

The elder of the two sons of Edward IV (q.v.), Edward was born in November 1470. When his father died on 9 April 1483, he was in the care of Anthony Woodville, Earl Rivers, at Ludlow. On the way to London to be crowned he was seized by his uncle, Richard, duke of Gloucester, and transferred to the Tower, where his younger brother, Richard, duke of York, was shortly to join him. Edward's coronation, planned for 22 June 1483, was cancelled and he and his brother disappeared from view even before Richard assumed the crown on 6 July. What sort of king the boy would have made we have few means of telling, but Dominic Mancini, an Italian visitor to London, commended his scholarly attainments and knowledge of literature.

The Usurpation of Richard III, ed. C.A.J. Armstrong, 2nd ed., Oxford, 1969.

EDWARD, THE BLACK PRINCE

Although the soubriquet 'the Black Prince' was not bestowed until the sixteenth century, Edward of Woodstock enjoyed almost legendary fame in his own lifetime as, in his biographer Chandos Herald's words, 'the perfect root of all honour and nobleness, of wisdom, valour and largesse'.

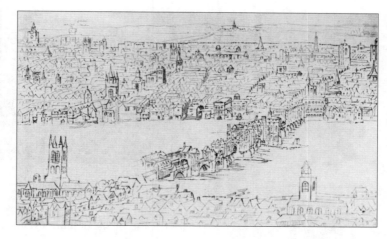

1 **London** Bridge *c.*1550 by Anthony van den Wyngaerde.

Above left: 2 A **Franciscan** by Matthew Paris.

Above right: 3 A folio from **William Langland**'s *Piers Plowman*.

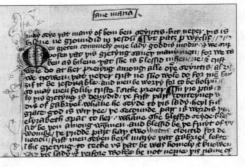

Left: 4 **Pilgrimages**. Some examples of pilgrims' badges.

Above: 5 Part of one of **John Wycliffe**'s tracts.

6 Seal of the city of **Canterbury**.

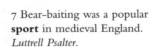

7 Bear-baiting was a popular **sport** in medieval England. *Luttrell Psalter.*

Left: 8 Richard, duke of York (d. 1460), father of **Edward IV** and Richard III. Statue formerly on the Welsh bridge, Shrewsbury.

Above: 9 **Richard Neville**, 'Warwick the Kingmaker', from the Rous Roll, late fifteenth century.

If it plese ony man spirituel or temporel to bye ony pyes of two and thre comemoracios of salisburi vse enpryntid after the forme of this preset lettre whiche ben wel and truly correct, late hym come to westmo; nester in to the almonesrye at the reed pale and he shal haue them good chepe .∴.

Supplico stet cedula

10 **William Caxton**'s advertisement.

11 Frontispiece to **Caxton**'s edition of *Aesop's Fables*.

12 **Diet**. A medieval banquet, from the early eleventh-century 'Psychomachia', a poem on the conflict between virtues and vices in the soul.

13 Great Seal of **Henry I**.

Above: 14 **Hospital** in London, founded by Queen Matilda *c.*1101. From the chronicle of Matthew Paris.

Right: 15 Enamel tomb plaque of Geoffrey 'Plantagenet', (1113–51), count of Anjou, husband to Empress **Matilda** and father of Henry II. Le Mans, France.

16 Great Seal of Empress **Matilda**, *c.*1140–*c.*1150.

Above left: 17 Seal of **Stephen Langton**.

Above right: 18 Seal of Oxford **University**, *c.*1300.

19 Seal of the city of **Oxford**.

20 Cricket may have developed from the medieval **sport** of club-ball.

21 Seal of a medieval Gloucester **guild** merchant.

22 Judicial combat between Walter Bloweberme and Hamo le Stare. Trial by combat was a Norman import to England's **justice** system.

23 **Coins** of William I, top, and William II, bottom.

24 **Coins** from the reign of John, top, and Edward I, bottom, demonstrate the switch from 'short-cross' to 'long-cross' coinage.

25 **Coins**. A noble of Edward III showing the king in ship.

26 Gold **coins** of the late fifteenth century: a 'rose noble or ryal' of Edward IV (top), showing the king's head in a rose motif, and a sovereign of Henry VII (bottom), featuring the Tudor king in majesty.

27 The **Jew**, Aaron of Colchester, late thirteenth century.

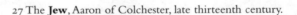

Above: 28 Archery as a **sport** was encouraged in medieval England as archers were crucial to to English success on the battlefields of France. *Luttrell Psalter*.

Left: 29 The murder of **Becket** by four knights from a painted wooden screen at the head of the tomb of Henry IV.

Above: 30 Great Seal of **Edward I**.

Above left: 31 **Humphrey, duke of Gloucester** (1391–1447), Henry V's younger brother. Drawing by the herald Jacques le Boucq (d. 1573) and possibly based on an earlier work of *c.*1425.

Above right: 32 Margaret of York, **Edward IV**'s sister and wife of Charles, duke of Burgundy in 1468.

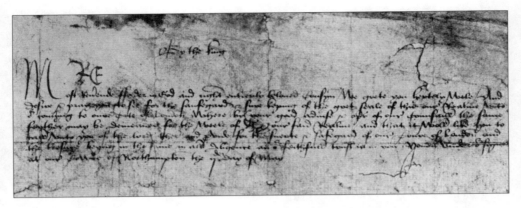

33 Letter from **Edward V** to Thomas Bourchier, Archbishop of Canterbury regarding the safe-keeping of the Great Seal, dated at Northampton, 2 May 1483 and signed 'R.E.'

Above: 34 The Great Seal of **Henry II** (obverse).

Right: 35 Seals of Henry as duke of Normandy (the future **Henry II**).

36 The Great Seal of **Henry II** (reverse).

37 **Henry II** in dispute with Becket.

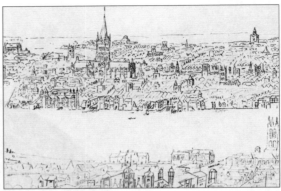

Left: 38 **Brasses** of Sir Hugh Halsham and his wife, 1441, West Grinstead (Sussex): London style 'B'.

Above: 39 St Paul's Cathedral *c.*1550 with its medieval steeple by Anthony van den Wyngaerde. **Architecture, ecclesiastical.**

Below: 40 Westminster *c.*1550, **London,** by Anthony van den Wyngaerde.

41 A late medieval representation of the community of scholars at New College, **Oxford**.

Right: 42 Effigy of **Henry II**, Fontevrault Abbey, France.

Far right: 43 Effigy of **Eleanor of Aquitaine**, Fontevrault Abbey, Anjou.

Far left: 44 **Brass** of the younger John d'Abernon (*c.*1340), Stoke d'Abernon (Surrey) showing armour worn at the beginning of the Hundred Years War.

Left: 45 **Armour and Arms.** Brass at Stoke d'Abernon (Surrey), showing armour worn at the time of the Scottish wars. Sir John d'Abernon I, *c.*1330.

Right: 46 **Brass** of Sir Robert de Bures, d.1331, Acton (Suffolk).

Far right: 47 **Heraldry**. Brass of Sir Roger de Trumpington, *c.*1325, Trumpington church (Cambs), showing the trumpet on his shield.

Left: 48 Effigy and arms of **Edward, the Black Prince**, d.1376, Canterbury Cathedral.

Below left: 49 Effigy of **Henry IV**, d.1413, Canterbury Cathedral.

Below: 50 Robert, duke of Normandy, d.1134, **William I**'s eldest son, as represented on his late thirteenth-century tomb effigy in Gloucester Cathedral.

51 Effigy of **Edward II** on his tomb in Gloucester Cathedral.

52 **Edward III** and Edward the Black Prince. This drawing was traced from wall paintings discovered in 1800 behind a coating of wood panelling in St Stephen's Chapel, Westminster. The paintings were lost in the fire that consumed Westminster Palace in 1834.

53 **Henry V**'s tomb in Westminster Abbey, from an engraving made in 1665 based on a painting then in Whitehall. Henry's effigy and tomb were gradually stripped bare (it was made of silver) from the 1460s onwards, the last pieces disappearing during a nocturnal raid in 1546.

The eldest son of Edward III (q.v.) and Philippa of Hainault, Edward was born on 16 June 1330 at Woodstock (Oxon). He owed his reputation in the eyes of contemporaries to the qualities of courage and generalship which he was to show in the Hundred Years War (q.v.) between England and France. His first experience of active service came at the battle of Crécy (q.v.) on 26 August 1346, when he commanded the right wing of the successful English army. Subsequently, he played a major role in the long siege of Calais.

In 1355 his father appointed him lieutenant of the duchy of Aquitaine. In this capacity he led a major *chevauchée* across southern France, reaching as far as the Mediterranean. In the following year he led a similar expedition northwards. His plan, it seems, was to link up with Henry, duke of Lancaster, who was ravaging Normandy and the Loire valley. However, the destruction by the French of the Loire bridges prevented such a junction, and instead the prince had to fall back south. Near Poitiers (q.v.), the French caught up with him and forced him to give battle. In the encounter which followed, the prince won the greatest victory of his career. The French king himself, John II, was taken prisoner. In 1359, when the negotiations for the king's release broke down, the prince and his father led a new expedition to France intended to bring about their adversaries' capitulation. The expedition was not as successful as had been expected and in the spring negotiations were opened. In the subsequent settlement Aquitaine was ceded to the English in full sovereignty.

The prince was now looking for a distinct political role of his own. In 1362, accordingly, his father created him Prince of Aquitaine with full responsibility for administering and defending the province. Aquitaine's security demanded that her two neighbours, France to the east and Castile to the south, be kept well apart. In 1366, however, the strongly francophile Henry of Trastamara seized the throne of Castile from his kinsman King Pedro, and it seemed that Castile would become a French satellite. The Black Prince reacted by leading a large Anglo–Gascon force into Castile and defeated Trastamara at Najera on 3 April 1367. Pedro was reinstated on the throne. Najera was to be the last victory of the prince's career. During his sojourn in Spain he contracted a painful and debilitating disease, probably dysentery, which was to prevent him from taking the saddle again. In 1371 he returned to England, and in the next year surrendered Aquitaine to his father. He died on 8 June 1376 and was buried in Canterbury Cathedral (plate 48).

The prince's fame rests on his reputation as the embodiment of fourteenth-century chivalry. He was renowned for his elaborate courtesy towards opponents. He entertained the French king lavishly after his capture at Poitiers. But there was a streak of harshness and cruelty in his character. He put the citizenry of Limoges to the sword after they had rebelled against him in 1370. He also treated his English tenants vexatiously. In 1353 he cancelled an eyre visitation of Cheshire when the Cheshiremen offered him a fine of 5,000 marks, only to inflict a trailbaston (q.v.) enquiry on them instead. In Aquitaine he ruled with a haughtiness that bred resentment among the province's independently minded nobility. It is doubtful whether he would have made a successful king.

The prince's piety appears to have been moralistic, anti-clerical and perhaps, too, anti-papal. His wife, Joan of Kent, who shared his sentiments, had in her service a group of knights closely associated with Lollardy. The Prince founded a house of the Bonshommes order at Ashridge (Herts). His devotion to the Trinity is reflected in a painting of the Trinity above his tomb at Canterbury.

His heir was his son, Richard II (q.v.).

R. Barber, *Edward, Prince of Wales and Aquitaine*, London, 1978.

ELEANOR OF AQUITAINE

Born *c.*1122, Eleanor was the sole daughter and heiress of William X, count of Aquitaine, and she succeeded to the duchy on her father's death in 1137. Her first marriage, to Louis VII, King of France, ended in divorce in 1152. In the same year she married Henry, count of Anjou, who two years later became Henry II (q.v.) of England. The marriage was a turbulent one, and for sixteen years Eleanor was imprisoned by her husband at Winchester. Although Eleanor was of spirited character, her political achievements were slight and she was overshadowed by her husband and her sons, in particular Richard and John, whose rebellions against their father she supported. As a cultural figure, however, she may have been of some importance. The movement of her court from southern to northern France helped to convey to a wider audience the ideals of courtly love which had grown up in the south. Eleanor died on 1 April 1204 and was buried alongside other members of her family in the Angevin mausoleum, Fontevrault Abbey.

G. Duby, *Medieval Marriage: Two Models from Twelfth-Century France*, trans. E. Forster, Baltimore, 1978.

ESCHEATOR

An escheat was a feudal tenement which lapsed in default of heirs or during the minority of an heir to the lord or descendant of the lord from whom it was held. To the greatest feudal lord of all – the king – escheated lands were a source of revenue of such importance that in 1232 responsibility for their collection was transferred from the sheriffs to newly established officers called escheators, two of whom (later reduced to one) were appointed in each county. When a tenant died, it would be the escheator's duty to take his lands into royal custody until it was ascertained by a local jury who was the next

heir and whether the king should exercise the right of wardship should that heir be under age. Unlike the coroner and other local officials who have survived to the present day, the escheator disappeared in 1660 when the feudal revenues he collected were abolished by parliament.

EXCHEQUER

See GOVERNMENT

EYRE

The eyre was the most powerful instrument of centralized government fashioned by the English crown in the Middle Ages. For over a century and a half, from the reign of Henry II (q.v.) to that of Edward II, the justices in eyre (Latin, *in itinere*) were sent on visitations of the shires to hear all civil and criminal pleas. Henry II was not the first king to send out his justices in this way. It is apparent from the exchequer pipe roll of 1130 that Henry I had been despatching justices to hear pleas in the counties, as the fines they collected are recorded in this exchequer account. But after the long civil war between Stephen and Matilda, Henry II had to construct the system all over again, and he appears to have done this by 1156.

A nationwide eyre visitation was an elaborate business. When the king announced such a visitation, he divided the country into circuits, each to be worked by a group of justices moving from one county to the next until they had completed their business. The justices held their sessions in a full meeting of the county court, and so long as they were there all subordinate courts suspended their hearings and handed over to them the indictments which had not yet been determined. When the juries from each hundred had assembled, the justices presented them with a series of questions known as the 'articles of the eyre', asking what crimes had been committed and what statutes contravened. The articles of 1194 served as the point of departure for all later sets of instructions to the justices. As the thirteenth century wore on, so many new articles were added, taking in business of an administrative rather than a judicial nature, that the eyre became bogged down in the sheer weight of its bureaucracy. It became less an instrument for enforcing the law in distant parts of the country than a means of keeping a check on local officials like the sheriff, and of raising money through the imposition of heavy fines. The oppressiveness of the eyre soon caused county communities to dread the coming of the justices. Sometimes they were prepared to pay a fine to the king in order not to receive a visitation. By the reign of Henry III it became the unwritten rule that no county was to have an eyre more than once every seven years.

In the reign of Edward II the crown finally abandoned eyre visitations altogether. The reasons for this seem to have been largely financial. For a century or more the main value of the eyre to the king had been the money that it raised in fines. By the 1290s, however, Edward I (q.v.) was turning regularly to parliament (q.v.) for grants of national taxation (q.v.). The counties would never have tolerated eyre visitations and taxation at the same time, so it was the eyre that had to go. There were just two eyres in Edward II's reign, in Kent in 1313 and London in 1321, and one right at the start of Edward III's reign in the East Midlands in 1329–30. After that the eyre to all intents and purposes was dead.

A. Harding, *The Law Courts of Medieval England*, London, 1973.

FASTOLF, SIR JOHN

A veteran of the Hundred Years War (q.v.), whose character and actions are documented in the Paston Letters (q.v.) and the recollections of his secretary, William Worcester (q.v.), Fastolf in real life was very different from the drunken debauchee to whom Shakespeare gave a corrupted form of his name. He was a successful knight and a shrewd businessman.

Born in about 1380, the scion of an old Norfolk family, he saw early service in the household of Henry IV's second son, Thomas of Clarence, but still ranked no higher than an esquire when he joined the Harfleur-Agincourt expedition in 1415. By 1416 he was finally knighted – hardly a premature honour for a man in his mid-thirties. His achievements were to come relatively late in life, in the reign of Henry VI (q.v.). At the battle of Verneuil (17 August 1424) Worcester tells us that 'he won by the fortune of war about 20,000 marks' – presumably meaning that he took prisoners whose ransoms came to that amount. Already it can be sensed that he was careful with money. The most distinguished prisoner whom he took at Verneuil, and potentially the most valuable, was the duke of Alençon; but after he was released a few years later, Fastolf complained that he had been deprived of his full share of the money. By 1426 Fastolf's reputation as a captain stood high enough to earn him election to the

Garter. But only three years later his honour was called into question after the battle of Patay (18 June 1429). It was alleged that he had beaten a hasty retreat from the field, leaving the Lords Talbot and Hungerford to be taken prisoner by the French. Talbot was certainly angry. Yet accusations of cowardice, such as those made by the chronicler Monstrelet, are hardly borne out by the evidence of continued confidence in him shown by the duke of Bedford, the English commander in France. Fastolf continued to be a member of Henry VI's French council until 1439, the year before he returned to England to invest and enjoy the profits he had made in France.

That he returned a rich man there can be no doubt. In 1445 his lands in England were worth £1,061 per annum, and to that total has to be added the income that he derived from the estates he held in France until the English collapse. Like most men of his standing in the Middle Ages, he invested his money in lands and in buildings. He spent no less than £13,855 on adding to his estates. In about 1430 he started to rebuild his fortified manor house at Caister, though how much money that absorbed in the course of a thirty-year building campaign is unclear. By his early seventies Fastolf had become, in K.B. McFarlane's characterization, 'a close-fisted, litigious and irascible old man', reduced to 'a state of querulous and unmanageable senility'. His final months were divided between worrying about the £11,000 the government still owed him and making last minute amendments to his will. Since he was childless, Fastolf proposed to use his money to endow a college of priests at Caister. But in November 1459, two days before his death, he revised his earlier plan so as to assign full responsibility for the foundation to his friend John Paston, who in return for 4,000 marks was to have in fee simple all the lands of which he was trustee. The validity of the second will was called into question, and for years ahead the Pastons (q.v.) were to be plagued by incessant litigation, documented in their family correspondence. Long after the dust had settled on Fastolf's deeds of conveyance, his fame was converted into notoriety by William Shakespeare. In the original draft of *Henry IV*, Hal's drinking companion in the London alehouses was called Sir John Oldcastle, but the name was changed to Falstaff when complaints about character assassination were made by Oldcastle's descendant Lord Cobham. There is some evidence for the youthful notoriety of young Prince Henry, but none at all to associate him with Sir John Fastolf, who was less than ten years his senior.

K.B. McFarlane, 'The Investment of Sir John Fastolf's Profits of War', *Trans. Roy. Hist. Soc.*, 5th series, vii (1957).

FEUDALISM

'Feudalism' is the term used to describe the decentralized political organization of early medieval Europe. The origins of the phenomenon are to be found on the continent in the age of the Emperor Charlemagne and his predecessors.

In the lands of the Frankish monarchy, particularly west of the Rhine, central authority was ceasing to be effective by the mid-eighth century. The kings of the Merovingian dynasty were too weak either to repel external aggression or to enforce internal peace. Men accordingly began to seek personal security by commending themselves to someone powerful enough to offer protection. In this process can be traced the origins of the feudal act of homage, whereby one free man became the 'vassal' of another, performing some agreed service, usually military, in return for the benefits of security and protection. To help his vassal to provide such military duties as might be demanded of him, the lord sometimes bestowed a benefice, or fief (*feudum* in Latin) as it later became known. Not least among such lords were the Merovingian kings themselves, who assembled an army by seizing the lands of the Church and granting them to vassals for the promise of military service. In the eighth century these estates were used to endow wellarmed soldiers; from the tenth century, usually knights. But later the kings also used them to provide maintenance for great officers at court. Vassals were granted fiefs, therefore, not just for the performance of military duties but for other specified forms of service too. Later on, such non-military forms of feudal tenure were known as sergeanties.

The deliberate policy pursued by the Frankish kings contributed to the spread of vassalage in the ninth century. Not only were the kings creating more vassals on royal and ecclesiastical estates but those to whom they granted benefices or fiefs then created vassals on their own lands. All that was needed to seal this process was a formal union between vassalage and the fief. This seems to have come by the early ninth century, when it was accepted that a vassal became liable for the performance of an agreed service once he had been granted a fief. In other words, feudalism was based on a contractual relationship between lord and vassal. This was created by the formal act of homage, when the vassal knelt down and placed his hands between those of his lord who received him as his man. After performing the act of homage, the vassal swore an oath of fealty, declaring that he would always be faithful to his lord.

Feudalism in this sense was a product of Frankish society in the eighth and ninth centuries, nurtured by the weakness of central authority and fostered by monarchs who granted fiefs in return for the performance of future military service. If they thought that by so doing they would buttress the authority of the crown, they were to be sadly mistaken. In law the vassal held only a life tenancy and on his death the fief reverted to the grantor, who was free either to retain it or bestow it again as he saw fit. In practice, however, the simple fact of possession came to favour the vassal, who could frequently regard the fief as his own and as his son's after him. The vassal's position was strengthened at the expense of his overlord's, even if that overlord was the king.

The structure of feudal relationships so far described developed in the lands of the Frankish monarchy but not in Anglo-Saxon England. In England, as elsewhere, it was becoming the practice by the tenth century for free men to commend themselves to the protection of powerful lords, but the notion of dependent land tenure in return for the performance of a stated personal service never developed here because the preconditions for its growth did not exist. Feudal relationships were introduced by the Normans after 1066. William I began to impose feudal structures on England soon after the battle of Hastings. And by dint of entering the country as a conqueror he was able to do so in a manner more thoroughgoing than had been customary in Normandy, where they had been the outcome of natural growth. Thus when he rewarded his followers for their success at Hastings William insisted that they should hold their newly won lands in return for the performance of future military service, usually knight service or castle guard. The

lords, whether secular or ecclesiastical, who held their lands in this way directly from the king were known as tenants-in-chief. They numbered about 150 in all. Each was made responsible for the provision of a certain quota of knights in the feudal host which, if all had assembled, would have totalled about 5,000. To perform this obligation, the tenants-in-chief could either keep the knights resident in their households or, more commonly as time went on, grant them fiefs from their own estates. By this process, known as subinfeudation, the feudal chain linking lord and vassal extended further and further down the hierarchy.

One of the most remarkable features of the Norman settlement of England is the speed with which tenants-in-chief are found granting out large tracts of their estates to dependent knights. This is of course understandable in the case of those monasteries on whom William had inflicted knight service. It is known from the history of one distinguished house that the existence of a large body of knights domiciled within the precincts could ruin monastic life. At Glastonbury the ham-fisted Abbot Thurstan once called in his knights to intimidate the monks and open fighting broke out in the church, where a number of them were gravely wounded. It is not surprising to find, therefore, that abbeys like Westminster and Bury St Edmund's which were assigned responsibility for a quota of knights started to solve the problem by granting them landed fiefs within twenty years of the Conquest.

However, it is less easy to understand why a powerful baron, proud of his standing in society, should wish to divest himself of a fair part of his estates merely to provide his knights with land of their own. Yet this is just what happened in the years after William's death. To understand the reasoning behind this subinfeudation we need to remember that when a lord granted a fief to a vassal he was not only providing for future military service but also creating a source of future income. How could a lord succeed in creating an income for himself at the same time as reducing his own landed resources?

The sources of income generally known as the 'incidents of feudalism' derived from the rights of ownership which a lord retained over a fief he had granted to a vassal. They were based on the belief, increasingly a fiction by the twelfth century, that the vassal was a life tenant, on whose death the fief would revert to the lord who had bestowed it. Theoretically, the lord was free to grant it out to anyone he chose, but it was the normal practice to allow the eldest son to succeed once he had paid an entry fine known as a 'relief'. Should the tenant die leaving a son under age, the lord was entitled to take the fief into 'wardship'. This afforded him the chance to exploit the estate for personal benefit until the son was old enough to succeed. If, on the other hand, the tenant died leaving only a daughter or daughters, their marriages were marketable commodities that could be used to make money. Faced in an emergency with a sudden need for cash, a lord was entitled also to take what was known as an 'aid' from his vassals. By the thirteenth century such occasions had come to be defined as the ransoming of the lord's person, the knighting of his eldest son and the marriage of his eldest daughter. These rules applied to the king in his dealings with his tenants-in-chief no less than to the latter in their own dealings with sub-vassals.

Seen from this point of view, feudalism was a nexus of financial privileges. It can be regarded not only as the means by which William I provided for his future military needs but also as a system of taxation. And it was in this direction that the future of feudalism was to lie. As early as 1100 it is known that the payment of scutage (literally 'shield money') was allowing the king's tenants to escape the performance of their obligations in the feudal host. Instead of serving in per-

son the tenants sent money which was used to hire mercenaries. The feudal host of 5,000 knights is therefore a product of the historical imagination rather than a reality rooted in contemporary military experience.

The dependence of the crown on its income from feudalism helps to explain why such perquisites as reliefs and wardships figured so prominently in disputes between king and baronage in the twelfth and thirteenth centuries. It was in the king's interest to mulct those who held from him – his tenants-in-chief – as intensively as he could. Indeed, he was limited only by the tenant's capacity to pay. For that reason it was laid down in 1100 that the king should charge only 'reasonable' reliefs. But since it was the king who decided what was 'reasonable', the barons were no better protected than before. Accordingly, it was decided in Magna Carta (q.v.) to lay down precisely what constituted a 'reasonable' relief, and figures were agreed of 100s for a knight's fee and £100 for a barony.

It was the financial worth of feudal ties that ensured their survival in skeletal form long after they had ceased to be the flesh and blood of medieval society. The principal turning point in the history of feudalism seems to have come in the reign of Henry II (q.v.). For a hundred years after the Conquest feudal society had centred on the honor, or barony, in other words, the assemblage of fiefs held from each tenant-in-chief of the crown. All the tenants of the honor were obliged to attend the meetings of the honorial court where matters of common interest were discussed and settled. Of the composition of the court and its procedure little is known, but the surviving evidence points to its importance in giving corporate expression to the ties forged between a lord and his vassals. After the reign of Henry II, however, the honorial court, and with it the honor, dwindled in importance as a result of the king's legal reforms which lured business from the feudal to the royal courts. Matters once settled by custom in the honorial courts were now being settled by means of the writs which Henry made available to initiate actions in the hearing of his own justices (q.v. JUSTICE). As a result of the process of judicial centralization, which strengthened the relationship between king and subject at the expense of that between lord and vassal, feudalism was dealt a lasting blow.

Surprisingly, feudalism was not formally abolished in England until 1660. Until then it had continued to form the basis of English land law, and as such it was valued by feudal lords for the lucrative rights which it gave them over their tenants. So far from dying, it actually enjoyed a revival in the age of the Tudors. In the reign of Henry VIII the two courts of Wards and Surveyors were set up to enable the crown to maximize its income from feudal rights. In the reign of Elizabeth, the queen's minister, Lord Burghley, was Master of Wards, a position which gave him control over the upbringing of such young noblemen as the dissolute earl of Oxford and the earl of Southampton, Shakespeare's future patron.

The posthumous history of feudalism is still more curious than its resurrection under the Tudors. The word 'feudal' did not exist in the English language until Sir John Spelman invented it in 1639. The 'feudal system' had to wait till 1776 for its first appearance in the writings of Adam Smith, while 'feudalism' itself did not appear until 1839. 'Feudalism' should not be seen as a theory or ethos; it is simply a conceptual tool for interpreting certain medieval structures and practices.

F.L. Ganshof, *Feudalism*, London, 1952; *Feudalism, English* ed. M. Bloch, London, 1960; *The History of Feudalism*, ed. D. Herlihy, London, 1979.

FINE

We sometimes find that in the Middle Ages a word conveyed a different meaning from the one it has today. A good example is the word 'fine'. The medieval equivalent of the modern term would have been 'amercement' (q.v.), that is to say, a payment imposed by a court on someone found guilty of a trespass. A fine (*<finis*) in its medieval sense was an agreement reached in the king's court at the end of a fictitious suit. The practice of using the royal courts in this way to register agreements over the tenure of land began in the reign of Henry II (1154–89), when the regular visitations of the justices in eyre (q.v.) encouraged litigants to seek licence to have their suit terminated and registered before a session of the court. At first the agreement was written down only in duplicate, one copy going to each of the litigants, but in 1195, probably at the initiative of the justiciar (q.v.), Hubert Walter, it was decided to make a third copy, known as the 'foot of the fine', which was filed in the treasury for easy reference in case of future disputes. By the thirteenth century most of the innumerable disputes which were terminated by fines were quite fictitious, undertaken solely for the convenience of having the conveyance registered in court. The feet of fines that survive in their thousands in the Public Record Office today are a valuable source for the study of family pedigrees and manorial histories.

FOOD
See DIET

FORESTS
Despite centuries of internal colonization, vast tracts of forest land still stretched across England on the eve of the Conquest. Here the king and his thegns were able to indulge their taste for hunting. Hunting was a sport particularly favoured by William the Conqueror and the Normans. William cleared a large area of south-west Hampshire to create what was to become known as the

'New Forest'. He and his advisers also gave legal definition to the forest for the first time. The forest was held to embrace those parts of the country subject to the forest law. As Richard FitzNigel put it a century later in his *Dialogue of the Exchequer*,

> The whole organization of the forests… is outside the jurisdiction of the other courts and solely dependent on the decision of the king… The forest has its own laws, based it is said, not on the common law of the realm, but on the legislation of the king.

The forest law, in other words, was a matter for the king alone, and nothing to do with the custom of the realm. Its purpose was the preservation of the vert and venison – that is, the natural habitat of the forest and the game which it sheltered – and to that end forest offenders were punished with a severity hardly known under the common law.

In the course of the next century and a half, however, the Norman and Angevin kings gradually realized that the forest law could be put to other and more practical uses than simply the punishment of those who dared to infringe it. It could be made to pay. It could be used to finance the needs of government. Accordingly, Henry I and his successors enforced the forest laws not so much by death or mutilation as by inflicting heavy fines. In 1130 one of the king's justices handed over no less than 500 marks to the exchequer in respect of the pleas of the forest which he had heard.

The more the forest law weighed down on its hapless victims, high and low alike, the more it became an object of popular dislike. But it was not only the stringency of the law which attracted criticism; it was also the limits within which it was applied. A medieval forest was not confined to the wooded area; it included much non-wooded land round about. Under William I, Henry I and particularly Henry II ever larger areas were brought

under forest jurisdiction, so that by the end of the twelfth century, when it reached maximum extent, it applied to between a quarter and a third of England. To the far-reaching legal consequences for the inhabitants was added the administrative dislocation caused to private landowners who now found themselves hemmed in by restrictions on the exploitation of their lands. It is hardly surprising, therefore, to find that in 1215 some of King John's leading opponents were lords with estates in northern England who had suffered from the enlargement of the forest. Nor is it surprising to find that a number of abuses arising from the forest administration were addressed in Magna Carta (q.v.). The barons dealt lightly with King John, however. Clause 47 required the king to disafforest all that he had afforested. But as it was not he but his father who had added most to the forest, that did not amount to much. He and his brother Richard (q.v.) had actually resorted to selling licences for disafforestation as a desperate means of raising money quickly. All the same, in the century that followed, the bounds of the forest and the law that applied within them remained as hotly contested as ever. Indeed, the subject was deemed to be of such importance that the clauses relating to it in Magna Carta were taken out in 1217 and enshrined in a separate document known as the Charter of the Forest.

It was in the reign of Edward III (q.v.) that the forest finally ceased to be a political issue. The reason for this was simple. The forest was no longer important as a source of revenue. The rise of parliamentary taxation (q.v.) in the later thirteenth century assured the king of a regular supply of money and freed him from dependence on the exactions of the forest justices. After the 1330s we hear little more of the bitter complaints that had been raised so vehemently in the past.

Concentration on the political wrangle concerning the forest can easily give the impression that in the twelfth and thirteenth centuries forest dwellers lived in unrelieved hardship. Doubtless they did suffer from the harshness of the law, otherwise they would not have complained. But the forest could also offer a life of freedom. It could give shelter to fugitives from justice. Sherwood Forest put Robin Hood (q.v.) and his men beyond the reach of the sheriff of Nottingham. And to Robin, as to many ordinary folk on the verge of the woodlands, poaching could provide a variety of diet (q.v.) denied to most peasants in medieval England: provided, that is, the poacher did not get caught.

C.R. Young, *The Royal Forests of Medieval England*, Leicester, 1979.

FORESTALLING and REGRATING

One of the duties of a municipal corporation in the Middle Ages was to ensure an adequate supply of food for its citizens. The interests of the consumers had to be protected against those of the merchant victuallers who could have taken advantage of their position as suppliers to force up the price. For that reason in codes like the Coventry Leet Book we often find that steps were taken to stamp out the twin abuses known as 'forestalling' and 'regrating'. Forestallers were those who bought up supplies before they reached the market place. Regraters were those who held back goods so as to sell them later at a higher price. How effective these measures were we have no means of telling; but we should not pitch our expectations too high.

FORTESCUE, SIR JOHN

Among political thinkers of the Middle Ages Fortescue was hardly one of the most original; but, not surprisingly for a man who was deeply involved in the political struggles of his day, he was one of the most practical-minded. Born in Devon in the 1390s, he joined Lincoln's Inn, and became a sergeant-at-law in about 1429. This legal training he pursued simultaneously with a political career which brought him to parliament as MP for a succession of West Country boroughs in the 1420s and '30s. Promotion in his chosen profession, when it came, was rapid. In 1441 he was appointed a king's sergeant and in the following year, without any intermediate step, Chief Justice of King's Bench. By now, Suffolk and the party dominant at Henry VI's (q.v.) court were coming under strong criticism for their alleged corruption and incompetence. But Fortescue was no trimmer. He was nothing if not a thorough-going Lancastrian. He was present at the Lancastrian debacle at Towton on 29 March 1461, and fled northwards to Scotland with the deposed Henry VI and his wife.

It may have been while on the run in the borderlands, or more plausibly while in exile in France after 1465, that he wrote the four tracts upholding the Lancastrian succession and the treatise *De Natura Legis Naturae*, in which he made his famous distinctions between *Dominium Regale*, or absolute monarchy, *Dominium Politicum*, or republican government, and *Dominium Politicum et Regale*, or constitutional monarchy. These ideas were taken further in the most popular of his works, *De Laudibus Legum Anglie*. He attributes the origins of absolute monarchy to military conquest, and of limited monarchy to the decision of a community of people to form themselves into a state. France he considered to be an absolute monarchy, England and Scotland (q.v.) constitutional monarchies. Fortescue came back with the temporarily ascendant Lancastrians in 1470-1, only to find himself on the losing side once again, this time at Tewkesbury on 4 May 1471. Edward IV (q.v.) now compelled him to make suitable amends for his past miscalculations. To recover his estates Fortescue had to refute his earlier writings and justify Edward's own title to the throne.

In the years that were left to him, in retirement at Ebrington (he died *c.*1476), Fortescue wrote his last work, *The Governance of England*. Many of the suggestions he makes in this treatise had already been voiced many times over in parliament and elsewhere: that the king should live of his own, that former royal lands should be resumed and made inalienable, that the power of the great magnates should be curbed. But more original was his proposal that the council should be transformed into a body of professional men, twelve secular and twelve clerical. Did he realize how far these measures to strengthen the crown would render more absolute the constitutional monarchy of which he had written so approvingly in his earlier works?

Sir J. Fortescue, *De Laudibus Legum Anglie*, ed. S.B. Chrimes, 1942; A. Gross, *The Dissolution of the Lancastrian Kingship: Sir John Fortescue and the Crisis of Monarchy in Fifteenth-Century England*, Stamford, 1996.

FRANCHISE

A grant of franchise gave a lord the right to exercise within his lordship those functions of justice or administration which would elsewhere be exercised by the king's ministers. Among the most important liberties or franchises in medieval England were the earldom of Chester, the palatinate of Durham and the Isle of Ely. If any reason can be offered to explain the creation of these privileged enclaves, it must be that they enabled the responsibility for administration in some of the more distant parts of the country to be delegated to a local magnate better placed than the king to exercise effective authority. This is not to say that a franchise holder could act as a free agent in his liberty. Far from it. By launching the so-called *quo warranto* proceedings (i.e., 'by what warrant') Henry III (q.v.) and Edward I (q.v.) sought to establish the principle that, however they might have originated, franchises could only be justified in future so long as they served the public good. The result was that by the late Middle Ages a franchise was just another piece in the vast mosaic of local administration in England.

H.M. Cam, *Law Finders and Law Makers*, Merlin, 1962.

FRANCISCANS

The Franciscans, or 'Grey Friars' as they were known from the colour of their habit, were the most successful of the orders of friars (q.v.) that settled in England. St Francis himself was less their founder than the source of their inspiration. What he believed in was teaching by example. In David Knowles's words, he had a purely spiritual conception of his friars as 'followers of Christ in perfect poverty and simplicity, a new leaven to the world'. He forbade them to own property. He wanted them to gain their living by work or, failing that, by begging. Difficulties were bound to arise from the practical operation of this doctrine, but they were eventually overcome by the legal fiction of vesting ownership of all the property needed by the friars in the Pope.

If the evangelical ideal could ultimately be modified like this to accord with reality, it was still revolutionary enough to provoke controversy. Even before St Francis's death in 1226 differences had arisen between those who wished to fulfil the founder's precepts to the letter and those who wished to relax them a little – differences which erupted into a bitter dispute that was only resolved a century later by Pope John XXII's bulls *Ad Conditorem Canonum* (1322), restoring to the friars full ownership of their property, and *Cum Inter Nonnullos* (1323), condemning the doctrine that Christ and the apostles had owned no possessions.

The English Franciscans were lucky enough to escape the worst excesses aroused by the debate on poverty on the continent. This is not to suggest that they were uninterested in the issues involved. Indeed, right from the start they had attracted to their ranks some of the most brilliant men of their day, such as Adam Marsh, an Oxford graduate, and Haymo of Faversham, who became sixth Minister General of the Order in 1240. They wanted to attract talent, and they had no trouble in doing so because they were strong in the universities. When they first arrived in England, in 1224, they made for Oxford. And thanks to the patronage of the learned Robert Grosseteste (q.v.), later bishop of Lincoln, the house they established there became a noted centre of learning. Among its most famous alumni could be numbered Roger Bacon (q.v.) and John Pecham, the first Franciscan Archbishop of Canterbury.

For all the advantages it brought, however, this close association with the universities would probably have met with the disapproval of St Francis himself. It had the effect of converting an order of simple evangelists into an order of intellectuals. St Francis wanted his followers to go from place to place inspiring devotion to the Christian faith by the very simplicity of their lives. The Lanercost chronicler tells the story of how an unfriendly knight was moved by the sight of two brothers walking barefoot near Oxford one winter, leaving bloodstains in the snow because their feet had been cut by the ice. But the more the Franciscans recruited from the universities, the more they risked forsaking apostolic simplicity for intellectual argument. What the Franciscans in fact were doing was usurping the role intended by St Dominic for his own order of friars.

Because the two mendicant orders chose to base themselves in the towns rather than the countryside, few of their buildings have survived. The most significant piece above ground is the choir of the Franciscan church at Chichester, a fine late thirteenth-century fabric. It is rather to excavations, such as those at Oxford, that we must look for any additions to our knowledge of the surroundings in which the Franciscans lived. It appears to have been between 1270 and 1320 that they undertook their biggest building programme. They had decided by then to settle down, rather than wander from place to place, and they wanted houses in which to live and work. One or two of their churches were quite large – up to a couple of hundred feet in length – but even so they were modest compared with the cathedrals, and hardly deserving of the strictures from the friars' opponents.

J.R.H. Moorman, *A History of the Franciscan Order*, Oxford, 1968.

FRIARS

The friars were those religious who combined, at least to begin with, a non-cloistered life with economic dependency on alms gained by begging (mendicancy, from Latin, *mendicare*, to beg). The Friars Preachers, or Dominicans (the Black Friars), were founded by Dominic of Caleruega (c. 1172–1221), and the Friars Minor, or Franciscans (the Grey Friars), by Francis of Assisi (c. 1181–1226). Although St Dominic conceived of his order primarily as a teaching institute, both founders wanted their followers to emulate the lifestyle of the apostles described in the New Testament. Later, these orders were joined by the Austin and Carmelite friars.

St Dominic was the first to seek formal papal approval for his order; St Francis followed in 1220. Both orders spread quickly across western Christendom. The Dominicans were the first to arrive in England. In 1221 a group of thirteen Dominicans landed at Dover. They travelled via Canterbury and London to Oxford, where they were attracted by the university. The Franciscans, who followed three years later, preferred to disperse more widely, and within six years of their arrival had founded communities as far apart as Norwich and Hereford, Bristol and King's Lynn. By 1255 there were forty-nine Franciscan houses in England, and by about 1260 some three dozen Dominican houses. A major element in the popularity of the friars was their willingness to settle in the rapidly growing towns, where they made good the gaps in the parochial system and performed valuable pastoral work.

At first, the friars were welcomed by the monks and the secular clergy. But as the years went by, their evident popularity with the laity bred resentment and jealousy. There were arguments between the friars and the parish clergy over burial rights: as is apparent from wills, people opted in increasing numbers for burial in the friars' churches, thus robbing the seculars of the burial fees to which they were entitled. The clergy in the parishes were also jealous of the friars' success in attracting audiences to their sermons while their own churches stood half empty. Rivalries between the secular clergy and the friars ate into the latter's early popularity; and so too did a growing perception that the latter were avaricious. By the fourteenth century, the first criticism of the friars is found in literature. Chaucer satirized his Friar in the General Prologue of The Canterbury Tales:

A very festive fellow.
In all Four Orders there was none so mellow,
So glib with gallant phrase and well-turned speech★

But Chaucer's contemporary Langland (q.v.) was equally scathing in Piers Plowman. Langland complained that the friars used all sorts of dubious devices to extract money from patrons, which they then lavished on building magnificent churches. In the universities Wycliffe (q.v.) was another vehement critic, accusing the friars of browbeating young people into joining their ranks.

The friars' critics, however, should not be seen as representing the mainstream of late-medieval opinion. There is evidence which points to the friars' continuing popularity. Most telling is the evidence of wills. A huge number of late-medieval testators left money to the friars. Indeed, there is hardly a will from a nobleman or knight in which the friars are not left something. In 1459 John Langley of Siddington (Glos) left 2s 6d each to the Dominicans at Gloucester and Warwick, to the Franciscans at Coventry and Bristol and to the Carmelites at Gloucester. In 1490 his grandson Edmund left 6s 8d each to the Franciscans, Dominicans and Carmelites in Gloucester. These examples are not untypical. In the decades before the Reformation there is little to suggest that the flow of benefactions was drying up. Friars' churches, such as that at Gloucester, were still being rebuilt. The zeal and freshness that had once commended the friars may have waned; but their admirers may still have outnumbered their critics.

C.H. Lawrence, *The Friars: the Impact of the Early Mendicant Movement on Western Society*, London, 1994.

★ G. Chaucer, *The Canterbury Tales*, ed. N. Coghill, Penguin, 1951, p.25

GASCONY

The duchy of Aquitaine, of which Gascony formed the largest part, came to the English crown by the marriage of Eleanor (q.v.), the duchy's heiress, to Henry of Anjou, later King Henry II (q.v.). In the twelfth century Gascony was an 'allod'; in other words, it was effectively independent. In 1259, however, as part of a more general settlement of Anglo-French differences, King Henry III agreed to hold it as a fief of the French crown, with the performance of liege homage – the most binding form of homage. The new relationship gave rise to all sorts of difficulties. The French king's exercise of his sovereign rights, his demands for service from his vassals and, in particular, his reception of appeals from the court of the seneschal of Gascony at Bordeaux all exposed the duchy to the centralizing activities of the French royal officers. The growing tensions led to outbreaks of war in 1294, 1325 and 1337. By the middle of the fourteenth century it had become apparent to the English that the only solution to the problem was to hold Gascony in full sovereignty, a notion that the French could never accept. The conflict over the status of Gascony was a major element in the Hundred Years War (q.v.), and it was only resolved with the final expulsion of the English from the duchy in 1453.

So long as it lasted, the link between England and Gascony was profitable to both partners. Bordeaux, the capital, was a large town of some 30,000 people which flourished by exporting wine to London and handling the cloth, leather, tin and fish which the ships brought in the return voyage. Bayonne, the next largest port, specialized in building and fitting out the ships that made the passage between Bordeaux and London. The Gascon elite, and in particular the merchant elite of Bordeaux, were strongly attached to the link with England. What they valued in it was the effective independence it conferred. Better a master 500 miles away in London than one half that distance away in Paris.

J.R. Studd, 'England and Gascony, 1216-1337', *England in Europe, 1066–1453*, ed. N.E. Saul, London, 1994.

GAUNT, JOHN OF

The third surviving son of Edward III (q.v.), John was born at Ghent in March 1340 while his father was based there in the early stages of the Hundred Years War (q.v.). A couple of centuries later, by the time Shakespeare was writing, the city of his birth had become corrupted on English tongues to 'Gaunt', and it is by that name that he is generally known today.

John gained the estates and title of the duchy of Lancaster in 1362 by virtue of his marriage three years earlier to Blanche, daughter and eventual heiress of Henry of Grosmont, the first duke. The vast estates which he inherited, spread across the Midlands and the north of England, brought him an annual income in the order of £12,000, considerably in excess of anything enjoyed by his peers in the nobility.

The duke rose to political prominence in the 1370s, when his father was in his dotage and his eldest son Edward, the Black Prince (q.v.), stricken with dysentery. This period was one of difficulty for the English, who were struggling to hold onto their conquests in France. In 1371 dissatisfaction with the handling of the war led to the replacement of Bishop Wykeham (q.v.), the chancellor, and Bishop Brantingham, the treasurer, by a group of secular administators who looked to Gaunt for leadership. But the new officers had no greater success than their predecessors. Popular discontent boiled over in the 'Good Parliament' of 1376, and Gaunt had the unenviable task of defending the court from the Commons' onslaught. The unpopularity that he incurred contributed to the hostile opinion formed of him by the chroniclers, in particular the most prolific of them, Thomas Walsingham of St Albans.

On Edward III's death in 1377, the ten-year-old Richard II (q.v.) became king. Gaunt now found himself pushed to the sidelines. The new king preferred to take counsel from his own intimates, chiefly the former retainers of his father, the Black Prince. A number of disputes broke out between Gaunt and those close to the king, culminating apparently in an attempt on the duke's life in February 1385. Partly in consequence, Gaunt decided to develop an outlet for his interests abroad, in particular in Spain. After the death of his first wife in 1368, he had married Constance, daughter of Pedro the Cruel, king of Castile. After Pedro's expulsion from his kingdom by his half-brother, Henry of Trastamara, and subsequent death, Gaunt claimed to be his

legitimate heir and assumed the title and arms of king of Castile. In 1386, taking advantage of the destruction of the Castilian army by the Portuguese at Aljubarrotta, he decided to mount an invasion of Castile in pursuit of his claim. Although his forces soon fell victim to disease, he remained sufficient of a nuisance to cause John I, Henry's successor, to make a settlement with him that paid him a substantial sum to depart.

In 1389, in response to the king's request, Gaunt returned to England. During his absence the country had been riven by a civil war in which Richard's opponents, the 'Appellants', had sought to remove his unpopular favourites, Robert de Vere and Michael de la Pole. Richard now appreciated the stability and moderating influence which his uncle's authority could bring. Relations between the two greatly improved. Gaunt now became the pillar of the state, the principal buttress of his nephew's regime. Nonetheless, the duke still took a Europe-wide view of his responsibilities. In recognition of his ambition, in 1390 Richard granted him the duchy of Aquitaine (q.v. GASCONY) for life. The grant was ill-received by the Aquitanians, however, for the local population cherished their direct link with the crown as a guarantee of their liberties. In 1394 the merchant elite of Bordeaux openly repudiated Gaunt's lordship and denied his officers entry into the city. Later that year Gaunt sailed to the duchy and spent fifteen months there restoring order. On his return he formalized his relationship with Katherine Swynford, his mistress of a quarter of a century's standing, whom he now took as his third wife.

In the next year, English political life was thrown into turmoil. On 10 July 1397 Richard arrested three of the former 'Appellant' lords who had rebelled against him ten years before. For the moment, Gaunt's son, Henry Bolingbroke, who had been one of the junior Appellants, was left at liberty. In the following year, however, he was sentenced to exile for ten years, following the outbreak of a quarrel between him and the other junior Appellant, Thomas Mowbray. When Gaunt died, on 3 February 1399, the awesome Lancastrian power, which had contributed so much to the recovery of royal authority, was under a shadow. In the following month it was finally eclipsed when Richard seized the Lancastrian inheritance for himself and extended Bolingbroke's exile to life.

For all his fame and eminence, Gaunt remains a rather enigmatic figure. No contemporary likeness of him survives, and the tomb effigies of him and his first wife in St Paul's Cathedral perished in the Great Fire. What emerges most strongly from the chronicle accounts of Gaunt is his aloofness. Gaunt was a very grand figure. He had aspirations to kingly title, albeit in Castile, and was suspected of harbouring them in England too. He lived in kingly style, and he had the largest indentured retinue in the land. Partly because of his aloofness he did not fit easily into English politics. He did not form alliances with other magnates, and he was strangely friendless. He is best seen as a figure acting on the European stage: the heir to those Europe-wide ambitions for the English monarchy espoused by his grandfather Edward III. If he was guided by any consistent principle, it was that of loyalty to the crown. He was aggrieved by his nephew's hostility to him in the 1380s and relieved by the favour shown to him in the 1390s. Yet at the heart of his career there was a paradox. Although the richest and most powerful magnate in the land, he was prevented by that very loyalty from halting the judicial liquidation of his son in 1398. The implications of this paradox were only to be resolved by his son's usurpation of the throne in 1399.

A.Goodman, *John of Gaunt. The Exercise of Princely Power in Fourteenth-Century Europe*, London, 1992.

GEOFFREY OF MONMOUTH

Geoffrey of Monmouth's *History of the Kings of Britain*, completed in *c.*1138, was a medieval bestseller. It was not a history in the conventional sense; it was more in the nature of literature. Indeed, as the chronicler William of Newburgh, one of its critics, noted, it was a 'figment of the imagination'. Geoffrey's work owed its popularity to its author's sense of the fantastic. The period he wrote about was obscure and ill documented. As a result, he was able to use author's licence to elaborate and embroider it as he saw fit. Geoffrey begins by explaining that the name 'Britain' was derived from Brutus, a descendant of Aeneas who settled here after the fall of Troy. He moves on through the story of King Lear to the Roman settlement and then the Saxon invasions in the time of King Vortigern. At this point he introduces his hero, King Arthur, son of Uther Pendragon. Arthur halts the Saxon onslaught and carries the war into Gaul, but at the battle of Camblan he is mortally wounded, and is carried away under mysterious circumstances to the Isle of Avalon. In this series of narratives the Arthurian legend (q.v.) is found developed for the first time in full. Geoffrey's sources are unclear. He tells us in his preface that Walter, archdeacon of Oxford, had presented him with an ancient book written in the British language which set out the deeds of all the kings from Brutus to Cadwallader. Whether this book ever existed or not is hard to say. No definite trace of it has been found. However, a Walter the Archdeacon is known to have existed, and Geoffrey is unlikely to have invoked his name unless they were both conspirators in an elaborate literary hoax.

Very little can be said about Geoffrey himself. He appears to have spent much of his life in Oxford, even if his name suggests Welsh extraction. Like most ambitious clerks of his day, he sought the favour of patrons in a position to offer him a benefice. Doubtless this explains why most surviving copies of his

History open with a dedication to Robert, earl of Gloucester, the bastard son of Henry I (q.v.). Eventually he obtained the bishopric of St Asaph, but the wars then being fought on the Welsh border probably prevented him from even visiting the see, let alone collecting its revenues, before his death in 1155.

Geoffrey of Monmouth, *The History of the Kings of Britain*, ed. L. Thorpe, Harmondsworth, 1966.

GILBERTINES

The one religious order of English provenance, the Gilbertines took their name from St Gilbert of Sempringham (Lincs), who in the 1130s founded some houses for the benefit of nuns and lay sisters. Gilbert wanted to create an opening for the many women for whom few opportunities existed in the male-dominated world of twelfth-century monasticism. The response was greater than he had expected, and before long he found himself at the head of a growing family of houses. Feeling himself ill qualified to provide the leadership now expected of him, he asked the General Chapter of the Cistercians in 1147 if they would agree to take over his community. They declined on the grounds that they could not admit women. It was almost by default, therefore, that Gilbert found that he would have to legislate for an order of his own.

In so doing he faced certain problems. The women of course could neither celebrate mass nor till the soil unaided. So he arranged for canons to minister to their liturgical needs, and followed the example of the Cistercians in introducing lay brothers to cultivate the land. In effect, he had revived the 'double' monastery, which had been a feature of seventh-century monasticism. At the time of his death in 1189, according to the chronicler William of Newburgh, Gilbert had founded more than a dozen monasteries, of which ten were 'double'. It is said that they catered for as many as 1,500 sisters but this figure, like most medieval statistics, may well be an exaggeration.

At the time of the Dissolution in the 1530s there were twenty-six Gilbertine houses in England. They were probably quite simple in construction and decoration, knowing as we do of Gilbert's respect for the Cistercian ideal of austerity. At Sempringham itself the church was 250ft long, and divided along its length by a solid wall broken only in the chancel by the saint's shrine. On the south side lay the nuns' church and on the north, that of the canons.

B. Golding, *Gilbert of Sempringham and the Gilbertine Order, c.1130-c.1300*, Oxford, 1995.

GLYN DWR, OWAIN

Owain Glyn Dwr (or Glendower) was the Welshman, immortalized by Shakespeare, who led the great national movement for renewal in Wales at the beginning of the fifteenth century.

Glyn Dwr was born around 1359 into a minor, but ancient, gentry family in north-east Wales. What led him to exchange the life of a landowner for that of a rebel was a dispute with a neighbour of his, Reginald Grey, Lord of Ruthin, whom he accused of seizing some of his lands. In 1400 Glyn Dwr and his men laid waste to Grey's estates, and Henry IV (q.v.), returning from Scotland, was obliged to march west to pacify the area. Henry's efforts were unavailing because the Welsh simply retreated into the mountains. By the end of the year Wales was in the grips of a major rising. In April 1402 Glyn Dwr had the good fortune to capture his adversary, Reginald, Lord Grey, and two months later he also took Sir Edmund Mortimer, uncle of the earl of March. The king and his counsellors were uncertain how to respond to the crisis. The Percys appear to have urged a conciliatory approach while others, including Grey himself until his capture, favoured a harder line. The danger posed by the crisis in Wales was made clear in 1403 when Glyn Dwr made the famous tripartite indenture with Mortimer and Henry's opponents, the Percys, whereby they agreed to divide the realm between them. After the defeat of the Percys' rebellion in July, Henry moved to the offensive. Glyn Dwr was at this time at the height of his power. Most of the Welsh castles had fallen to him, and he was powerful enough to establish a shadow government in the principality. He was even communicating with the Scots, the French and the Irish to widen the revolt. By 1406, however, he was on the retreat. The king's son, Prince Henry, the future Henry V (q.v.), led a series of campaigns which in the next few years succeeded in reimposing English rule. The fall of Aberystwyth in November 1407 and Harlech in the following year marked the final collapse of a rebellion that had dragged on for seven years.

Glyn Dwr himself, however, like the old soldier, did not die; he only faded away. When Henry V came to the throne, he was still at large. The new king offered to receive him back into his allegiance before setting out for France in 1415, but he heard nothing. Rumour had it that he died at the home of one of his daughters, the wife of a Herefordshire squire, at Monnington in the Golden Valley. Tradition holds that he is buried in Monnington churchyard. The aura of mystery surrounding his end, reminiscent of that surrounding the end of King Arthur, could hardly be more appropriate for one who was seen by his fellow countrymen as a saviour in the tradition of the legendary British king.

R.R. Davies, *The Revolt of Owain Glyn Dwr*, Oxford, 1995.

GOVERNMENT

In the Middle Ages the king was the personification of government, and the branches of his household were the first government ministries. This was why medieval government retained a domestic and informal quality right down to the sixteenth century. It may have been ramshackle and ill co-ordinated, but the dependence of its parts on the king's will gave it a consistency of purpose which prevented it from sliding into chaos.

The origins of the medieval system of government may be traced to the later Anglo-Saxon period. By the late tenth century the growing use of charters to guarantee title to land had led to the organization of a royal writing office, and the levying of taxes to the establishment of a treasury. The early history of these two institutions is obscure. But that very obscurity suggests that bureaucratization could not have gone very far: otherwise more written evidence would have survived.

In the decades before the Conquest the pace of bureaucratization quickened. The first governmental office to acquire a formal existence was the chancery or writing office. This was staffed by the clerks of the royal chapel, and headed by an official known as the chancellor. Although an important figure, the chancellor was not yet the great officer of state that he was to become later. He was usually one of the king's chaplains, and would be rewarded for his service with elevation to a bishopric. Herfast, the first chancellor known to us by name, was appointed to the East Anglian diocese of North Elmham in 1070. The writing office which William the Conqueror took over in 1066 was the most advanced of its day in northern Europe, chiefly because it had solved the problem of how to communicate the king's wishes to his subjects. This it did by means of the writ, a formalized written notification usually addressed to the officers and suitors of the county court. The office then went on to solve the problem of authentication by attaching a two-faced pendant seal to the bottom of the writ. Custody of this seal was the most important of the chancellor's duties.

As the scope and activity of government increased under the Norman and Angevin kings, so too did the number of writs produced by the clerks in chancery. If government were not to lose its sense of memory, it would be necessary to keep copies of these letters and to file them according to their subject matter. In 1199, therefore, the year of King John's (q.v.) accession, the charter roll was started for copies of charters. This was followed in 1201 by the patent roll for copies of letters issued 'patent', i.e. open, and finally in 1204 by the close roll for letters issued 'close', i.e. sealed. Strangely, these copies were not kept in registers, in the manner of the papal chancery, but were transcribed onto long parchment membranes which were then stitched head-to-tail to form continuous rolls, one for each year.

For the first two centuries of its existence, the chancery itinerated with the rest of the king's household, but as its records grew ever bulkier, it became necessary for it to settle down. By the fourteenth century the chancellor had established himself in Westminster Hall, and was sealing at least some of the king's letters there. The massive enrolments were found a resting place in the 1370s in the House of the Jewish Converts in Chancery Lane – the building on the site of the later Public Record Office (which in the 1990s moved to Kew).

In parallel with the bureaucratization of the writing office, there grew up a system of financial organization. As early as the tenth century the Saxon kings were levying a complex land tax known as the geld (q.v. TAXATION), the proceeds of which were paid into a treasury at Winchester. The Winchester treasury was no more than a storehouse kept under lock and key by a local worthy who held the title of 'treasurer'. In the early twelfth century, by an initiative that may be associated with the justiciar Bishop Roger, a regular auditing process was introduced at a new office called the 'exchequer'. The exchequer gave the king what he had hitherto lacked: a means by which he could ensure that his officials paid over every penny of what they owed him. The exchequer's machinery was cumbersome and slow, but it was also thorough. Sessions of the exchequer were held twice yearly. At the Easter session, known as the 'view of account', each sheriff paid in the first instalment of his 'farm', or income due from his shire. When he returned in Michaelmas, he paid over the final instalment, at the lower exchequer, where the sums were notched up on wooden tallies. He then went to the upper exchequer for his accounts to be audited. This was an occasion he very likely dreaded. He sat before a table covered by a chequered cloth (hence 'exchequer'), the vertical columns of which stood for units, tens, hundreds and so on. Since it was impossible to do complex sums in Roman numerals, adding up and subtraction were done by placing or taking away as many counters in each column as were required. On one side of the table sat the sheriff. On the other sat the treasurer and barons of the exchequer, that is, the lawyers who dealt with any litigation that arose. When the accounts had been audited to the treasurer's satisfaction, they were transcribed onto long membranes of parchment secured at their heads with cords, and known from their appearance when rolled up as 'pipe rolls'.

The strength of the exchequer was its ability to maximize the yield from existing sources of revenue, and its weakness, on the other hand, the length of time that it took to collect that revenue. Like the chancery, in the thirteenth century the exchequer 'went out of court', and settled down at Westminster. Again like the chancery, its machinery quickly became cumbersome and inflexible. The Angevin kings felt the need for a smaller and less rigid financial office to provide them with cash as they travelled around the country. At the beginning of the century King John made use of the chamber. However, under his successor, Henry III (q.v.), the chamber was gradually supplanted by the wardrobe. The reason for this may have been the wardrobe's closer relationship with the exchequer, which was the source of most of its money. In the reign of Edward I (q.v.) the wardrobe developed into a major department of state. From the 1280s on, Edward needed to mobilize, and to pay for, large armies in Wales and Scotland. He realized that the exchequer could not adequately cope and so expanded the wardrobe into a war treasury in all but name. Theoretically subordinate though the wardrobe's officials were to the exchequer, in practice they acted as free agents, organizing the collection of taxes and customs revenues and disbursing the wages to the troops. This system worked satisfactorily so long as wardrobe income was sufficient to meet expenditure. But by Edward I's final years this was not the case, and the wardrobe had to borrow heavily. For that reason, under Edward II (q.v.) there was a reaction in favour of exchequer supremacy, and the wardrobe's brief heyday as a war ministry was over.

If the king was to make use of more informal financial offices than the exchequer for disbursing money, then he would likewise need to have some means of passing on his instructions more quickly. It was no longer possible for him to turn directly to chancery, for this office had 'gone out of court'. Accordingly, he introduced a new seal, the 'privy seal', to authenticate letters which he dictated personally. John is the first king known for certain to have had a privy seal, because he used it to give warrants for the issue of letters under the great seal of chancery. For the greater part of the thirteenth century the privy seal was kept wherever the king happened to be, at first in the chamber and later in the wardrobe. But in Edward II's reign the reforming committee of

Ordainers (q.v. ORDINANCES) decided to transfer its custody to a specially appointed official called the keeper of the privy seal. The privy seal, like the great seal, had become institutionalized. It had 'gone out of court'.

What happened next was a resumption of the familiar process of evolution. Deprived of the privy seal as an instrument for his personal use, the king commissioned a new seal, which was known as the 'secret seal'. This first appears to have been used in 1313, two years after the Ordinances. The secret seal was kept in the most private place available to the king – the chamber, the financial office from which he met such expenses as presents for his wife and children. Edward III (q.v.), however, entertained plans for the expansion of the chamber, and the secret seal was closely associated with them. Edward wanted to make the chamber the lynchpin of his system for mobilizing England's resources for the Hundred Years War (q.v.). He accordingly assigned lands for the chamber's support, and told the chancery and exchequer to recognize the secret seal, or 'griffin' as it was now called, as the official warrant for its business. The exchequer put up with this arrangement for as long as it had to, but finally in 1356 reasserted its supremacy. The chamber's existence as an estate office came to an end, and with it the use of the griffin seal.

When the secret seal made a reappearance in the 1380s, it was under a different name and in a new guise. Richard II (q.v.) called this seal the 'signet', and entrusted it to the custody of an official known as the 'secretary'. The use to which the young king put this seal was not to everyone's liking, as he made it the instrument of his autocratic will both to give direct orders to local officials and to 'move' the great and privy seals. Thus when his opponents came to power in 1386, Archbishop Arundel, their nominee as chancellor, refused to accept the signet as a warrant for the issue of letters under the great seal. After this setback both signet and secretary receded into the background, and it was not until the reign of Henry VI (q.v.) that they experienced a revival. Thomas Beckington, who was appointed secretary in 1437, made himself a great man of affairs. But his successors were figures of less importance, and it was not yet clear whether the man made the office or the office the man. Certainly, the successive bouts of insanity which afflicted Henry VI in the 1450s diminished the standing of the secretary as the official closest to the king.

Wielded by an able and vigorous king, however, the signet could be made the means to get the administrative machine moving again. After he recovered the throne in 1471, Edward IV, who was such a king, used the seal to initiate more and more business. Indeed, the signet came close to overshadowing the privy seal in importance. The keeper of the signet, the secretary, was a major figure in government, and in the late fifteenth-century keepers may be discerned the forebears of Thomas Cromwell and William Cecil in the sixteenth. Important as the signet was, however, it was only an instrument, a means to an end. It was the policies which it initiated that mattered. And what contributed most to the success of the Yorkist and early Tudor kings was the expansion in their revenue from land through the chamber. Realizing as some of their predecessors had that the exchequer was utterly inadequate to the task of increasing royal income, Edward IV and Henry VII turned once again to the household agencies to engineer a recovery. Lands were transferred from the control of the exchequer and entrusted to the management of specially appointed keepers who were accountable to the chamber for the rents they collected. This very personalized approach to government reached its culmination in the age of Thomas Cromwell. The final reassertion of exchequer control was not to occur until 1554 in the reign of Mary.

S.B. Chrimes, *An Introduction to the Administrative History of Medieval England*, Blackwell, 1952; W.L. Warren, *The Governance of Norman and Angevin England, 1086–1272*, London, 1987; A.L. Brown, *The Governance of Late Medieval England, 1272–1461*, London, 1989.

GRANGE

The economic organization of the estates of the Cistercian (q.v.) monasteries centred on the unit known as the grange. What distinguished the Cistercians from the Benedictines (q.v.) was the fact that they established their houses outside the reach of feudal society, in uncultivated districts which could be organized as a single estate. Dependent though such an estate would be directly on the monastery, if it was of some size the more distant parts would need to be administered from a farm – in other words, a grange. The buildings of the grange would have comprised storerooms, an oratory and sleeping accommodation for the lay brothers on whom the Cistercians relied for manual labour. So well suited was the grange to the administration of a large estate that it was soon adopted on the estates.of other orders, and one of the best examples to survive to this day is the grange of the Benedictine nuns of Shaftsbury at Tisbury (Wilts).

GROSSETESTE, ROBERT

Robert Grosseteste was the most distinguished intellectual on the English episcopal bench in the thirteenth century, and one of the greatest scholars of his day. But his early life is obscure, and much about his intellectual development is the subject of controversy.

Traditionally, Grosseteste has been seen as a normative figure: as someone who stood in the mainstream of contemporary scholasticism on the continent and who exercised a key influence on its dissemination in

England. In 1986, however, this view of him was challenged in a major study by Sir Richard Southern. Southern saw Grosseteste as essentially an outsider, cut off from the main tradition of scholastic debate by his humble origins, the product of a provincial education, and as a theologian largely an autodidact, who had never attended the schools of Paris and came late to a teaching career at Oxford. These views are lent support by Grosseteste's scholastic thought, which shows unusual independence and originality. All the same, it is difficult to demonstrate Southern's view of Grosseteste's intellectual development conclusively. Grosseteste's early career is ill documented. There is no evidence to indicate where he was educated. His first recorded appointment was as a clerk in the household of the bishop of Hereford in 1193. By 1225 he had become a leading master in the Oxford schools. Sometime in the 1220s – probably in the later part of the decade rather than the earlier – he was elected chancellor of Oxford in opposition to the wishes of the bishop of Lincoln. By this time he had become a great figure, attracting growing attention by his sermons and lectures. In the 1230s he held a lectureship with the Oxford Franciscans (q.v.), encouraging and assisting them in their studies. He was beginning to break new ground in his theological studies and he also undertook Europe's first full translation of Aristotle's *Ethics*.

In 1235 he was elected bishop of Lincoln, a see with which he had previous connections. He was almost certainly aged at least sixty. He quickly established a reputation for himself as a conscientious and hard-working diocesan. He hardly courted popularity, however, by his keenness to reform the morals of both clergy and laity and by his inflexible insistence in 1239 on making a visitation of the cathedral of Lincoln in defiance of the wishes of the dean and chapter. The principle which guided him in the exercise of his pastoral duties was, as he put it, 'the supreme importance of the cure of souls'. It was this belief which enabled him to combine devotion to the idea of papal supremacy with ringing denunciation of the Pope when the latter's 'provision' (q.v.), or appointment, of an unworthy candidate to a benefice placed the cure of souls in danger.

Grosseteste died on 9 October 1253 and was buried in Lincoln Cathedral. Almost immediately there were attempts to promote his canonization. It may have been in this connection that around 1255 a tomb of notably shrine-like character was erected to his memory over his resting-place in the south-east transept. Although lost, the tomb is known from a seventeenth-century drawing.

Robert Grosseteste: Scholar and Bishop, ed. D.A. Callus, Oxford, 1955; R. W. Southern, *Robert Grossesteste. The Growth of an English Mind in Medieval Europe*, Oxford, 1986.

GUILDS

Medieval guilds were many-faceted institutions. Their functions were a mixture of the social, religious, political and economic. In essence, guilds were voluntary associations formed by people who had interests in common. However, they tended to vary widely in character and nomenclature. Besides guilds, they could be called fraternities and misteries. Although predominantly urban institutions, they could also be found in the countryside.

Guilds made their first appearance in early medieval England as social institutions whose activities sometimes stretched to the defence of their members' trading interests. In this sense, they anticipated the 'guilds merchant' which emerged in many large towns after the Norman Conquest. The 'guild merchant' in the twelfth century was the body of all the leading merchants of the town. It normally acted in defence of the trading privileges of its members, but it could also become the spokesman for the town as a community. It was often through the guild merchant that a town obtained its charter of incorporation. In towns where this was the case, the same men would be found holding office in both the guild merchant and the borough.

With power in the towns coming to be concentrated in the hands of small elites, the members of the lesser crafts often felt left out. This was particularly the case in the cloth towns, where urban affairs were dominated by the wealthy merchants who made their money in the finishing trades. The people engaged in the earlier stages of production – the weavers and the fullers – lacked a forum in which to express their own views. Their response was to form guilds of their own (q.v. INDUSTRY). It was these bodies which are generally referred to as 'craft guilds'. Commonly craft guilds sought to secure for their members the monopoly of engaging in that particular trade in the town.

Not all the early guilds lasted for very long, and even the mighty guilds merchant died away once the boroughs had won the right to run their own affairs and to choose their own officers. The guilds or fraternities of the later Middle Ages were bodies rather different in character from their predecessors. In part, they were semi-religious. As people tended to think more about how to ease their sufferings in the afterlife, so guilds or fraternities took on the responsibility of securing burial for their members and arranging intercession for them at side-altars or in chantries (q.v.). Such guilds or fraternities need not necessarily have been craft-organized, but very often they were. At the same time, these bodies

were made the instruments of a policy of urban regulation. It was through enforcement of rules of formal apprenticeship that a system of quality control was maintained. While the urban elites were ruthless in establishing local monopolies of trade, they used the system of guild ordinances to ensure that the consumer did not unduly suffer.

By the fourteenth century many of the larger guilds had become considerable property owners as a result of donations and bequests from their members. The guild officers used this wealth to build halls and chambers where feasts could be celebrated, for example on the anniversary of the patron saint of the body. The guildhalls at York, Leicester and Stratford-on-Avon are good examples of these. Once the guilds became property owners, they needed protection at law. Like the borough communities of which they formed part, they achieved this by seeking incorporation by royal licence. In 1453, for instance, Henry VI granted permission to fifteen tailors of York to found a guild of a master and four wardens 'of the said Mistery and other persons, brethren and sisters, in honour of St John the Baptist in York'. Of the many social activities of the guilds the most familiar are the drama productions known as the 'mistery plays' (q.v.). The religious side of their work was curtailed at the Reformation when the chantries were dissolved and all property held by the guilds for devotional purposes was confiscated. In London and other cities, however, the guilds have survived to the present day in the guise of the livery companies.

H

HASTINGS

The engagement fought on 14 October 1066 and known as the battle of Hastings took place on a ridge of the Weald where the town of Battle now stands. On Edward the Confessor's death on 5 January 1066, Harold, earl of Wessex, had seized the throne, but before long his title was challenged by two claimants, Harold Hardrada, king of Norway, and William, duke of Normandy (q.v.). The Norwegian invasion came to a bloody end at the battle of Stamford Bridge near York on 25 September, when Hardrada himself was killed and his army shattered. No sooner had Harold recovered from this challenge, however, than news reached him of William's landing on the Sussex coast at Pevensey on 28 September. The king immediately marched southwards, reaching London on or about 6 October and setting out for the Weald a day or two later. His aim was probably to blockade the invaders on the Hastings peninsula and in this way force them to surrender or withdraw. William could not permit himself to be blockaded and sought an early engagement. On or around 13 October he took his army northwards into the Weald. The English, now in the Weald, were caught unawares. At dawn on 14 October they awoke to find the Normans facing them across the valley. Harold lined his men in a strong defensive position on a broad ridge, with his housecarls in the front. His force was composed entirely of foot soldiers. Duke William's force, however, included some 2,000–3,000 heavily armed cavalrymen. At the commencement of hostilities, Duke William launched first his infantry and then his knights against the English, but to little avail. At one point, the Norman left flank began to give way, and some of Harold's men came pouring down the hillside in hot pursuit. It is said to have been this episode which gave William the idea, once order had been restored, of luring his enemy from the ridge by the ruse of a feigned retreat. Although some of Harold's men were rash enough to abandon their hill-top security only to be cut down by the Normans, the majority stood firm. William therefore rallied his cavalry, and sent them once more against the English. At the same time he ordered his archers to fire their arrows high into the air so that they rained down on Harold and his men. It was presumably at this stage that Harold himself was killed. The English position finally broke, and by nightfall William was in command of the field.

According to the most reliable estimates Harold's force may have numbered about 8,000 men, and William's perhaps as many as 10,000. The Conqueror commemorated his victory by founding the monastery known as Battle Abbey, the high altar of which was reputedly raised on the place where Harold met his death.

See also BAYEUX TAPESTRY

J. Bradbury, *The Battle of Hastings*, Stroud, 1997.

HENRY I

Few monarchs of comparable importance have left so faint an impression on the pages of history as Henry I. The king's personality emerges only imperfectly from the chroniclers' narratives. Although he was clearly effective as a ruler, he inspired little affection and was considered harsh. Yet his reign was imbued with a warm afterglow by the anarchy which followed in Stephen's (q.v.) reign.

Henry was the youngest of the three sons of William the Conqueror (q.v.) and, if the tradition is true that he was born at Selby in 1068, the only one of the Norman kings to have been born in England. He was probably bilingual, although the later legend that he was a considerable scholar (which by the fourteenth century had earned him the surname 'Beauclerk') rests on no firmer foundation than that he could read Latin.

When the Conqueror died in 1087, his dominions were divided between his two elder sons, Robert and William (Rufus). Henry received nothing but a legacy of £5,000 in silver. However, he invested this money wisely, and by 1088 had established himself in the Cotentin peninsula in Normandy, which he had purchased from Duke Robert. On 2 August 1100 he was in Rufus's company when the latter was killed in the New Forest. Whether or not he was involved in procuring his brother's death, he quickly had himself crowned as his successor. He needed to act with all haste because Duke Robert had just returned from crusade, and was considering bidding for the crown himself. Henry secured his position by offering a series of concessions. He published a charter offering liberties to his subjects; he welcomed back Archbishop Anselm (q.v.), who had gone into exile rather than endure Rufus's attacks on the Church; and he ordered the imprisonment of Ranulph Flambard, Rufus's unpopular minister. When Robert finally mounted an invasion of England in 1101, he attracted support from a small group of barons, notably the powerful earl of Shrewsbury, but rather than risk a pitched battle, he decided on compromise. He signed away his claim to the crown in return for an annuity of 3,000 marks. In consequence, the final resolution of the struggle between the brothers was postponed until 1106, when Henry invaded Normandy and defeated Robert at Tinchebrai. The duke was captured in the battle and imprisoned in Cardiff Castle, where he languished till his death in 1134.

For the remainder of his reign Henry ruled England and Normandy jointly as king-duke. He spent roughly equal time in the two dominions. While he was in Normandy, he relied on Roger, bishop of Salisbury, the justiciar (q.v.), to oversee the government of England. It was Roger's responsibility not only to supervise the judicial machine but also to provide the king with a constant stream of money for war. Henry's main enemy was King Louis VI of France, who was keen to see Anglo-Norman power diminished and to that end was constantly launching incursions into the duchy. Henry was intermittently at war with Louis until he scored a decisive victory over his adversary at Bremule in 1119. Henry's heavy demands for taxation led to a formalization of financial procedures in England. Onto the long-established treasury at Winchester, which received the king's revenues, was grafted the exchequer, where the accounting was done by the justiciar and his staff (q.v. GOVERNMENT). Henry, however, needed not only institutions but men – reliable men, like Bishop Roger. Here he was able to turn to his advantage the rebellions against him in the early years of the reign.

Seizing the lands of those who had rejected his rule, he granted these out to his supporters, the 'men raised up from the dust' in the words of one chronicler, who owed everything they had to Henry. These men became the chief instruments of his rule. Never again would he have to face a rebellion in England.

Although he was highly successful in the art of government, the permanence of Henry's achievement was called into question by an accident at sea which effectively changed the course of twelfth-century history. On 25 November 1120 Henry's only legitimate son, William, was killed in the wreck of the White Ship off the Normandy coast. Henry had lost his heir. In the following year Henry remarried, but there was no more legitimate issue. He therefore brought back from Germany his daughter Matilda, widow of the emperor, and made the barons swear that they would uphold her succession to the throne. To neutralize the threat from Anjou, Normandy's traditional enemy on the south, Henry married her to Geoffrey, the son of the count of Anjou. In the eyes of the nobility, the arrangements which Henry had made were not only offensive, but positively dangerous, carrying as they did the prospect of an Angevin succession. It was small wonder, then, that after Henry died on 1 December 1135, they forgot their oaths to Matilda and welcomed Stephen as king instead.

For Henry the tragedy was that, though he had fathered more bastards than any other English king – nineteen in all – he had only two legitimate children, William and Matilda. Both were borne by his first wife Edith, a descendant of the Saxon royal house, who assumed the name Matilda on her marriage. His second wife was Adeliza, daughter of Godfrey, duke of Louvain. With Henry, the Norman house came to an end in the male line. He was the most competent of the Conqueror's sons, a ruthless and effective ruler. Yet in the end his legacy was a mixed one. His administration was too harsh and predatory to command long-term acceptance. A proportion of the nobility felt that they had lost out to Henry's 'new men' and were itching to recover lost privilege. It is possible that baronial disaffection would have followed his death even if there had not been a disputed succession.

C.W. Hollister, *Henry I*, New Haven and London, 2001.

HENRY II

One of the most able and energetic of England's medieval rulers, Henry II was a monarch whose rule extended over so many territories and whose career embraced so many fields of activity that it is hard to form an overall view of his reign. The quarrel with Becket (q.v.) is accordingly treated separately.

Henry was born on 4 March 1133 at Le Mans, the eldest son of Geoffrey of Anjou and his wife Matilda, Henry I's daughter and designated successor. His earliest involvement in English affairs came during the civil war occasioned by his mother's bid to wrest the crown from Stephen (q.v.). In 1147, shortly before Matilda abandoned the struggle, he crossed to England with a small force but, inferior in resources to Stephen, he accepted the latter's money to return home. He crossed again in force in 1152. By this time many of the aristocracy were forming the view that the only way to end the war was by allowing Stephen to rule for his lifetime while designating Henry his successor. In July 1153 Henry's army confronted Stephen's across the Thames at Wallingford. Neither of the forces would fight, obliging the two principals to negotiate. A draft treaty was agreed, subsequently finalized at Westminster, which provided for a settlement on this basis: Stephen would remain king but Henry would be his successor.

Stephen died less than a year later, on 25 October 1154, and Henry found himself the ruler of dominions stretching from the

Scottish border to the Pyrenees. From his father he had inherited Anjou and Maine, from his mother England and Normandy, and from his wife Eleanor (q.v.), whom he had married in 1152, the duchy of Aquitaine in south-west France.

Henry's first task in England was to restore order after the long civil war. He needed to act with care because the resources of the crown were much diminished and his position as king was weak. In making his first governmental appointments, Henry ensured that all the main interest groups were represented – the baronage by Robert, earl of Leicester, the knights by Richard de Luci, co-justiciar with Leicester, and the Church by Thomas Becket, his chancellor. Although the new king drew support from all sectors of political society – from former adversaries as well as allies – he soon showed his intention to be master in his own house. In 1155 he expelled the Flemish mercenaries whom Stephen had employed, and set a time limit for the demolition of all unlicensed castles that had been erected during the Anarchy.

A particularly urgent issue was the need to sort out the conflicting claims to land that had contributed to the feuding in Stephen's reign. Disputes over the descent of land at this time were heard in the court of the feudal superior from whom the fief was held, whether the king's court in the case of tenants-in-chief or the honorial court in the case of sub-tenants (q.v. FEUDALISM). Normally it was not open to a plaintiff dissatisfied with his lord's justice to appeal to a higher court. In the unsettled conditions of the time, however, such an arrangement was unsatisfactory. Accordingly, Henry introduced the writ 'of right' which ordered the lord to do right to a plaintiff, if the sheriff were not to take up the case himself. Although intended to remedy only defects of justice, the writ of right eventually undermined the feudal courts by destroying their finality: it was now open to any aggrieved plaintiff to transfer an action to the royal courts.

In the 1160s Henry introduced a speedy remedy to those who had been ejected from (or 'disseised of') their lands. The Assize of Novel Disseisin instructed a jury to enquire before the king's justices if the plaintiff had been unjustly disseised. Other 'assizes' followed in the 1170s, the most important of these being Mort d'Ancestor, which enabled a deprived heir to recover his inheritance. These actions all involved the use of a jury, empanelled by the sheriff, to decide a simple question of fact. If, however, a more complex case were to reach the courts, it would normally have been settled by ordeal or by battle. With judicial procedures becoming increasingly sophisticated, this method appeared outdated, and in 1179 Henry II offered trial by jury as an alternative. This was known as the 'grand assize'.

Henry's reforms laid the foundations of an effective system of common law. What had once been separate Old English, Danish or Norman customs were now welded into a unified legal code regulated by the writs activating the king's assizes. The king's courts, however, were only open to those of free condition. Thus a side effect of the reforms was to emphasize the difference between the freeborn and the villeins: the latter could proceed no further than their lord's court. The increasing popularity of royal justice had major implications for the future of baronial justice itself. As the courts of the barons lost their finality, so too they lost attractiveness. In the long run they were fated to wither away. And simultaneously, as the royal courts became busier, so the king became more powerful. The lives of more and more people were affected by his judgements (q.v. JUSTICE).

These developments did not pass unnoticed by contemporaries. The steady drift of power from the barons to the king, which took place in the first twenty years of the reign, helps to explain why so many lords were prepared to support the rebellion – the 'great war' as it was known – against the king in 1173-4. Although this was in origin a family quarrel, it developed into a major rebellion which convulsed all the Angevin lands and exposed them to attack from the king of France. Once Henry had overcome the rebels, he made sure that never again would they be able to mount such an assault on royal authority. He received former opponents with favour, but he ordered the demolition of their castles. At the same time, he embarked on a massive castle-building programme of his own. Newcastle-on-Tyne and Dover are two of the most notable fortresses that he built.

The last years of the reign were marred by bitter family quarrels between husband and wife, father and sons. Henry's marriage to Eleanor of Aquitaine (q.v.), the former wife of Louis VII of France, was tumultuous. By the early 1170s the two were living apart, Henry with his mistress, Rosamund Clifford, and Eleanor in confinement in Winchester. At the same time, Henry was at odds with his sons. He failed to create a political structure which satisfied their growing aspirations to rulership. In the 1170s Henry, the young king, his eldest son, rebelled in order to win a share of power. In 1183, after the death of the young king, Richard (q.v.), the second-born, became heir. But by 1189 he too had rebelled, allying himself with Philip of France; the two, indeed, were marching into Anjou when Henry died on 6 July 1189.

Henry II, Eleanor and Richard are all buried at Fontevrault Abbey in France. Henry was a mighty king, yet curiously unkingly in manner. He was unkempt in appearance and indifferent to what people thought about him. Pomp and display were qualities that in the 1150s he had left to his chancellor, Becket (q.v.).

W.L. Warren, *Henry II*, 2nd ed., New Haven and London, 2000.

HENRY III

Henry III's reign was marked by unprecedented peace and prosperity, but in its later years it was marred by the period of bitter strife associated with the name of Simon de Montfort (q.v.).

Henry was born at Winchester on 1 October 1207, the son of King John (q.v.) and his second wife, Isabella of Angoulême. His accession to the throne in 1216 on the death of his father inaugurated the first royal minority in English history since the Conquest. For its duration the country was governed by a regency council, initially under the leadership of William Marshal, earl of Pembroke (d.1219), whose task it was to negotiate a settlement of the civil war that had broken out between King John and the barons. The council brought the minority to an end in two stages, the first in 1223, the second in 1227 when the king declared himself of full age.

The early years of Henry's reign were largely concerned with sorting out his father's chaotic inheritance. After the Marshal's death the justiciar (q.v.), Hubert de Burgh, applied himself to the task of rebuilding royal authority. Gradually, royal demesne lands were recovered, and royal income built up. But Hubert made enemies – in particular, the late king's two Poitevin counsellors, Peter des Roches and Peter des Rivaux. In 1232 the Poitevins brought about Hubert's downfall and assumed power themselves. A couple of years later they were overthrown in turn by Richard Marshal in a revolt which drew on the growing anti-alien feeling in the country. Since Normandy's (q.v.) loss to the French in 1204, the sense of national identity in England had been increasing apace.

The early years of Henry III's personal rule from 1234 to 1258 witnessed a gradual relaxation of these tensions. Henry fostered good relations with his subjects, in particular with his higher nobility. There were fewer external wars and fewer demands for money. However, rivalries in the elite were fed by the arrival of newcomers from abroad. In 1236 a group of Savoyards arrived in the retinue of Henry III's queen, Eleanor, notable among them Boniface, later Archbishop of Canterbury. A little under a decade later Henry's half-brothers, the Lusignans, arrived in England too. This last clique were particularly unpopular. Not only were they highly ambitious and self-seeking; they were also thought to profit unduly from the king's favour.

Political tensions were further generated by the expectations raised by Magna Carta (q.v.). The Charter, which had been reissued in 1225, provided Henry's subjects with a touchstone of good government. In the years of his personal rule Henry's kingship was considered in some respects to fall short of the standards which it set. Complaints were made that the king appointed unsuitable sheriffs, that his justice was corrupt, that his forest administration was oppressive, and so on. In 1258 growing frustration with the king's government combined with factional rivalry at court to produce a major political crisis.

In a parliament held at Oxford in April 1258, Henry had requested a grant of taxation to pay for the installation of his second son Edmund on the throne of Sicily. The barons disapproved of the king's scheme and wanted it cancelled. More substantially, they wanted reforms. Their demands were twofold: that the Lusignans be expelled and that the king accept a reforming constitution, the Provisions of Oxford (q.v.). The Provisions were more radical than Magna Carta. Where the latter had left the king in full control of the country, the Provisions took matters of day-to-day governance out of his hands. In effect, the king reigned while the council ruled. Henry took an oath to uphold the Provisions, but did so reluctantly. Ahead lay a long period of instability and jockeying for position between the two sides.

In the two years from 1259 Henry skilfully reconstructed his political base. By 1261 he had won sufficient backing to throw off the Provisions. However, the reform movement, in which Simon de Montfort had become increasingly dominant, was not spent. By the autumn of 1263 king and reformers were deadlocked. As a result, they agreed to submit their differences to the French king, Louis IX. Louis' arbitration, given in January 1264, gave Henry everything he could have asked for, and his opponents realized that they would have to take to arms. At Lewes (14 May 1264) the baronial army gained a decisive victory over the royalists, and both the king and his son Edward (q.v.) were taken prisoner. After managing to escape, however, Edward rallied the royalists, and led them to victory at Evesham on 4 August 1265. During the closing years of his father's reign, which ended in 1272, it was Edward who exercised the decisive influence over policy.

Henry III derived his political ideas both from home and abroad. His devotion to the cult of the Saxon king, Edward the Confessor, was rooted in a desire to identify with English traditions which found expression in the choice of name for his eldest son and in the rebuilding of Westminster Abbey, where the Confessor was buried. But at the same time he sought inspiration in the court of Louis IX of France (St Louis). This explains the seemingly paradoxical choice of a French model – Rheims Cathedral – for Westminster Abbey, which was the coronation church of the English kings.

On his death in 1272 Henry was buried in a fine tomb in the abbey; he was the first post-Conquest monarch to choose the abbey as his burial place. His widow, Eleanor of Provence, who died in 1291, was buried at the nunnery of Amesbury, in which she had spent her retirement.

F.M. Powicke, *King Henry III and the Lord Edward*, Oxford, 1947; D.A. Carpenter, *The Reign of Henry III*, London, 1996.

HENRY IV

The 'unquietness' of Henry IV's reign, so memorably captured by Shakespeare, resulted from the weakness of the king's title, which left him vulnerable to criticism and attack from his enemies.

Henry was born in about 1366, the only legitimate son of John of Gaunt, duke of Lancaster (q.v.) by his wife Blanche. His relations with his cousin, Richard II (q.v.), were uneasy, and in the 'Appellant' crisis of 1387–88 he ranged himself alongside the king's opponents. After Richard's reassertion of power in 1389 and the consequent easing of tensions, Henry found an outlet for his energies abroad. In 1390 he went on a crusade to Prussia, fighting alongside the Teutonic Knights against the Lithuanians. In 1392 he went to Prussia for a second time but, finding that his services were not needed, embarked instead on a pilgrimage to the Holy Land, visiting a number of courts on the way.

In 1397 English politics entered a period of instability. On 10 July Richard arrested the three former senior Appellants – Gloucester, Arundel and Warwick – a move which left Henry and Mowbray feeling isolated. Mowbray warned Henry of his suspicion that the king planned next to destroy him and his father. Henry, for his own security, reported Mowbray's warning to the king and Mowbray panicked. A quarrel erupted between the two men, and Richard ordered them to settle their differences by a duel. At the last moment, Richard called the duel off, and sent them both into exile, in Henry's case for ten years.

The question of Henry's future was reopened barely five months later when the duke's father, 'time honoured Lancaster', died (3 February 1399). Richard had to consider whether to allow the duke to return to recover his lands or, alternatively, to extend his exile to life. There were dangers attendant on both courses. If he were to allow the duke to return, he would be acquiescing in the emergence of a potential rival; on the other hand,

if he were to extend his exile, he would be disseising a lord and offending against the deepest sensibilities of the age. In the event he opted for the latter course. On 18 March he took possession of the Lancastrian inheritance and extended the duke's exile to life. Two months later he set sail for Ireland. While he was away, Henry returned to England. Landing at Ravenspur, he declared that he had come solely to recover his birthright. He obtained the crucial support of the Percy family, and quickly took control of the realm. At Conway Richard surrendered to his challenger. By this time Henry had decided to venture a bid for his crown. At the end of September, in parliament, Richard was deposed, and Henry staked his own claim – one justified, so he said, partly by right of descent and partly by conquest. On 13 October he was crowned king as Henry IV.

Henry's reign turned out to be a troubled one. Richard's policy of ruling by faction and feud had left him with a baneful inheritance. From the very beginning there were challenges to his title. In January 1400 a group of Richard's courtier lords plotted to restore the former king, but Henry quickly disposed of them. The rebellion of the Percys in 1403 was a more serious affair. The Percys and their allies attracted widespread support in the north and west, and their challenge culminated in a bloody encounter at Shrewsbury (1 July 1403). Henry emerged the victor from the battle, in which Henry Percy ('Hotspur') was killed. Hotspur's father, however, the earl of Northumberland, who was not present at the battle, remained at large, fomenting discord. In 1405 he conspired with Richard Scrope, Archbishop of York, to lead yet another rising. Henry nipped this in the bud, and had the archbishop executed. Northumberland himself was captured and killed at Bramham Moor three years later.

In addition to these challenges to his title, Henry had to deal with Owain Glyn Dwr's (q.v.) massive rebellion against the English ascendancy in Wales. Drawing on widespread resentment against English lordship, the rebellion dragged on for nearly eight years. After 1408, however, when the rebellion collapsed, Henry's problems gradually eased. In the second half of his reign his kingship was more secure. Yet his own health began to deteriorate. From 1406 he suffered long periods of illness which left him incapacitated. He found travelling on horseback difficult and he was often confined to his bed. The signs are that he suffered from a thrombosis in the leg.

Throughout his reign Henry had to face constant criticism in parliament because of his recurrent requests for taxation. In his later years he had to face, additionally, the criticisms of his eldest son, the future Henry V, who wanted to secure a more active role for himself in government. For a year, from 1410 to 1411 the prince and his allies controlled the council. In November 1411, however, the king dismissed them and appointed councillors of his own. In the last year of his life he regained full control of affairs. Henry died on 20 March 1413, and was buried in Canterbury Cathedral.

Henry IV's problems were considerable, yet it is possible to exaggerate them. By June 1405, with the despatch of Archbishop Scrope, he had effectively disposed of the challenges to the Lancastrian title. From 1405, disagreements in government were ones within the Lancastrian family itself. The Lancastrian dynasty was secure. Although Henry's reign was politically disturbed and, to a degree, disappointing, he passed on a secure crown to his successor.

K.B. McFarlane, *Lancastrian Kings and Lollard Knights*, Oxford, 1972.

HENRY V

Henry V, like Richard I (q.v.) was a king virtually lionized by his contemporaries. He has been hardly less highly regarded by posterity.

The second Lancastrian found his Elizabethan apotheosis in the hero of Shakespeare's play. But Shakespeare's picture of a dissolute youth turned good bears little relation to the historical figure.

Henry V was born at Monmouth on 16 September 1387, the son of Henry, earl of Derby, Gaunt's heir, and his first wife, Mary Bohun. After his father became king in 1399 as Henry IV, the young Henry was made prince of Wales. He was heavily involved in the struggle against the Percys and suffered severe injury in the face at Shrewsbury. Subsequently he was given charge of suppressing Owen Glyn Dwr's rebellion in Wales. By 1408 he had brought most of the province back into English lordship. It was in his Welsh campaigns that he learned the military skills which he was to put to such devastating effect in France.

By 1410 he was growing impatient with the governance of his father's ministers. As his father's health deteriorated, he wanted to assume greater responsibility himself. In 1410–11 he and his allies took control of the council. Henry effectively dismissed them a year later, but the differences between the two parties were not deep. When the old king died in 1413 there was a smooth transfer of power to his son. Shakespeare's picture of Hal repenting of a dissolute youth has little foundation in fact. Shakespeare wanted to make the transformation of Hal a metaphor for the transformation of the realm. The accession of the new king certainly had the effect of bringing a quickened pace to government. There were major initiatives to restore law and order, and new measures were taken to suppress heresy. But the old reign still cast its shadow. In 1415 a plot was hatched by the earl of Cambridge to murder the king and replace him by the earl of March. This was the last echo of the dynastic disputes that had plagued the last reign.

Henry's main aim was to renew the English claim to the crown of France. After the failure of negotiations with the Dauphin, Henry led an expedition to France in August 1415. Landing in Normandy (q.v.) he laid siege to the port of Harfleur. The siege turned out to be a lengthier affair than expected, and by the time the town fell (22 September) the English forces were riddled with dysentery. Despite his losses Henry decided to march across northern France to Calais. He was closely trailed by a Franco-Burgundian army, which caught up with him at Agincourt (q.v.). In the battle of Agincourt (25 October) he scored the most celebrated English victory of the Middle Ages. When he returned in triumph to England, Chancellor Beaufort (q.v.) claimed that the victory indicated God's blessing for the king's cause.

Agincourt, although a brilliant victory, strategically counted for little. It failed to bring Henry any nearer to winning the French crown. Accordingly, in 1417 Henry embarked on a new expedition. This time his strategy was different. Instead of launching the traditional hit-and-run raid, or *chevauchée*, he attempted territorial conquest. His aim was to effect the complete takeover of Normandy – to rule it in person as duke and to partition its land among his nobility. By 1419 he had largely succeeded. After a long series of sieges, he had captured the main cities – Caen, Evreux, Rouen – and French resistance had collapsed. His success owed much to his military genius. But it was also greatly assisted by internal divisions within France. French political society was divided between two competing factions, the Armagnacs and the Burgundians. When the Armagnacs murdered the duke of Burgundy in 1419, the Burgundians entered into an alliance with the English and assisted in their occupation of Paris. A settlement was agreed between Henry and the enfeebled Charles VI at Troyes in 1420, whereby Charles remained king for his lifetime while Henry was recognized as his heir and successor. Only Henry's premature death at

Vincennes on 31 August 1422 robbed him of the chance of uniting England and France under his rule.

In less than nine years Henry V had succeeded where his predecessor Edward III had failed; he had won the French crown. Yet in the end his achievement was to be transient because he left a one-year-old child to succeed him. It is tempting to wonder if the enterprise could have succeeded had he lived. The task facing Henry was huge. The whole of southern France lay in Dauphinist hands. Continuing war would have been slow and costly. However, in the face of the English advance the Dauphinist lords might have been brought to submit. Henry was a vigorous, determined and purposeful man. He was driven by an austere piety, and he was convinced of divine support for his work. He saw his mission in France as a natural extension of that in England. Nonetheless, the processes of national development were working against him. At the very time when he was seeking to bring England and France closer together, increasing divergences of language and culture were driving them apart.

C. Allmand, *Henry V*, 2nd ed., New Haven and London, 1997.

HENRY VI

'Woe to thee, O land, when thy king is a child', said Thomas Kerver of Reading in 1444. By that time Henry VI had all but lost the crown of France, and fifteen years later he had lost the crown of England as well.

Born on 6 December 1421, the only son of Henry V (q.v.) and his French bride, Catherine of Valois, Henry became king when he was only nine months old. He was heir to the dual Anglo-French monarchy founded by his father. For the fifteen years of his minority the administration in France was led by his elder uncle, John, duke of Bedford, and in England by his other uncle,

Humphrey, duke of Gloucester (q.v.). Inevitably, the conciliar government was divided by rivalries between the great lords, notably between Duke Humphrey and the crown's biggest creditor, Cardinal Beaufort (q.v.), but considering the many difficulties they faced, they coped adequately enough. In France Bedford proved an effective regent. He managed to finance the continuing war without asking for heavy taxes. But, try as he might, he could only delay and not halt the slow erosion of Henry V's conquests. At Arras in 1435 the Burgundians, who had sided with Henry V in 1420, decided to switch allegiance to Charles VII of France, the king they had once helped to disinherit. And in April the following year the French re-entered Paris.

Matters were not helped by Henry VI's coming of age in 1437. Although the king was well educated 'in good manners and letters' and had received careful instruction from his father's executors, he turned out to be naïve, incompetent and lacking in warrior instincts. By the 1440s he was pressing hard for a settlement with the French. In 1444 he sponsored a two-year truce at Tours and in the following year he took a French bride, Margaret, the daughter of René of Anjou. His peace initiatives prompted little response from the French, however. The tide of war had turned sharply in their favour. In 1449 they overran Normandy, and in the following year Aquitaine. Only Calais remained to the English.

The collapse of English rule in France did enormous damage to Henry's prestige. However, the shortcomings of his government at home did considerably more. Henry increasingly limited the taking of counsel to a small circle composed of the queen, the duke of Suffolk and the Beauforts. He conspicuously ignored the duke of York, his heir presumptive since 1447 and an advocate of a stronger line in France. When Jack Cade (q.v.) and his fellow rebels in Kent took over London in 1450, York's admission to the council was among the first of their demands.

Popular support, however, counted for little in the face of Henry's and Margaret's firm hostility. It was only the onset of Henry's insanity in 1454 that rescued York from oblivion. In March of that year York was named Protector of the Realm, a title that he held for the next nine months. As soon as Henry recovered his senses, however, he found himself excluded again. In May 1455 Margaret and the court summoned a council at Leicester at which York feared that he would be arrested. Accordingly, he and his men planned to intercept the king at St Albans. The battle that followed in the streets of the town (22 May) is considered to be the first engagement in the long struggle known as the Wars of the Roses (q.v.). However, it was not immediately followed by further hostilities. Four years of uneasy calm followed, until a further attempt by the queen to marshal her supporters, at Coventry in November 1459, convinced the Yorkist leaders that they would have to flee the realm. They returned in the following year, and at the battle of Northampton (10 July 1460) captured Henry VI's person. Paradoxically, it was a Lancastrian success that brought his unhappy reign to an end. At Wakefield on the last day of 1460 York was killed, and two months later Henry was retaken by his wife. Without an anointed king to legitimize their actions, the Yorkists had to make one of their own. On 4 March 1461, therefore, York's son was crowned king as Edward IV (q.v.).

Henry's deposition marked the beginning of a ten-year exile, spent mainly in Scotland. Margaret, acting on her husband's behalf, planned his return to power. The chance was given to her in 1470 when Richard Neville, earl of Warwick (q.v.) – the Kingmaker – overthrew Edward IV and reinstated Henry. The 'readeption', as it was known, stood little chance of lasting. In April the following year Warwick fell at the Battle of Barnet, and Edward re-entered London on 21 May. This event really did spell the end for Henry VI who was executed shortly afterwards. His remains were interred in Chertsey Abbey, and later transferred to St George's Chapel, Windsor.

It is possible that Henry VI's bouts of insanity were inherited from his maternal grandfather, Charles VI of France. However, contemporary descriptions give the impression that his ailment was different from Charles's. What Henry suffered from in 1453–4, and seems never fully to have recovered from, was sheer mental collapse. He looked blankly at people and did not respond. The problem for the historian is to decide whether in his saner moments he was downright malevolent or just a helpless simpleton. It is clear that he was intensely devout. His concern for good works was reflected in his twin foundations of Eton and King's College, Cambridge. But he was also prurient and responsible for allowing a gross misdirection of patronage. The Yorkist claim to the throne would surely never have been heard of had it not been for his appalling exercise of kingship.

B.P. Wolffe, *Henry VI*, London, 1981; R.A. Griffiths, *The Reign of King Henry VI*, 2nd ed., Stroud, 1997.

HERALDRY

Heraldry may be described as a system of identifying individuals by means of hereditary devices placed upon a shield.

The placing of the devices on a shield is a significant pointer to the military origins of the science. In the twelfth century, when knights rode into battle covered from head to foot in mail suits and with their faces concealed beneath closed helms, identification became impossible. To overcome this difficulty they adopted the simple expedient of showing a pictorial device which everyone would recognize. This would be displayed on the shield and, additionally, on the linen surcoat worn over the armour – hence the familiar terms 'coat armour' and 'coat of arms'.

In an illiterate society armorial bearings provided the means by which a knight could not only identify himself in the field but also authenticate charters and other important documents. Because charters were preserved as deeds of title, the personal seals attached to them by witnesses provide the earliest evidence of the use of heraldry in England. The first surviving armorial device comes from Stephen's (q.v.) reign, just before the outbreak of the civil war, when Waleran, count of Meulan and earl of Worcester, made a seal (*c.*1136–8) showing him on horseback, holding in one hand a shield and in the other a lance flag, on both of which can be discerned the checky coat used by his family. Across the Channel, the first evidence of the adoption of hereditary armorial devices comes from roughly the same time. At Le Mans there remains the famous enamelled plate said to have been over the tomb of Geoffrey, count of Anjou (d.1151) and now preserved in the local museum. The count is shown beneath a semicircular arch holding a shield of golden lions on a blue field and wearing a cap also charged with a lion. This device, like the checky coat of Count Waleran, can be accepted as truly heraldic because it was transmitted from one generation to the next: on the Great Seal of King Richard I (q.v.), Count Geoffrey's grandson, we find the arms three lions passant guardant destined to become famous as the lions of England.

By the thirteenth century there is clear evidence that heraldry was becoming an established science: it was acquiring a technical vocabulary of its own. The first usage of this corrupted French jargon is found in the Rolls of Arms drawn up by the heralds to record the arms of knights present at some special occasion like a tournament. The vocabulary adopted in the Middle Ages is still the language of heraldry today. At the same time, a series of rules was worked out governing the design of a shield. These rules, like the language used to describe them, are still in use today. The rules, though seemingly abstruse, are in fact precise and straightforward.

The colours or 'tinctures' of a shield are classified as two metals and five colours. The two metals are gold (or) and silver (argent), and the five colours red (gules), black (sable), green (vert), blue (azure) and purple (purpure). To eliminate possible confusion in the identification of a shield, the convention was accepted that a colour should never be placed on a colour, nor a metal on a metal. Very few shields, however, had a plain field. If the danger of overlapping was to be eliminated, 'divisions' had to be introduced for sake of variety. The divisions are eight in number, and are best represented diagrammatically.

From the divisions of the shield we come to the 'ordinaries', which are the oldest and most important of the charges on a shield. Once again, there is an exact terminology, generally similar to, and derived from, the descriptions of the principal divisions. Simple forms like these, variously arranged, proved perfectly adequate for the construction of some of the earliest and most beautiful coats of arms. Practical necessity, however, led in the direction of greater complexity. How, for example, were the arms of a son, a brother or a nephew to be distinguished from those of the head of the family? Since the purpose of heraldry was to identify individuals, differences were introduced, known in the case of children as 'marks of cadency':

a. The eldest son, a label.
b. The second son, a crescent.
c. The third son, a molet.
d. The fourth son, a martlet.
e. The fifth son, an amulet.

The evolution of this body of rules begs questions about the degree of control exercised over the adoption and use of arms in the Middle Ages. How was it that two knights did not by accident adopt the same device? On some occasions they did, but on the whole such occurrences were rare. Part of the explanation may lie in the way in which heraldic devices were adopted. Camden observed in the 1580s in an oft-quoted passage how men began 'to bear arms by borrowing from their Lords Arms of whom they held in fee'. He was almost certainly right in his observation. In the fifteenth century the Talbots of Fincham (Norfolk) were using the device six gauntlets, in the order, three, two, one, which clearly followed the arms of the Wauncy family from whom they held their lands. In Cheshire a number of gentry families derived their arms in the same way from the earls of Chester. Arms thus derived from a common root would usually be differentiated adequately enough to prevent overlapping. Then again there were what are known as 'canting' coats of arms, those which involved a pun on the owner's name: the shells of Shelley and the trumpets of Trumpington are two of the best known examples (plate 47).

If overlapping and confusion were generally avoided, it is still unclear who was entitled to bear a coat of arms in the Middle Ages. Contemporaries themselves were perplexed by this. In the 1380s the French writer Honoré Bovet had to admit that the issue was treated satisfactorily in none of the earlier textbooks. One of the books known to Bovet was that of the celebrated jurist Bartolus of Sassoferrato, who came to the conclusion in 1356 that any man could assume arms on his own initiative, but that those granted by a prince were of higher authority than the others. On the other hand, only active knights who used arms for identification on the field would really need them. A stay-at-home knight could manage with a signet ring. Someone of this sort could perhaps sympathize with the predicament of Otto de Maundell, who in 1393 obtained from Richard II confirmation of arms granted to his father because the original letters patent had been lost. From what evidence there is for England it seems that arms could be bestowed by the king (though royal grants are rare) or by earls and barons on their retainers, or could simply be assumed, as Bartolus said, without authority. The consequence, as Nicholas Upton complained in the 1440s, was that many humble men were taking up arms on their own initiative. What caused such freedom to be curtailed was the growing assumption by the fifteenth century that possession of a coat of arms implied the quality of noble birth. Some of the early writers had been conscious that there might be a connection between dignity of blood and a grant of arms by the king. This is certainly the assumption behind the letters patent that Richard II issued in 1389 in favour of John Kingston, saying he would receive him into the estate of gentleman and make him an esquire with the right to bear the arms argent, a chapeau azure with an ostrich feather gules. The knights and esquires, born of noble and gentle blood, felt that their superiority over those of merely free birth was marked by their armigerous status. If armorial bearings were to become a mark of privilege, then it followed that the right to assume them would have to be limited. In England this was done by delegating to the heralds sole responsibility for the granting of arms. The first moves in this direction came in the reign of Henry V (q.v.), when the responsibilities of the heralds were defined. In 1417 the king created the new office of Garter King of Arms, with jurisdiction over the other heralds. A few months later the duke of Clarence published a set of ordinances defining the relations of Garter and the other kings-of-arms and enjoining them all to seek out the noble and gentle men living in their respective provinces, especially those who ought to bear coats of arms in the service of the king. In this ordinance can be discerned the origins of the later system of heralds' visitations.

How did the heralds come to be given these duties? Such evidence as there is suggests that the heralds' earliest duties were connected with the organization of tournaments (q.v.). When a tournament was to be held, heralds were sent far and wide to summon knights to take part, and when the day came they were expected to recognize the combatants and to exercise whatever control they could over the conduct of these often disorderly occasions. Once it was all over, their knowledge of armorial insignia made them the obvious people to ask to draw up a roll of arms celebrating the occasion. Somewhat later the heralds were entrusted with undertaking diplomatic errands, and finally in 1417 they were assigned responsibility for not only identifying but granting coats of arms.

At just this time, as we have seen, the duke of Clarence was seeking to clarify the relative claims to precedence of the various officers of arms. He did this by assigning a territorial jurisdiction to each of the senior heralds, known as kings, under the overall primacy of the newly created Garter King of Arms. North of the Trent lay the province of Norroy, and south of it the province of Clarenceux King of Arms. The kings were the principal officers of what was later to become by incorporation in 1484 the College of Arms.

It is worth stressing in conclusion how unique the English system of heraldry is in European historical development. Only in England was the granting of arms delegated by the king to an institution like the College of Arms; and only in England were the claims of the armigerous investigated regularly by heralds' visitations of the shires.

Boutell's Heraldry, revised by C.W. Scott-Giles, London, 1950; A. Wagner, *Heralds and Heraldry in the Middle Ages*, 2nd ed., Oxford, 1956.

HERIOT

Heriot was a death duty paid by a tenant to his

lord (Old English, *here*, army, and *geature*, military equipment). Thus a lord would be entitled to a suit of armour, for example, on the death of one of his military tenants. More usually, however, heriot described the payment due to a lord whenever a villein tenant died and on some estates, also, whenever villein land changed hands between tenants. The heir would be expected to hand over the best beast or chattel to the lord, and the second best beast to the parson as a mortuary payment. By the thirteenth century liability for such payments as heriot and merchet (q.v.) was one of the distinguishing marks of villein (i.e. unfree) status. After the Black Death (q.v.), when the position of the tenantry was much improved, villeins struggled to shake off these burdens, and heriot often gave way to an agreed money payment that soon became incorporated within rent.

HERLAND, HUGH

Medieval England excelled above all in the art of carpentry. Some of the finest medieval woodwork was the creation of three men who successively held the office of king's carpenter in the fourteenth century – William Hurley (d. 1345) and William and Hugh Herland. Hugh was probably born in about 1330. By 1366 he had been in royal employment for some time because in that year he received a grant of 10 marks (£6 13s 4d) in recognition of his long service. In 1383 he retired on the grounds that he was getting old, but was back at his job again in the 1390s when Richard II (q.v.) commissioned him to design the roof for Westminster Hall. Herland, like most of the master craftsmen in the king's pay, also did part-time work for other clients, most notably in his case for William of Wykeham, bishop of Winchester (q.v.), with whom he dined several times in the 1390s. It may well have been his work on the chapel of the bishop's new college at Winchester which persuaded Richard to invite him to crown the newly rebuilt Westminster Hall with a magnificent timber roof. This roof was to be his masterpiece. It was the earliest large-scale design of hammer-beam construction in England, and measures 240ft in length and 70ft across.

Herland died in 1405. He is very likely the *carpentarius* whose kneeling figure appears in the east window of Winchester College Chapel, alongside those of two men he must have known, William Wynford (q.v.), Wykeham's architect, and Simon Membury, his clerk of the works.

HOSPITALS

Medieval hospitals were very different in character from their modern counterparts. They were almost always religious institutions, either part of a monastery or run by clergy on behalf of pious layfolk. Their function was different too. They cared not so much for the very ill as for the aged and infirm and those who could not afford medical treatment: they were more in the character of modern almshouses. Special hospitals were set up for the isolation of lepers.

Well over 750 hospital establishments were founded in England in the Middle Ages. This high number owed much to the keenness of founders and benefactors to arrange for the performance of good works to assist in the salvation of their souls. A number of well endowed hospitals, such as that at Ewelme (Oxon), founded by William de la Pole, duke of Suffolk, in 1437, were conceived as part of chantry foundations. The inmates were required to take part in a ceaseless round of intercession for the souls of the founder and his kin. The attractive fifteenth-century buildings of Ewelme survive almost unaltered. Other fine medieval hospital buildings can be seen at the Great Hospital, Norwich (founded 1249), where the great 200ft-long infirmary hall survives.

N. Orme and M. Webster, *The English Medieval Hospital, 1070-1570*, New Haven and London, 1995.

HUMPHREY, DUKE OF GLOUCESTER

Soldier, political adventurer and patron of learning, Duke Humphrey was one of the most significant and versatile figures of fifteenth century England.

The youngest son of the future Henry IV (q.v.), Humphrey was born in 1391. When his elder brother, Henry V (q.v.), died in 1422, leaving a nine-month old child as his heir, he claimed the office and title of Protector of the Realm, citing as his authority a codicil added to the late king's will. Such bold pretensions were not well received by the lords of the council, who chose instead to divide the powers of government between Humphrey and his brother, John, duke of Bedford. Significantly, one of Humphrey's critics on this occasion was Bishop Beaufort (q.v.), the man destined to be his lifelong rival and adversary. The differences between the two were both personal and political. Beaufort was judicious, Duke Humphrey impetuous. Beaufort believed in extricating England as honourably as possible from the war in France, Duke Humphrey in prosecuting the war vigorously and in defending English maritime interests in the Channel. Humphrey could argue a good case for his views, but confidence in his judgement was weakened by the failure of his expedition in 1424–5 to recover the inheritance of his wife, Jacqueline of Hainault. Jacqueline had already been married to John, duke of Brabant, but Humphrey claimed the contract to be invalid. He lost the argument, and afterwards married Eleanor Cobham, one of Jacqueline's ladies-in-waiting. For all his impulsiveness, however, Gloucester was a force to be reckoned with, as the support he enjoyed in the country balanced, if it did not outweigh, his unpopularity at court. Henry VI (q.v.) was clearly suspicious of him. In 1447 he summoned him to a parliament at Bury St Edmund's, and had him arrested. He died a few days later (23 February) under circumstances that suggested foul play.

Among the many mourners must have been the chancellor and scholars of the University of Oxford. Over the years the university had benefited much from the duke's generosity in gifts of books and manuscripts, and it was to house these that they built another storey over the Divinity School known to this day as 'Duke Humfrey's Library'. History, science and rhetoric were among the duke's special interests, but the books which he donated included works on theology and the classics too. Humphrey is supposed to have been no less devoted to pleasures of the flesh, but it is as a sponsor in England of the new learning of the Renaissance that he best deserves to be remembered. He was buried in St Albans Abbey, where his chantry chapel can still be seen.

K.H. Vickers, *Humphrey, Duke of Gloucester*, London, 1907.

HUNDRED

The hundred (or its alias in the Danelaw, the wapentake) first emerged as the main administrative unit below the shire in the tenth century. Its two principal officers were the bailiff, who served writs on behalf of the sheriff, and the constable, who was responsible for the hue and cry. According to ancient custom, the hundred court met every four weeks, when those who attended would transact a wide range of minor administrative and judicial business. By the later Middle Ages the court met less often because by then its importance lay not so much in the business actually determined before it as in the drawing up of indictments which would be heard later before a session of the JPs or the king's justices. The empanelling of juries from the hundreds was the standard means by which thirteenth- and fourteenth-century governments collected the information they needed. Rarely was the crown's appetite for information demonstrated more dramatically than in the enquiries launched by Edward I (q.v.) when he returned from crusade (q.v.) in 1274. Commissioners were appointed in each county to investigate allegations of corruption and malpractice, and they did this by putting a series of questions, or 'articles', to the hundred juries who came before them. The replies, submitted in writing and known to us today as the Hundred Rolls, were lengthy and detailed enough to convince Edward that reforms were needed, and over the next ten years the Statutes of Westminster I (1275), Gloucester (1278), and Westminster II (1285) were published to rectify the encroachments and injustices uncovered.

H. Cam, *The Hundred and the Hundred Rolls*, London, reprinted 1963.

HUNDRED YEARS WAR

The term 'Hundred Years War' describes the period of Anglo-French hostilities which opened with Philip VI's confiscation of Gascony (q.v.) on 24 May 1337 and ended with the final expulsion of the English from France (except Calais) in 1453. Although the period lasted for more than a hundred years, and was by no means one of continuous war, it nonetheless had a coherence of its own. The contest was not about the feudal status of Gascony, as previous Anglo-French conflicts had been; rather, it was chiefly about the English king's claim to the crown of France.

The causes of the war were complex. Long before the claim to the crown of France became an issue, the status of Gascony was a recurrent source of tension with the French kings. Gascony (or Aquitaine) had come to the English crown by Henry II's marriage to Eleanor of Aquitaine, the heiress of the duchy. In the twelfth century Gascony had been an allod: it was effectively independent. In 1259, however, by the Treaty of Paris, Henry III

(q.v.) submitted to become a vassal of the king of France, from whom he was to hold Gascony as a fief in return for the performance of liege homage. The assumption behind any feudal relationship was that the interests of lord and vassal were identical. But those of the king of France and his vassal in Gascony were not. So successive French kings engaged in undermining the authority of the English, in particular by hearing appeals from aggrieved Gascons who wanted to overturn judgements given in the ducal court at Bordeaux. If goodwill had existed on both sides, the feudal relationship could have been made to work, but as the interests of the two kings diverged, goodwill evaporated. In the peace negotiations of 1359–60, therefore, the English demanded that Gascony be held in full sovereignty.

An issue that increasingly complicated matters in the fourteenth century was the French determination to link the Gascon question with a settlement of the long-standing Anglo-Scottish dispute. Ever since Edward I had begun subduing the northern kingdom in the 1290s, the Scots had turned to France for help, and by the Treaty of Corbeil (1327) they were committed to intervening on the French side in the event of any future Anglo-French conflict. In May 1334 David Bruce, driven from power in Scotland (q.v.) by Edward III, took refuge in France, where he was welcomed by Philip VI and allowed to set up court. Thereafter the French insisted that there could be no settlement in Gascony without a concomitant settlement in Scotland. And when in 1336 Philip moved what had been intended to be a crusading fleet from the Mediterranean to the Channel, Edward had good reason to fear that an invasion of England was imminent. His own invasion of the Low Countries in 1338 may well have been undertaken to head off that eventuality.

The third factor that contributed to the outbreak of the war was Edward's claim to the crown of France. Edward assumed the title and arms of king of France at a ceremony in Ghent market place on 26 January 1340. His claim, although late in coming, was well founded. In 1328 Charles IV, the last in the direct line of the Capetians, had died childless. His nearest heir in blood was his sister Isabella, widow of Edward II of England. The French council, however, had awarded the crown to Charles's cousin, Philip of Valois, who became Philip VI. In 1328 Edward had been too young to enter a claim himself. A decade later, however, he made good his omission. His motives were very likely mixed. He may have genuinely believed himself to be the rightful French king: there is evidence that he saw the dispute as a legal one. Alternatively, he may have conceived the claim as a bargaining counter to be discarded when necessary in favour of a more tangible concession – for example, possession of Gascony in full sovereignty. Edward did eventually surrender his claim for this in 1360. A third possibility is that he was thinking of diplomacy. In diplomatic terms, the claim offered him one great advantage. It cut through all the technical legal arguments about Gascony. The dispute with the French king was lifted to a higher plane. Edward could invest himself with legitimacy. He could claim the allegiance of vassals himself.

After a lengthy round of diplomatic preliminaries, hostilities were initiated in 1338, when Edward transported himself and his army to Flanders. His strategy was the time-honoured one, practised long before by King John in 1214 and by Edward I in the 1290s, of the mobilization of a grand Low Countries and German coalition. It all turned out to be wildly overambitious. The local princes took the pensions Edward offered but declined to move. All through the winter and spring of 1338–9 the king was condemned to idleness. When in September he finally marched into the Cambresis he was abandoned by the count of Hainault, and such remaining hopes

of success as he had were dashed by the refusal of the French to meet him in open battle. The first, inconclusive phase of the war was terminated by the truce of Esplechin (25 September 1340). When Edward returned to England, he had little to show for his efforts apart from the naval victory off Sluys on Midsummer Day 1340.

In the 1340s Edward reviewed his strategy. Abandoning the idea of a frontal attack from the north-east, he decided instead to launch a simultaneous series of assaults from bases on the French periphery. Gascony itself, although much shrunken by the 1340s, gave him one such foothold. Brittany provided another. In Brittany a bitter succession dispute between Charles of Blois and John de Montfort, who held the English earldom of Richmond, provided Edward with the opportunity to intervene on the latter's behalf in return for recognition as king of France. Elsewhere in France, Edward was able to draw on the assistance of such malcontents as the Norman lord, Godfrey d'Harcourt, and Charles the Bad, king of Navarre. The essence of the new strategy lay in exploiting the resentments felt by the provincial nobility against the centralizing policies of the Capetian and Valois monarchs. The Hundred Years War became a French civil war.

Over the next two decades Edward and his commanders launched a series of attacks on France from their bases in Gascony, Brittany and Normandy. Their general aim was to divide and distract the French forces, so that the latter hardly knew whence to expect the next attack. In the summer of 1346 Edward fielded two substantial armies, one under himself in Normandy and the other under Henry of Grosmont in Gascony. Philip and his commanders decided to concentrate on repelling Edward's own force. In mid-August the king sacked the town of Caen. Afterwards he marched eastwards, and Philip forced him to give battle at Crécy (q.v.). The result was a crushing English victory, one of the most remarkable of the age. Ten years later, Edward employed broadly the same strategy again. On this occasion Henry of Grosmont was deployed in the north, and the king's son, Edward, the Black Prince (q.v.) in the south. On 19 September 1356 the prince scored a decisive victory over the French at Poitiers, even capturing King John himself. Edward now saw the crown as within his grasp. In 1359 he headed an expedition which he thought would culminate in his coronation at Rheims Cathedral. Rheims, however, resisted assault, and at Brétigny in the following spring Edward was obliged to come to terms. The agreement reached there, subsequently ratified at Calais, granted Edward an enlarged Aquitaine in full sovereignty in return for surrendering his claim to the throne.

The Brétigny settlement, though arguably giving Edward less than he had wanted, marked, for the English, the end of the most successful period of the war in the fourteenth century. When hostilities were reopened in 1369, in the years of Edward's decline, the advantage in leadership had passed to the French. Gradually, the English gains were whittled away until only the Gascon coastal strip was left. In the 1370s the English decided to reopen negotiations. Twenty years later, a draft peace treaty was agreed, in which the English finally surrendered their claim to hold Gascony in full sovereignty. The treaty failed to win parliamentary approval, however, and in 1396 a twenty-eight-year truce was agreed instead, sealed by a marriage alliance between Richard II and Isabella, the six-year-old daughter of the French king Charles VI.

In the fifteenth century the outbreak of a bitter civil war in France gave the English the opportunity to reopen the struggle. With Charles VI mentally incapable, two competing factions, the Armagnacs and the Burgundians, struggled for control of the state. In 1413 the new English king, Henry V (q.v.), renewed the claim to the French crown, negotiating with both parties simulta-

neously. When his grossly extravagant demands were, as he expected, rejected, he landed at the mouth of the Seine, besieged the port of Harfleur and after capturing the town embarked on a *chevauchée* to Calais. Near Agincourt, in the Pas de Calais (25 October 1415), he was forced to give battle and, although heavily outnumbered, won a justly famous victory over his enemy. In 1417 he led a new expedition to France and began the systematic conquest and settlement of Normandy. The continuing divisions among the French played into his hands. In September 1419 the Armagnacs murdered the duke of Burgundy at Montereau-sur-Yonne. In consequence, the Burgundian party were driven into the arms of the English. By a settlement with Charles VI at Troyes in May 1420 the Dauphin was disinherited, and Henry recognized as heir to the crown of France.

Charles VI died only a couple of years later in 1422. Henry himself had died two months before. The heir to the dual monarchy was thus Henry's son, a nine-month-old boy, Henry VI (q.v.). For the next thirteen years, during the king's minority, the conduct of affairs in France lay in the capable hands of John, duke of Bedford, who appreciated that continued success depended on the Anglo-Burgundian alliance. So long as the Burgundians maintained their quarrel with the Dauphin, now Charles VII, the English were safe. But Philip, the new duke, could not ignore the revival in Charles's fortunes following Joan's relief of Orléans. If he wanted to retain any influence in French affairs, he would have to come to terms with his kinsman. At the Congress of Arras in 1435, not unexpectedly, he changed sides. The loss of the Burgundian alliance and the collapse in morale under the incompetent Henry VI sealed the fate of the English in France. What is surprising is not so much that the French recovered their strength but that they took so long to do so. Normandy fell in 1450 and

Gascony in the next year. John Talbot, the famous war veteran, tried to stage a comeback in 1452 by leading an army to Gascony in support of a local uprising; but at Castillon on 17 July 1453 he was defeated and killed. This setback really did mark the end. Only Calais was left.

The French monarchy, whose abasement had given the English their opportunity, recovered because it became symbolic of the national will to expel the invader. In the demands made by Charles and his ministers for taxation and service were laid the foundations of the *ancien régime*. No peace treaty followed the conclusion of hostilities. The French did not need one; and the English could not make one. It was not until 1802 in the Treaty of Amiens that an English king in the person of George III finally surrendered his title to the crown of France.

C.T. Allmand, *The Hundred Years War. England and France at War, c.1300–c.1450*, Cambridge, 1988; A. Curry, *The Hundred Years War*, Basingstoke, 1993.

I

IMPEACHMENT

The idea of a prosecution in parliament (q.v.) by the lower house before the upper emerged for the first time in the 'Good Parliament' of 1376 when the Commons, led by their Speaker, Sir Peter de la Mare, were seeking the removal of a group of Edward III's ministers. The Commons decided to bring a list of charges against the ministers, first and foremost against the chamberlain, Sir William Latimer. When Latimer asked who was accusing him, de la Mare, speaking on behalf of the Commons, said that they would maintain the charges together. This was the essence of impeachment: the Commons, acting in the king's name, assuming the role of a community of accusers. In proceeding in this way, de la Mare and his friends had fashioned a useful parliamentary instrument for putting unpopular ministers on trial. They used it again to prosecute Michael de la Pole, the chancellor, in 1386. However, its future value for this purpose was effectively undermined by the ruling of the judges in 1387, when questioned by Richard II (q.v.), that ministers and justices could not be put on trial by the Lords and Commons without the king's assent. After an unsuccessful revival in 1450 against the duke of Suffolk, impeachment lay dormant until the seventeenth century, when it was resurrected in James I's reign to bring Sir Giles Mompesson to trial.

INDUSTRY

Although the majority of England's medieval population worked on the land, the needs of society were sufficiently varied and sophisticated to stimulate the growth of a modest industrial sector.

The industry which developed furthest along capitalistic lines based on the division of labour was clothmaking. In the thirteenth century the industry was centred chiefly in the old-established towns of eastern England: Beverley, York, Lincoln and Northampton. A major advantage which it enjoyed was an ample supply of wool from the sheep flocks for which England was famous. Oddly enough, however, the cloth towns lay at some distance from the main wool-producing areas, which were over in Herefordshire, the Cotswolds and on the Pennines.

The first stage in the manufacture of cloth was sorting, because the mixture of different qualities of wool in a single cloth was forbidden. Next came carding or combing, the purpose of which was to make the wool ready for spinning into yarn. Spinning itself was traditionally done by women. The yarn was then ready to be woven into cloth. For this operation a horizontal, flat-bed loom was used, at one end of which was the warp beam and at the other a roller onto which each section of finished cloth was wound. The weaver operated his loom by using pedals to raise the lower alternate warp threads, at the same time as passing the shuttle with the weft threads across them from one side to the other. Next, the raw cloth had to be fulled – in other words, thickened – by being beaten in troughs flowing with water and fuller's earth. The latter was an absorbent form of earth found in deposits at Nutfield and Reigate in Surrey. The cloth would then be stretched back to its original shape and passed onto the finishers whose business it was to draw all the loose fibres by using teazles. By now it was ready for dyeing, a process which involved both colouring the raw material and fixing it. Madder was used for scarlet, vermilion for bright red, saffron for yellow and woad for blue. The woad plant had been grown in this country at least from Saxon times, but by the late Middle Ages the dyers were finding themselves ever more reliant for this, as for other dyes, on imports from abroad. Whatever colour was chosen, it was fixed by a mordant, usually alum for scarlet and potash for other colours. All that remained, then, once the cloth had dried, was for it to be packed and sent off to market. The standard broadcloth woven in England by these methods was 24 yards long and 1½-2 yards wide.

The cloth trade was probably medieval England's biggest industrial employer. One estimate is that it gave jobs to some 15,000 people in 1400 – although this statement needs to be qualified by saying that some of those would only have worked part-time. Cloth production was also a long and complex business. That very complexity soon encouraged the growth of specialization, to the extent that by the thirteenth century each stage of the process was performed by artisans skilled in their own craft. Of these, the men who emerged as the most powerful were the dyers, because the necessity of importing dye materials from abroad gave them international trading links. In many of the biggest cloth towns the dyers took on the character of

mercantile entrepreneurs controlling not only the local production of cloth but also the marketing of it. The weavers and fullers were prepared to put up with the dyers' dominance only for so long. In the thirteenth century they responded by forming themselves into guilds (q.v.). But the very strengthening of their position encouraged the dyers to transfer their custom to textile workers in the countryside, who could be paid less. As imports from Flanders grew in volume in the thirteenth century, it became all the more important for them to cut their costs. The erection of fulling mills on country streams, which historians once considered so important, was therefore less a cause than a consequence of the general decline of urban textile making.

Despite these setbacks, the cloth industry survived to flourish another day. But when it experienced a revival, as it did under the stimulus of providing cheap clothing for the armies of Edward I and Edward III, its geography looked very different from before. Some of the old-established manufacturing towns, like Salisbury, were still flourishing, but it was the newer centres that were meeting the mass demand for cheaper cloths. First and foremost, there were the West Country centres – Stroud and Cirencester in Gloucestershire, Bradford and Castle Combe in Wiltshire, and Frome in Somerset. But there were also significant centres in East Anglia – Sudbury, Lavenham, Worsted and other villages, whose late medieval prosperity is attested by the magnificence of their parish churches.

If we turn to other medieval trades, we find that the numbers employed were fewer, and the methods involved usually less sophisticated. One exception was glazing. The glaziers' trade did not employ great numbers but it did require a measure of specialization. Glass making was carried on at Chiddingfold in Surrey. It involved taking sand, lime and potash and melting them in a clay pot in a furnace. Glass painting, on the other hand, was a quite separate process carried on in the workshop of a master glazier at somewhere like London, Norwich, Coventry or York (q.v. STAINED GLASS). Although armorial windows became very popular in upper-class houses in the late Middle Ages, the main demand for painted glass came, as it always had, from the Church. Bell founding was another industry that flourished under ecclesiastical patronage. Richard Tunnoc, goldsmith and bell-founder of York, was so proud of his trade that he donated the so-called 'bell-founder's Window', in the north aisle of York Minster (*c.*1320). This depicts various stages in the craft of bell making. In one panel, the master and two assistants are shown casting the bell, and in another Tunnoc and an assistant either polishing or tuning it.

Another significant industry was metalworking generally. In the thirteenth and fourteenth centuries the iron and metal trades may very likely have employed more men in the Midlands city of Coventry than textiles did. The supply of iron came from the Forest of Dean, which contained the most extensive mines in medieval England. By the fifteenth century, however, the Dean mines were being matched by the Wealden workings in Kent and Sussex which supplied the London market. Tin, another component in bell founding, came from Devon and Cornwall. Since 1198 the tin-miners of these counties had been organized under the aegis of the Stanneries Court, which guaranteed them immunity from villein (q.v.) dues and exemption from normal taxation. Instead, the crown levied a due on all tin produced. It is hard to be certain about levels of tin production in the Middle Ages. However, we know that in the early fourteenth century, a period of unusually high production, between 560,000 and 817,000 pounds of tin were being presented each year to be taxed.

For warmth in their homes people relied on charcoal and wood. In the north-east of England the coal mines that had lain idle since the departure of the Romans were brought back into use in the twelfth century, but mainly to supply the kilns that were used for lime-burning, brewing and baking. Coal was apparently not popular as a heating fuel, at least not with the Londoners who complained in 1307 that it was infecting and corrupting the air. There is no evidence that coal-mining in the Middle Ages was a highly capitalized activity, and it was presumably only the seams close to the surface that were exploited. All the same, enough coal was extracted to bring prosperity to late-medieval Newcastle-on-Tyne, which was the centre of the coastal carrying trade.

Finally, mention should be made of the salt trade. In the Middle Ages salt was the essential preservative. Along the east coast of England it was produced by the process of evaporation from seawater; inland it was extracted from the brine springs of Droitwich (Worcs) and Nantwich (Cheshire). In the early Middle Ages England was probably self-sufficient in the commodity, indeed a net exporter, but by the fourteenth century was reliant on imports from the Bay of Bourgneuf area of western France.

See also BUILDING

English Medieval Industries, ed. J. Blair and N. Ramsay, London, 1991.

IRELAND

Medieval Ireland had many of the characteristics of a colonial society. The majority of the native population were of Gaelic blood, but political overlordship was exercised by the English. Politically, Ireland was fragmented. While English settler lords were dominant in the east, native rulers, or 'kings', held sway elsewhere.

Between the sixth and the eighth centuries the Irish, who had developed a highly sophisticated local culture, had been instrumental in spreading Christianity in England and north-west Europe. Irish missionaries had travelled as far as Germany. From the ninth century, however, this delicate culture decayed. Many of the monasteries were ravaged by war. Underdevelopment took its toll. While Viking colonies were established on the eastern seaboard at towns like Dublin and Waterford, there was little development inland. Economically, Ireland began to lag behind England.

The later twelfth century saw the establishment of the Anglo-Norman lordship. The background to the settlement lay in the rivalries of the native princes. In 1152 Dermot McMurrough, king of Leinster, had abducted Devorgilla, wife of Tiernan O'Rourke of Breifne in Meath. Although Devorgilla soon returned to her husband, Tiernan was determined to gain revenge, and in 1166 he allied with Rory O'Conor, the 'high king', to drive his rival out. Dermot turned to Henry II of England (q.v.) for assistance. The latter was not prepared to intervene himself, but allowed the Irishman to enlist the support of members of his baronage. Among the first to go, in 1169, were Robert FitzStephen and Maurice FitzGerald. However, the largest contingent to answer Dermot's call was that led by Richard de Clare, earl of Pembroke, known to history as 'Strongbow'. By the end of 1170 Strongbow had taken Dublin and Waterford. He married Dermot's daughter Eva, and on her father's death in 1171 succeeded to the kingdom of Leinster. The string of successes proved too much for Henry II. Concerned that the adventurers might become too powerful, he crossed to Ireland in person in 1171 to secure the submission of both the new settlers and the native princes. 'Strongbow' had to surrender Dublin to the king; but he was re-enfeoffed with the rest of Leinster. Thus he could consider himself well satisfied.

While in Ireland, Henry established the rudiments of a national administration in Dublin. In the next generation his son King John (q.v.), who visited Ireland in person, was responsible for putting the Anglo-Norman colony on a firmer basis. The new administrative structures were simple. The crown was represented by a justiciar – or lieutenant, as he was known by the fourteenth century. The rest of the Irish government mirrored its counterpart in England (q.v. GOVERNMENT). There was a council, which advised the justiciar or lieutenant, a chancery, which wrote his letters, and an exchequer, which collected the revenues. By the thirteenth century there was also a parliament, to which in due course (though later than in England) representatives of the Commons were summoned.

If the future of the Anglo-Irish colony looked promising when John returned to England in 1210, that appearance was deceptive. The 'conquest' of Ireland had little or nothing in common with the conquest of England in 1066. When Harold fell at Hastings, England fell with him. But Ireland had not one king but many, and these were all still in power. Moreover, the Norman conquest of England was a state-directed enterprise. The Anglo-Norman settlement of Ireland was a private affair, and largely allowed to remain as such. By the mid-thirteenth century, the momentum that had earlier driven the settlement forward was beginning to falter. Ireland, a century after Strongbow's visit, remained only half-conquered. The task of governing Ireland involved the justiciar and his staff in a delicate exercise of compromise, negotiation and balance. The Dublin government had to recognize the severe constraints on its power.

By the early fourteenth century English-ruled Ireland was in crisis. An invasion by Robert Bruce's brother Edward in 1315, undertaken with the aim of unsettling the English, had stimulated a major Gaelic revival. By the 1350s there was a remarkable upsurge of Gaelic literature and the Gaelic sense of identity became sharper. In the face of these developments, many of the English aristocracy left the province for the mainland, while others allowed their identity to merge with that of the Irish. The Dublin administration, in alarm, reacted by passing the Kilkenny statutes (1366), which prohibited the settler population from marrying into the native Irish or adopting their way of life. The statutes, although draconian-sounding, were more defensive than aggressive. All the same, the government at Westminster made a fresh attempt to buttress the English position. In 1361 Edward III (q.v.) sent his son Lionel of Clarence to Dublin as lieutenant. Despite the many advantages which he brought to the job – for example, his marriage to the heiress of the earldom of Ulster – Clarence failed to make much headway before returning to England in 1366. Undeterred, Edward tried again three years later. In 1369 he appointed William of Windsor as lieutenant, with £20,000 to spend on supporting the Irish administration. Generous though the subsidy was, it proved insufficient, and Windsor's aggressive efforts to raise money from the Irish aroused such opposition that he was recalled in 1371. By this time, the reopening of the Hundred Years War (q.v.) prevented the English government from undertaking any fresh initiatives, and the problems of Ireland were relegated to the background.

The most serious attempt to address the problems of Ireland in the late Middle Ages was made in the next reign, that of Richard II (q.v.). The long truce negotiated with France in 1389 allowed Richard to make the first personal royal intervention in Irish affairs since John's two centuries before. In 1394 the king led a major expedition to Ireland, at the conclusion of which he received the submission of the Gaelic chiefs.

By making the chiefs his vassals Richard elevated them in status and gave them a vested interest in his rule. All the same, the settlement quickly unravelled after his departure. The Irish chiefs quarrelled with the English over rights to land and in 1399 Richard had to cross to Ireland again. This visit, however, was cut short by Bolingbroke's arrival in England. Richard returned precipitately to England, and Ireland was left in confusion.

The new government of Henry IV (q.v.) lacked both the resources and the commitment to uphold the Ricardian settlement. In the fifteenth century Ireland was left largely to its own devices. It played some role in English affairs. In the struggles between Lancaster and York Ireland lent its support to York, who held large estates there, inherited from his Mortimer ancestors. After the accession of Henry Tudor in 1485 Ireland became, almost literally, the home of lost causes. In 1487 Lambert Simnel made Ireland the base for his attempt on the throne. A few years later in 1491 Perkin Warbeck arrived in Cork claiming to be Richard, duke of York. It was the fear that the Irish parliament might lend its support to these pretenders that lay behind the passing in 1494 of a law which allowed the Dublin assembly only to pass such measures as had first been approved by the king and council in England. This famous law perpetuates the name of Sir Edward Poynings, who was deputy lieutenant at the time. The subordination to the authority of Westminster which the law created was to last for three centuries until 1783.

A.J. Otway-Ruthven, *A History of Medieval Ireland*, London, 1968; *A New History of Ireland, II. Medieval Ireland, 1169–1534*, ed. A. Cosgrove, Oxford, 1987.

J

JEWS

In the Middle Ages, when usury was condemned by the Church, moneylending was conducted mainly by the Jews. That is not to say that there were no Christian moneylenders. On the contrary, Henry II (q.v.) borrowed heavily from William Cade of St Omer, a usurer who had agents in every part of western Europe. In England by the thirteenth century Italian lenders were very active. Nonetheless, between the eleventh and the thirteenth centuries the Jewish community in England was more prominent than it was across the Channel in France.

The Jews had been introduced into England after the Norman Conquest. Although free in law, they technically belonged to the king, who commended them to the protection of the keepers of his castles. In the reign of Henry I (1100–35) Jews were resident only in London, but in the civil war of Stephen's reign a process of dispersal took place. By the early years of Henry II's reign communities were established at Norwich, Lincoln, Cambridge, Thetford, Northampton, Oxford and in Gloucestershire, Wiltshire and Hampshire. In 1221 there were recognized communities in seventeen of the larger towns – a recognized community being one which possessed an archa, or office for the registration of Jewish bonds.

It would be wrong to suppose that the Jews derived their entire livelihood from usury. If

Aaron of Lincoln (d.1186) and Jurnet of Norwich (d.c.1197) had cash to lend, it was because they had already amassed a fortune from trade (though virtually nothing is known of which trades they engaged in). But once they had acquired enough capital, they used this to earn more. In the thirteenth century their clients ranged from monasteries in need of money to improve their buildings to hard-up knights reduced to paying off one debt by contracting another. If a borrower entered into a bond for a capital sum, he could pledge either land or moveable property as security. Should he then default in payment, the Jewish creditor would simply sell the moveables or make arrangements for the disposal of the land. Being a town dweller, the Jew did not usually enter into possession himself. One consequence, accordingly, of the failure of improvident borrowers to acquit themselves was the growth of an active market in encumbered estates, which enabled a skilful speculator like Bishop Walter de Merton in the 1260s to accumulate the properties that went to endow his college in Oxford.

Their trade as moneylenders did not necessarily make the Jews unpopular. A few of them were on close, though perhaps not intimate, terms with the great. The reign of Henry II (q.v.) was their heyday. After Henry's death and the accession of Richard the Lion Heart (q.v.) the rise of crusading fervour bred a wave of anti-semitic hysteria. In 1190 the Jewish community at York was massacred. Hostility towards the Jews gathered strength again in the baronial wars of the following century. In 1264 there were pogroms in London and other towns. In November 1278, after peace had returned, Jews all over England were arrested on suspicion of coin-clipping. The end finally came in 1290 when Edward I (q.v.) expelled them.

Why should the king turn against a community which his ancestors had striven for so long to protect? One possibility is that he was coming to the relief of hard-pressed landowners driven by necessity into dependence on the moneylenders. This possibility is unlikely, however, since the king took over the bonds himself: the debtors simply exchanged one creditor for another. In reality, the expulsion was a straightforward act of plunder. By 1290 the Jewish community, which had once numbered 3,000 or so, was reduced in both numbers and wealth. Edward had no need of their money-lending facilities. Italian bankers could provide him with extensive credit on the security of parliamentary taxation (q.v.). The Jews no longer played a significant role in the national economy. So he could take what was left of their wealth and expel them.

H.G. Richardson, *The English Jewry under the Angevin Kings*, London, 1960; R. Mundill, *England's Jewish Solution, 1262–1290: Experiment and Expulsion*, Cambridge, 1998.

JOHN

King John's notoriety hardly does justice either to the complexity of his personality or to the scale of the political problems he faced. Although a cruel and untrustworthy ruler, he was an efficient administrator who came up with intelligent responses to the crisis of the Angevin monarchy.

Born in 1167, probably at Oxford, John was the youngest and favourite son of Henry II (q.v.). When his three brothers had been given a landed endowment, John still lacked any of his own – hence his nickname, John Lackland. In 1172 his father decided to give him the castles of Chinon, Mirebeau and Loudon. The scheme, however, ran into opposition from John's elder brother Richard (q.v.), who claimed the castles as his own, and civil war followed. A few years later Henry granted Ireland (q.v.) to John. The grant did not satisfy his ambitions, however, and by the time of his father's death in 1189 he had joined Richard in rebellion. In Richard's own reign he schemed to further his own interests. He was a man who set little store by loyalty.

When news was received of Richard's death in 1199, it was unclear who the next king would be. Richard had designated John, but Arthur, the son of John's elder brother Geoffrey, had a good claim. John for once acted decisively, seizing the Angevin treasure at Chinon and sailing for England, where he was crowned on 27 May. The hapless Arthur was rounded up in 1202, and died in captivity a year or two later. There were widespread and justified suspicions that Arthur had been murdered; certainly many of his fellow prisoners had been killed. The distaste which the episode provoked led to a rebellion against John in Normandy, and Philip of France, who had long had the ambition of driving the Angevins from Normandy (q.v.), now moved in for the kill. The Normans' will to resist crumbled and by midsummer 1204 the duchy and its capital had fallen to the French.

The loss of Normandy was a major humiliation for John. Not only did it expose his poor tactical sense; it deprived him of vital resources. For the next ten years he worked hard to get the duchy back. The strategy he employed was an intelligent one, which was to be used by later English kings such as Edward I (q.v.). John aimed to launch an invasion of France from the south-west himself and to build a coalition of allies in Germany and the Low Countries to do likewise from the north-east. The drawback to the scheme was that it was very expensive. John needed to raise large sums of money in taxation. And, unfortunately for him, England was suffering from severe inflation at the time. Simply to keep pace with prices John needed to increase his income proportionately; to pay for his ambitious plans on the continent he had to push his demands still further.

Simultaneously, John was misguided enough to become embroiled in a dispute with the Church. When the archbishopric of Canterbury fell vacant in 1205, John was anxious to secure the election of his counsellor John de Gray, bishop of Norwich. The pope, however – Innocent III – overruled de Gray and insisted on Stephen Langton (q.v.), an Englishman influential in the papal Curia. John was bitterly opposed to Langton and denied him entry to the realm. In 1208 Innocent responded by imposing an interdict: all the churches were closed, and the clergy stopped performing their duties; in 1209 John himself was excommunicated. The interdict caused major disruption in the life of the Church; but a paradoxical side effect was that it eased John's financial problems as he was able to collect the revenues of the Church.

By 1213 John's problems were in danger of multiplying. Innocent, impatient with John's defiance, forged an alliance with King Philip of France, whom he empowered to invade England and depose the king. John, operating on the principle of 'divide and rule', now decided to submit to the Pope, who now became his ally. Philip continued fitting out his invasion fleet nonetheless, and moved it to Damme in Flanders. There it was discovered at anchor by John's fleet and attacked with the loss of 100 ships and many more cut adrift (30 May 1215). Encouraged by this success, John decided in the following year to launch the invasion of France for which he had been so long preparing. But his efforts were to no avail. When he got to south-western France, he was deserted by the local barons. And in the Low Countries, his German allies were defeated so decisively at Bouvines (27 July 1214) that his own hopes were shattered in the bargain.

Even before news of the Bouvines defeat reached England, opposition to John was building up. Since 1212 the king had encountered resistance from the northern lords, who objected to serving abroad, but in the wake of his measures to pay for the campaigning a more general opposition movement built up. By early 1215 full-scale civil war had broken out, and after the fall of London to the rebels in May John was obliged to negotiate. At Runnymede in June he agreed to the famous charter of liberties known as Magna Carta (q.v.). The charter was a kind of peace treaty. But while ending one war it started another; too extreme to satisfy the king, it was too moderate to satisfy the extremists. In the autumn hostilities resumed. John sought release from the Pope from his oath to uphold the charter and was still fighting his opponents when he died at Newark in October 1216.

In many ways John was the most resourceful of the sons of Henry II. He understood administration and did much to rationalize it. He created a precedent, in the thirteenth of 1207, for a system of national taxation (q.v.). And he brought into being the navy that thwarted King Philip's projected invasion. However, he failed in the art of managing men. Too often, he was slippery and untrustworthy.

John's failings help to explain why he was so unpopular in his own day. But they do not properly explain why he has suffered such a bad press. John's problem was that he incurred the ire of the ecclesiastical writers. He had been on the wrong side of a dispute with the Pope and so they got their own back by savaging his reputation. The most vehement of the writers was Roger Wendover of

St Albans. It is Wendover who tells us that John extracted teeth from the Jews, slitted the noses of papal servants and imprisoned Geoffrey of Norwich in a leaden cope. Wendover's epitaph on the king was: 'Foul as it is, hell itself is defiled by the fouler presence of John'. John was certainly no angel, but he appears to have evinced a conventional piety. In his will he asked to be buried in Worcester Cathedral between the shrines of St Oswald and St Wulfstan. He was devoted to the cult of Wulfstan because Wulfstan was reputed to have upheld the royal appointment of bishops. John's tomb at Worcester is the earliest surviving royal effigy in England.

W.L. Warren, *King John*, 2nd ed., New Haven and London, 1997.

JOHN OF SALISBURY

Perhaps the most learned man of his day, John of Salisbury was not only a scholar and writer but a man of affairs too. His modern reputation rests principally on two works, the *Polycraticus* and the *Metalogicon*, both completed in 1159 and dedicated to his friend and patron, Thomas Becket (q.v.), at that time Henry II's chancellor.

All that is known of John's early years is told to us by John himself in an autobiographical chapter in the *Metalogicon*. He was born between 1115 and 1120 at Salisbury. In 1136 he went abroad to continue his studies, drawn to the Hill of St Genevieve in Paris, like so many of his contemporaries, by the reputation of the great Abelard. When Abelard gave up teaching in the following year, John went to the school at Chartres, where the study of classical literature had been revived by such men as Bernard and William of Conches. His years at Chartres were important for his intellectual development, for it was very likely there that he acquired the unaffected Latin style, so unusual for a medieval scholastic, which distinguishes his writing.

In 1140 or 1141 he returned to Paris. By the time he left again in about 1148 he had spent twelve years of his life in study. All this was a more than adequate preparation for the career that he was to pursue in ecclesiastical administration. After attending the Council of Rheims in 1148, he spent the next four years at the papal Curia, where his experiences were to inspire him to write the *Historia Pontificalis*. Then, in 1153, he took advantage of letters of recommendation he had acquired from Bernard of Clairvaux to become the counsellor and secretary of Theobald, Archbishop of Canterbury.

It was while he was at Canterbury that he wrote the two works for which he is chiefly remembered. The first of these, the *Polycraticus*, is a discursive treatise in nine books, five of which deal with the idle vanities that beguile the courtier and the other four with theories of the state. John takes an organic view of society. The commonwealth is likened to a human body in which the priesthood corresponds to the soul, the prince to the head, the judges to the eyes, the soldiers to the hands and the husbandmen to the feet. Written more than half a century before Aristotle's *Politics* became available in the West, the *Polycraticus* is wholly medieval in outlook, and not in the least influenced by the revival of classical ideas that began in the twelfth century. John's other great work, the *Metalogicon*, by contrast, equally medieval though its philosophical preoccupations are, succeeded in breaking new ground. It was the first work to make use in their entirety of Aristotle's philosophical treatises known as the *Organon*.

John's political views determined his attitude to the struggle between Becket (q.v.) and Henry II (q.v.), which he was privileged to observe at close quarters. He believed that human laws could only be derived from the Christian faith; in that case the Church was entitled to have a say in their formulation. Church and state, in other words, were both part of the same commonwealth. Whatever misgivings he may have felt about Becket's handling of the dispute, John had no alternative but to support his stand and to share with him his years of exile. When in 1170 it seemed that a settlement was close and Becket returned, John almost certainly came back with him. He was only a few rooms from him on 29 December 1170 when the archbishop met his death.

In the early 1170s John probably remained at Canterbury. But in 1176 he was elected to the bishopric of Chartres, an office that he held until his death four years later on 25 October 1180. He was buried at the monastery of Josaphat, just outside the city. Less original than the famous Abelard, John was nevertheless a learned and widely read scholar, an accomplished letter-writer and a perceptive commentator on the world around him.

C.C.J. Webb, *John of Salisbury*, London, 1932; *The World of John of Salisbury*, ed. M. Wilks, Oxford, 1984.

JUSTICE

In few areas has the medieval period made a more lasting contribution to modern life than in those of law and judicial administration. The English system of common law is essentially a creation of the Middle Ages.

The foundations of the English legal system were laid in the pre-Conquest period. In Anglo-Saxon times law was mainly unwritten. It took the form of the customs which people knew and accepted, and which were declared when necessary in the folk moot. Law was there to be discovered, not made or created. With the arrival of Christianity in the seventh and eighth centuries, Mediterranean influences began to permeate Saxon society, and kings like Ethelbert of Kent and Ine of Wessex followed the example of the Roman emperors in publishing written law codes.

The coming of Christianity also promoted the idea that new laws could be made, because the institution of Church property created the need for legislation that would have been inconceivable in pagan society. A further twist was given in the ninth and tenth centuries when the tie of lordship gradually superseded that of kinship as the principal bond of society. In the early Middle Ages people thought of the law, and the duty of preserving the peace, as belonging to someone, usually to the person in whose court infringements of that law were punished. Thus the king reserved to his own court cases which he considered to be breaches of his own peace, such as fighting at court, robbery on the highways and obstructing his officials. This category was to be the basis of the 'pleas of the crown' which are encountered later on – namely, those crimes serious enough to be heard by the king's professional justices in the court of King's Bench.

On the eve of the Conquest there was a hierarchy of courts in England, ranging from the king's court at the top, through the shire court, down to the hundred court and the private court of the manorial lord. William the Conqueror took over this system largely as he found it, and made few alterations except to transfer the hearing of spiritual pleas from the shire court to the jurisdiction of the Church. In this move are to be found the origins of the separate Church courts of the later Middle Ages. If the Conqueror tampered little with the existing public courts, he was nonetheless responsible for erecting alongside them a system of feudal justice, based on the courts of the 'honors', to adjudicate pleas arising out of feudal tenure (q.v. FEUDALISM). The settlement in these courts of matters of mutual interest to the tenant-in-chief and the honorial barons who held their lands from him was to form the essence of life in a feudal society for the next hundred years.

The main turning point in English legal history came with the reign of Henry II (q.v.), a period often said to have witnessed a 'great leap forward' in the development of royal justice. The civil war of Stephen's reign presented Henry on his accession with a legacy of violent crime and conflicting claims to land to which he responded by making changes in the law known as 'assizes'. A key innovation in the handling of criminal business was provided by the Assize of Clarendon in 1166, which provided for juries from each of the hundreds (q.v.) to present the names of suspected wrongdoers to the sheriff. This assize can be seen as marking the beginning in England of the idea of the public prosecution of crime, conducted moreover in the peculiarly English form of the 'grand jury' – a system which still lives on in the United States long after it has vanished in its country of origin. Juries were also used in the so-called 'possessory assizes', which rank as Henry II's greatest achievement in the area of civil (as opposed to criminal) jurisdiction. These were legal actions intended to resolve the conflicting claims to land which had built up during the civil war and before, and their novelty lay in the employment for the first time of the returnable writ and the jury of recognition. The Assize of Novel Disseisin can be taken as an example of how these actions worked. A plaintiff recently disseised (i.e., dispossessed) of his land would purchase from the king a writ of Novel Disseisin instructing the sheriff to summon a jury to decide the simple question of whether he had been ejected unjustly and without the judgement of a court. If the answer was yes, the sheriff was obliged to reinstate him. One or two observations need to be made about the implications of these procedures. Firstly, they asked the jury to decide not a question of right but one of fact: had the plaintiff been disseised or not? That made for speedy settlement of the case. Secondly, these writs were obtainable from the king and could be heard only in his courts. The effect of this was to attract before the king's justices a vast and

increasing volume of business which would once have been heard in the honorial courts. If Henry II did not set out intentionally to undermine feudal justice, he made the superiority of royal justice so apparent that the honorial courts of the tenants in-chief went into a slow but definite decline. Thirdly, the royal courts were only open to men of free birth. Those who were unfree – that is, the villeins – were confined to litigating in the court of their lord, which usually meant the manorial court.

The enormous popularity of his new assizes gave Henry II the opportunity to carry out a policy of judicial centralization. He did this by reviving Henry I's policy of sending out the royal justices on periodic visitations, known from a corruption of the Latin word *iter* as 'eyres' (q.v.). From 1166 until their cessation in the early fourteenth century the eyres were the most dramatic manifestation of the king's judicial omnicompetence, welcomed at first for their success in deterring the violent criminals, but later resented for the element of fiscal extortion that entered into their work. By the later thirteenth century the county communities were offering fines to the king in order not to be visited by the eyre justices.

The breakdown of the eyre in the 1320s, although a setback, was by no means a major blow to the judicial and administrative power of the crown because other agencies stepped into its place. Most obviously, there were the two central courts of Common Pleas and King's Bench into which the former 'curia regis' (king's court) had been divided in 1234. In the fourteenth century King's Bench, although normally based at Westminster, undertook periodic visitations of the shires in much the same way as the eyre justices once had. There were also the commissions of oyer and terminer which could empower one or two of the king's justices with a few laymen to hear and determine a specific case. And finally there were the keepers of the peace, or the justices of the peace as they became in 1361, when they acquired the power to pass judgement on, and not just to receive, the indictments brought before them. In the fifteenth century it was the JPs who took over the shire court's position as the centre of social, political and judicial life in the shire. The JPs' quarterly sessions became a major local event.

From the voluminous legal records of medieval England it is possible to learn much about how this system worked in practice. Let us consider what would have happened to a malefactor suspected, say, of larceny in the reign of Edward III (1327–77). Had the malefactor been apprehended in the act, and the coroner (q.v.) called in, the case would have been straightforward: he would have been indicted. But, if he had escaped in possession of stolen goods, and was pursued in vain by the local constable after the hue and cry had been raised, then a number of courses would be open. The plaintiff could, if he or she wished, proceed by way of appeal (q.v.), which would entitle him formally to accuse the suspect in the county court according to certain precisely regulated rules and then offer to support the charge by combat. In fact very few appeals ended in a duel, for there were procedures which allowed the issue to be decided by an inquest jury or terminated by out-of-court settlement. Although appeals were still being heard at the end of the Middle Ages, a more common way of proceeding was by indictment. The offender, suspected of the crime either because he had been witnessed in the act or because he was a notorious malefactor, would have been named either by the hundred jury next time the sheriff made his tourn of the hundred courts or by the keepers of the peace. All medieval crimes fell into the two broad categories of felony and trespass, and under which heading a case of larceny came depended very much on the preference of the jurors. If the malefactor were indicted of a plea of trespass, he would

probably be summoned to appear before the shire court at an appointed date. Had he been caught in the act, the sheriff could detain him in prison pending trial. But if he had been lucky enough to escape – and here was the main weakness in the medieval system – there was no incentive for him to attend in court at all. Under normal circumstances a trial could not proceed in the absence of the accused. In that case, process of outlawry would be invoked entailing the seizure of the accused's goods and chattels until such time as he did appear in court.

If the jurors felt that the larceny case was serious enough to be considered a breach of the king's peace, then the indictment might well go to King's Bench for hearing before the justices in Westminster or in the shire concerned next time a visitation was undertaken. In the central courts, whether King's Bench or Common Pleas, the pleading would be undertaken by the sergeants-at-law. These were the men who would aspire in due course to become judges: the link between bench and bar which has endured to the present day was forged in the Middle Ages, probably before the mid-fourteenth century. The case was then put to the jury – the petty jury, as it was called, to distinguish it from the grand or indictment jury. The use of juries to establish the matter of guilt or innocence gradually replaced the old-fashioned methods of trial by ordeal. But it should not be supposed that medieval jurors were models of impartiality or that they were denied contact with the parties to the dispute as jurors are today. Quite the contrary: both parties were expected to acquaint the jury with their version of events, to 'labour' them, in the language of the day, although not to offer them bribes.

If the jury returned a verdict of guilty on the accused, then he could consider himself distinctly unlucky. In pleas of felony, guilty verdicts were very few. The main reason for this was that conviction for felony automatically carried the death penalty, and jurors were naturally reluctant to condemn a man so long as there was the slightest chance of his innocence. In pleas of trespass, there was commonly no verdict at all. Generally, cases did not come to a conclusion; they just disappeared from the rolls. The lawyers would arrange for adjournments from term to term, usually for procedural reasons, then either the plaintiff or the defendant would give up and settle out of court. The delays and the apparent ineffectiveness of the courts have often been criticized; and certainly they were criticized at the time. But the stituation was not necessarily as dire as it seemed. The aim of medieval dispute settlement was to promote reconciliation between the parties. Litigation in the courts was but one means to this end. Outside the court there was a complementary system of informal justice. This took the form of the structures of conciliation and arbitration – both of these commonly offered as an aspect of lordship. Common-law litigation was often undertaken simply to bring pressure on an opponent to settle out of court. If a case disappeared from the rolls because it was settled in this fashion, it could be seen as a triumph for the system, not a mark of its failure.

F. Pollock and F.W. Maitland, *The History of English Law*, 2nd ed., Cambridge, 2 vols, 1898; A. Harding, *The Law Courts of Medieval England*, London, 1973; P. Brand, *The Origins of the English Legal Profession*, Oxford, 1992; W.L. Warren, *The Governance of Norman and Angevin England, 1086-1272*, London, 1987.

JUSTICIAR

For more than a century the justiciar was the highest officer in England under the crown. The origins of the office are to be found in the early twelfth century when England and Normandy (q.v.), divided after 1087 between the sons of William the Conqueror (q.v.), were reunited by Henry I (q.v.). In the long period of internal peace that followed England had to accustom itself to the periodic absence of the king-duke in Normandy, and Normandy to his periodic absence in England. So how was government to be carried on if the king was away? In England Henry I solved the problem by delegating to someone who could act in his name. After about 1120 that person was Roger, bishop of Salisbury, who is generally reckoned as the first of our justiciars. It is not clear that a successor was appointed to Roger after his arrest by King Stephen (q.v.) in 1139, but when peace was restored by Henry II (q.v.) in the 1150s not one but two co-justiciars were appointed: Robert Beaumont, earl of Leicester, an erstwhile supporter of Stephen's, and Richard de Luci, a member of the knightly class. After Earl Robert's death in 1168, Richard served alone until his retirement ten years later. He was then succeeded by Ranulph Glanvill, the reputed author of the famous treatise on the laws of England.

So long as the king had to divide his time between his English and his continental dominions, a justiciar would continue to be needed. But when Normandy fell to the French in 1204, and the king was henceforth resident in England, the office became unnecessary. In 1234 it was allowed to lapse. After 1258 it experienced a brief revival, however, when Hugh Bigod was appointed by the baronial reformers to investigate the many complaints that were made against Henry III's government.

F.J. West, *The Justiciarship in England, 1066-1232*, Cambridge, 1966.

KEMPE, MARGERY

Controversial mystic and author of the first extant autobiography in English, Margery Kempe (*c.*1378–after 1438) was the daughter of John Brunham, mayor of King's Lynn (Norfolk). Married at the age of twenty to one John Kempe, she suffered a mental breakdown after the birth of her first child and experienced a mystical conversion. Eventually, at her request, her husband released her, and she began a life of travel, visiting shrines both in England and abroad and going as far afield as the Holy Land, Santiago

and, eventually, Danzig. For her fellow pilgrims she was a difficult companion, and her constant weeping inspired many to revile her and to question her orthodoxy. Her autobiography, *The Book of Margery Kempe*, is both a mystical treatise, consisting of the author's visions and conversations with Christ, and a narrative of her life, recording the story of her conversion and pilgrimages. Margery was illiterate and dictated the work to scribes.

The Book of Margery Kempe, ed. B.A.Windeatt, Penguin Books, 1985.

L

LANFRANC

An Italian clerk of legal background, Lanfranc was appointed by William the Conqueror (q.v.) as Archbishop of Canterbury and was responsible for the post-Conquest Normanization of the English Church.

Lanfranc's early career is ill documented. His father was a 'lawman' of Pavia in Italy and the young Lanfranc may initially have pursued legal studies himself. However, in about 1030 he made a break with the past and crossed the Alps to France. Here he travelled for some time before settling at Avranches in Normandy, where he became a schoolmaster. In about 1042 he experienced a religious conversion, and joined Herluin and the band of monks who had recently founded the abbey of Bec. Three years later he became prior. Bec represented a new depature in the history of Norman monasticism. It had been founded by Herluin, a retired knight who, like the Cistercians in a later generation, longed to return to the life of simplicity and seclusion from which he felt that the monks of his own day had strayed. But, however strongly Lanfranc may have been attracted by the ascetic ideal, he also wanted to start teaching again, and he obtained Herluin's permission to open a school at the abbey. In the course of these years at Bec he acquired a formidable reputation as both a teacher and a scholar. Today, he is overshadowed by the fame of his pupil Anselm (q.v.) but it is hard to ignore the word of those contemporaries to whom he was the brilliant star that God had given to lighten Europe's darkness.

In his later years at Bec Lanfranc became drawn into a celebrated dispute with his former master, Berengar of Tours, on the nature of the Eucharist. Berengar had argued that the bread and wine were only symbols of Christ, and that they could not be changed materially into the flesh and blood of His body. Though the doctrine of transubstantiation had not yet been clearly formulated, Berengar's views and the force with which he propounded them caused sufficient alarm for him to be summoned to recant in 1059. He complied, but subsequently repudiated his oath and continued to debate the Eucharist. At this point, Lanfranc brought his forensic powers to bear on the matter in his treatise *The Body and Blood of the Lord*. The argument he put forward, that though their outward appearance remains the same, the bread and wine are converted in their being into the flesh and blood of Christ by ways beyond our comprehension, was to be regarded by his own and subsequent generations as the definitive orthodox reply to Berengar.

By the time he had finished writing the book, in 1063, Lanfranc had been appointed first abbot of Duke William's new foundation of St Stephen's, Caen. He spent the next seven years of his life at this house, until he was summoned to become Archbishop of Canterbury. Apparently he only accepted appointment with reluctance; nonetheless, he turned out to be one of the most outstanding holders of the office. The key to his success lay in his harmonious relations with his friend and patron, King William. The partnership flourished at precisely the time when Pope Gregory VII (1073–85) was calling into question the very right of a lay ruler to intervene in the affairs of the Church. Lanfranc ignored some of the more radical demands of the Pope, while showing in his reforms that he was fully aware of the need to bring English usages into line with those in the rest of western Europe. He held three important synods, at Winchester in 1072 and 1076 and at London in 1075, at which measures were taken against such abuses as simony, clerical marriage and vagrant clerks and monks. As for the monasteries, Lanfranc was limited in his scope of action. The right of appointing bishops and senior abbots was one that the king chose to exercise himself – although no doubt after consultation with his archbishop. Normans or Frenchmen were invariably appointed, among them Lanfranc's own nephew, Paul, to St Albans. The archbishop's influence was most widely felt in two ways: in the letters that he wrote to those who turned to him for advice and in the Monastic Constitutions he composed for Canterbury Cathedral Priory, which were later adopted by at least nine other communities including St Albans, Durham and Westminster.

Lanfranc survived the Conqueror to die on 24 May 1089. What is known about his career leaves unresolved a number of questions. Why did he leave his native Pavia? Why did he then abandon his career as a teacher in favour of the monk's habit at Bec? And how did he come to be such a close friend of Duke William? It is difficult to reconcile the young Lanfranc, the dialectician and wandering scholar, with the pragmatic statesman of later

years. He remains a curiously elusive figure. The truth of the matter may be that, judging by his surviving work, he was never quite the profound scholar that some of his pupils and contemporaries took him to be. His writings, although competent, are marked by a slight superficiality. And his policy as archbishop is characterized by an aloof detachment from the Gregorian reform movement that was to render his kind of personal solution to the problem of Church/state relations obsolete by the time of his death. Arguably his weaknesses as a scholar proved to be his strengths as a politician.

M. Gibson, *Lanfranc of Bec*, Oxford, 1978.

LANGLAND, WILLIAM

Virtually all that is known about William Langland is derived from the autobiographical passages in *Piers Plowman*, the poem that was his life's work. As a boy Langland was provided with some schooling in the Scriptures, at the expense, so he tells us, of his father and some friends. When these friends died, he was left without any patrons. He moved from the West Midlands to London and there sank into the clerical underworld, making such money as he could from saying offices for the souls of the dead in St Paul's and other churches. He could hardly have risen above Minor Orders because on his own admission he kept a wife and daughter.

His experience in life no doubt led him to identify with the poor and downtrodden, whose sufferings he describes with such insight in *Piers Plowman*. The popularity which this poem enjoyed down to the sixteenth century (by which time its dialect was found too difficult) is evidenced by the large number of manuscripts which have survived – no fewer than fifty-one, in three different versions. The earliest, the so-called A-text, was composed in the 1360s. Langland was evidently dissatisfied with this because he rewrote it at greater length in the 1370s in the form known as the B-text. He then subjected it to further revision, so as to achieve clarification of the main theme, in the C-text of around 1387. The poetic form that Langland adopted was alliterative verse. Relying for its effect on the repetition of the initial letter or syllable of a number of words in the line, this was a favourite literary form of the Anglo-Saxons, kept alive in northern and western England in the years after the Conquest to blossom forth again in the fourteenth century (q.v. LANGUAGE). Although it would have been regarded as old-fashioned by a courtly poet like Chaucer (q.v.), alliteration provided a perfect vehicle of expression for Langland's great allegory.

Structurally the poem falls into two halves, 'The Vision of Piers the Ploughman', comprising the first seven books or *passus* of the B-text, and 'The Vision of Do-Well, Do-Better and Do-Best', comprising the last thirteen. The allegory is described and interpreted by Langland's persona, who falls asleep one May morning on the Malvern Hills and dreams of a plain thronged with people going about their worldly business. After the allegorical figure of Lady Mead has been introduced to symbolize the corruption of society caused by love of money, Reason calls on the people to begin the quest for Truth. Piers speaks up, and offers to guide the people to the Mansion of Truth. As remission for his sins, he is given a pardon by Truth, but finds himself tricked by its promise of salvation only to those who do well. Piers now disappears from the poem and the dreamer begins the long search for Do-Well. Two friars suggest that he should turn to Thought and Intelligence, but their answers proving unsatisfactory he consults instead the representatives of Learning, Study, Clergy and Scripture. The poem approaches its climax in the Founding of the Holy Church on earth, but the dreamer falls asleep in the middle of the Mass and sees the Holy Ghost equipping Piers to establish a Christian society. The conclusion finds Conscience still searching for Truth, personified by Piers the Plowman, just as humans are still searching for the religious meaning that lies behind their lives.

Piers Plowman does not make easy reading. It requires perseverance, but if we make the effort we are rewarded by a poem rich in satire, humour and imagery. For the historian it is valuable for the author's comments on contemporary grievances. Langland is critical equally of the papal taxers, the friars and the cardinals. Yet he does not descend into heresy: it is significant that he is as remote from the Eucharistic beliefs of the Lollards (q.v.) as he is from the courtly circles of Geoffrey Chaucer. Nor does he favour social revolution; he looks for inner reformation under the healing power of the Trinity.

W. Langland, *Piers the Ploughman*, ed. F. Goodridge, Penguin, 1959; F.R.H. Du Boulay, *The England of Piers Plowman*, Woodbridge, 1991.

LANGTON, STEPHEN

Though known chiefly in the Middle Ages as a preacher and biblical commentator, Langton is remembered today more for his part in the political struggles of John's reign.

Stephen appears to have been the son of one Henry de Langton of Langton-by-Wragby (Lincs). He was probably born in the late 1150s. Nothing is known about him before his arrival at the schools in Paris. At Paris he studied, and later lectured, on theology. His reputation was such that in 1206 Pope Innocent III summoned him to Rome to become a cardinal. He had only been at the Curia for a few months when, at the Pope's initiative, he was chosen by the monks of Canterbury to be their next archbishop. King John (q.v.), however, was opposed to Langton. His own preferred candidate was his close adviser John de Gray, bishop of

Norwich. There was a clear conflict of interest here, and neither party was prepared to give way. When John denied Langton entry into the country, Innocent retaliated by imposing an interdict.

Like Becket before him, Langton spent his years of exile at the abbey of Pontigny in France. John was perfectly content to hold out so long as the Pope was acting in isolation. But in 1213 a papal sentence of deposition was passed against him, the execution of which was entrusted to King Philip of France. An alliance between France and the papacy was too dangerous to contemplate. So John, performing a volte-face, gave in and allowed Langton to enter England.

On his return in July 1213 Langton tried to heal the wounds that had been opened over the previous five years, but it was difficult. Quite apart from the problems raised by the lifting of the interdict, the baronial opposition to the king was building up. John was forced to negotiate with his opponents, and settlement terms were agreed in Magna Carta (q.v.). Langton now had to choose between his conscience and his duty of obedience to the papacy. In the eyes of Innocent III the barons were rebelling against a king who since his submission had become a vassal of the Church, and moreover a crusader. But Langton was the man on the spot. He could see what John was really like. By the autumn of 1215 he found himself at such variance with the Pope's declared policy that he was suspended from office. He went to Rome to plead his case, and in due course obtained the revocation of the sentence on condition of his staying away from England. He was not able to return to his see until the restoration of peace in 1218.

In the closing years of his life Langton immersed himself in the day-to-day affairs of the Church, to which through force of circumstances he had been able to devote little time hitherto. In 1222 he called a council of the English Church at Osney Abbey, Oxford, to discuss the application in this country of the important decrees passed at the Fourth Lateran Council at Rome in 1215. If, today, historians are inclined to question the effectiveness of the constitutions passed at this and later councils, there is no need to doubt the sincerity of Langton's personal commitment to the cause of reform. He died on 9 July 1228 at his manor of Slindon (Sussex), and was buried in Canterbury Cathedral. His Purbeck marble tomb in the south-west transept is modest, but his greatest witness in the cathedral was, in a sense, the shrine of St Thomas, the making and installation of which he had masterminded in 1220.

F.M. Powicke, *Stephen Langton*, London, 1928, repr., 1965.

LANGUAGE and LITERATURE

The medieval period saw a wide extension of literacy across English society. By the fourteenth century the clergy, the nobility and gentry, the burgess class and the upper peasantry were all functionally literate. Over the same period, a process of linguistic simplification took place. In the aftermath of the Conquest two vernaculars were spoken, French and Old English, with Latin as the language of government. By 1400 only one vernacular was spoken – English in the form known as Middle English; and this was used as the language of government.

In pre-Conquest England there was a long tradition of writing in the vernacular. The earliest fragment of poetry to have come down to us dates from the seventh century. This is the song of Caedmon of Whitby which Bede preserved in his *Ecclesiastical History*. The language in which it is written is a Northumbrian dialect of 'Old English' (OE). Not surprisingly, since the Anglo-Saxons were of Germanic origin, OE bore strong similarities to German. It was an 'inflected' language; that is to say, it identified

54 Tomb of King **John** in Worcester Cathedral.

Far left: 55 Effigy of **Richard I** in Fontevrault Abbey, France.

Left: 56 Tomb effigy of **Henry III** in Westminster Abbey.

Below: 57 Monument of Eleanor of Castile, **Edward I**'s queen, in Westminster Abbey.

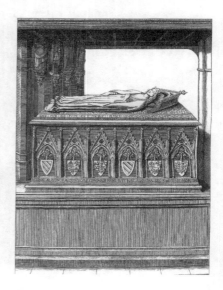

Far left: 58 Tomb effigy of **Edward III**'s queen, Philippa of Hainault, in Westminster Abbey.

Left: 59 Tomb effigy of **Edward III** in Westminster Abbey.

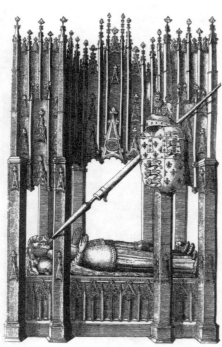

60 Tomb of **John of Gaunt** and Blanche of Gaunt in Old St Paul's *c.*1665; it was destroyed in the following year in the Great Fire.

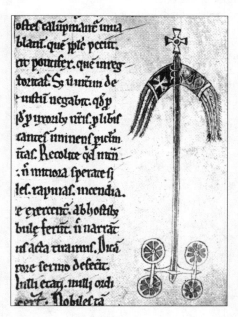

61 Tomb of Katherine Swynford, **John of Gaunt**'s third wife, and their daughter, Joan Beaufort, in Lincoln Cathedral (now lost).

62 The Standard. From a near-contemporary manuscript by Aelred, abbot of Rievaulx, containing a description of the battle of the Standard fought in 1138 between the forces of King **Stephen** and David I, king of Scotland.

63 Henry II doing penance at the shrine of **Thomas Becket**: stained glass panel in the Bodleian Library, Oxford. Becket's shrine in Canterbury Cathedral was the most popular English destination for pilgrims.

64 A fragment of a drawing of the shrine of Becket at Canterbury. Within a few years of his death at the hands of Henry II's knights Becket's tomb was the focus of one of the most important cults in western Christendom. In 1174 Henry II came to Canterbury as a penitent **pilgrim** and was flogged before the shrine of the martyr, a king of England truly humbled.

Left: 65 The **Magna Carta** of 1215, the product of an extraordinary moment in English history.

Below: 66 The future **Henry V** in action against his father's opponents Henry Percy and his son 'Hotspur' at the battle of Shrewsbury on 21 July 1403. From the *Beauchamp Pageant*, a life of Richard Beauchamp, who fought in the battle.

Above left: 67 The battle of the Seine, August 1416. As a result of this naval victory by **Henry V**'s brother John, duke of Bedford, the French blockade of Harfleur was ended and the way opened up for the king's subsequent invasion and conquest of Normandy. From the *Beauchamp Pageant*.

Above right: 68 The siege of Rouen, July 1418 to January 1419. The capitulation of the 'master city of all Normandy' on 19 January 1419, after a long and implacable blockade by **Henry V**, made the duchy's conquest by the king virtually inevitable. From the *Beauchamp Pageant*.

69 **Hundred Years War.** The marriage of Henry V to Catherine of Valois, which cemented peace between England and France and raised the prospect of a united crown, from the *Beauchamp Pageant*.

70 The birth of **Henry VI**, the only child of Henry V and Catherine of Valois, born at Windsor Castle on 6 December 1421. The treaty agreed between the French and English at Troyes in 1420 stipulated that a son of the Princess Catherine and Henry V should be king of both England and France. Henry V's death from dysentery when his heir was less than a year old made it impossible to sustain the dual monarchy.

71 The coronation of **Henry VI**, the only English monarch ever to be crowned king of France, in Paris, 16 December 1431. From the *Beauchamp Pageant*.

Far left: 72 Henry V and to his left, the chancellor, **Henry Beaufort,** who is presenting to Richard Beauchamp, earl of Warwick. From the *Beauchamp Pageant*.

Left: 73 Portrait of **Edward IV**. Stained glass, Canterbury Cathedral *c*.1480.

74 Portrait of Elizabeth Woodville, **Edward IV**'s queen. Stained glass, Canterbury Cathedral *c.*1480.

Left: 75 Duke William bestowing arms on King Harold before he bacame king. From the **Bayeux Tapestry.**

Below: 76 During the heat of the battle at **Hastings,** William the Conqueror raises his helmet to dispel a rumour that he has been killed; this was a critical moment in the battle after which the Normans are shown advancing. Scene from the Bayeux Tapestry.

77 The death of Harold. From the **Bayeux Tapestry**.

Above: 78 **Duke William** enthroned. From the Bayeux Tapestry.

Left: 79 **Henry VI** depicted as a royal saint on a screen at Ludham (Norfolk) of *c.*1500.

Above left: 80 Seal of Battle Abbey. **Hastings**.

Above right: 81 The coat of arms of **Henry III**.

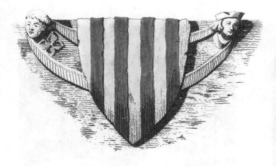

Clockwise from above left:

82 The coat of arms of Eleanor of Provence, **Henry III**'s queen.

83 The coat of arms which **Edward III** adopted after assuming the title of King of France.

84 The coat of arms of Philippa of Hainault, queen of **Edward III**.

Above left: 85 The coat of arms of Joan of Navarre, **Henry VI**'s second queen.

Above right: 86 **Richard III** with the Tudor-invented deformation of his back.

Above left: 87 Badge of **Richard II** from MS Vincent 152 at the Heralds' College.

Above right: 88 Badge of **Richard III** from MS Vincent 152 at the Heralds' College.

89 **Monasticism**. Bermondsey Abbey from Wyngaerde's *Panorama of London, c.*1543. Bermondsey is now vanished without trace.

90 In 1290 Edward I expelled England's **Jews**. Here we see the multi-faced, wheeler-dealer Isaac of Norwich, crowned in mockery in a record of 1233.

Above: 91 **Black Death** from a broadsheet on mortality in Oxford in 1577.

Right: 92 **John Wycliffe** in a sixteenth-century likeness.

93 The duke of Gloucester and the earls of Warwick and Stafford chase the duke of Burgundy from the walls of **Calais** in 1436. From the *Beauchamp Pageant*.

Above: 94 **Armour and Arms.** An eleventh century manuscript showing warriors in battle.

Right: 95 Unarmoured Scottish soldier *c*.1300 with spear and exaggerated sword. Such soldiers fought at the battle of **Bannockburn**.

96 Initial letter of **Edward II**'s charter to Carlisle in 1316. The Scots are shown attacking the city with a 'machine for casting stones', while a miner with a pick works at the foot of a wall.

Above: 97 **Wales**. Unarmoured Welsh soldiers of the thirteenth century.

Left: 98 The battle of **Hastings**. Page from Simeon of Durham's *History of the Kings of England*, describing the Norman Conquest. Simeon wrote this chronicle at the beginning of the twelfth century.

99 Seal of **Owain Glyn Dwr**.

Above left: 100 **Hundred Years War**. Richard Beauchamp, earl of Warwick, at the siege of Caen, 1417, from the *Beauchamp Pageant*.

Above right: 101 **Chaucer**: the portrait commissioned by Thomas Huccleve so that no one would forget what the great poet looked like (early fifteenth-century).

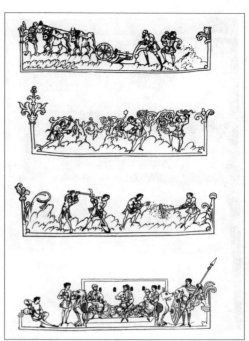

Clockwise from right:

102 An eleventh-century Old English calendar, showing typical **agricultural** scenes, January–April.

103 An eleventh-century Old English calendar, showing typical **agricultural** scenes, May–August.

104 An eleventh-century Old English calendar, showing typical **agricultural** scenes, September–December.

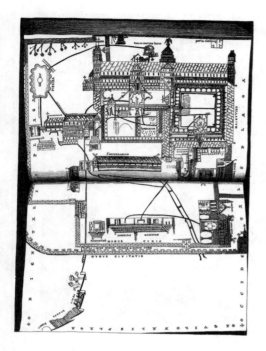

105 **Architecture, Ecclesiastical**. Plan of Canterbury Cathedral Church and monastery *c.*1150.

Above: 106 A thirteenth-century drawing of **London** from the margin of a page of Geoffrey of Monmouth's *History of the Kings of Britain*.

Right: 107 **Wales**. Gruffydd, son of Llewelyn, trying to escape from the Tower of London in 1243, from Matthew Paris, *Chronica Majora*.

the relationship of one word to another not by its position in the sentence but by use of case endings. Likewise it employed gender, and required each adjective to agree with the noun it qualified. In the tenth and early eleventh centuries the coming of the Vikings to eastern and northern England added a distinctly Scandinavian flavour to the vernacular spoken in those parts of the country. But, as Alfred and the Wessex kings gradually extended their rule into Danish England, so they took with them their own dialect of the OE tongue. It is that dialect which became the language of government in the century or more before the Conquest.

Literature at the end of the OE period was either heroic or religious – concerned, that is, with celebrating noble feats of arms or with imparting Christian beliefs. For poetic effects the Anglo-Saxon writers, from Caedmon on, relied on alliteration, or the repetition of a letter or set of letters usually at the start of each word. The following lines, taken from the *Song of the Battle of Maldon*, written soon after the event in the 990s, illustrates the point well:

Thaer geflymed weard
Nordmanna brego, nede gebaeded
to lides stefne lytle weorode;
cread cnear on flot, cing ut gewet
on fealone flod, feorh generede

(There the leader of the Northmen was put to flight, driven by necessity to the prow of the boat with a small troop; the galley hastened to sea, the king went out on the dark sea, [and] saved his life.)

Each line was broken in the middle by a caesura, the two halves being held together by the use of alliteration. In other words, the effect was created not, as might be the case today, by rhyming sounds at the end of each line but by the repetition of stress within the line or group of lines. This absence of rhyme makes the distinction between prose and poetry much less clear in OE literature than in modern. Tenth- and eleventh-century writers like Aelfric and Wulfstan relied on alliteration so much in their sermons that it is often difficult for modern editors to know whether to print their texts in verse or prose.

The Norman Conquest dealt a savage blow to OE. Its ascendant position was lost. The Normans made their own tongue (a version of French developed on English soil) the language of polite society and Latin the language of government. The kings themselves spoke mainly French. OE, once a medium for both business and literature, was now condemned to a period of cultural eclipse. By the time it emerged from this three centuries later, in the form we know as Middle English (ME), it was a different language. Inflection had gone, and meaning was determined largely by the position of words in the sentence.

Within half a century of the Conquest alliterative poetry, at least in its OE form, was a dying art. However, it had by no means died out completely. The great alliterative revival of the fourteenth century cannot be explained without supposing that an informal tradition of such writing survived during the centuries after 1066. One of the most notable works of the period was Layamon's *Brut*, an isolated piece of historical writing in vernacular alliteration composed by a priest of Areley King's (Worcs) in or around 1200. Telling the history of Britain from the time of the supposed landing here of Brutus (hence the title), a descendant of Aeneas, it was the only important vernacular chronicle written in the early ME period (*c.*1100–*c.*1300). And from the literary perspective it is important in marking a transition between old-fashioned alliteration and the new, rhymed verse which was coming in from France.

For our knowledge of the vernacular literature of this period we are entirely dependent on the extant manuscripts, which in their uneven incidence of survival may give a sadly incomplete picture of what people read. The many short popular songs and poems which a great lord and his servants heard in a baronial hall were rarely written down; they were transmitted orally. What we know most about is the sermons and religious treatises that circulated in written form. Judging from the number of manuscripts of it which have survived, one of the most popular works of the period was the *Ancren Riwle (Anchoresses' Rule)*. Written originally in about 1100 by an unknown author for the guidance of three well-born young ladies who had become anchoresses, this attractive piece was revised between about 1215 and 1222 for the benefit of a wider community in the form known as the *Ancrene Wisse*. The work is written in a West Midlands dialect, a point of some significance when we remember that Layamon, author of the *Brut*, and William Langland (q.v.) came from that part of England too. Internal evidence suggests that it may have been composed by a canon of Wigmore Abbey for the benefit of one or other of the two groups of nuns who were living nearby and to whom he probably acted as confessor. As a devotional manual the *Ancrene Wisse* acquired a wide circulation, and was read well into the fifteenth century. It was matched in popularity in the fourteenth century by the works of the mystic writers, of whom the most important was Richard Rolle of Hampole (Yorks), who died in 1349. Rolle wrote several prose tracts in his native Yorkshire dialect, which for their quality and style have earned him a justified place in the history of English prose and religious thought.

In the period in which these religious works were written a major change was taking place in the nature and content of secular European poetry. It was a change only to be fully felt in English poetry in the fourteenth century. In the early medieval period most secular poetry had been heroic; it had taken the form of the epic, the saga. But in the twelfth century, in the French-speaking world, the place of the epic had been taken by the romance. This was the most profound shift in European sensibility to have occurred between the antique period and the rise of the Romantic movement. Broadly speaking, it can be associated with that general cultural rebirth known as the 'Twelfth Century Renaissance'. The first stirrings of the new mood can be heard in Provence and Aquitaine in the late eleventh century, when the troubadours began composing their love lyrics. The troubadours emphasized the gentler side of life. Their knights did not engage in blood feuds or slaying dragons; they performed valorous deeds for their ladies. The character and conventions of this poetry varied according to time and place. In the context of ME literature, it is the romances inspired by the legend of King Arthur – the so-called 'Matter of Britain' – which figure most.

That Arthur should have occupied such a prominent position in English literature right down to the age of Tennyson was largely due to Geoffrey of Monmouth (q.v.), who first presented the legendary sixth-century king to a medieval audience in the 1130s. In the course of time, as the legends became embroidered, the emphasis passed from the king himself to his companion knights – the Knights of the Round Table – whose exploits were the subject of celebration in their own right. The greatest ME poem deriving from this tradition is *Sir Gawayne and the Green Knight*, written in about 1370 in a north-west Midlands dialect. The poem tells of the arrival in King Arthur's hall of the Green Knight, clad in green armour, with green hair and astride a green horse. He challenges any of King Arthur's knights to attack him with his huge axe – a challenge accepted by Sir Gawayne who strikes off his head. Little good does this feat do him because the Green Knight picks up his head and rides off, challenging Gawayne to meet him in a year's time at the Green Chapel. The rest of the poem describes Gawayne's journey, his encounter with the Green Knight and his failure in a chastity test. The poem has preserved the secret of its inner meaning as successfully as its author has preserved his anonymity. All that can be said for certain about this talented man is that he also wrote *Pearl*, *Patience* and *Cleanness*, three poems so-called from their opening words which are found with Sir Gawayne in the same manuscript. Although these poems are inspired by the alliterative revival of the fourteenth century, they experiment in breaking the monotony of the long line by combining rhymed and alliterative verse. In the case of Sir Gawayne, for example, the long alliterative lines are followed by a sequence of five short ones, rhyming 'ababa'.

The most celebrated poem of the alliterative revival is Langland's *Piers Plowman*, a great allegory which stands comparison with *The Pilgrim's Progress*. Once again there is a connection with the West Midlands. The setting is the Malvern Hills, where the poet falls asleep and dreams of Piers's quest for truth. Langland's world is very different from that of the Arthurian romances. No longer are we in the company of the knights and damsels at court but with the common people. *Piers Plowman* is a work of social satire. But, if it shows sympathy with the labouring folk, it is devoid of sentimentality, because Langland (q.v.) is prepared to criticize all the ranks of society. *Piers Plowman* was one of the most popular of all medieval poems, not least with John Ball and the peasant rebels who quoted it in 1381.

The author of *Sir Gawayne and the Green Knight* is unknown, and William Langland remains a shadowy figure. The most familiar writer of the period, however, Geoffrey Chaucer (q.v.), falls into an altogether different category. Chaucer's career is copiously documented. He was a courtier, a king's esquire: someone who mingled with the rich and powerful. We know a great deal about his public appointments. He was an MP in the parliament of 1386 and, for some years, a justice of the peace in Kent. Yet there seems little connection between the public figure and the gentle ironic figure who was the poet. Chaucer, unlike most of his predecessors, was not writing for a didactic purpose but, rather, partly for pleasure and partly in response to the demands of his friends and patrons. Chaucer was the first 'courtly maker'. *The Canterbury Tales* was his most ambitious work: indeed too ambitious as it was left unfinished. However, it was preceded by a number of earlier poems of which *The Book of the Duchess*, *Troilus and Cressida* and *The House of Fame* are the most important.

Chaucer's place in the history of English literature is, in a sense, a strangely isolated one. As several writers have commented, the two great poets of the age – Chaucer and Langland – contemporaries and both at some time residents of London, seem to have had no knowledge of each other's work. They inhabited different worlds, not only socially but intellectually. Although a poet who was to enjoy a long popularity, Langland was himself old-fashioned to the extent that in England if not in Scotland he was among the last of the long line of alliterative poets. Chaucer, on the other hand, stands at the head of a line of versifiers stretching down to Wyatt and the earl of Surrey in Tudor England. All the same, he remains in a class of his own. John Gower (c.1330–1408), a friend of his, was a competent enough though not brilliant poet who could write equally well in English, French or Latin – the last English author of note to be able to do so – and he included some valuable political comment in his work. In the next generation or two, the poets were of much lower calibre. There was Thomas Hoccleve (c.1368–c.1450), a clerk in the privy seal office who regarded himself as a disciple of Chaucer. His main work, *The Regement of*

Princes, was addressed to the future Henry V (q.v.) and written in an easy, rather slipshod style, which is at least devoid of the scholarly pretence that besets John Lydgate (*c.*1370–1452). A monk of Bury St Edmund's, Lydgate was a prolific poet whose popularity is attested by the patronage he received from magnates like Humphrey, duke of Gloucester (q.v.), and even from Henry VI himself (q.v.). To the modern reader, however, he comes across as long-winded. It was probably after ploughing through his main work, *The Troy Book*, a history of the Trojan Wars in no fewer than 29,626 lines, that Joseph Ritson, a nineteenth-century critic, spoke of 'this voluminous, prosaick and driveling monk'. The fifteenth century certainly produced no Brahms to follow Chaucer's Beethoven. But by way of compensation it did succeed in bringing the Arthurian legends to a fitting climax in Sir Thomas Malory's *Morte d'Arthur* (q.v. MALORY). A great work of prose, this poem is the fullest exposition of the Arthurian romances in the Middle Ages, and its appeal was recognized by Caxton (q.v.) who printed it in 1485.

Until the arrival of printing, which had the effect of introducing standardization, great variety was to be found in ME spelling and vocabulary. Chaucer had certainly succeeded in making ME a respectable language of literature once more, but that is not to say that he had found it ready for use, for its vocabulary was as yet incomplete. Every time that ME could not supply him with the word he needed, Chaucer had to borrow one from French or Latin. It has been calculated that of the 4,000 words from Romance languages found in Chaucer, as many as a thousand had not appeared in any English text before. The possibility needs to be borne in mind that a number of these words might have passed some time before into spoken use, or even into written use in texts that have not survived. But the most recent work done in this field suggests that French loan-words passed into the vernacular later rather than earlier in the ME period. French and English lived alongside each other for a long time, and the former only began to influence the latter in terms of vocabulary when its dominance was beginning to wane.

The process by which the upper classes began speaking English once again is one that by its very nature is ill charted. What people read is attested by written evidence; what people said is not. If the records of the royal government are any guide, the changeover came quite late. Henry V (1413–22) was the first king since the Conquest to use the vernacular as the everyday language of government. But an indication that English had come to prevail over French in polite speech much earlier is given by a famous passage which the Berkeleys' chaplain John Trevisa interpolated into his translation of Higden's *Polychronicon*:

> For Johan Cornwal, a mayster of gramere, chayngede ye lore in gramerscole and construccion of Freynsch into Englysch; and Richard Pencrych lurnede that manere techyng of hym, and other men of Pencrych, so that now, the yer of oure Lord a thousand threehondred foure score and fyve [1385], of the secunde kyng Richard after the Conquest nyne, in al the gramerscoles of Engelond childern leveth Frensch, and construeth and lurneth an Englysch...

In 1385, then, it was general for schoolchildren to translate from Latin into English, and not French. It is interesting to find as well that a couple of decades earlier in 1362 a statute was passed permitting the use of English in courts of law; and from *c.*1370 we have the first surviving monumental inscription in English, on a brass to John the Smith at Brightwell Baldwin (Oxon). In the keeping of records, particularly those of the crown, the competition was not only between English and French, as it was in speech and informal writing, but also between English and Latin. The weight of bureaucratic inertia ensured that in this particular area change would come later than elsewhere, but a turning point was reached in the reign of Henry VI (1422–61): the main government offices started using English in the 1420s and in the next decade English petitions started appearing in the official roll of parliamentary proceedings.

The English language as it re-emerged in the later fourteenth century was very different from the form spoken by the Anglo-Saxons. We have seen that before the Conquest the Wessex dialect was winning general recognition. But when English became respectable again in the later fourteenth century, it was a Midland dialect which triumphed. It needs to be borne in mind that in the Middle Ages, as in modern Chinese society, the written and the spoken forms of the language did not necessarily coincide. Thus while modern English is based on a uniform written standard which emerged towards the end of the Middle Ages in London, the dialectal forms from which that standard evolved were transmitted by the spoken word. Until the mid-fourteenth century it was the East Anglian dialect which exerted greatest influence on English as spoken in the capital. After the mid-fourteenth century it was the dialect of the east Midland counties of Northamptonshire, Huntingdonshire and Cambridgeshire. In the age of Chaucer, however, wide variations in spelling are still found, indicating that written uniformity had not yet been achieved. What completed the process was the adoption in the 1430s by the scribes in the king's chancery of a form of the language, combining both London and east Midland forms, that was to become the basis of modern English. Immigration into the capital, substantial in the post-Black Death period, must have substantially contributed to this evolution.

See also ARTHURIAN LEGENDS; KEMPE, MARGERY; MISTERY PLAYS

D. Pearsall, 'Language and Literature', in *The Oxford Illustrated History of Medieval England*, ed. N.E. Saul, Oxford, 1997; J.A. Burrow, *Medieval Writers and their Work*, Oxford, 1982; *Cambridge History of Medieval English Literature*, ed. D. Wallace, Cambridge, 1999; M. Clanchy, *From Memory to Written Record: England, 1066-1307*, 2nd ed., Oxford, 1993; *Cambridge History of the English Language, 1066-1476*, ed. N.F. Blake, Cambridge, 1992.

LAW
See JUSTICE

LITURGY
The term 'liturgy' describes the forms of worship used in the Church. In the pre-Reformation period the basic structure of the liturgy was uniform throughout western Christendom, comprising as the latter did a single community dependent on the authority of the Pope. Yet within that structure there was almost infinite scope for local variation. The rites practised in England differed from those in Norway and Spain, and within England the rites practised at, say, Salisbury differed from those at York or Hereford. Eventually it was the Salisbury arrangements – the Use of Sarum – that triumphed over all the others and came to be adopted in cathedrals and parish churches as far apart as Glasgow and St David's.

The liturgical programme used in the cathedrals and secular churches followed the basic routine mapped out many centuries before by the Benedictine monks (q.v. MONASTICISM). In other words, the clergy were committed each day to celebrating High Mass and to saying the eight canonical offices, or 'hours'. At Lincoln in 1400 High Mass was celebrated at 10 a.m. and Evensong at 3 p.m. In this daily ritual the Mass was naturally accorded a position of special importance. In the late Middle Ages popular veneration for the mass

greatly increased, following the pronounce-
ment of the doctrine of transubstantiation at
the Fourth Lateran Council in 1215. The Mass,
it was officially taught, was a re-enactment of
Christ's supreme sacrifice for the purpose of
obtaining the forgiveness of sins. The regular
performance of masses was thus seen as a vehicle for drawing down the Almighty's forgiveness. In the fourteenth and fifteenth centuries
it became common for testators who could
afford it to provide for the regular celebration
of soul-masses in the hope of curtailing the trials of Purgatory. Private masses of this sort
would typically be sung by chantry (q.v.)
priests at side altars in churches or in chapels
built specially for the purpose, like those
which today line the aisles of Winchester
Cathedral. As belief in the potency of the Mass
intensified, so it seems that churchgoers
received the sacrament less often. This was
because communion was administered only
after the faithful had confessed their sins to the
priest, an operation so thorough that it was
normally undergone only once a year, before
Easter. This in turn meant that most people
communicated only once a year. It was again
this respect for the Host which explains why
the Church slowly abandoned administering
the sacrament in both kinds. Until the twelfth
century the congregation had been given both
the bread and the wine. Thereafter it was normal to offer only the bread, concealing
beneath it the flesh of Christ.

High Mass on Sunday was invariably the
best attended service of the week. The faithful were naturally encouraged to attend the
other services, particularly Matins, but the
indications are that they hardly ever did so. In
1291 Archbishop Pecham wrote to his
archdeacon at Canterbury complaining that
Sunday was being poorly observed and urg-
ing him to persuade more people to attend
church. Such injunctions were common. But
it was the clergy's usual practice to recite the
daily offices alone. A priest would normally
say Prime and Terce before the congregation

arrived for Mass, and then Sext and Nones
after they had gone.

A church needed a whole repertory of
service books for the purposes of daily worship. The most important of these was the
Missal, or Mass book. This contained not only
the words said or sung by the celebrant but
also the text of the two scriptural lessons and
of the four chants: elements that, with the celebrant's three or four variable prayers, were
specific to each liturgical day or occasion. This
material alone made for a sizeable book, but
where the mass was celebrated with music
and special solemnity there could also be separate codices containing the Epistles and
Gospels. The deacon might have a Gospel
Book, from which he would read a passage
appropriate for the day, the sub-deacon an
Epistle Book, containing the New Testament
Epistles, and the choir the Gradual, setting out
the music. Apart from the Mass, there were
sacramental services of an occasional form –
baptism, marriage, visitation of the sick and
burial of the dead. For these a separate book
was provided, known as the Manual. This had
to be small enough for the parson to carry
around, because he would need to take it
when, for example, going to a house to
administer the last rites to a dying parishioner.

The non-sacramental service, or 'daily
office', consisted of 'hours' of prayer officially
eight in number: Matins, Lauds, Prime, Terce,
Sext, Nones, Vespers and Compline. When
sung, these services would require the use of
many books: Bible, psalter, legendary, homil-
iary, and a collection of office chants and
texts. For private or non-choral recitation, the
basic elements of these books were abstracted
in a volume known as the 'breviary' or 'porti-
forium'. This, too, could be a big book, and it
was sometimes split up into a winter half and
a summer half.

For private devotions in their chapels, the
well-to-do laity used principally two books:
the Psalter and the Book of Hours. The former
brought together all the Old Testament

psalms in a form convenient for private devotion, while the latter, a very popular devotional book, included the Hours of the Blessed Virgin, the seven Penitential Psalms, the fifteen Gradual Psalms, the Litany, the *placebo* and *dirige* and the commendations. The office in honour of the Blessed Virgin reflected the enormous popularity of the Virgin's cult in later medieval England.

The richness of the medieval liturgy can immediately be sensed by looking at the beautiful service books that have come down to us: for example, the *St Omer Psalter* and the Winchester Bible. Not all service books, however, would have been so richly ornamented. A breviary used in a small parish church would have matched the humility of its surroundings. Indeed, it must be remembered that, if the liturgy meant something to the literate and the educated, it may have meant little or nothing to the humble bulk of the congregation. Most of those in the nave would hardly have been able to see what was happening in the chancel, much less to hear it — large parts of the service were whispered by the celebrant and, of course, were in Latin. The effect on the congregation may well have been principally one of mystery and symbolism, reinforced by the message conveyed to the more sensitive of the congregation by sculpture (q.v.), painting (q.v.), music (q.v.) and stained glass (q.v.).

J. Harper, *The Forms and Orders of the Western Liturgy from the Tenth to the Eighteenth Century*, Oxford, 1991; C. Wordsworth and H. Littlehales, *The Old Service Books of the English Church*, London, 1904; E. Duffy, *The Stripping of the Altars: Traditional Religion in England, c.1400–1580*, New Haven and London, 1992.

LOLLARDY

The fourteenth-century Oxford theologian John Wycliffe (q.v.) inspired a movement of disciples known as the Lollards. This nickname was probably derived from the Dutch *lollaerd*, meaning someone who mumbled his prayers; but it had the advantage too, from the point of view of their detractors, of sounding conveniently like the English 'loller', a loafer or idler.

The Lollards comprised three main groups of people, each of whom may have had little or no contact with any of the others. To begin with, there were Wycliffe's immediate followers at Oxford. Among them could be numbered men like Philip Repton, Nicholas Hereford and John Aston, all faithful to the master so long as he was in Oxford, but forced to reconsider their positions once he had left. The effect of Archbishop Courtenay's visitation of the university in 1382 was to produce submissions from Repton and Aston that autumn and from Hereford a few years later in 1391. Lollardy's link with the academic community at Oxford was largely broken.

The second group was never fully brought into the open by the Church. This was the handful of knights serving at the court of Richard II (q.v.) whom the chroniclers accused of harbouring Lollard sympathies. That there was substance to the chroniclers' accusations is indicated by other evidence which testifies to the knights' heretical beliefs. Three of the knights, for example, made wills which contain Lollard characteristics like the prohibition of funerary pomp and contempt for the flesh; another, Richard Stury, was obliged by King Richard himself to abjure his heresy. How long these influential knights were able to escape censure is hard to say, but there is nothing to suggest that their sympathies ever brought them into open collision with the Church.

The third group were not so fortunate. These were the humbler followers whom Lollardy attracted and on whom the mantle of Wycliffe's faith descended once his disciples in the university had been broken or dispersed. Among them were men like William Swinderby, nicknamed William the Hermit, an unbeneficed preacher from Leicester whose activities across central and western England continued to make him an embarrassment to the authorities until his final disappearance into Wales in 1392. It was people like Swinderby who seem to have been most attracted by the puritanical, evangelical streak in Lollardy. Nor were they always clerks. The passage of Lollard beliefs owed as much to the laymen, often literate laymen, who would meet in small groups or congregations to discuss the Bible, which had so recently been made available to them in its entirety in English. Ill educated these sympathizers may have been, but they had that insatiable appetite for first-hand knowledge of the scriptures which was to be shared by the Puritans in the seventeenth century.

This characteristic of the Lollards introduces us to one of the central tenets of their philosophy. They respected the Bible as the sole authority for the Christian religion. It followed that the Vulgate should be made available to all in the vernacular. At first the Church was slow to react, since partial translations had been made before, at the initiative of princes and members of the nobility, without repercussion. The Lollards themselves had made two translations before the clampdown came in 1407. By then the implications for the Church of making the Bible available to all had become apparent. Once the Scriptures were respected as the sole source of authority, the mediatory role of the priest was bound to be called into question. The next demand would be to get rid of the clergy altogether and to redistribute their wealth among the people. But there was more to Lollardy than just old-fashioned anticlericalism. It was anti-sacramental, and openly sceptical towards Catholic teaching on the doctrine of transubstantiation. And last but not least it drew on a strong fund of anti-papalism: in Lollard epistemology the Bishop of Rome was denounced as Antichrist.

Unaccustomed to coping with heresies, the English Church was at first slow to react to this novel phenomenon. A vigorous example was set by Archbishop Courtenay in 1382 in reimposing orthodoxy at Wycliffe's own university of Oxford, but the other bishops were slower in stirring themselves into action. The earliest Lollards, like Hereford and Aston, were therefore permitted considerable freedom of action and expression before the long arm of the ecclesiastical law finally began to catch up with them in the later 1380s. The problem that then exercised the minds of the authorities was the absence of any penalty that would deter others from straying along the path to heresy. How could the Church's armoury be reinforced? The remedy was provided in the reign of Henry IV (q.v.) in 1401 when burning was for the first time in England made the penalty for obdurate heretics.

In the event the fires were only kindled twice in the reign of Henry IV. Lollardy was by then a nuisance rather than a serious threat, not so much a nationwide movement of dissent as a discredited rag-bag of doctrines shared by scattered communities of believers. Still, it retained sufficient strength to mount an organized rebellion against Henry V (q.v.) in 1414. The ringleader was Sir John Oldcastle, a Herefordshire knight who wanted to replace the house of Lancaster with a Lollard state. He planned to kidnap the king and his brothers and occupy London, but the government, evidently forewarned, experienced no trouble in rounding up the motley army of rebels that converged on St Giles's Fields on the night of 9-10 January 1414. That Oldcastle was able to assemble any rebel gathering at all nevertheless implies that local congregations were able to keep in touch with each other, perhaps through the network of Lollard preachers. He drew little support from his own county of Hereford, rather surprisingly in view of William Swinderby's missions there, but perhaps it was too far for sympathizers to make their way to London. Bristol, on the other hand, still a good way from the capital, provided the largest single contingent of all. In eastern England there were again marked local disparities, with Essex providing generous support and Norfolk and Suffolk very little. In the Midland counties Lollardy drew its strongest support from the towns, Leicester and Coventry for example.

These were roughly the localities that were to afford continued evidence of Lollard attachment for the rest of the fifteenth century. But there were smaller, more localized pockets as well. Indeed, Lollardy was something of a hydra-headed monster. As soon as it was suppressed in one area, it sprang up in another. In the Thames valley, for example, the Buckinghamshire Chilterns sheltered a colony of Lollards until 1414, thanks to the patronage of the Cheyne family; but once the heretics there had been stamped out, a new colony popped up south of the river in Berkshire. That Lollardy did live on in the fifteenth century in such areas as these can hardly be doubted, since recent research has thrown up so much evidence of prosecutions for heresy. In that case how far did the lingering influence of the Lollards shape the early stages of the English Reformation? The very least that can be said is that some of the essential doctrines of Protestantism had been anticipated a century and a half earlier in the writings of John Wycliffe, and that the survival of Lollardy helped to prepare the ground for the reception of Lutheranism. But this is not to say that the work of Wycliffe and his disciples helped to advance the Reformation. Quite the contrary. Lollardy failed because it became proletarian. The Reformation succeeded because it was promoted by the king.

K.B. McFarlane, *John Wycliffe and the Beginnings of English Nonconformity*, London, 1952; J.A.F. Thomson, *The Later Lollards*, Oxford, 1965; A. Hudson, *The Lollard Reformation*, London, 1988.

LONDON

London was much the largest city of medieval England, and one of the largest cities of Europe. Current estimates suggest that its population peaked in 1300 at around 80,000, falling rapidly after the Black Death (q.v.) to around 40,000. A couple of miles to the south-west of the city proper was the suburb of Westminster, which was rapidly emerging as the kingdom's administrative capital (plates 1 and 106).

It was the Romans who first appreciated London's geographical advantages. The city was conveniently sited opposite the ports and cities of north-west Europe; it was the first point at which the Thames could be bridged; and it could be made the focus of a major road (q.v.) system. The Roman city was large: its walls were nearly three miles in circumference. The city was linked to the south bank by the first bridge over the river. Apparently this was a wooden structure a little to the east of the present one. This structure lasted until the 1170s when, according to the Waverley Abbey chronicler, Peter, the vicar of St Mary, Colechurch, began rebuilding it in stone. It was this stone bridge which spawned the crowded superstructure of buildings so familiar from Hollar's engraving of 1647. At the southern end of the bridge lay Southwark, never formally a part of London in the Middle Ages but nonetheless a busy community in its own right. It boasted the Tabard Inn, whence Chaucer's (q.v.) pilgrims set off for Canterbury (q.v.). Southwark was also home to the city's brothels.

In the south-eastern corner of medieval London lay the great fortress built by William the Conqueror (q.v.) known as the Tower of London. The battlemented skyline of the Tower figures prominently in contemporary views of the Thames-side scene. But what above all dominated the city skyline was the great cathedral of St Paul's, at 644ft the longest ever built in England. Thanks once again to Hollar's engravings it is possible to gain an idea of the cathedral's appearance before its destruction. Inside the west door the view extended eastwards along the Norman nave, past the choir and lady chapel, rebuilt in the Decorated style between 1251 and 1312, towards the lovely rose window at the end. On the south side lay the chapter house and cloister, rebuilt in the 1330s and among the earliest essays in Perpendicular architecture (plate 39). The cathedral and many of the city churches were destroyed in the Great Fire. But, despite these losses, a good deal of medieval ecclesiastical work survives. St Olave's, Hart Street, St Helen's, Bishopsgate, and the priory church of St Bartholomew's, Smithfield, are three that are virtually intact. It goes without saying that London, like most medieval English towns, was almost overendowed with parish churches: by the thirteenth century there were at least a hundred, or one for every 3½ acres.

Being populous and close to the seat of government, medieval London exercised a weighty influence on the affairs of state. In 1135 the citizens helped to secure the throne for King Stephen (q.v.). In 1141 they expelled his rival Matilda when she was on the point of being crowned. In 1215 they lent support to the barons who had taken up arms against King John (q.v.). But if the Londoners were capable of speaking with one voice at a time of national crisis, particularly when their own liberties were at risk, on other occasions they were torn apart by internal feuds and rivalries. There were the familiar struggles of rich and poor, rulers and ruled. But in the fourteenth century it was the ruling class itself that was divided. In Richard II's reign the victualling guilds, led by Nicholas Brembre, a grocer, tried to win a monopoly of the import of foodstuffs into the city. They were challenged by an alliance of rival guilds led by John of Northampton, a draper, who whipped up popular agitation against his rivals. Brembre being a protégé of the king, Northampton turned for support to his opponents. Although Northampton's cause was eventually to fail, he had his moment of satisfaction in 1388 when the Appellant earls, temporarily in the ascendant, had Brembre and other of Richard II's friends executed.

These political ups and downs prompt consideration of how London was governed in the Middle Ages. In the Norman period the most important officials were the two sheriffs, who were responsible for collecting the farm, or sum of money, that the city owed to the king. The first major concession made to the citizenry (in Henry I's reign) was that of choosing their own sheriffs and raising the money themselves. By the end of the twelfth century, however, civic aspirations had advanced very much further. In 1191, while Richard I was in the East, the Londoners created their city a 'commune', in other words, a self-governing community under a mayor. In John's reign the Londoners won the right to choose the mayor themselves. The mayor eventually superseded the sheriff as the most important official in the city, and his installation each year on October 28 provided the occasion for a major display of pageantry that has lasted to this day. Once elected, the mayor found himself presiding over an intricate structure of courts and councils that had been grafted onto the city's government one by one whenever it was found necessary. The oldest was the folkmoot, where outlawries (q.v.) were promulgated. Nearly as old was the court of husting, which assembled in the Guildhall to hear pleas relating to land, debts and rents. The affairs of these assemblies were guided, if not managed, by the aldermen who formed an inner council of twenty-four (later twenty-five), one from each of the city's wards. These were the men who counted for most in medieval London, the charmed circle from whom most of the mayors were chosen. It was to counter this tendency towards oligarchy, common to all medieval urban administrations, that the 'common council' was formed in the fourteenth century. Like the court of aldermen its members were elected by the wards, apart from a period of eight years between 1376 and 1384 when they were chosen by the crafts.

For administrative purposes Westminster was never a part of the City of London; on the other hand, it naturally developed close social and commercial links with its larger neighbour. The king was dependent on the city merchants for loans; and they were dependent on him for business. For that rea-son if no other it worked to their advantage when king and government settled down at the then ramshackle palace between the Abbey and the Thames.

City of London: from Prehistoric Times to c.1520, ed. M.D. Lobel (Historic Towns Atlas Series), London, 1989; G. Rosser, *Medieval Westminster, 1200-1500*, Oxford, 1989; C.M. Barron, *London in the Later Middle Ages: Government and People 1200–1500*, Oxford, 2005.

M

MAGNA CARTA

Magna Carta – the Great Charter – is the name given to the charter of liberties issued by King John (q.v.) at Runnymede in June 1215 in the hope of ending the baronial rebellion which had broken out against him in the previous autumn.

The crisis out of which the Charter arose had its origins in causes both long-term and short-term.

The main long-term cause of the crisis was to be found in the arbitrary nature of Norman and Angevin government. It is interesting to see a number of the grievances aired in the charter anticipated in the concessions made by Henry I (q.v.) in his coronation charter of 1100. The difficulty which faced the Norman and Angevin kings was that they had to resort to irregular and highly unpopular financial exactions in order to pay for their military ambitions. The fiscal structure at their disposal has been described as 'less a system of taxation than a system of plunder'. The one source of national taxation (q.v.) which they had inherited from the Saxon kings – the geld – had been allowed to fall into disuse from the 1160s because its yield was so low. Consequently, Henry II and his successors became ever more reliant on the profits of justice (q.v.) and the lucrative but irregular sources of revenue refererd to as the 'incidents of feudalism' (q.v.). These included relief (paid by a son who succeeded to his father's lands), wardship (custody of lands during a minority) and aids (emergency taxes). The main drawback to these feudal revenues was that they fell not on all of the king's subjects but only on those who held their land on feudal terms from the king – in other words, the tenants-in-chief, a group largely synonymous with the barons.

By the reign of Henry II the barons were well aware that they were being squeezed for every penny by the king. The financial pressure was intensified in the 1190s under Richard I (q.v.), when money had to be found to pay for the king's ransom. By John's reign the financial position of the crown had become still more precarious, because strong inflationary pressures had set in. Between about 1180 and John's death in 1216 prices rose at least threefold. Simply in order to maintain the level of his income, therefore, John needed to increase his receipts proportionately. But the sheer scale of John's appetite for money was such that he needed to increase his income much more than that. In 1204 Normandy (q.v.), his family's patrimony, had been lost to the French. John spent the next ten years trying to get it back. The amount of money that he spent on assembling a military coalition and despatching an army to Poitou led to massive demands on his vassals. His exactions might have been accepted had he met with success. In fact, however, he did not. Defeat abroad was inevitably accompanied by demands for reform at home.

The draft of Magna Carta presented to John in June 1215 was not produced in a vacuum. It was the product of many months' work by the barons. The first draft, known as the Unknown Charter, was probably formulated in the early months of 1215. It consisted of Henry I's coronation charter supplemented by a dozen new clauses. By June, however, events had moved on so fast that the Unknown Charter had become obsolete and a new document, known as the Articles of the Barons, was drawn up. This contained most of the main clauses that were to be in Magna Carta, with a few more extreme ones that were not, indicating that in the course of the next few weeks initial demands were watered down in order to produce a document on which both sides could agree. Magna Carta in its final form was not a document forced on the king by a group of hardline militants but a charter of liberties secured by a broadly based opposition movement. John had to accept the document because the tide of war had turned against him. At Brackley in April the barons had met to perform the act of *diffidatio* – that is, to renounce homage to him – and in the following month they took London (q.v.). The loss of London was a fatal blow for John. By June, when he was staying at Windsor, he decided to negotiate. At that time the barons were based at Staines, and they met the king at Runnymede because it was halfway between. It is difficult to reconstruct in exact detail the progress of the negotiations there, but it seems likely that there were several meetings between the two sides. At the first, on 10 June, broad agreement was reached on the basis of the Articles of the Barons; at the second, five days later, further discussion produced the document we know as Magna Carta; and at the third, on 19 June, a firm peace was made and homage renewed.

Almost certainly John never signed anything at Runnymede; and he may not have sealed anything either.

To a modern reader the terms of Magna Carta may come as a disappointment. There is nothing in it to match the rhetoric of the American Declaration of Independence. There are no grand-sounding Jeffersonian declarations of liberty. It is not a charter of liberty; it is a charter of liberties. The major role that financial oppression played in provoking the crisis is recognized in the large number of clauses limiting the king's ability to exploit the 'incidents of feudalism'. For example, reliefs, which in the past had been regulated only by the convention that they should be 'reasonable', were now fixed at £100 for a barony and 100s for a knight's fee (cl. 2). The rights of minors were safe-guarded during a wardship (cls. 4 & 5), and the rights of widows were protected (cls. 7 & 8) so that they would not be sold against their will to the highest bidder. Such apparently dry details addressed issues at the heart of feudal society. Other clauses were intended to prevent King John's corruption of the workings of justice which, again, had been occasioned by his need for money. Thus in clause 40 John agreed, 'to no one will we sell, delay or deny right or justice'. The extension of royal justice (q.v.) in his father's reign had given John ample opportunity to take bribes and fines. It is by looking at these clauses about justice that we can understand how Magna Carta acquired its lasting fame. In clause 40, for example, we read that 'No free man shall be taken or imprisoned... except by the lawful judgement of his peers or by the law of the land.' The barons could not afford to allow Magna Carta to become a purely sectional document, securing only their own privileges, otherwise they would have lost support. The concessions they extracted from the king were therefore made applicable to all free men. For the villeins, however – for those who were not free – the Charter offered nothing. But they would not have expected anything from its terms.

The barons hardly expected King John to abide by the terms of the Charter for any longer than was necessary. To prevent him from going back on his word, they introduced a security clause (cl. 61). This set up a committee of twenty-five to whom breaches of the Charter were to be referred. If within forty days John failed to offer redress, the committee were empowered to move against him. The limited object of this procedure was to ensure that John restored the castles which he had confiscated in the course of his reign (cl. 52), but it set in motion the events that led to renewed war. In the summer John naturally seized every opportunity to drag his feet. By August aggrieved barons like Nicholas de Stuteville were complaining that they had still not recovered their property. To force John to comply, the twenty-five began ravaging his lands. It was therefore the operation of clause 61 that provided the legal cover for the renewal of hostilities that ended only after John's timely death in October 1216.

Magna Carta was born in a crisis, and so far from ending it, it merely provided additional material for argument. Nevertheless it survived to become one of the cornerstones of the constitution. Insofar as England can be said to have a written constitution, it consists of such documents as Magna Carta, 1215, and the Bill of Rights, 1689. But Magna Carta became permanent only in proportion as it became less contentious. When it was reissued in 1216 and 1217 it was reissued by the king's friends. As a result, the radical clauses restricting royal power were removed. The process was taken further still in 1225 when the slimmed-down Magna Carta was republished and its forest clauses hived off and supplemented in what became known as the Charter of the Forest. Thereafter, in any settlement of grievances between king and baronage, as in 1297 and 1311 for example, it was the custom to begin by confirming 'the

Charters'. Magna Carta was launched on its career as a document of symbolic significance.

Magna Carta survives in four 'originals', two preserved in the British Museum, one at Lincoln Cathedral and one at Salisbury Cathedral. Historians now doubt whether there was ever a master copy, which King John or one of his clerks would have been called on to seal at Runnymede on 15 or 19 June. Later in the month, however, copies of it were certainly being written out for distribution to the shires, and it is these which are the four surviving contemporary versions we have today (plate 65).

J.C. Holt, *Magna Carta*, 2nd ed., Cambridge, 1992.

MALORY, SIR THOMAS
The association of Malory's name with *Le Morte d'Arthur* rests on a paragraph at the end of the edition which Caxton (q.v.) printed in 1485, where the author reveals his identity, prays for deliverance from prison and says that he wrote the book in the ninth year of Edward IV's reign (1469). Malory is usually identified with the Warwickshire knight, Sir Thomas Malory of Newbold Revell, a lawless character whose criminal career affords little promise of the creative turn which his mind was to take in confinement. He first appears as a young esquire in the service of Richard Beauchamp, earl of Warwick. In 1443 he succeeded to his family estates. Two years later he was returned to parliament as a knight of the shire (i.e. MP) for Warwickshire. After this his career took a turn for the worse. In August 1451 an indictment was submitted at Nuneaton (Warks), accusing him of a succession of violent crimes over the previous eighteen months, culminating in two attacks on Coombe Abbey. Soon afterwards he was arrested, and he spent the next few years in and out of prison. After Edward IV came to

the throne in 1461 he received a pardon, but there is no firm evidence that he was ever at large again. Although he had once enjoyed the favour of the Beauchamp earls of Warwick, he seems to have been regarded as expendable by their Neville successors. He died in 1471, and was buried at Greyfriars, Newgate, which suggests that he must have spent his last days behind bars in the sheriff of London's prison at Newgate.

It was in the unlikely surroundings of prison that Malory whiled away his time writing the stories of King Arthur (q.v.). Malory's career affords a reminder that, however ruffianly the medieval gentry may appear, they were well acquainted with ballads and romances. In the preface to his edition of *Le Morte d'Arthur* Caxton hints at the sources which Malory had consulted. He says that the 'copye' he was publishing was one which Sir Thomas 'dyd take oute of certeyn bookes of Frensshe and reduced it into Englysshe'. These French books are not known by name today, but probably included the most popular French versions of the Arthurian romances, most of them obtainable easily enough in fifteenth-century London. All the same they were not the only sources Malory used. 'The Tale of King Arthur and the Emperor Lucius', for example, was derived from a fourteenth-century English poem, the alliterative *Morte Arthure*. Malory's achievement was to rewrite these earlier chivalric romances in a form acceptable to a late fifteenth-century audience. This involved rejecting the old-fashioned narrative technique of interweaving one story with another in favour of the 'modern' technique of progressive exposition. In other words, Malory started with Arthur and Lucius, moved onto the stories of Sir Lancelot and Sir Tristram, and ended up with Mordred's treachery and the deaths of Arthur and Guinevere.

For over four centuries Malory's great work was known only from Caxton's edition of 1485; no autograph manuscript is extant.

But in 1934 a manuscript was discovered in the library of Winchester College which brings us significantly closer to the lost original. The Winchester manuscript contains a text slightly different from Caxton's, including fuller versions of eight addresses by Malory to the reader at the end of each section known as explicits (*explicit*, it is finished). It was once thought, on the evidence of the explicits, that Malory had in fact written a set of separate stories. This hypothesis is now rejected. However, scholars do accept the episodic nature of Malory's work and the existence of inconsistencies both between and within the main sections.

Although Malory can no longer be credited with welding all the Arthurian legends into a coherent whole, his achievement was real none the less. He was a skilful writer bringing to his art a fluent English prose style, the development of which can be well appreciated from a reading of *Le Morte d'Arthur*.

See also ARTHURIAN LEGENDS; LANGUAGE AND LITERATURE

Le Morte D'Arthur, ed. J Cowen, Harmondsworth, 1969; P.J.C. Field, *The Life and Times of Sir Thomas Malory*, Cambridge, 1993.

MANOR

Although often used as if synonymous, the terms 'village' and 'manor' describe different, but related, concepts. A village is a small rural community in which agrarian occupations predominate. A manor, on the other hand, is a unit of lordship which may or may not happen to coincide with the village. If manor and village do coincide, the chances are that the lord will derive his income from three sources: the sale of produce grown on the home farm or demesne (q.v.), rents from the dependent tenantry and the profits of jurisdiction exercised in the manorial court. These constituents would have varied in importance, of course, according to the relative proportions of demesne and tenant land in the manor. When we talk about the estates of a particular lord, we mean the collection of manors that he held.

MATILDA, 'The Empress'
See STEPHEN

MERCHET
This was a licence paid by a villein (i.e., unfree) tenant to his lord for permission to marry off a daughter. Like heriot (q.v.), it was a mark of unfree condition, and by the fifteenth century became incorporated with the money rent, or disappeared altogether. On the manor of Minchinhampton (Glos) in the thirteenth century merchet payments varied from 1s 6d to 6s 8d.

MISERICORDS
Some of the most attractive medieval wood carvings are to be found on 'misericord' seats in churches. In characteristic medieval fashion these liftable seats provided the carver with the chance to turn practical need to creative advantage. The monks or canons who had to spend many hours singing in the choir needed some way of easing the strain on their feet; and this was achieved by so constructing the seats that when tipped up they exposed on their underside a bracket against which the priest could lean during the long service (Latin, *misericordia* = act of pity).

The first mention of misericords occurs in the twelfth century in connection with the convent of Hirsaugh in Germany. In England the earliest seats to survive are the thirteenth-century set in Exeter Cathedral (*c.*1230–70). The shape of the seats usually provides a rough guide to their date. In the thirteenth century the front edge was normally carved in convex form; in the fifteenth, seats were more commonly of polygonal shape with a pointed projection in the centre. Whatever the date of construction, however, misericords followed a consistent pattern of design, involving a central feature flanked by supporters. The subject matter of the carvings was derived from the entire range of Christian imagery, secular literature and drama. One of the most popular sources was the Bestiary, a Christian text available in the vernacular which used animals to illustrate the perennial theme of good and evil. On the other hand, there can be no doubt that a good many misericord subjects were carved for no better reason than that they appealed to the carver's fancy. How else are we to explain the carving at Beverley Minster of a wife thrashing her husband? Or of the knight falling from his horse at Lincoln Cathedral?

Sets of misericord seats survive in many of our cathedrals and greater churches, notably at Exeter, which has fifty, Beverley Minster and Winchester, which have sixty-eight each, and Lincoln Cathedral with no fewer than 108. Perhaps the best of all are those for which a talented school of carvers was responsible in northern England, at Ripon, Chester, Manchester and Carlisle. These four churches offer a dazzling display of the carpenter's art.

C. Grossinger, *The World Upside Down. English Misericords*, London, 1996.

MISTERY PLAYS
A rich corpus of religious drama has survived from the later Middle Ages in the form of the plays performed by the craft or 'mistery' guilds (*mistery*, *métier* = trade). Like so much of the medieval cultural heritage, the plays were devotional in inspiration and didactic in purpose. In other words, they set out to convey the Biblical message to an audience many of whom would have been illiterate.

The mistery plays had their origins in the dramatic dialogues which had from time to time been interpolated into the liturgy (q.v.)

to make the events of the Mass more real to ordinary lay folk. In these dialogues the parts would have been taken by clerics speaking in Latin. The transition to outdoor drama was intimately connected with the rise of the feast of Corpus Christi in the late Middle Ages. Corpus Christi, falling as it did on the Thursday after Trinity Sunday, so close to midsummer, afforded an excellent opportunity for processions and outdoor pageants. From this ritual, centred on the completion of the sacrifice of Christ, developed, appropriately enough, the idea of presenting a dramatic cycle extending from the Creation through the life and death of Christ to the Last Judgement. It is this extended theme which provides the subject matter of most of the plays, and accounts for their sometimes enormous length.

The English Corpus Christi plays are always thought to have been acted as processional cycles. A cycle was composed of a series of plays, each one assigned to a guild or group of guilds (q.v.). The plays were performed on horse-drawn wagons, or pageants, which were moved from station to station through the town, so that an audience at any one station would see the entire cycle acted out in full in front of them, provided that they were prepared to wait long enough. Estimates which have been made suggest that if they had wanted to see an entire cycle, the onlookers, whether standing or looking from upstairs windows, would have had to rise at daybreak for the first performance and wait till late into the night for the last. At Chester, indeed, the performance was spread over three days. These very practical problems of production have led to the suggestion that one of the longest cycles – that of the York guilds – must have been performed indoors, but in the absence of any conclusive evidence either way the question must remain open. Whatever may have been the case at York, it seems that generally the plays were performed outdoors, in prominent positions around the town. When Margaret, Henry VI's queen, visited Coventry in 1457 to see the Corpus Christi cycle, she stayed at the house of Richard Woods, which overlooked the first of the stations or acting-places. It is reported that she witnessed all the plays except Doomsday, which could not be performed for shortage of daylight.

Official texts of the cycles, copied from manuscripts in the hands of the guilds themselves, were kept by the town authorities, and were added to and altered from time to time. During the Reformation these texts were called in so that expressions of religious sentiment contrary to reformist ideas could be eliminated. Stripped of their 'popery', however, the plays lived on, and indeed experienced a revival early in Elizabeth's reign. After the 1580s, however, nothing more is heard of performances.

Bearing in mind their instructive purpose, the mistery plays come across, even today, as works of extraordinary force and power. It is fair to assume that the plays were the works of clerics, and in view of the orthodox nature of their content, rather conservative ones at that. They relied for their success on powerful visual effects, achieved through the use of stage props, and on strong characterization, communicated not only by speech but by gesture and expression. Herod, for example, the first medieval villain, was depicted as a ranting tyrant. In the work of the Wakefield Master, perhaps the most remarkable playwright of the fifteenth century, he was transformed into an overbearing magnate. Never one to stand back from his work, the Wakefield writer used his medium to complain about such contemporary grievances as unruly magnate retainers and the corruptibility of ecclesiastical lawyers. Like all medieval artists he chose to present the past in terms of the present. The strength of these plays lay in their very directness. How much more dramatic still they must have been when performed with all the paraphernalia and props on which the guilds lavished so much of their money.

A.H. Nelson, *The Medieval English Stage, Chicago and London*, 1974; *English Mystery Plays*, ed. P. Happé, Harmondsworth, 1975; G. Wickham, *Early English Stages, 1300-1600*, 3 vols, London, 1959-81; *The Cambridge Companion to Medieval English Theatre*, ed. R. Beadle, Cambridge, 1994.

MONASTICISM
Monasticism involved a communal life of prayer and devotion in accordance with the triple vows of poverty, chastity and obedience. The origins of monasticism are to be found in the early Christian East, where ascetics like St Anthony sought the hermit lifestyle in the belief that only by withdrawing from the temptations of the world could the Christian attain a proper understanding of God. Anthony inspired many to follow him into the desert. Some of these folk lived singly; others, however, joined together to live as communities, or monasteries as we call them.

In the course of the fourth and fifth centuries the contemplative life started by the desert fathers spread to western Europe, where it was given the shape it was to have for the rest of the Middle Ages in the Rule of St Benedict of Nursia (*c.*480–550). Although Benedict's Rule was not a work of such originality as was once thought, it still remains fundamental for establishing a moderate, balanced set of guidelines adapting the eremetic tradition to the communal approach favoured in the West. In Benedict's view a monastic community should be self-supporting, dependent only on homegrown produce, and self-contained, because it was not the task of monks to undertake social or pastoral work. Benedict laid down guidelines for an horarium, or division of time within the day. Some four hours were to be spent in prayer in the church, four hours in reading and private prayer and the remaining six waking hours in manual labour. Almost certainly the labour intended by St Benedict was not heavy work in the fields but domestic or artistic work.

In the early Anglo-Saxon period monasteries were founded in Kent by Augustine and his fellow missionaries soon after their arrival in 597, and in the north by Celtic missionaries coming from Iona. But these abbeys, particularly those in the north, suffered badly from Viking invasions, and despite a revival in the tenth century it was left to the Normans after 1066 to infuse new life into English monasticism.

In 1066 about forty-eight monasteries were still functioning in England, all of them south of a line drawn from the Humber to the Severn. After the Conquest the Normans quickly made their mark in founding new monasteries and reviving old ones. Battle, Shrewsbury, Chester, Colchester, St Mary's, York, and Tewkesbury were all new foundations of the late eleventh century: Whitby, Jarrow and Wearmouth were revivals of previously vigorous northern communities that had lapsed in the Viking period. Equally striking was the increase in the number of recruits to the cloister. The house of Worcester rose from twelve to fifty under Bishop Wulfstan (1062-95), Rochester from twenty-two to over sixty under Bishop Gundulf (1077-1108) and Gloucester from ten to a hundred under Abbot Serlo (1072-1104). Many of the newly appointed Norman abbots were enthusiastic builders. The abbey churches of Tewkesbury, Ely, Peterborough and St Albans were all rebuilt in this period. But the new abbots also reformed the internal regime of their houses, introducing the customs and observances of the Norman houses from which they had come.

In the years immediately following the Conquest, the main source of inspiration for monastic reform came from Normandy. But in the later eleventh and twelfth centuries a wider variety of influences was felt. As society grew more diverse and sophisticated, the varying monastic impulses could no longer be contained within the traditional Benedictine frame. The monopoly of the old Benedictine Order was broken, and new orders came into existence. One of the first of these was the Cluniac Order – the family dependant on the great Burgundian abbey of Cluny (q.v.) – which established several dependent houses in England, notably those at Lewes (1077) and Reading (1121). An altogether more radical departure was represented by the Cistercian Order (q.v.), which came into existence in the early twelfth century. The puritanism of the Cistercians, abrasive and uncompromising, represented a major challenge to traditional Benedictinism and evoked an enthusiastic response from founders. By the time that St Bernard, the founding father of the Cistercians, died in 1153, there were 343 houses belonging to the order, of which thirty-six were in England. A very different approach to monasticism was represented by the Canons Regular, who came into existence around 1100. The canons, while following a version of the monastic Rule, were allowed more compromises with the world and could undertake pastoral duties, whereas monks were confined to the cloister. Many of their early canons' houses were founded in the towns, an example being Osney Abbey, Oxford. The two main orders of canons were the Augustinians (q.v.) and the Premonstratensians (q.v.), both of whom made swift advances in England in the reign of Henry I (1100–35).

There were numerous smaller monastic orders; England, indeed, gave birth to an order of its own, that of St Gilbert (q.v.) of Sempringham, which revived the idea of the double monastery embracing both men and women. But the principal orders represented in England by the late twelfth century were the Benedictines, the Cistercians and the Augustinian Canons. After about 1200 the pace of monastic expansion slowed. In the later Middle Ages the only order to experience significant growth was the Carthusian Order (q.v.), perhaps because it preserved its original purity longer than the others. After 1300, it is true, the monasteries continued to prosper: the richer abbots and priors were still great figures in society. But monasticism was no longer at the cutting edge of spiritual life. Over time, the monks lost the intellectual primacy which they had enjoyed in the age of Lanfranc and Anselm (q.v.). With the establishment of the universities (q.v.) in the thirteenth century, the most gifted thinkers of the period – men like Wycliffe and Bradwardine – were to be found in the lecture rooms of Oxford and Cambridge.

An innovation of the thirteenth century was the establishment of the mendicant orders – the orders of friars. The friars, unlike the monks, were not permitted any ownership of property; they were dependent on alms originally gained by begging (mendicancy). The two main orders of friars were the Dominicans (q.v.) and the Franciscans (q.v.). In England, as elsewhere, the friars quickly became very popular because they represented a return to the apostolic ideal. By the end of the thirteenth century there were mendicant houses in almost every English town. Many of these became fashionable burial places for the wealthy. Though criticized by writers like Langland, the mendicants retained their hold on popular favour for longer than did the monks.

The monks were committed to a life of prayer and contemplation. Their daily regime was governed by the horarium or timetable that prescribed the offices to be celebrated in the church. These offices were composed of psalms, lessons and anthems (q.v. LITURGY). The horarium varied according to the season, but the winter arrangement can be taken as an example. The day would begin at about 2 a.m., with the singing of Nocturns, or Matins. Lauds, the next office to be recited, came at dawn, followed by Prime at about

6 a.m. The monks would then read in the cloister until 8 a.m., when they would return to the dormitory to wash. Their next office in the church was Terce, following which the monks would assemble in the chapter house for the daily meeting or 'chapter' of the community. Between chapter and Sext, at midday, the monks would devote themselves to pursuits like reading, writing or illumination of manuscripts. The singing of Sext was closely followed by High Mass and the recitation of Nones. Then at 2 p.m. (or midday in summer) the community would proceed to the refectory for dinner – probably not without haste, for this was the first meal of the day. After dinner they would devote themselves to reading until about 5 p.m. Then came Vespers, and at 6.15, following some refreshment, Compline. The community retired to the dormitory at about 6.30 for some seven hours' rest before the routine began again at 2 the next morning. The peculiarities of the horarium, and in particular the provision of a siesta after dinner in summertime, arise from the origins of monasticism in the hot climates of the east and the failure to make adjustments to the cold north. To what extent flexibility was introduced into the monastic observance is a question to which no certain answer can be given. However, it seems likely that by the thirteenth century the rules on silence would have been eased. Discussion would need to take place not only about matters spiritual or scholastic but also in a great Benedictine house about the innumerable business transactions created by the day-to-day running of an extensive estate.

St Benedict provided simple but lasting guidelines for the administration of the monastery. He envisaged that the monks would be ruled by an abbot, assisted by a prior and by no more than one or two officials such as the cellarer, who provided for the material needs of the community. By the eleventh century, as houses grew larger and their needs more complex, further officials were needed.

Typically, there were the precentor, who supervised the liturgical and literary activities, the sacrist, who took charge of the fabric and contents of the church, and the infirmarer, who looked after the hospital. The most important of these officials was always the cellarer, for he controlled the purse-strings. By the twelfth century in most houses centralized models of administration were beginning to break up. There were a number of reasons for this. Firstly, it was becoming usual to divide the lands of the monastery between those of the abbot and those assigned for the support of the community; and, secondly, the revenues assigned to the monastic portion no longer typically passed through the hands of the cellarer but were divided among separate departments headed by monk 'obedientiaries', who derived their income either in money or in kind from lands and manors allotted for their support. This new model could have provided a convenient structure, but its disadvantage was a lack of central direction. As a result, in some houses there was a return to something like the old centralized pattern. At Canterbury Cathedral Priory, for example, the obedientiary system, which had been instituted by the 1130s, was amended sometime between 1163 and 1167 to allow the appointment of central (monastic) treasurers from whom the cellarer, chamberlain and sacrist each received their rents. The new arrangements, coupled with the elaborate audit each Michaelmas, prevented overspending by the subordinate obedientiaries.

An idea of the surroundings in which the monks lived can be gained from the many surviving monastic fabrics. In one of the larger houses the precincts were usually entered through a fine gateway like those at Ely or Bury St Edmund's. The gateway typically gave access to an outer courtyard containing the stores, granary and guesthouse. Further in would be the main monastic buildings, ranged around the cloister garth. Unless, as at

Malmesbury or Canterbury, the local topography dictated otherwise, the cloister was usually placed to the south of the church, to gain maximum hours of sunlight. Generally, cloister walks were open to the elements, but in some richer houses in the late Middle Ages glass was inserted into the openings. Immediately adjacent to the cloister was the church, where so much of the day was spent. Typically, the interior of a monastic church was broken up by screens and partitions, as can still be seen at St Albans. At the far end of the nave there was the rood screen, so named from the rood or crucifix which towered above it, and to the west of this a nave altar, for use by the local people if the abbey doubled as a parish church or by the lay brothers if it was Cistercian. East of the rood screen was an open space under the tower, and east of this again a second screen, the pulpitum, which gave access to the monks' choir. To the south-east of the church, and entered from the east walk of the cloister, would be the chapter house. Here the community would meet each day, and here too, as at Rievaulx, the early abbots would be buried. The rest of the east walk was usually taken up by the dormitory and the south walk by the refectory. Along the west range of the cloister the ground plan was subject to greater variation. In Benedictine or Augustinian houses the abbot's quarters or the cellarium might be found here. In Cistercian houses, however, the space was almost invariably occupied by the lay brothers' quarters – a good example being the range at Fountains (W. Yorks). The infirmary and calefactory would then be tucked away outside the cloister, often, as at Sherborne and Fountains, behind the east range (plate 138).

The English monasteries were dissolved in the reign of Henry VIII, the lesser ones in 1536, and the greater in 1538-40. Their buildings met with differing fates. Five abbey churches became cathedrals of newly created dioceses. A few more, chiefly situated in the towns, were taken over for use as parish churches, as for example at Selby and Tewkesbury. But all too often abbeys which were not reused in this way were pounced on as quarries by the local townsfolk. For this reason hardly a trace remains of the once great abbeys of Burton, Abingdon or Winchcombe. With the buildings of the Cistercians, which were usually situated in the countryside, it was a different story. Some, like Buckland (Devon) and Forde (Dorset), were converted by their new owners into country houses. Others survived roofless, but otherwise intact. In the eighteenth and early nineteenth centuries monastic ruins exerted a powerful appeal over the Romantic imagination. Tintern inspired Wordsworth to write some of his finest lines, while Fountains and Rievaulx were made the centrepieces of arcadian landscapes.

D. Knowles, *The Monastic Order in England, 940–1216*, 2nd ed., Cambridge, 1963; *The Religious Orders in England*, 3 vols, Cambridge, 1948–59; J. Burton, *Monastic and Religious Orders in Britain, 1000–1300*, Cambridge, 1994; C.H. Lawrence, *Medieval Monasticism: Forms of Religious Life in Western Europe in the Middle Ages*, 2nd ed., London, 1989.

MONTFORT, SIMON DE

A Frenchman by birth and upbringing, Simon became an Englishman by adoption. Authoritarian by temperament, he became a populist by necessity. These paradoxes lie at the heart of Earl Simon's career.

Born around 1208, Simon was a younger son of Simon IV de Montfort, who had led the crusade against the Albigensian heretics in southern France. The younger Simon's interest in English affairs arose from the marriage of his grandfather, Simon III, to Amicia, daughter of Robert Beaumont, earl of Leicester. When the last of the Beaumonts died childless in 1205, the inheritance should, strictly, have been divided between his two sisters, but Amicia's portion was taken first by the king and then by the earl of Chester. Simon accordingly had to come to England in person to claim what he regarded as his rightful inheritance. In 1231 he was granted the lands, and in 1239 the title, of the earl of Leicester.

For a man whose origins were unpromising, Simon did remarkably well for himself in England. In 1238, the year before his recognition as earl of Leicester, he married Eleanor, King Henry III's sister (q.v.). Although endorsed by the king, this marriage aroused the hostility of the aristocracy, who complained that they had not been consulted. At this stage of his career Simon was seen firmly as a king's man, someone tarred by the same brush as the rest of Henry's foreign-born favourites. His disaffection with the court appears to have sprung from a dispute over his wife's dower claims. Eleanor had been previously married to the younger William Marshal, earl of Pembroke, and she was entitled to a third of her former husband's estates. Henry, however, proved reluctant to hand over the lands, because his treasury was benefiting from the income, and the dispute became a running sore in relations between the two parties. For many years, however, Simon enjoyed the king's favour. In 1248 he was sent as lieutenant to Gascony (q.v.), to restore order in the duchy. He set about the job with ruthless efficiency, and complaints about him were sent back to England. After four years he was recalled and summoned to answer the charges. Henry's treatment of his brother-in-law did much to widen the rift between the two.

In 1258 the Provisions of Oxford (q.v.) were published, subjecting the king's government to conciliar supervision. Simon played little part in the crisis leading to the Provisions as he had gone to France to help negotiate a peace treaty between Henry III and Louis IX. Nevertheless, Henry's comment that much as he dreaded lightning, he feared Simon even more, suggests that he regarded the earl as a potential adversary even at this stage. In the years which followed Simon stood foursquare behind the Provisions. But his colleagues found him a difficult man to work with, and the disunity which weakened the baronial ranks enabled Henry to regain control in 1262. Simon took refuge in France. What brought him back in April 1263 was the crisis unleashed by a rising in the Welsh Marches. Edward, the future Edward I, tried to restore order in the area but his efforts were unavailing because he offended the Marcher lords by bringing along a force of foreign mercenaries. The Marchers now gave their backing to Simon as the man most likely to restore order. His ascendancy did not last long, however. By the end of the year Simon was forfeiting support because of his personal acquisitiveness and his involvement in attacks on aliens. As his power base shrank, he agreed that the differences between himself and the king should be submitted to Louis IX of France for arbitration. Louis's judgement (the Mise of Amiens, January 1264) was a decisive statement in favour of Henry. Simon had little option but to fight. He marched south to head off a French invasion force, while Edward simultaneously moved west from Winchelsea. The two armies met at Lewes on 14 May 1264. The battle was a mighty victory for Simon, and Henry III and Edward were taken prisoner. The earl used his moment of triumph to impose a new constitution known as the Mise of Lewes, which appointed a Council of Nine to govern in the king's name. But he was in a difficult situation. He could neither legalize his authority nor surrender it. Supreme as he was for the moment, his position was quickly undermined by the defection of his leading supporters in the Marches. His ambitions to establish his family territorially in this area aroused resentment among the local aristocracy. By the spring of 1265 the

Marches were ablaze. Simon marched west to quell the disorder. With his power base disintegrating, he appealed to a wider public by summoning representatives from the shires and the boroughs to a parliament (q.v.) in June. This was a bold propagandist move, yet insufficient to save him from the armed challenge of Edward and the Marcher barons. On 4 August 1265 the two sides met in battle at Evesham, and Simon was defeated and killed.

Before long the monks of Evesham, who had taken the earl's body for burial, found themselves growing rich from offerings made at his tomb. A cult of Simon the martyr developed. Pilgrims, such as the earl of Oxford, came to his tomb from afar. But the cult was never officially recognized.

Simon's undoubted idealism appears to have been fed by a deeply felt piety. According to the Melrose chronicler, he wore a hair shirt by day and by night and knew the primer and the psalter by heart. His piety underpinned his campaign for the Provisions. He was convinced of the rightness of his cause. But he was also driven by material self-interest: he fought long and hard for a settlement of his wife's dower claims and at the height of his power struggled to establish his sons in the aristocracy. He apparently saw nothing wrong in pursuing grievances and high principles in parallel. But these weaknesses in his stance cost him support. His rapacity bred resentment, and so too did his authoritarianism. He was the vehicle for high-minded reform, but as a campaigner he was fatally flawed.

J.R. Maddicott, *Simon de Montfort*, Cambridge, 1994.

MORTMAIN

Alienation into mortmain (literally 'dead hand') describes the conveyance of land to the Church. In England, by the thirteenth century the loss of land to the Church was giving rise to concern. If an estate was granted to the Church, it was lost to the land market for ever; while if it was held in frankalmoign (free alms), as most Church land was, the crown lost knight service; moreover, the Church being an undying corporation, the overlord lost the feudal incidents to which he was entitled. It was very likely to meet the objections of landlords concerned at the loss of feudal income that Edward I enacted the Statute of Mortmain in 1279. Echoing similar legislation passed in other countries, the statute prohibited all acquisitions of land by the Church in future. Draconian though its terms may have sounded, it in fact did little more than introduce a licensing system. Before an alienation was made, an inquisition *ad quod dampnum* was held in the appropriate shire to determine what feudal incidents would be lost. The alienor would then be charged a fine roughly in proportion to the scale of financial loss involved. If it ever had the serious object of limiting the acquisition of land by the Church, the Statute came much too late in the day: by 1279 the Church had already acquired most of the land it was ever to acquire in the Middle Ages.

S. Raban, *Mortmain Legislation and the English Church, 1279–1500*, Cambridge, 1982.

MUSIC

What did most to shape the character of early medieval music was its association with the Church. The link between music and worship had been forged by the Jews, and it was to be reinforced by the Christian community. Much of the music that has come down to us from the Middle Ages is therefore religious. But not all of it is. Medieval people liked to relax to the sound of light music as much as people do today; the Middle Ages gave us the love lyric. But what is common to practically all surviving medieval music, whether religious or secular, is that it is vocal.

The oldest form of Christian music is known as plainchant. In a large basilica the spoken voice would soon have been lost in the aisles. So, to improve audibility and to lend an air of solemnity, it was decided to intone the texts. In simple plainchant a melody of two phrases is sung without accompaniment and repeated for each verse of the text, the two melodic phrases corresponding to the two halves of a verse. Plainchant, though associated with the name of Pope Gregory the Great (590-604), was in existence well before his time. As it spread throughout Europe, it became the standard chant for the divine offices sung in Church; and at the hands of the monks, whose principal employment was to sing it, it became a musical form of singular beauty.

The essence of the chant was its simplicity but, human nature being what it is, before long men thought to improve on it. The liturgy (q.v.) was enriched by interpolations of melody or text, or both, which are known as 'tropes'. By the beginning of the twelfth century, when the fashion had run its course, every office had been troped, and even the tropes themselves were troped.

If we look at the earliest manuscripts of plainchant, what immediately stands out is that rhythm is not indicated at all, and pitch not very exactly. This must mean that both pitch and rhythm were part of what is called 'performance practice': that is, they were learned, understood and passed on orally, and did not need to be codified. What these early sources tell us is the shape of the melody and its construction, that is all. They were an adjunct to a tradition that was still basically oral. But once a composer, no longer satisfied with simply interpolating a trope, chose to superimpose one tune on another, written notation was bound to become necessary if singers were to keep in time with one another. So in the course of the next century western music acquired the written forms it still uses today. And once that was done, the way was open to polyphony. The two Winchester Tropers, dating from the late tenth and early eleventh centuries, contain a number of polyphonic settings which were used for the major festivals of the Church year. There are indications, however, that the Normans may not have viewed polyphony with such favour. And, besides, the Church did not allow every part of the liturgy to be elaborated without limit by the addition of more voice parts.

One of the happiest forms of medieval polyphony was the motet. This entailed a tenor chanting plainsong as a background to one or more upper voices, each with a different text. The potential for variation was almost limitless. The sacred tenor could find himself accompanied not by a devotional text but by a love poem, sung not in Latin but in the vernacular. This combination might be one which modern listeners would find bizarre. The modern preference is for harmony. The medieval audience, however had an ear for contrast. Most of the early vernacular motets to survive are in French. Almost the only one in English is 'Worldes blisse, have good day' over the tenor '*Benedicamus Domino*', which dates from the later thirteenth century. The secular motet apparently exercised less appeal in England than it did on the continent. But another polyphonic form – the round or canon – took no time to establish itself in the English repertory. A round is a song in which the singers come in one after the other with exactly the same text. The most famous example is '*Sumer is icumen in*', written at Reading Abbey in about 1240. It is unlikely that this attractive piece was the spontaneous work of a monk overjoyed one afternoon by the thought of summer approaching. In the manuscript the English poem is written above a Latin text, '*perspice Christicola*'. The evidence suggests that the Latin text is the earlier and that the composer then made a setting of the English poem as a *contrafactum*. If that is the case, then the composer was a very skilled artist indeed.

By the time that 'Sumer is icumen in' was written, major changes were taking place in the content and form of secular music. In the twelfth century, a period of cultural renaissance, Europe had awoken to the sound of the courtly love lyric (q.v. LANGUAGE AND LITERATURE). The troubadours of southern France had begun to sing of beauty and love. Their tender songs began to filter northwards after 1137, when Eleanor of Aquitaine (q.v.) married Louis VII, king of France, Bernard of Ventadorn, one of the greatest musicians of the day, coming north with her. A decade and a half later, Eleanor was divorced by Louis and married the Angevin Henry II (q.v.), who inherited the English crown in 1154, but the second marriage does not seem to have borne the fruitful musical consequences of the first. Even though French was, and was to remain for another century or more, the vernacular language of the English nobility, the troubadour genre did not strike roots here. Nonetheless, it can be inferred from the famous story of Richard I (q.v.) that Eleanor's favourite son inherited her musical interests: while a captive of Leopold, duke of Austria, Richard was discovered by his faithful minstrel Blondel, who went from castle to castle singing a song known to them both until finally a refrain from a tower told him he had reached his master's prison. One or two songs composed by Richard have in fact survived. Yet his tastes do not seem to have been shared to any extent by the nobility. English composers could turn their hand to some delightful rounds like 'Sumer is icumen in'. But before the late fourteenth century there is an almost total absence of anything corresponding to French courtly polyphony. It is conceivable that this is just an optical illusion caused by the loss of the music. However, had many more songs been written, they would surely have survived in greater number than they have. The preponderance of Mass pieces and Latin motets may be a not unfaithful reflec-

tion of what was composed in England in the Middle Ages. Part of the problem may have lain in the king's own choir – the Chapel Royal – in the fourteenth century. None of the minstrels whose names are recorded in the account books of the king's household can be connected with any piece of written music that has come down to us. Nor for that matter can the name of any clerk be connected with any non-sacred composition. John Aleyn, a canon of Windsor (d.1373), wrote a liturgical motet but there the list ends. A gulf separates performance from composition. With the approach of the fifteenth century, however, the story changes. From the 1390s there survives a collection of songs made by Thomas Turk, a Fellow of Winchester, to pass away the long evenings around Christmas and the New Year. And at court the king himself was a source of inspiration, to judge from the two compositions in the Old Hall manuscript ascribed to 'Roy Henry', probably Henry IV or V.

Shortly before 1400 the influence of Ars Nova began to be felt in England. Ars Nova was a new current of musical thought which took its name from a highly influential book written by the Frenchman Philippe de Vitry in about 1325. Philippe sought to distinguish the old method of notating motets in longs and breves from the new one in shorter values, of semibreves and minims. The new rules he prescribed encouraged musicians to break free from the old rhythmic patterns and to employ all types of semibreve and minim combination. The Old Hall manuscript mentioned earlier is the best collection of English music illustrating the new influences. It contains an important composition ('Veni creator spiritus/Veni sancte spiritus') by John Dunstable, the most distinguished English composer of the fifteenth century. But the bulk of Dunstable's work, amounting to some sixty compositions in all, is preserved in foreign manuscripts, an indication perhaps that his influence was felt more directly in France and Burgundy, where he spent the most active years of his life, than it was in England.

In conclusion, something should be said of developments in instrumental accompaniment in this period. By the ninth century there is evidence that organs were being made in England. By the time of Bishop Athelwold (963–84) Winchester Cathedral had an organ so big that we are told seventy men stood perspiring as they worked its bellows. The church organ quickly established itself as an indispensable accompaniment to sacred music. For the performance of secular music there was a dazzling array of instruments to choose from. String instruments included the rebec, held to the chin like a violin, and the viele, which was held upright on the lap. Both were played with a bow. The psaltery, which is known to have been played by St Dunstan (d. 988), is an example of a string instrument that was plucked. The range of wind instruments included the flute and the recorder, and of percussion instruments, the triangle, cymbals and castanets. But in the Middle Ages instrumental sound served mainly as an accompaniment to voices, and not as a musical form in its own right. The move towards independence was to come later, during the Renaissance.

The Pelican History of Music: i, ed. A. Robertson and D. Stevens, Harmondsworth, 1960; Medieval English Songs, ed. E. J. Dobson and F. Ll. Harrison, London, 1979; A. Wathey, Music in the Royal and Noble Households in Late Medieval England, New York and London, 1989; J. Caldwell, The Oxford History of English Music, i. From the Beginnings to c.1715, Oxford, 1991.

NEVILLE, RICHARD, EARL OF WARWICK

'Warwick the Kingmaker' is the most notorious 'over-mighty subject' of the English late Middle Ages. Although undeniably ambitious, he usually acted defensively rather than out of a desire to accumulate power in his hands.

The Nevilles of Raby (Co. Durham) were an active and widely ramified family. They had held estates in the north since at least the twelfth century. But only with Ralph Neville, earl of Westmorland (d. 1425) did they rise from regional to national prominence. Earl Ralph married twice. From his first marriage, to Margaret Stafford, descended the senior line of the family, the earls of Westmorland. From his second marriage, to Joan Beaufort, descended the junior line from which Warwick sprang. Richard, Joan's eldest son, became earl of Salisbury; this man's son and heir, also Richard, was Warwick 'the Kingmaker'. Warwick inherited his father's earldom and went on to acquire that of Warwick by his marriage to Anne, daughter and eventual heiress of Richard Beauchamp.

Warwick played a prominent part in the Wars of the Roses (q.v.). He shared in the triumph of the Yorkist lords when they invaded England from Calais (q.v.) and he defeated the Lancastrians at Northampton on 10 July 1460. Early the following year, however, he was less successful. At the second battle of St Albans (17 February) he was defeated by Queen Margaret's force. Although valorous, he showed little tactical and strategic talent. Even so, there is no denying the role that he played in putting Edward of York on the throne in 1461.

In the 1460s Warwick gradually became disenchanted with Edward's policies. He favoured closer ties with Louis XI of France, whereas the king favoured Louis's rivals, the Burgundians. He also had a private grievance: he felt that the king was not promoting satisfactory marriages for his daughters. In 1469, accordingly, he formed an alliance with Clarence, Edward's feckless brother, to reassert his influence over the king. Warwick and Clarence invaded England from Calais, defeating Edward at Edgecote, but the king escaped their clutches. Warwick fled into exile, and in France he transferred his support to Queen Margaret and the Lancastrians. On 13 September 1470 he invaded England again, restored Henry VI (q.v.) to the throne, and forced Edward abroad once more. His second exercise in king-making proved to be short-lived, however. Edward, equipped and supported by his Burgundian allies, returned in the following spring, and Warwick was defeated and killed at Barnet (14 April 1471).

The bare outlines of Warwick's career are quickly narrated. However, it is more difficult to form a clear view of the man's character. Warwick was brave and glamorous, and he knew how to court popularity. However, he had a cruel side. His merciless attitude to his opponents contrasts sharply with Edward's generosity: after triumphing at Edgecote he executed Earl Rivers, the earls of Devon and Pembroke, Sir Thomas Herbert and Sir John Woodville. He lived in a competitive age, and he was highly competitive himself. He gives the impression of a man of little principle, and it is true that he switched sides. His one lodestar was self-preservation. When he felt that his interests were challenged, he acted; and in 1470 he acted decisively.

M. Hicks, *Warwick the Kingmaker*, Oxford, 1998.

NORMANDY

The origins of Normandy are to be found in the Treaty of St Clair-sur-Epte, 911, by which the Carolingian ruler, Charles the Simple, granted the lands east and west of the Seine estuary to Rollo the Viking and his descendants. Rollo's successors proved effective and dynamic rulers. By the later eleventh century the impact of Norman expansion was being felt in almost every part of Europe.

The conquest of England in 1066 has to be seen in the context of the much wider experience of Norman expansion. It was part of a movement which embraced the Norman settlement of Sicily and southern Italy and Norman participation in the First Crusade. Spearheaded by the duke himself, it was carried out by an aggressive military aristocracy.

The effect of the Norman Conquest of England was to create a kind of cross-Channel Norman empire. The Conqueror treated his dominions as one, ruling them as king-duke. However, it is doubtful if he intended this novel arrangement to last. After his death, his eldest son Robert succeeded him in Normandy and his second son William Rufus (q.v.) in England. This division of lands followed the customary Norman rules of inheritance, whereby the family patrimony passed to the eldest son and heir, and any lands acquired by the father in his lifetime to younger sons. The division between the brothers set up tensions. Robert was naturally keen to win England, and William to win Normandy. William achieved his aim of securing Normandy in 1096 when Robert pawned it to raise money for the crusade (q.v.). However, the period of reunification was brief. Robert returned from the crusade in 1100 to recover his inheritance. Only a short time before, Rufus had been killed in the New Forest and was succeeded in his kingdom by the third brother, Henry (q.v.). Henry and Robert now competed for each other's lands, as Robert once had with Rufus. This period of competition ended in 1106 when Henry defeated Robert at Tinchebrai, cast him into prison and brought Normandy and England together again.

The period of 'Norman empire' ended amidst the civil turmoil of Stephen's reign. By the mid-1140s Stephen's rival, Matilda, and her husband, Geoffrey of Anjou, had effectively overrun Normandy, separating it from England and annexing it to the Angevin lands. In 1154 their son, Henry – Henry II (q.v.) – having succeeded his father in Anjou, succeeded Stephen in England. The reconstituted union of England and Normandy thus became one link in a much larger chain of territories that included Maine, Anjou and Aquitaine. This larger entity survived until 1204 when King Philip of France completely overran Normandy and annexed it to his own kingdom. Normandy was thus linked to the English crown, on and off, for a period of a century and a half. The cement which held the two dominions together, and drew them back after separation, was the cross-Channel aristocratic estates. When William had conquered England in 1066, he had seized the estates of the English aristocracy and given them to his own followers. The great Norman baronial families, the Beaumonts, the Lacys and the Montgomerys, henceforth held lands on both sides of the Channel. It was accordingly in their interest to see the two dominions ruled by the same man, for as soon as they were partitioned, with each ruler wanting the other's half, a conflict of loyalties was bound to arise. This was why the prolonged separation in the civil war of Stephen's reign was so disastrous for them. It forced them to make choices. Many of them resolved the issue by dividing their lands between different branches of the family.

To recognize that it was convenient to have England and Normandy under the same ruler is not to imply that much administrative assimilation occurred. Progress to assimilation was slight. England had its own institutions of government, and Normandy likewise. The link between the two dominions was found solely in the person of the ruler. The king-dukes gave expression to their will and their lordship by constant travel backwards and forwards across the Channel. Both Henry I and Henry II spent much more of their time south of the Channel than north of it.

The Angevins' claim to Normandy was surrendered by Henry III in the Treaty of Paris in 1259 as part of a more general settlement of Anglo-French differences. A century and a half later, however, it was to be resurrected by Henry V (q.v.). When renewing the English claim to the crown of France, Henry made a special claim for the cession to him of Normandy. In 1417, when he invaded France, he made a priority of conquering and settling the duchy. What he carried out was a kind of Norman Conquest in reverse. He divided the lands of the duchy among his senior commanders, much as Duke William had divided England's among his. The apportionment gave the recipients a vested interest in maintenance of the conquest. But the English occupation of Normandy was not to last long. The duchy was recaptured by the French in the course of 1449-50.

J. Le Patourel, *The Norman Empire*, Oxford, 1976; *England and Normandy in the Middle Ages*, ed. D. Bates and A. Curry, Woodbridge, 1994.

NORWICH

Norwich, the capital of East Anglia, first appears in the records in the early tenth century, which suggests that its origins lay in the Danish settlement of eastern England from c.870 to 917. By 1086 Norwich was the third or fourth largest town in England, a reflection of the importance which it derived from being the economic and administrative centre of a large and prosperous hinterland. Although the Normans inherited a town already well established, they transformed it socially and topographically. By 1075 they had built a castle and had founded a new borough alongside the old one; twenty years later Bishop Herbert de Losinga moved the seat of the East Anglian diocese there from Thetford and began work on the present cathedral. The works undertaken in the first half of the twelfth century at both the cathedral and the castle represented the biggest building programme Norwich was to see until the circuit of stone walls was erected between 1297 and 1344. These walls enclosed an area as big as the city of London, while containing only a quarter of its population. Medieval towns may have been squalid and unhygienic but in Norwich at any rate overcrowding was not a problem except in the market area.

In the later Middle Ages the production of worsted cloth was the main manufacturing trade carried on in the city. The wealth which the trade brought to the city is reflected in the rebuilding of many of its churches. Norwich has more medieval churches than any other city in England, but before the late-medieval population decline the tally was even higher. The church of St Peter Mancroft, in the market place, is one of the largest parish churches in England, and its east window, a product of the city's glaziers, is particularly fine. Many of the other parish churches are characterized by high towers and grand clerestories. Central Norwich offers a number of good late-medieval townscapes, Elm Hill and Princes Street being particularly attractive.

J. Campbell, 'Norwich' in *The Atlas of Historic Towns*, London, 1975; *Norwich Cathedral. Church, City and Diocese, 1096-1996*, ed. I. Atherton, E. Fernie, C. Harper-Bill, H. Smith, London, 1996.

OCKHAM, WILLIAM OF

Ockham was one of the greatest English thinkers of the Middle Ages: a logician without rival and a philosopher of European importance.

The facts of Ockham's life can be summarized quickly. Born in about 1288 at Ockham in Surrey, he became a Franciscan and was educated at Oxford. While studying for his Master's degree he began writing a treatise on theology, the allegedly heretical implications of which were drawn to the attention of the papal Curia in 1324. William was summoned to Avignon for examination. During his period of residence at the city, he met Michael of Cesena, the Franciscan minister-general who was struggling to uphold his order's traditional ideal of absolute poverty against Pope John XXII, who was equally determined to secure its revision. Ockham shared Michael's doubts about the orthodoxy of the papal arguments. Fearing they might soon be arrested, the two fled from Avignon in 1328 and found refuge at Pisa with Pope John's implacable enemy, the Emperor Lewis. Ockham spent most of the rest of his life at the latter's court conducting pamphlet warfare with the papacy. He died in about 1349, probably a victim of the Black Death (q.v.).

The tracts that flowed from his pen over a period of more than twenty years were numerous and often difficult. But the logic which they employed was rigorous – hence the term 'Ockham's razor'. What Ockham did was demolish the synthesis between faith and reason carefully assembled between 1266 and 1272 by Thomas Aquinas. The gradual reception over the century or so before 1250 of the large corpus of Aristotelian thought had posed a problem for thinkers steeped in the tradition of St Augustine. Augustine had taught that divine inspiration was the source of all knowledge. In the twelfth century Anselm (q.v.) had expressed a similar idea when he spoke of 'faith seeking to understand'. Anselm believed that a deeply spiritual personality could with the powers of reason attain a knowledge of God; for him as for Augustine, truth could only be revealed by truth. The reception of Aristotelianism, however, changed all this. It dignified the human intellect by recognizing its autonomy; but at the same time it questioned the capacity of that intellect to comprehend divine truths of which it could have no direct experience. The task that faced thirteenth-century writers was thus to reconcile intellect and faith, Aristotle and Augustine. Aquinas's solution to this problem can be summed up in his famous sentence, 'Grace does not destroy nature; it perfects her'. Aquinas worked from effect to cause in discussing how to approach God. The material world around us is an effect deriving from God as first cause. This world of matter is something unaided reason can understand; but the divine mysteries, incapable as they are of proof or comprehension, can only be approached through faith. In Thomism, therefore, reason and faith each found their own sphere.

Ockham blew this synthesis sky high. He went to the very foundations of Thomism by attacking its metaphysic of being. Every finite being, Aquinas had said, is made up of essence and existence. For example, we could conceive of the essence of a dinosaur, while acknowledging that dinosaurs are extinct and no longer exist; this is because, though existence is unstable, the essence of a thing is found in God. But such thinking, argued Ockham, is incapable of proof. The mind cannot abstract essence from the thing known because the mental process of abstraction cannot be shown to exist. 'Nothing', he wrote, 'can be known in itself naturally save by intuitional knowledge.' This 'Nominalist' epistemology denied to the thinker any right to knowledge of the extrasensory universe save the intuitive knowledge of individual things, and in effect therefore denied that any metaphysical knowledge at all was possible. The existence of God was not demonstrable by the powers of reason. It could only be accepted as a matter of faith. Hence all the proofs for God's existence which had been worked out over the centuries, whether by Anselm, Aquinas or anyone else, were invalid.

Reason and faith, which Aquinas had laboured so hard to reconcile, were therefore driven as far apart as possible. As a result of confining the mind to the realm of human experience, Ockham awarded to God an absolute power, an absolute freedom to act as He would. Pursued to its logical conclusion, this doctrine carried devastating implications. It followed, for example, that God could, if He so wished, command a man to hate Him. He could dispense with charity and grace if He wanted. Grace as a quality of the soul was superfluous; it existed only as long as God pleased. So the whole system of merit and reward fell to the ground.

A consequence of God's freedom of action was man's freedom of action too. And when dealing with men Ockham saw no distinction between the Pope and any other mortal. The pope had no claim to infallibility, so it made better sense to vest supreme authority in the Church in a general council. At the same time, Ockham and Marsilius of Padua, a fellow exile at Lewis IV's court, developed an autonomous secularist view of the state which, they said, should be free from any subjection to ecclesiastical sovereignty. One consequence of Ockhamist political thinking was to be seen in the early years of the fifteenth century when the idea of a general council was revived as a means of healing the Great Schism in the Church. In the field of theology, however, the effects of 'Nominalism' were to be shattering. The Thomist synthesis, one of the most accomplished intellectual creations of the Middle Ages, was gone forever. But the older tradition was not without its defenders, the most important of whom was Thomas Bradwardine (c. 1290–1349), an Oxford mathematician and Fellow of Merton. Bradwardine's answer to Ockham's emphasis on free will was an assertion of divine determinism, which later in the century in the hands of John Wycliffe (q.v.) was to become what McFarlane called the 'grisly creed' of predestinarianism.

D. Knowles, *The Evolution of Medieval Thought*, London, 1962; G. Leff, *Medieval Thought: St Augustine to Ockham*, Harmondsworth, 1958.

ORDINANCES

The Ordinances of 1311 represented the last major attempt at baronial 'constitution-making' in the Middle Ages. On 16 March 1310 the committee of Lords Ordainers was appointed by an unwilling Edward II (q.v.) to reform the state of the realm. The committee produced the first six Ordinances within a few days of their appointment, and the remaining thirty-five eighteen months later.

The appointment of the Ordainers was prompted by dissatisfaction with Edward II's government. In the north the war with the Scots was going badly and was bankrupting the exchequer, while at court the king's infatuation with his favourite Piers Gaveston was alienating many of the aristocracy.

The Ordainers, led by the earls of Lancaster and Warwick, drew up a lengthy code of reforms. Their main aim was to reinvigorate the crown's finances by removing those who had been responsible for its impoverishment. So Gaveston and his friends were expelled from the kingdom (cls. 20-22); and the lands and gifts which the king had wasted on them since March 1310 were recovered, or 'resumed', to replenish the royal demesne (cl. 8). To ensure the king's compliance with the Ordinances, a system of supervision was set up. Sessions of parliament were to be held once or twice a year (cl. 29), the officers of state were to be appointed in the presence of the baronage in parliament (cl. 14), and a committee of lords was to be named in each parliament to receive complaints against the king's ministers (cl. 40). Through supervisory structures of this kind the Ordainers hoped to be able to enforce their programme.

Their hopes were only imperfectly fulfilled. From the start the king's lack of cooperation rendered much of their work nugatory. Moreover, the earl of Lancaster was the only one of the Ordainers prepared to take a stand on the reforms, and he alone could do little because of the distrust with which he was viewed by the king. After the king's defeat at Bannockburn (q.v.) in 1314 Lancaster and his allies were given the opportunity to enforce the Ordinances, but their efforts were undermined by the terrible famine of those years. In 1322 Lancaster led a rebellion of Marchers and northerners against the king, but he was defeated at Boroughbridge and executed shortly afterwards. A few months later, the Ordinances were repealed. Unlike Magna Carta (q.v.) the Ordinances did not enter popular mythology, but the doctrines which they embodied continued to be voiced by the Commons in parliament (q.v.) until the 1340s, and the idea of 'resumption' was revived in the fifteenth century.

English Historical Documents, iii, 1189–1327, ed. H. Rothwell, Eyre Methuen, 1975.

OUTLAWRY

Under the English system of common law, if an accused failed to attend the shire court to answer charges against him, sentence could not be pronounced in his absence; instead, the process of outlawry had to be invoked. A writ of capias was issued ordering the sheriff to attach him, and if on the third summons he still could not be found, then the 'exigent' was issued, this being a formal demand that he be exacted, or compelled to attend. After the award of the first exigent, the accused forfeited his goods and chattels to the king, and after the fifth he was outlawed. Until such time as he answered for himself in the court to which he had been summoned, he was placed outside the protection of the law. The consequences of outlawry could be serious: until 1329 a man outlawed for felony could be killed with impunity. However, in practice the severity of the system was tempered. Outlawry applied only to the county in which it had been pronounced; so, to escape its consequences, an outlaw simply had to flee from his own county to the next. In late medieval England the outlaws amounted to a considerable band because, roughly speaking, for every man convicted by the courts another ten were outlawed. Some of the most prominent outlaws, as we know from the Robin Hood (q.v.) ballads, were lionized and elevated to hero status. So many contemporary lawyers were corrupt and oppressive that those who defied conventional 'justice' won the admiration of the downtrodden and oppressed.

OXFORD

In the twelfth century Oxford had been just

one of a number of English towns sheltering congregations of masters and scholars. Within a century, however, it had all but seen off its rivals; only Cambridge (q.v.) was left. Oxford possessed a number of advantages over the other schools. It was conveniently situated and well served by communications. It lay on the edge of a diocese (Lincoln) and was thus relatively free from episcopal supervision. But probably the most important reason for its success was its ruthlessness in securing privileges. Through adroit exploitation of influence in high places, it was able to secure a near monopoly in the granting of degrees.

Oxford's progress to educational distinction, however, was by no means smooth or unchecked. In 1209 a feud between town and gown resulted in the temporary dispersal of the university, and the secession of some of the masters to Cambridge. The stability – indeed the very existence – of the university was threatened by the periodic rivalries between the northern and southern scholars which turned particularly violent in the fourteenth century. It was, indeed, to ease the tensions between the rival groups that the first proctors were appointed, one to represent the northern masters, and the other the southern. The proctors are first heard of in 1248, and they still remain the principal disciplinary officers of the university today.

Surprisingly few of the buildings which make a visit to Oxford such a memorable architectural experience actually date from the Middle Ages. The main reason for this is that the first colleges were not founded until the later thirteenth century. The colleges were originally communities of graduate scholars. The undergraduates lived in houses around the town known as 'halls' – essentially properties rented by principals who provided instruction for their student tenants. Of the medieval halls only St Edmund Hall survives by name (its buildings are later) – although remains of many others lie hidden behind later shop fronts on the High Street.

What prompted late-medieval benefactors to endow the colleges was a wish to provide for hard-up graduates wishing to pursue the long courses of study that led to the higher degrees. University (1249), Merton (1270, 1274), Balliol (1282), Exeter (1314), Oriel (1324) and Queen's (1341) were the first of the colleges to be founded, but the chapel, hall and Mob Quad of Merton are the only buildings to come down to us from this period. The Merton buildings were irregularly planned. The foundation of William of Wykeham's (q.v.) New College in 1379 marked a breakthrough in architectural planning. Wykeham's buildings, designed by the mason William Wynford (q.v.), offered a study in ordered symmetry. The chapel and the hall were placed back-to-back on the northern side of the main quadrangle. Wykeham's foundation was also innovative in its arrangements for teaching. The senior members of the college were charged with giving instruction to the junior. In these arrangements it is usual to find the origins of the later Oxford tutorial system (plate 41). The two main fifteenth-century foundations – All Souls (1438) and Magdalen (1458) – both owed a great deal to the inspiration of New College, particularly in their ground plan and architectural conception. Of the university (as opposed to college) buildings of the period, the most important survival is the Divinity School, with Duke Humfrey's Library above it, built in the fifteenth century when, paradoxically, theological studies in Oxford were at their lowest ebb of the Middle Ages.

See also UNIVERSITIES; SCIENCE; WYCLIFFE, JOHN

The History of the University of Oxford, I: The Early Oxford Schools, ed. J.I. Catto, Oxford, 1984; *The History of the University of Oxford, II: Late Medieval Oxford*, ed. J.I. Catto and T.A.R. Evans, Oxford, 1992.

OXFORD, PROVISIONS OF
See PROVISIONS OF OXFORD

P

PAINTING

Medieval art has come down to us in many forms, notably in frescoes, wall paintings, stained glass (q.v.) but most important of all, in illustrated (or 'illuminated') manuscripts. In interpreting medieval art, a number of points need to be borne in mind. Firstly, it should be remembered that medieval art is Christian art. It is the essentially religious content of medieval art which distinguishes it from that of later periods. The best artists of the day were engaged to decorate Bibles, Psalters and towards the end of the Middle Ages Books of Hours (q.v. LITURGY). Even though they were working in a religious setting, however, the medieval painters seized every chance to introduce picturesque vernacular detail into their work. The second thing that should be remembered is that medieval art was in a sense abstract. The artist did not portray nature as he saw it, but as he needed to represent it for his purpose. In this respect the Renaissance marks a turning point in Western history. Before the Renaissance period it was considered no part of the artist's job to portray man as man or, for that matter, a city as a city. Symbolism was what mattered. Thus anatomical modelling was ignored, and the rules of perspective undreamed of. For the Heavenly City it was sufficient to show a collection of roofs and towers crammed within a circular wall. Medieval art was art as vision.

Partly for this reason it possesses an emotional intensity which has never been surpassed.

The earliest flowering of English medieval art came in seventh-century Northumbria, where Saxon, Celtic and Mediterranean influences came together to produce such masterpieces as the Lindisfarne Gospels. The Northumbrian school was extinguished by the Viking onslaught of the ninth century, and when artistic excellence reappeared it found its centre in southern England at Winchester. In the reign of King Edgar (959–75), Dunstan, Archbishop of Canterbury, and Athelwold, bishop of Winchester, led a revival in monastic life which stimulated the production of illuminated manuscripts. The artists responsible for this work evolved a style, known as the 'Winchester style', which prevailed in England until a generation after the Conquest. This represents a break with the Hiberno-Saxon art of three hundred years before. The chief characteristics of the Winchester style can be seen in one of its finest manuscripts – the foundation charter of New Minster, Winchester (966). In the centre of this, King Edgar is shown presenting the charter to Our Lord, who is enclosed within a mandorla supported by winged angels. The figures themselves are full of movement, easily recognizable for their swirling, fluttering drapery, and enclosing the scene is a rich border, loaded with heavy acanthus ornament (plate 142). The most enduring legacy of the Winchester school was its technique of outline-drawing, employed on the New Minster charter for the angels. Sketched in ink and only lightly coloured, these rely for their aesthetic effect solely on the use of line. The artists of Winchester and Canterbury probably derived the 'outline-drawing' style from continental exemplars, but they invested it with such vigour that it became a characteristically English idiom.

The Norman Conquest had relatively little influence on manuscript illumination in England. The next main changes were to come in the twelfth century and are associated with the wider cultural revival known as the 'Twelfth Century Renaissance'. In this period English art was subjected to a wave of continental influence that was strongly Byzantine in inspiration (not surprisingly, considering that the Crusades were bringing Europe into closer contact with the Near East). As a result the informal sketchiness of the Winchester style became more severe and more monumental. This transformation first found expression in about 1120 in the *Albani Psalter*, a volume produced at St Albans but now preserved at Hildesheim (Holland). In place of the gaiety which had invigorated Saxon art, it is solemnity that pervades the work of the *Albani* artists. Perhaps for that reason the *Albani* style represented too strong a reaction from the traditional tastes of the English artists, and in the later work of the twelfth century its rigidity gave way to a style more rhythmical while still monumental. This is the style found in the greatest Romanesque manuscript produced in England – the Winchester Bible (begun *c.*1140–60), preserved in the library of Winchester Cathedral.

The Winchester Bible, like many medieval books, has been shown to be the work of not one but a number of artists, very likely drawn to Winchester by the patronage of Bishop Henry of Blois, King Stephen's brother. Of these men the most brilliant was the so-called Master of the Leaping Figures who began, but did not finish, the two capital 'B's at the head of the Psalms. The name by which the artist is known to scholars sums up his style. His figures, though intended to be clothed in the characteristic twelfth-century 'damp-fold' drapery, have overcome the early stiffness and instead leap and swirl in a highly emotional manner. Under powerful continental influence, the heavy acanthus leaf borders of the Anglo-Saxon artists disappeared in the twelfth century. Instead, the miniatures of the period are neatly surrounded by frames within which the familiar Hiberno-Saxon interlace pattern made a reappearance. From the small corpus of wall-painting which has come down to us from this period it is clear that the monumental style was not confined to manuscripts. High on the wall of St Anselm's Chapel, Canterbury Cathedral, is a high-quality painting of St Paul shaking the viper into the fire. The convention in which the draperies are shown points to a hand closely associated with the Master of the Leaping Figures, a hand clearly capable of combining careful modelling with powerful and dramatic handling of design. It is these qualities which make the painting one of the masterpieces of late twelfth-century art.

At the beginning of the thirteenth century English art sustained another wave of influence from abroad. This time it was largely French-inspired and was associated with the evolution from Romanesque to Gothic. The movement that in architecture saw heavy Norman buildings give way to lighter Gothic structures also saw the profound, monumental style of the twelfth century in illumination give way to a smaller-scale, more human form in the thirteenth. The main features of the new mood are well illustrated in the Fall of Man from a Bible of *c.*1230–50 in the Fitzwilliam Museum, Cambridge. The grandiose proportions of the Winchester Bible (23in x 15½ in) have given way to more modest dimensions (10in x 7in). And this preference for a smaller format was accompanied by a change in the manner of illumination. Artists came to favour a narrative approach, enclosing each scene within a medallion – a technique often found in the stained glass of the period. In the Fitzwilliam Bible, for example, the six oval medallions down the centre of the page portray scenes from Genesis and the roundels along the border tell the story of Adam and Eve. This manuscript and, even better, the Bible of Robert de Bello serve to demonstrate the main decorative change that becomes noticeable in the thirteenth century – the reappearance of the wide border that had distinguished the pre-Conquest 'Winchester style'. It was in the border that ever-increasing decorative embellishment was to be concentrated as the century wore on. What this reflected was a release from the serious mood of the twelfth century, which allowed the artist to lavish as much if not more attention on the periphery as he did on the central subject of the page. He was able to indulge his taste for the irrelevant once more. He introduced rabbits, squirrels, monkeys, not to mention animal grotesques, all of them creeping in and out of the luxuriant foliage. For the moment, though, we must note that it is in the thirteenth century that we can start identifying some of the artists who worked on these manuscripts. For example, the Bible in the Fitzwilliam was signed by 'W de Brailes', perhaps William de Brailes, the illuminator who is known to have worked in Oxford. Another artist who signed his work was Matthew Paris (q.v.), the chronicler, in whose scriptorium at St Albans there began a revival of the technique of outline-drawing.

These characteristics of thirteenth-century art form the background to the evolution after 1300 of the 'East Anglian style', so called from the number of works produced there, in which English medieval illumination found its most glorious expression. By the early fourteenth century there was a shift in the nature of the market for manuscripts. Painters were spending less time working on Bibles than on devotional books like Psalters and Books of Hours commissioned by private lay patrons. Of the devotional books the finest of 'East Anglian' origin is the St Omer Psalter, begun in about 1330 for the family of that name resident at Mulbarton (Norfolk). All the essential elements of the style are represented on its 'Beatus' page, the Psalter's opening folio on which the illuminator lavished all his skills. The capital 'B' encircles a Jesse tree in which the interlace technique puts in another appearance. Small and intricate as it is, the letter is matched by the exquisite medallions which adorn the border; and out of the interstices between them grow a variety of foliage motifs in which a peacock, a snail, a stag, a monkey and even a unicorn can be identified. With the St Omer Psalter the East Anglian artists produced a masterpiece that was never to be surpassed (plate 144). In some of the later manuscripts of the school signs of decadence are evident. The Luttrell Psalter (c.1340), though one of the most popular of medieval manuscripts for its delightful scene of Sir Geoffrey being armed by his wife and daughter-in-law, is nevertheless the first major manuscript of the school to show unmistakable marks of this decline. Its margins are filled with babewyns, like the famous monkey wagoner, which draw on the contemporary fascination with the grotesque.

Just as in architecture the exuberance of Decorated gave way to the rectilinear simplicity of Perpendicular, so in painting the richness of East Anglian work gave way mid-century to a simpler style in which these decorative borders received less emphasis. In the 1350s, in the wake of the Black Death, few works of importance were produced, and it took a wave of French and Italian influence to breathe new life into English art in the 1360s. The principal characteristics of the new 'International' style, as it is called, can be seen in the Bohun Psalter of c.1370–80, the Italian inspiration of which is suggested by the beady black eyes and black hair of Christ and his apostles. However, English artists were not to be content for long to borrow directly from foreign models. By the final decades of the century they were forging an attractive new style of their own – a style at once cosmopolitan and yet distinguishable from the output of France or the Rhineland. The most celebrated painting in this genre is the Wilton Diptych in the National Gallery, a folding altarpiece showing Richard II (q.v.), flanked by three saintly sponsors, kneeling to the Virgin and Child and a company of angels. The Diptych is a work of exquisite beauty and refinement. Although the names of a number of Richard's painters are known from exchequer accounts, it is hard to say which of them, if any, was responsible for the work. Only one major English artist of this period is known to us by name and this is John Sifrewast, a Dominican friar. Sifrewast and his assistants were responsible for the *Sherborne Missal* in the British Library, a superb manuscript decorated with elaborate borders containing beautifully drawn birds. Sifrewast also decorated the *Lovell Lectionary*, which was commissioned by John, Lord Lovell of Titchmarsh for Salisbury Cathedral. In this work, Sifrewast included a portrait of himself presenting the volume to his patron – a celebrated and attractive scene, but how far an exercise in self-portraiture is unclear.

Sifrewast was effectively the last in a long line of English illuminators. He had no distinguished successors, much less did he found a school. Such achievements as the fifteenth century has to show in manuscript art come not so much in painting as in the revival of outline-drawing. In the 1440s a school of artists had perfected their own form of this, known as the 'tinted outline style' from the shading which was introduced so as to give a fully modelled appearance. A delightful example is the miniature of John Lydgate presenting his book *The Pilgrim* to Thomas Montacute, earl of Salisbury. Outline-drawing

remained popular into the 1470s when John Rous executed his historical pageant roll of the earls of Warwick in this style. Some of the figures – those of the duke of Clarence and his wife, for example – are attractive enough, but hardly rank as artistic masterpieces.

It may well have been the 'tinted outline' technique in manuscript illumination which set the fashion for monochrome wall paintings like those in the chapel of Eton College for which two artists, Gilbert and William Baker, were paid between 1479 and 1488. Despite the impression given by the unmistakeably English names of these two men, the inspiration for their work was clearly continental. If Flemish painters were not called in, then at least Flemish cartoons must have been used. In fact, the paintings at Eton make an apt commentary on the decline of English art at the end of the Middle Ages. Even though English artists seem to have been engaged for the work, the style in which they worked was Flemish. This is hardly surprising when it is remembered that Jan van Eyck and Roger van der Weyden were making the Low Countries the centre of a new approach to painting based on a sense of perspective and a keen observation of the human figure. Not until after Holbein's visits to the court of Henry VIII in the next century was there any sign of a recovery in English art.

A certain incompatibility between the English and Flemish approaches helps to explain the decline in English art in the fifteenth century. But it is not the whole story. The problem was that methods of production had changed in the course of the Middle Ages. In the Romanesque period illuminated manuscripts were produced in the monasteries, chiefly at houses like Winchester, Canterbury and Peterborough which had a long tradition of artistic excellence. But during the twelfth and thirteenth centuries, as the demand for service books by private as well as institutional patrons increased, so the place and mode of production changed.

Illumination moved out of the cloister. What had once been a skill now became a trade. It could be carried on in workshops, like those in Oxford for example, where the 'lymenours' or illuminators are known to have been centred in Catte Street. And if a London ordinance of 1403 is to be taken as typical, 'leymenour' and scribe were likely to be two different men, even if they were enrolled in the same guild. Mass production and the division of labour led to a coarsening of the quality of the work.

M. Rickert, *Painting in Britain: The Middle Ages*, Harmondsworth, 1954; R. Marks and N. Morgan, *The Golden Age of English Manuscript Painting, 1200–1500*, London, 1981; N. Morgan, *Early Gothic Manuscripts, 1190–1285*, 2 vols, London, 1982–88; L.F. Sandler, *Gothic Manuscripts, 1285–1385*, 2 vols, London, 1986.

PARIS, MATTHEW

Matthew Paris was one of the greatest English historians of the Middle Ages. He was a prolific writer and his work is informed by a sustained and consistent outlook on the world (plate 145).

Most of what is known about Matthew he tells us himself. He says that he became a monk of St Albans in 1217, which means that he must have been born around 1200. He mentions visits he made to Canterbury and Westminster and on one occasion to Norway. Apart from these outings he seems to have spent the whole of his life at St Albans.

Matthew's enduring fame rests on his writings. He took over the scriptorium at St Albans from another monk, Roger of Wendover, in 1236, and he remained in charge of it till his death (*c*.1259). His magnum opus was the *Chronica Majora* (*Great Chronicle*), the largest and most detailed narrative to survive for the middle years of Henry III's reign (q.v. CHRONICLES). Like many medieval chroniclers, Matthew aimed to write a universal history embracing everything from the Creation onwards. For the period to his own day he needed to do no more than transcribe the *Flores Historiarum* (*Flowers of History*) of his predecessor, Wendover. But when he incorporated an earlier work, he did not simply fit it into his own narrative. He rewrote it and improved it. Thus many of the most famous stories about King John's (q.v.) wickedness, most of them anyway apocryphal, were further embroidered in Matthew's pages. As soon as he moves onto writing about his own times Matthew becomes not only more valuable but also more self-revealing. Though his life at St Albans was sheltered, Matthew knew a great many people who were in a position to provide him with information about events at home and abroad. His appetite for news was insatiable. And not only that: the intrusion of his own personality into his writings distinguishes him from most other writers. He lambasts the king and the Pope; he attacks the friars; he resents taxation and condemns the justices in eyre (q.v.). Matthew is nothing if not trenchant. But he was not a genius. His views were instinctive rather than well thought out. To suggest, as some have done, that he had a theory of constitutional monarchy in which the king would govern with the advice of the barons, his 'natural counsellors', may be according his ideas a dignity they do not deserve. The pro-baronial viewpoint which was to characterize the St Albans chronicles in the Middle Ages is found well before Matthew's time in the work of Wendover.

The highest compliment that can be paid to Matthew is that his work is compelling to read. In addition to that, he was a good artist, as can be seen from the delightful drawings that adorn the margins of his manuscripts.

R. Vaughan, *Matthew Paris*, Cambridge, 1958, repr. 1979; V.H. Galbraith, *Roger of Wendover and Matthew Paris*, Glasgow, 1944, repr. 1970.

PARLIAMENT

The earliest occurrence of the word 'parliament' is found in 1236, when a case in the court of King's Bench was adjourned to a session of 'parliament' (*parliamentum*). A decade later the word appears for the first time in a chronicle. Matthew Paris (q.v.) says that Henry III (q.v.) summoned a parliament of all the English nobility, ecclesiastical as well as secular, to London. Twelve years after that, a clause in the Provisions of Oxford laid down that parliaments were to be held three times a year. Parliaments, by the mid-thirteenth century, had evidently become an established part of English political life.

Parliaments were the creations of royal power. Although much later they were to place limits on the crown's freedom of action, originally they were called into being to enlarge it. Parliaments were summoned by kings to extend and formalize their authority, to publicize their policies, and to assist in what was usually referred to as 'the great business of the realm'. Few records survive from the earliest parliaments. Most of the exiguous documentation to have come down to us from the thirteenth-century assemblies concerns the settling of pleas. On the strength of this evidence, the suggestion has been made that the earliest parliaments were summoned principally to advise the king on judicial matters: that parliament was in essence a court. This view is strongly challenged by those who stress instead the much wider range of business transacted in parliament – political and fiscal, as well as judicial – to which the chronicle evidence bears witness. It is apparent from the work of writers like Matthew Paris that kings summoned parliaments to seek counsel on such matters as military strategy, the conduct of foreign policy, the drafting of statutes and other matters. One area of business above all, however, gave parliament its essential place in the life of the realm, and that was the king's need for taxation. It was generally accepted in the Middle Ages that, if

the king wished to tax his subjects, he needed to obtain 'common consent'. In 1225, 1232 and 1237 Henry III obtained such consent from an assembly of lords. By the 1250s, however, the lords were doubting whether they alone had the power to sanction a tax the incidence of which fell not only on them but on the whole community. In 1254, when they were again approached for a tax, the lords told the king that he should summon, in addition, representatives of the shires and the clergy. It was in this way that the shire representatives – the future Commons – were first invited to attend parliament. They were summoned again in 1264 and 1265, at the behest of Simon de Montfort (q.v.), and on these occasions they were joined by the burgesses, the representatives of the towns. It was the kings' ever-growing need for taxation (q.v.) which gave the lower house, the Commons, an established place in parliamentary life and ensured that parliament would develop as a bicameral institution. The last parliament to which the Commons were not summoned was probably that of midsummer 1325.

The upper house, the Lords, consisted of the lords spiritual and temporal. All the archbishops, bishops and senior (or 'mitred') abbots received summonses to attend. The temporal lords, who sat alongside them, consisted of the earls and other senior magnates and the king's leading friends and counsellors. Increasingly, membership of the parliamentary nobility was defined by the hereditary principle. Membership of the lower house was decided by election. Two knights were elected from each shire and two burgesses from each parliamentary borough or city. In the early days, the 'electoral' process must have been more akin to selection. The lack of interest which electors could sometimes show is attested by the complaint made against the sheriff of Cambridgeshire in the 1330s that he simply returned his own nominees. By the end of the fourteenth century, however, as parliament's importance increased, the level of interest increased. Occasionally, parliamentary elections were contested, and rival candidates are found bringing posses of supporters along to meetings of the county court. More commonly, however, matters of representation were settled informally beforehand. Nonetheless, it is evident that the gentry saw election to parliament as an honour.

By the mid-fourteenth century sessions of parliament had settled into a routine. Typically, a session was opened by a speech from a minister of the crown delivered to both Lords and Commons together in the Painted Chamber of the Palace of Westminster. The minister, normally the chancellor by the reign of Richard II, explained the reasons for their meeting and invited petitions to be submitted. 'Common' petitions were sent via the clerk of parliament to the king and his council, who used them as the basis for drafting legislation, while 'singular' petitions (relating to the grievances of individual persons) went to the receivers, who sorted them and passed them onto the triers. Both assemblies would spend several days discussing the matters or 'points' on which the king and his ministers wanted their advice. One important 'point' would often be a request for taxation, to which it was unlikely that a reply would be given before the Lords and Commons had 'intercommuned' or conferred. Sometimes, as the needs of business required, there would have to be a more formal consultation of king, Lords and Commons assembled together, usually in the White Chamber. On one such occasion, in the Good Parliament of 1376, the Commons all went along together, only to find that some of their number were admitted and the rest excluded. Accordingly, their spokesman, Sir Peter de la Mare, declared that he would not deliver his message until they were all let in. Evidently a forceful man, Sir Peter, a knight of the shire for Herefordshire, is considered to have been the first of the long line of Speakers of the House of Commons. It was also in this parliament (the longest till then held) that the Commons used the process of impeachment (q.v.) for the first time, to indict Lord Latimer and other unpopular royal officials before the assembled Lords on charges of corruption.

By the end of Edward III's reign the Commons had acquired all the powers they were to enjoy for the next 200 years, the most important being control over the supply of funds to the crown in taxation (q.v.). The position of the Commons was assured once Edward III had given up bargaining for money independently – with the county communities for direct taxation and the merchants for indirect – and it was substantiated in 1407 when it was established that the Lords should merely assent to what had been granted independently by the Commons. Furthermore, the right of announcing the final grant had for some time been the privilege of the Speaker of the Commons.

The development of the English parliament stands in sharp contrast to that of its namesake in Paris, which also emerged for the first time in the 1230s. Although the two institutions were initially not dissimilar, they developed along different lines. The omnicompetence of the English parliament was not paralleled in France, where the 'parlement' of Paris remained a purely judicial body composed of professional lawyers. The tax granting powers of the English parliament were exercised in France by the Estates General, which took on the character of a representative assembly. In the fourteenth century a French king who needed money would begin by convening a session of the Estates General, but would move on to negotiating with local or regional assemblies to ensure actual collection of the money. Not least among the factors which contributed to the growth of royal absolutism in France was the absence of a national assembly which could set redress of grievance against supply of money.

J.G. Edwards, *The Second Century of the English Parliament*, Oxford, 1979; G.L. Harriss, *King, Parliament and Public Finance in Medieval England to 1369*, Oxford, 1975; *The English Parliament in the Middle Ages*, ed. R.G. Davies and J.H. Denton, Manchester, 1981.

PASTON LETTERS

The Pastons owe their fame to their great collection of letters and papers, now mostly in the British Library, which are a vital source for the study of fifteenth-century local society and of medieval manners and life more generally. The often turbulent lives of the Pastons and their associates have done much to colour the impression of late medieval England as a lawless society.

The Pastons were an arriviste Norfolk gentry family. The effective founder of the line was Sir William Paston, a justice in the court of Common Pleas. William's son and heir, John, was a country gentleman and a justice of the peace. Through his wife Margaret (née Mautby), John was introduced to Sir John Fastolf (q.v.), the war veteran, whose legal adviser he became. By the 1450s John sufficiently enjoyed the confidence of the old knight that by the terms of a nuncupative will made two days before his death Fastolf granted him all of his estates in Norfolk and Suffolk except those assigned to the endowment of a college of priests at Caister, the foundation of which he wanted John to complete (54).★ John was the only one of Fastolf's staff to benefit financially from his years of service to a master renowned for his meanness. Various other of the executors, like William Worcester (q.v.), were jealous, and raised objections to the will. John accordingly moved quickly. Dismissing the objection that the will was a

★ References in brackets are to the numbers assigned to the letters in *Paston Letters and Papers of the Fifteenth Century*, ed. N. Davis, 2 vols, Oxford, 1971, 1976

forgery, he took possession of the lands bequeathed to him. In this way a dispute was inaugurated which was to dog the Pastons for the better part of the next twenty years. The struggle was to involve them in a combination of lobbying, litigation and hand-to-hand fighting. The Pastons' mistake was to over-reach themselves. Trying to seize all, they in the end gained only a little. But along the way they fought their corner doggedly. John and other members of the family spent a great deal of time in London and Westminster, championing their cause. Indeed, that is the main reason why so many letters came to be written. John wanted to keep in touch with his wife, and she with him, John II with his parents and brothers, and so on.

The story of the Pastons' struggle may be summarized as follows. John Paston found his title to the Fastolf estates challenged by a number of powerful adversaries. The most determined of these were a slippery judge, Sir William Yelverton, another of the executors, who laid claim to the manor of Cotton in Suffolk (644, 645); a local magnate, John de la Pole, duke of Suffolk, who claimed the manors of Hellesdon and Drayton, near Norwich; and later, as he grew to manhood, John Mowbray, duke of Norfolk. The first of these men to take action was Yelverton, who seized possession of Cotton. A few years later, the duke of Suffolk sent a raiding party to occupy Hellesdon and Drayton (196). John was obliged to spend much of his time in the capital fending off challenges to the will in the court of Arches. For the most part he was successful. However, the constant worry wore him down and in 1466 he died – quite young, at the age of forty-five. John was succeeded by his son, John II. This John was a very different man from his father. Where the father had been dour and inflexible, the son was pliable and subtle. He had a gift for winning allies. In his youth he had served in the royal household. The connections which he forged there he now put to good use by securing Edward IV's recognition of his title to Caister (896). But his efforts enjoyed only limited success. Edward would not offend a magnate who was shortly to emerge as the Pastons' most intransigent opponent – John, duke of Norfolk. Norfolk had set his sights on Caister. In 1469 he occupied the castle by force (332, 334). The scandal of the castle being stormed over a decade after its owner's death caused alarm in government. In 1470, therefore, the chancellor, Bishop Wainfleet, and another of the executors, cut the Gordian knot by proposing to relieve Paston of all the estates except for Caister, Hellesdon and Drayton, and to transfer the proposed college of priests to Wainfleet's own foundation of Magdalen College, Oxford (252). Norfolk took absolutely no notice of the proposal. When he briefly withdrew from Caister in 1471, it was less out of deference to Wainfleet than as a response to the temporary loss of the throne by his patron, Edward IV (q.v.). When Edward IV stormed back a month or two later, Norfolk entered into possession again. John Paston II could do nothing to resist him, for it was his misfortune to have fought at Barnet on the losing side, the Lancastrian. Though forgiven by Edward IV, he had no credit to draw on. The end of the Pastons' long struggle finally came in 1476 when Norfolk died. John entered his claim to the property immediately and the king's council ruled in his favour (268, 299, 300).

John I's widow, Margaret, like many medieval widows, long survived her husband – in her case, by nearly two decades – and she lived to see the triumph. It was her resolution and good sense that had seen the family through many crises. In the early 1470s, for example, her son, John II, was running up debts, and could not even ensure that his late father's memory was properly honoured. 'Yt is a schame', his mother wrote, 'and a thyng that is myche spokyn of in this countre [i.e. county] that your faders grave ston[e] is not mad[e]' (212). Admittedly, though, John had

been enquiring only a couple of months before how much space was available for the tomb in Bromholm Priory (264). It is details of family business of this sort, not to mention Margaret Paston's concern for her children's love affairs, that make the letters so fascinating. The Pastons were facing problems on all fronts. Yet, there were always opportunities for reading and other leisure pursuits. An inventory of John Paston II's books made shortly after his death in 1479 show that his tastes included Arthurian romances (q.v.), Cicero, heraldry, *The Game and Playe of Chesse* and a book of statutes, no doubt for reference (316). Among the menfolk's favourite outside recreations were hunting and hawking (269, 270, 354, 574). Marriage in the right social circles was one of Margaret Paston's main concerns. Margaret strongly disapproved when her daughter Margery insisted on marrying Richard Calle, the family bailiff (203, 245, 332). On the other hand, prison does not seem to have carried much stigma, for the gentry at least. John Paston I was committed to the Fleet in London no fewer than three times and appears to have been little the worse for it. He could dictate business letters, and amuse himself and his wife by writing doggerel verses (77). His contemporary, Sir Thomas Malory (q.v.), tells us that he composed *Le Morte d'Arthur* in Newgate Prison.

Paston Letters and Papers of the Fifteenth Century, ed. N. Davis, 2 vols, Oxford, 1971, 1976; C. Richmond, *The Paston Family in the Fifteenth Century. The First Phase*, Cambridge, 1990; C. Richmond, *The Paston Family in the Fifteenth Century. Fastolf's Will*, Cambridge, 1996; H. Castor, *Blood and Roses*, London, 2004.

PATENT ROLLS

Letters issued patent from Chancery were those which were so wrapped that they could be opened and read without breaking the seal. They communicated matters of public business, such as appointments of justices of the peace and commissioners of array, grants of licences and so on. From 1201 copies of these letters were made on parchment sheets stitched head to tail to form rolls.

See also GOVERNMENT

PEASANTS' REVOLT

In several parts of Europe in the late fourteenth century social harmony was shattered by outbreaks of peasant discontent – the Ciompi in 1378 at Florence, the Jacquerie in 1358 and the Maillotins in 1382, both in France, and the Peasants' Revolt in England in 1381. Each of these rebellions drew on conditions unique to its own time and place. But, generally, the underlying cause of the instability of the period was the transformation of the economic order brought about by the fall of population. In England, the Black Death had reduced numbers by between a third and a half, from 5-6 million to about 3½ million (q.v. POPULATION). Landowners who before 1348 had been assured a plentiful supply of labour now found themselves in difficulties. Rental income was threatened by the shortage of tenants, and demesne husbandry by rising wage bills. If the landowners were to maintain their living standards, they needed to cut their costs. In the 1350s they had sought to do this by the Ordinance and then the Statute of Labourers, which had pegged wages at their pre-plague rates. But the landowners had other weapons in their armoury. Above all, they had the apparatus of villeinage. Landowners reinforced their hold over their unfree or 'villein' tenants. They compelled them to perform labour services which had been commuted for money back in the days of cheap labour; they forced them to take up vacant holdings; they held them liable for such payments as heriot (q.v.) and merchet (q.v.); and they sought to prevent them from leaving the manor. Through such means landlords went a long way to minimizing the impact on

them of the population fall caused by the Black Death. Not surprisingly, then, the abolition of villeinage was in the forefront of the peasants' demands in 1381.

The event which precipitated the revolt, however, was the levying of the poll taxes. In the 1370s the government was faced with the problem of financing the war with France at a time when it was going badly for England. The yield from the traditional fifteenths and tenths on moveable property had fallen since the Black Death. A new and more lucrative form of taxation was needed. The one which found favour was the poll tax, first levied in 1377 on everyone over fourteen at the rate of 4d a head. It was levied again in 1379, at a graduated rate, and in 1380 for a third time, on this occasion at a flat rate of 1s a head, the rich in each village helping out the poor. The 1380 levy raised problems. It was grossly inequitable, and it was levied at a high rate. Not surprisingly there was widespread evasion. The yield from the tax was much less than expected and in spring 1381 new commissions were appointed in certain counties to investigate corruption and negligence. It was the assault launched at the end of May on a session of the Essex commissioners at Brentwood that precipitated the rising.

Within days of the Brentwood incident acts of disobedience were occurring all over Essex. On 2 June a group of rebels assembled at Bocking, and four days later they assaulted the sheriff of Essex at Coggeshall. On 10 June a larger group attacked and destroyed the Hospitallers' preceptory at Cressing Temple. From Cressing the rebel band began to advance on London. At the same time the men of Kent were stirring. On 6 June a rebel gang stormed Rochester Castle. On the following day, under their inspirational leader, Wat Tyler, they marched to Maidstone and Canterbury. From Canterbury they moved west to Blackheath, overlooking the Thames – a distance which they covered in only two days (evidently they had horses). By now panic was spreading in the capital: Tyler and his followers opened the Marshalsea prison at Southwark, and the men of Essex were gathering on the eastern outskirts of the city at Mile End. The rebels appear to have had sympathizers within the city. One of these people lifted the gate, admitting the Kentishmen on Thursday 13 June. Later the same day the men of Essex broke in as well, and John of Gaunt's (q.v.) palace of the Savoy was burned to the ground.

The small group of magnates and counsellors attending the thirteen-year-old Richard II (q.v.) in the Tower had to decide what to do. According to the chronicler Froissart, a number of them urged a sortie from the Tower to slay the rebels while they slept; others, however, inclining to caution, urged a more conciliatory approach. The latter party won the day. The counsellors agreed that next morning Richard should meet the rebels at Mile End. Richard rode out to the rendezvous with a small retinue. He gave his consent to the rebel demands for the abolition of villeinage, fair terms of employment and land at 4d an acre and urged them to depart. Heady with excitement, the rebels went off in all directions. Some of them made for the Tower, where they captured and executed the Archbishop of Canterbury, while others set about massacring all the foreigners they could find. The strategy of persuading the rebels to leave peacefully had failed. Accordingly, a new meeting with the rebels was set for the next day (Saturday) at Smithfield, and this time an ambush was arranged. Richard's men were ranged on the east side of the field, while the rebels under Tyler stood on the west. Tyler rode forward to present his demands, which went further than those of the previous day; and at some stage in the parleying a member of Richard's retinue, apparently Walworth, lunged forward to stab him. Within minutes the city levies had sallied forth and the rebels were surrounded. By evening the city was emptying. The most

dangerous moment had passed. The king and his government had re-established control. On 2 July the order was given for the charters of manumission to be revoked.

As the main chronicle accounts make clear, there was regular contact between the rebels in London and dissident groups in other parts of the country. So, after the storming of London, rebellions quickly broke out elsewhere. In East Anglia a particularly determined group of rebels, led by one Geoffrey Litster, enjoyed a brief moment of triumph until they were crushed by Henry Despenser, the bishop of Norwich. At St Albans the townsfolk, led by William Grindcob, invaded the precincts of the abbey and extracted a charter from Abbot Thomas de la Mare. At Bury St Edmund's, another Benedictine house faced with assertive townsmen, events took a more violent turn. Prior John de Cambridge and his friend Sir John Cavendish, the Chief Justice, were both captured, and their heads stuck on spikes in the pillory: 'and they put the prior's head next to the justice's, now to his ear as if seeking advice, now to his mouth as though showing friendship, wishing in this way to make a mockery of the friendship which had been between them in life'. Antagonism towards the king's justices, and towards the legal system more generally, was a major element in the revolt. The peasantry resented the collusion between the lawyers and the great lords, which had the effect of corrupting the courts, and the justices paid the price with their lives.

Of the chroniclers who wrote about the revolt the most perceptive in his analysis of its causes was Jean Froissart, the Hainaulter, who pointed to the 'ease and riches that the common people were of'. Paradoxically the uprising came not at a time of hardship, such as had been felt in the early fourteenth century, but at a time when wages were rising and prices falling. In the short term the peasants gained little or nothing from the revolt.

But in the longer term the movement of wages and prices worked in their favour. Large-scale demesne cultivation, in the form in which it had been long practised, no longer offered landowners the prospect of profit. Accordingly, by the end of the century most of the big demesnes had been put out to lease and labour services abandoned. At the same time, 'villein' or customary tenure slowly evolved into copyhold tenure – tenure by the custom of the manor – which gave tenants a measure of security and protection. The revolt had a more immediate impact in challenging the complacency of the upper classes. Ministers and landowners alike were given a shock. In consequence, the poll taxes were abandoned; experimentation with new taxes was brought to a halt; and there was an effort to clean up the dispensation of justice. For the next decade or two the upper classes lived in fear of another uprising. That there was none did not make that fear any the less real.

The Peasants' Revolt of 1381, ed. R.B. Dobson, 2nd ed., London, 1983.

PERPENDICULAR

See ARCHITECTURE, ECCLESIASTICAL

PILGRIMAGES

Like the Crusades (q.v.), pilgrimages were a remarkable manifestation of the intense popular piety of the Middle Ages. From all over Europe, pilgrim bands, like the one familiar to readers of Chaucer, thronged the well-worn routes to such favoured shrines as those of St Peter at Rome, St Thomas at Canterbury (q.v.) and St James at Santiago de Compostela.

What lay at the root of the pilgrimage ideal was a belief in the potency of saints' relics. This had been shown as early as AD 156, when the Christians of Smyrna had taken possession of the bones of their murdered bishop Polycarp, saying they were 'more valuable than refined gold'. Relics, it was believed, brought success in war, conferred protection in times of adversity and restored health to the infirm. A reliquary or shrine was considered to contain not just a collection of bones but the very person of the saint himself. His living presence protected the church where his tomb lay, and it was to him personally that offerings were made. This attitude of mind led to the localization of a saint's cult, even in the case of those like the Virgin Mary whose lives were not associated with a particular sanctuary. Men spoke, for example, of 'Our Lady of Chartres' because what was claimed to be her tunic was preserved in that cathedral. Those sceptical of cults were apt to warn that veneration of relics was in danger of becoming an obstruction to the true understanding of God. But the Church said in reply that people should not worship relics for their own sake, but should look to them to help in the veneration of those who had lived lives of undoubted holiness or had died for the faith.

This official line – one which was notable for its caution – was in danger of being overtaken by the enthusiasm of the laity. It failed to take account of the miracle-working quality of the relics. Christ in His own mission had resorted to miracles to demonstrate the power of the one true God, His Father. The apostles and the earliest missionaries had likewise performed miracles to prove the superiority of their God to the numerous gods of the pantheistic societies in which they moved. It was believed that in those early and difficult times miracles were necessary to assist in spreading the faith but that once the Conversion was over, they would cease. In fact, of course, they did not, because of the continuing popular demand for miraculous demonstrations of the faith. And the commonest such demonstrations were cases of healing.

How are these cases to be explained? They could only be accepted in the number that they were in an age when medical knowledge was limited. A visit to a shrine was considered to be more beneficial than a visit to a doctor. If the disease was psychological or psychosomatic, the experience of visiting, say, Canterbury and the shrine of St Thomas might well be enough to do the trick. But there was more to it than that. According to a decree of the Fourth Lateran Council in 1215 illness sprang not from physical ailments but from sin. It followed, then, that the malady was less likely to be cured by the application of medicine than by a visit to the tomb of a saint. Hence the vast crowds of sick and dying who crowded at the gates of a cathedral on the feast day of the blessed martyr contained within its walls.

Not all of those who visited a shrine were in need of a cure, however. Chaucer's pilgrims, as we know, were fit enough. Another reason for going on pilgrimage was a desire to obtain forgiveness, to perform a penance. By about the eleventh century it was generally accepted that a man could seek remission for his sins by visiting a shrine, usually one named by his bishop or confessor. Thus the way lay open to using pilgrimages as a form of punishment for particular crimes. It is known, for example, that in the twelfth century Scottish convicts were required to visit the shrine of St Cuthbert in Durham Cathedral.

Just as a pilgrimage might enable the penitent to atone for past sins, so it could gain him early remission from the trials of Purgatory. King Robert of France made a tour of nine shrines before his death in 1031 in the hope that he would 'evade the awful sentence of the day of judgement'. In the event that a penitent were to agree to go on a pilgrimage and then die before performing it, the Church would allow a vicar to fulfil the obligation on his behalf. Exploiting that loophole to the full, testators regularly from the fourteenth century took the precaution of leaving a sum of money in their wills for someone – a relative or a clergyman, for example – to make the pilgrimage on their behalf. It could be argued that this was a major step towards debasing the original idea of pilgrimage as an act involving sacrifice or hardship. Once it was accepted that a testator could arrange for someone else to go in his name, then it would not be long before the living made similar arrangements too – hence the so-called vicarious pilgrimages.

Pilgrimages could be to local shrines or to shrines far away, like Rome, Santiago or the Holy Land. The motives that led pilgrims to choose one destination in preference to another remain obscure. Factors of convenience and fashion probably counted for most. Those who could afford it, like Henry of Derby, the future Henry IV (q.v.), in 1393, and some less able to afford it, like Margery Kempe (q.v.) in 1413, went the whole way to the Holy Land. Chaucer's pilgrims, on the other hand, were content to go to Canterbury (q.v.). Becket's tomb was easily the most popular of English shrines, although much less so on the eve of the Dissolution than in the aftermath of the martyr's death. One of the remarkable things about medieval saints' cults is just how short-lived many of them were. An example is the cult of Thomas Cantilupe, bishop of Hereford. After Cantilupe had died in Italy in 1282 his bones were brought back to his cathedral church at Hereford, which was taking over £178 in offerings by 1290. In 1320 the dean and chapter finally secured his canonization. But by 1336 the saint's cult was already in decline, and by 1388 the annual total of offerings at the shrine only came to £1 6s 8d. Even at Canterbury trade fell off in the late Middle Ages. In the later twelfth century offerings averaged £426 per annum and in 1220, the year of the translation of the relics, they totalled no less than £1,142 5s. But at the Dissolution they averaged a paltry £36 a year. In the late Middle Ages newer shrines came into being. In the thirteenth century the fashionable centre was Bromholm Priory, which sheltered the Holy Rood. A century later it was Walsingham, where the shrine of Our Lady was bringing the canons as much as £260 a year in offerings in 1535.

Before commencing a journey a would-be pilgrim needed to make considerable preparations. First, it was essential that he obtain the blessing of his parish priest and confess the wrongs which he had committed. Then, if he had property to bequeath, he would make his will. When ready to set off he would don the special garb that symbolized his admission to the pilgrim's order. This consisted of a long, coarse tunic, known as the sclavein, a staff and a broad-brimmed hat turned up at the front on which on the return journey he would sport his pilgrim's badge. For reasons of safety the pilgrims would travel in groups, in early times probably on foot, later more usually on horseback. They would seek hospitality at monasteries or at inns along the road (q.v. ROADS).

Although shrines like Walsingham and Hailes were still attracting crowds at the end of the Middle Ages, the cult of relics and the miracles associated with them were beginning to incur criticism, and not just from implacable enemies like Wycliffe and the Lollards (q.v.). The claims of the credulous were treated with more scepticism than before, and the authorities conducted full and thorough examination before recognizing any newly proclaimed cult. As Bishop Grandison of Exeter said on one occasion, 'I find these miracles hard to believe and impossible to prove... I fear that the people have given themselves over to idolatry.' And yet pilgrimages were still offering people hope. In Worcester Cathedral around 1500 a man was laid to rest wearing the full pilgrim garb. He had probably just returned from a pilgrimage to Santiago: he was carrying a cockleshell. On the eve of the Reformation, the pilgrimage trade was still flourishing in England and abroad

J. Sumption, *Pilgrimage: an Image of Medieval Religion*, London, 1975.

POITIERS

Poitiers was the greatest victory in the career of Edward, the Black Prince (q.v.). The prince, who had been appointed lieutenant of Gascony by his father, Edward III, had landed at Bordeaux in September 1355, and later that autumn led a *chevauchée* towards Narbonne and the French Mediterranean coast. In the next year he turned northwards, possibly with a view to linking up with Henry of Grosmont, duke of Lancaster, in the Loire valley. In the event the destruction of bridges across the Loire frustrated his plan, and he retreated southwards trailed by an army led by King John of France. At Maupertuis near Poitiers on 19 September 1356 the English were forced to give battle. Each side employed much the same tactics as at Crécy (q.v.) ten years before, and for much the same reasons. The English adopted a defensive strategy because they were numerically inferior, and the French an offensive one because they were numerically superior. The prince stationed his archers in front and his knights and men-at-arms, dismounted, in the rear. King John began by sending in his cavalry as his father had done at Crécy, only to find that they, like their forebears, got mown down by the English archers. John then ordered the knights to dismount, little realizing that unless they were then combined with the archers there was little point in this manoeuvre. In the course of the battle King John himself was taken prisoner. The terms for his release were to be the subject of detailed negotiations between the English and the French over the next four years.

POPULATION

Estimating the level of England's population in the Middle Ages is an exercise fraught with difficulty. There are no census-like data for the Middle Ages: the regular ordering of censuses did not begin until the nineteenth century. Nor, for the medieval period, are there any parochial records of the kind which demographic historians use for the period from the sixteenth century to the nineteenth. Essentially, only two main sources are available: Domesday Book (q.v.) for the early part of the period and the poll tax returns of 1377–80 for the later.

Domesday Book records about 275,000 people in England in 1086. The Conqueror's great book, however, was conceived principally as a fiscal survey. For this reason it records landholders only, and a multiplier has to be found to convert this figure into a figure for the whole population. J.C. Russell, who supposed the medieval family to be no larger than its modern equivalent, suggested a multiplier of about 3.5. This figure, however, is now generally considered too low, and the modern preference is for a multiplier somewhere in the region of 4.8 to 5.2. Using a multiplier of this size, England's population in 1086 may be said to have been in the order of 1.75–2.25 million.

Three centuries later, the returns of the first poll tax of 1377 suggest that there were 1,355,201 taxpayers in England – a figure that represents all male and female laypersons aged fourteen and upwards, except for the most needy. Once again estimates have to be made of family size and of such other variables as the number of clergy. When the necessary adjustments have been made, a figure of between 2.5 and 3 million can be posited for this date.

In the period between the making of Domesday Book and the compilation of the late medieval poll tax returns population had both risen and fallen. From the evidence of assarting and agrarian expansion it is evident that there was a rapid population rise in the twelfth and thirteenth centuries. However, in the fourteenth century there was an equally rapid decline. In the 1310s and 1320s a series of famines had led to starvation in the countryside, and in 1348–9 the Black Death caused massive and well attested mortality. It is obviously desirable to form an idea of the level of population on the eve of these twin crises. It is fair to assume, on the evidence of ecclesiastical and manorial records, that the death rate caused by the plague was something in the order of 40%. If we then project back from the evidence of the poll tax returns, we arrive at a population figure of some 5–6 million in the 1340s. A generation earlier the figure would have been a little higher still.

Population remained low for the rest of the Middle Ages. Indeed, in the fifteenth century it may have fallen. A number of factors offer a possible explanation for this. In the first place, there were renewed visitations of the plague – some of these, although localized, were still severe. According to the chroniclers, children and adolescents were particularly vulnerable to the plague bacillus. Secondly, there appears to have been a sharp decline in the birth rate. Men and women, it appears, were marrying later and in consequence having smaller families. There is little evidence of a definite recovery of population until the closing decades of the fifteenth century. But in the century and more that followed population rose sharply. By the end of Elizabeth's reign population levels were again approaching those of the 1200s. It is these crowded conditions which provide the background to the poor law legislation of the 1590s.

See also AGRICULTURE

J. Hatcher, *Plague, Population and the English Economy, 1348–1530*, London, 1977; *Before the Black Death: Studies in the Crisis of the Early Fourteenth Century*, ed. B.M.S. Campbell, Manchester, 1991.

PREACHING
See SERMONS

PREMONSTRATENSIANS

The Premonstratensians, or White Canons, took their name from the abbey of Premontré near Laon, founded in 1121 by a German, St Norbert of Xanten (c.1080–1344). The order came from the same stable as the Augustinians (q.v.) or Black Canons. In other words, they were one of the new orders called into being by the renewed spirituality of the twelfth century. Like the Augustinians, they sought to offer a semi-monastic way of life to the secular clergy. But, unlike them, they chose to imitate the simplicity and austerity of the Cistercians (q.v.). This placed them in a good position to benefit from the prohibition on new foundations passed by the General Chapter of the Cistercian Order in 1152: the piety which had once fed the Cistercians could from now on go to feed the Premonstratensians instead. Between 1170 and 1216 more than fifteen of their houses were founded in England, colonized for the most part from the existing houses of Newhouse (Lincs) or Welbeck (Notts). The Premonstratensians looked for inspiration to the Cistercians not only in their austere manner of life but also in the centralized constitution they adopted, based on visitations and general chapters. Their abbeys in the British Isles were for the most part of modest size and modest wealth. Few have left extensive remains, but Dryburgh (Scotland) and Bayham (Sussex) are important, and picturesque, exceptions.

D. Knowles, *The Monastic Order in England*, Cambridge, 2nd ed., 1966.

PRISES

The royal right of 'prise', or compulsory purchase, bulks prominently in English politics under the three Edwards. The king had long exercised the prerogative right of requisitioning victuals and means of transport for the maintenance of his household on its travels around the realm. No one denied him that right. But its extension and abuse during the Welsh and Scottish wars of the later thirteenth century led to demands for it to be defined more clearly. Statutes prescribed that goods should never be taken without the owner's consent; they should be paid for; and they should be taken only for the use of the household, not for the whole army. In 1362 the Statute of Purveyors brought together the earlier enactments and proved to be the definitive statement on the subject for the Middle Ages. The term 'prises' is often used by historians as if synonymous with 'purveyance'. Until about 1310 it probably was, but by then a distinction had been formulated between purveyance as legitimate purchase in time of emergency and prises as illegal seizure of the subject's property. It was this distinction which the king's critics wanted him to observe.

G.L. Harriss, *King, Parliament and Public Finance in Medieval England to 1369*, Oxford, 1975.

PRIVY SEAL

See GOVERNMENT

PROVISIONS OF OXFORD

The series of two dozen Provisions agreed at Oxford in the spring of 1258 represent the most radical attempt made in England in the Middle Ages to limit the powers of the crown.

In April 1258 dissatisfaction with Henry III's (q.v.) distribution of patronage and, in particular, his generosity to his Poitevin half-brothers led to the appointment of a committee of twenty-four to draw up proposals for reform. Twelve of the committee's members were to be named by the king and twelve by the baronage.

The committee's proposals, published in June, were far-reaching. The principal recommendation was that a council of fifteen should be appointed 'to advise the king in good faith on the government of the kingdom and on all things touching the king and the kingdom'; and that the council should authorize use of the great seal. The committee made other recommendations. The old vice-regal office of justiciar was revived (cl. 6); the other officers of state – the chancellor and treasurer – were to be subjected to the authority of the king and council jointly (cls. 14 & 15); castles were to be put under the control of new castellans who had strict instructions not to give them up (cl. 8); and finally parliaments were to be held three times a year (cl. 21).

The Provisions went very much further than Magna Carta (q.v.) half a century before. Their radicalism had its origins in a number of sources. The suggestion that the barons should nominate counsellors to watch over the king can be traced back to the 'Paper Constitution' of 1244 – indeed, beyond that to the experience of Henry's minority, the first royal minority since the Conquest, when the magnates were given a real taste of government. But there were broader influences too. The leading reformers on the baronial side were heavily influenced by the thinking of the churchmen. The notions of election and accountability articulated in 1258 had been central to the ecclesiastical reform movement of the twelfth century. Very likely, men like Simon de Montfort (q.v.) were heavily indebted to the informal influence of churchmen like Robert Grosseteste (q.v.) and Adam Marsh.

Like Magna Carta in 1215, the Provisions, so far from settling matters, only made them worse. Henry was determined to recover the authority he had lost to the council, and in 1261 he succeeded in obtaining papal absolution from his oath to uphold the reforms. Two years later war broke out between the king and his opponents, and after de Montfort's defeat and death at Evesham the Provisions were formally annulled.

Documents of the Baronial Movement of Reform and Rebellion, 1258–1267, ed. R.F. Treharne and I.J. Sanders, Oxford, 1973.

PROVISIONS, PAPAL

'Provision' describes the system by which the Pope would override the rights of an ordinary 'collator' or patron to appoint a nominee of his own to an ecclesiastical benefice; the Pope, in other words, would use his authority to 'provide' a candidate.

Papal intervention in the disposal of livings was one aspect of the centralizing tendency which concentrated more and more power in the hands of the Pope from the early twelfth century onwards. The first provisions had been made under Innocent III, who directed bishops to confer prebends and other benefices on his nominees. In 1245 the system of provisions was legitimized in Clement IV's decretal *Licet Ecclesiarum* which claimed that the Pope alone could fill those benefices vacated in the Roman Curia. Under the Avignon Popes John XXII (1316-34) and Clement VI (1342–52) the system was carried still further.

The spur to this centralization was found in the plight of those thousands of well-trained, and yet under-endowed, young clerks who came to Rome desperate to seek preferment. Often these men were graduates. Lacking patrons, however, they had little expectation of a benefice unless the Pope overturned the normal patterns of patronage in their favour.

The system of provisions was highly unpopular with the English landowning class who normally appointed to benefices, and it gave rise to a series of critical parliamentary petitions. There was a spate of these petitions between 1343 and 1347. Edward III encouraged the expression of such sentiment. In 1343 he told the Commons that alien appointees did not know the faces of their flocks, much less speak their language, and as a result there was a decline in devotion among the people. What was worrying Edward was that he would not be able to get his own nominees appointed to bishoprics if the Pope kept filling them. Thus he was happy to satisfy the Commons by conceding the Statute of Provisors (1351), which allowed clerks appointed by the Pope to be imprisoned and held liable to pay compensation. Two years later, in 1353, he approved the first Statute of Praemunire which limited appeals to Rome. A second such statute followed in 1393. In practice, Edward III had little intention of enforcing these laws to the letter. He was prepared to invoke them on those occasions when he wanted to extract concessions from the papacy, but once a healthy compromise had been reached, he would relax them again. The usual kind of arrangement was that a vacant see would be filled by provision, and that the candidate provided would be the king's nominee. Such laws existed principally for the king's convenience, and they were to prove particularly convenient to Henry VIII in the 1520s when he invoked Praemunire against no less a man than Cardinal Wolsey.

G. Barraclough, *Papal Provisions*, Oxford, 1935.

RICHARD I

Richard the Lionheart became a legend in his own lifetime, and has remained one ever since. Largely for that reason he remains one of the best known, and yet one of the least known, of our kings.

Richard was born on 8 September 1157 at Oxford. His father, Henry II (q.v.), the first Angevin king, ruled a sprawling confederation of territories stretching from the Scottish border to the Pyrenees and including the duchy of Aquitaine which had been brought to him by his formidable wife, Eleanor (q.v.). Richard, their second son, was his mother's favourite. Consequently he responded to her influence, and when in 1173 she and Henry, her eldest son, stirred up a rebellion against Henry II, he joined in on her side. The rebellion lasted for eighteen months, and was known to contemporaries as the 'great war'. By the summer of 1174, however, Henry had succeeded in re-establishing his authority. At Montlouis on 30 September he was formally reconciled with his sons.

Henry II's family, however, rarely co-existed peacefully for long. Within a few years the sons were taking up arms again, this time against each other. Henry 'the Young King' was thirsting to share some of his father's power. Richard had been given Aquitaine to rule and Geoffrey, the third son, Brittany. Yet the 'Young King' had nothing: no lands at all

that he could call his own. Idleness bred resentment, and in 1183 he joined those of the Aquitainian baronage who had rebelled against Richard's heavy-handed rule. What threatened to develop into another major crisis for the Angevin family was averted only by the timely death of the 'Young King' on 11 June.

Richard then found himself in the position which his elder brother had once occupied. He was his father's heir, and yet denied any share of power so long as the old man lived. His feelings of frustration need to be understood if the significance of what followed is to be appreciated. On 18 November 1188 Richard, Henry II and Philip Augustus of France met at Bonsmoulins in the Loire. Richard asked his father to recognize him as his rightful heir. When Henry refused, he turned to the French king, his father's mortal enemy, and did homage to him for all the lands he held on the continent. This ceremony inaugurated the last war that Henry was called upon to fight. He died at Chinon on 6 July 1189.

On hearing of his father's death Richard went straight to the Angevin mausoleum of Fontevrault to pay his last respects. He crossed to England on 13 August, was crowned in the following month, and left again on 12 December. He was subordinating everything to a bold plan for a joint Anglo-

French crusade (q.v.) to recover the cities of Acre and Jerusalem recently taken by Saladin. To oversee the government of the country in his absence he appointed Hugh Puiset as justiciar and William Longchamp, bishop of Ely, as chancellor; but the two did not get on, and in 1191 Richard, by now in Sicily, had to despatch Walter of Coutances, Archbishop of Rouen, to England to sort things out.

In July 1190 Richard and Philip finally embarked on their journey. Their progress east was dogged by interminable disputes which extended even to the terms on which Richard could renounce a precontract to Philip's sister to marry Berengaria, daughter of the king of Navarre. Richard's marriage to Berengaria finally took place in May 1191, a month before the expedition reached its destination, the port of Acre. Richard's achievements in the East certainly justified his reputation as a great soldier. Five weeks after arriving he had recovered Acre from the Muslims, to whom it had fallen four years before. Encouraged by this success he was minded to push on quickly to Jerusalem. With the hot eastern sun beating down, he led his troops to within sight of the Holy City; but as he no longer had the manpower or logistical support necessary to undertake a long siege, he had to settle for a three-year treaty. On 9 October 1192 he set sail for home. En route he was captured by Leopold, duke of Austria, whom he is supposed to have insulted on the crusade. The duke transferred him to the custody of the Holy Roman Emperor, Henry VI, and from this time on the argument over the terms of his release became ensnared in the wider – and more difficult – issue of Anglo-French-German relations. Eventually a ransom of 150,000 marks was agreed.

On 13 March 1194 Richard returned to an England which had been taxed to the hilt to secure his release. But he was away again two months later, this time to Normandy to pro-

tect his continental dominions from the continuing attacks of the king of France. It was Philip's ambition to cut the Angevins down to size and to sever the link between Normandy and England. But in Richard he had more than met his match. Not for nothing was Richard known as 'Coeur de Lion', the Lion-Heart. He was much the ablest soldier of his age. Castles held to be invincible fell before him; Acre surrendered little more than a month after his arrival there. Moreover, he had a shrewd strategic sense. He knew intuitively where the weak links in the Angevin empire were. Thus he strove to safeguard the southern approach to Normandy by building the great stronghold of Chateau Gaillard at Les Andelys. And towards the end of his life he concentrated his energies on defending the Limoges area, south of the Loire. In the Limousin Philip had forged an alliance with a group of rebel barons with a view to driving a wedge between the northern and southern lands of the Angevin empire. Richard marched south to besiege one of the rebels at Chalus. In the course of the operations he sustained an arrow wound from which he died on 6 April 1199. He was buried alongside his father and mother at Fontevrault.

Richard, unusually for an English ruler, was a figure in world history. What he did had an impact on much of Europe and the Middle East. He faced enemies on a host of fronts and saw them off. The challenge which increasingly dominated his life was the power of France. Yet, to the end, he successfully defended his inheritance. Only in the time of his less able brother and successor, John (q.v.), did it fall apart.

J. Gillingham, *Richard I*, New Haven and London, 1999; R.V. Turner and R.R. Heiser, *The Reign of Richard the Lionheart. Ruler of the Angevin Empire, 1189–1199*, Harlow, 2000; N.E. Saul, *The Three Richards*, London, 2005.

RICHARD II

Richard II sought to create a stronger and more authoritarian style of kingship in England by placing a novel emphasis on the prerogative. His efforts, tactlessly implemented, were to cost him his throne.

Richard was born at Bordeaux on 6 January 1367, the son of Edward, the Black Prince (q.v.) and Joan of Kent. He became heir apparent to the English throne on the death of his father in June 1376. Twelve months later, on Edward III's death, he became king. For the first three years of the reign the country was governed in fact if not in theory by a minority council which continued the policies pursued in Edward's later years. The cost of maintaining the late king's conquests in France led to the imposition of the notorious poll taxes which were to provoke the Peasants' Revolt (q.v.) in 1381. The revolt was a major upheaval in the south-east. Rebels poured into the capital from Kent and Essex and captured the Tower. Richard rode out to meet them, and by promising to accede to their demands persuaded them to disperse. The chroniclers, rightly or wongly, portray him as one of the few members of the ruling class to show any powers of leadership in the crisis.

In the years that followed, Richard chose to rely on a small circle of close friends, some of them contemporaries of his like Robert de Vere, others men like Sir Simon Burley who had served his father and from whom he may have picked up his advanced notions of regality. Growing dissatisfaction with foreign policy, parliamentary allegations of corruption and criticism of extravagance in the royal household led to the impeachment of the chancellor, Michael de la Pole, in parliament in October 1386 and to the appointment of a committee of government, resident at Westminster, which was to hold office for one year. Richard avoided its supervision by travelling round England, and sought to clarify the legality of his position by putting to the judges a series of questions about the nature of the royal prerogative. The judges' answers offered the strongest statement of the prerogative that Richard could have desired. De Vere, meanwhile, was bringing an army to the king's assistance, but after its defeat at Radcot Bridge (20 December 1387) the king was obliged to submit to his opponents, the so-called Appellant lords. In the aptly named 'Merciless Parliament' which followed, the lords 'appealed' de Vere and other supporters of Richard and sent them to the executioner's block.

The rule of the Appellants lasted until 3 May 1389, when Richard asserted his majority by dismissing the Appellants' councillors and appointing councillors of his own. Over the next eight years, while showing himself more conciliatory than before, he pursued policies designed to reinforce the authority of the crown. In a major initiative, he launched a baronial-style affinity (identified by the white hart emblem) so that a king would never again be powerless in the face of his opponents. At the same time, he encouraged lofty new forms of address – 'your majesty' instead of 'my lord' – to encourage the better performance of obedience. Externally, he promoted the making of peace with the French so that the crown could avoid impoverishment from spending on war.

In the summer of 1397 Richard suddenly shook off the restraint of earlier years: he arrested his former opponents, Gloucester, Arundel and Warwick. All three lords were charged with treason and condemned; Arundel was executed, Warwick imprisoned on the Isle of Man, and Gloucester disposed of at Calais. Richard's coup puzzled contemporaries. Nonetheless, the ideas which informed it represented the fulfilment of aims which he had long pursued. In letters sent to foreign rulers shortly afterwards he said that he was promoting obedience and punishing rebellion. His ministers had been enjoining obedience on the king's subjects for years; and he himself had urged obedience on the Irish when he had pacified the province in 1394-5. In the same letters he proclaimed that he was bringing 'peace' to his realm. By 'peace' he meant unity, the elimination of dissent. This again was an aim that he had been pursuing for some time.

In early 1398 Richard's new political dispensation was threatened by a quarrel between Henry Bolingbroke, duke of Hereford, John of Gaunt's son, and Thomas Mowbray, duke of Norfolk. Mowbray had warned Bolingbroke that Richard was plotting the destruction of the house of Lancaster – a charge that was probably true. Bolingbroke had then reported this to the king. The issue between the two lords being a matter of honour, it was resolved that their quarrel should be settled by trial by battle, but when the duel scheduled for 16 September 1398 was due to begin Richard stayed the proceedings and pronounced sentences of exile, on Norfolk for life and on Hereford for ten years. However, just four months later, John of Gaunt (q.v.) died, and Richard had to weigh the advantages to be gained from seizing the Lancastrian inheritance against the fears that would be aroused by so blatant a threat to the rights of property. Richard decided to take the risk. In March 1399 he took the Lancastrian lands into royal possession. This act did more than any other to seal his fate. In July 1399, while Richard was in Ireland, Bolingbroke landed on the Yorkshire coast, ostensibly to claim his rightful inheritance. He won the support of the earl of Northumberland, marched south to Bristol and then swung north-westwards to Chester, which he entered on 9 August. Richard, in the meantime, had returned from Ireland. He found security in the walls of Conway. Had he remained at Conway, he could have called Bolingbroke's bluff. However, he allowed himself to be persuaded to leave, and at Chester he became Bolingbroke's prisoner. Bolingbroke summoned a parliament to meet in Richard's name. Under duress Richard was persuaded to abdicate, and his supplanter claimed the throne as Henry IV (q.v.). Richard was imprisoned at Pontefract, where he died (or was murdered) in 1400. His remains were interred at King's Langley until they were brought to Westminster Abbey by Henry V.

Richard's kingship had a number of characteristics in common with that of contemporary European monarchs. Virtually all the kings and princes of the day, faced with noble or popular disaffection, sought to elevate themselves above their subjects; and some at least, in particular Charles V of France, shared Richard's fascination with authoritarian portrait images of themselves. Richard's exalted conception of his office was not unique. But in the context of the English polity his rule was almost certain to fail. Not only was it internally inconsistent – for example, the emphasis placed by the king on 'peace' and unity was at odds with the factional nature of his rule – but more importantly his sympathy with civil law – he is reported to have said that the laws of England were in his mouth or in his breast – challenged the tradition of 'constitutional' kingship inaugurated by Magna Carta.

Richard's kingship was informed by an intense, even cathartic piety, which contributed to the sacral conception of his office. Sacred and secular ideas were inseparably fused in his mind. He strongly identified his cause with that of the Almighty. In the letters which he sent to fellow rulers in 1397 he accused his enemies of rebelling against 'King Christ the Lord'. He saw heresy – in its English form Lollardy (q.v.) – as the twin sister of rebellion because it too involved the rejection of authority. On his tomb epitaph in Westminster Abbey he prided himself on 'laying low the heretics and scattering their friends'.

Richard was married twice, firstly to Anne of Bohemia, daughter of the Emperor

Charles IV, and secondly to Isabella, daughter of Charles VI of France. Both marriages were childless. The king's childlessness may have contributed to his close identification with his Saxon predecessor Edward the Confessor, another childless monarch, although it is more likely that this sprang from the Confessor's association with Richard's own ideal of peace.

N.E. Saul, *Richard II*, New Haven and London, 1997.

RICHARD III

The character and personality of Richard III have aroused interest out of all proportion to the duration of his reign, which lasted for little more than two years (1483–5). Popular interest in the king centres chiefly on the question, who killed the princes in the Tower? Contemporaries, too, saw that issue as central to any assessment of his suitability to rule.

Richard was born on 2 October 1452 at Fotheringhay (Northants), the youngest of the surviving children of Richard, duke of York, and his wife Cecily. In 1461 his eldest brother became king as Edward IV (q.v.) and during the twenty-two years of his reign Richard, as duke of Gloucester, supported him loyally. After 1471 he was entrusted with sweeping powers in the north as Warden of the Western Marches. From his seat at Middleham Castle he held sway over the most lawless part of England with a firmness and fairness that won him the respect of the local inhabitants and the favour of the city of York (q.v.). Contrary to Shakespeare's version of events, Richard was not the éminence grise behind the execution of his brother, Clarence, in February 1478. The slippery Clarence was charged with treason, and had only himself to blame. If anything, there may well be some truth in the reports that Richard pleaded for his life.

When Edward IV died on 9 April 1483, he left a thirteen-year-old son to succeed him as Edward V. Had the terms of his will been followed, Richard would have become Protector, but the larger grouping on the council in London, composed of Queen Elizabeth Woodville's relatives, preferred a conciliar form of government which would have reduced Richard to the position of chief councillor. It was apparent that the differences which had built up in Edward IV's lifetime between Richard and his ally Buckingham on the one hand and the Woodville clan on the other were coming into the open in a struggle for control of his young heir. When news broke of the king's death, Edward V was at Ludlow, whence the Woodvilles planned to spirit him to London for an early coronation. Richard intercepted the party at Stony Stratford on 30 April, and despatched Earl Rivers and Sir Thomas Vaughan to the north for execution. On hearing of the arrests the queen fled into sanctuary at Westminster, taking her second son Richard with her. The young Edward was placed in the Tower.

So far Richard had acted ostensibly as the defender of his nephew's interests against the intrigues of the queen and her Woodville relatives. In so doing he enjoyed the support of the duke of Buckingham and Lord Hastings. But from now on his ambitions began to arouse suspicion. Lord Hastings suspected him of designs on the throne and Richard found it necessary to remove him. On 13 June Hastings was charged with plotting with the queen and executed. Thereafter events moved rapidly. On 16 June the queen agreed to hand over her younger son, who joined his brother in the Tower. Then Buckingham made his famous speech at the Guildhall, immortalized by Shakespeare, in which he peddled the story that the children of Edward IV and Elizabeth Woodville were bastards because of a precontract between the king and Eleanor Butler, thus making Richard of Gloucester the legitimate heir to the crown. On 25 June the Commons and Lords assented to Richard's succession and on 6 July he was crowned.

Richard's was destined to be a troubled reign, and contemporaries were not slow to connect the misfortunes that afflicted the king with the unscrupulous way he had climbed to power. In October 1483, only four months after he had so signally assisted Richard's usurpation, Buckingham raised a rebellion in the Midlands and West Country. Buckingham's support was drawn from those who had been closest to Edward IV. Heavy rain in the Severn valley prevented the rebellion from getting anywhere, and the duke himself was captured and executed. But the effect of events was to drive Richard into ever-greater reliance on his own affinity, which was composed principally of northerners; this, in turn, was to cost him support in the south.

To the difficulties that Richard had of establishing his regime securely were added personal tragedies. In April 1484 the death occurred of his only son Edward (b. 1473), followed less than a year later by that of his wife, Anne Neville, the Kingmaker's daughter. Inevitably rumours abounded that the usurper was now earning retribution for his evil deeds. Though the country was internally peaceful at the beginning of 1485 Richard could never in fact feel secure so long as the pretender Henry Tudor, earl of Richmond, remained at large in Brittany and France. In August 1485 Henry decided to try his luck by landing with a small army at Milford Haven. As he marched across central Wales he picked up enough support to have a respectable army under his command when he met Richard at Bosworth (q.v.) on 22 August. In the battle that followed, tactical mistakes and the difficulties encountered in fighting on a constricted site cost Richard the day. He fell in the thick of the fighting. Henry had his body carried naked to Leicester where it was interred at the Greyfriars.

Richard's reign was thus over in two years. But what had happened to the princes in the Tower? Concern for the boys' safety was voiced even before Richard's coronation. Dominic Mancini, an Italian visitor to England in 1483, reports that before he left London (in July 1483) they had disappeared from view. In a passage remarkable for the evidence it affords of public sympathy for the princes he goes on to say that men wept when talking of Edward V's disappearance, and that suspicions arose that he had been *sublatum* ('disposed of'). It is one thing, of course, to say that the princes were never seen again after Richard became king and quite another to assert his responsibility for killing them. But, despite all the work that has been done in recent years to exonerate Richard, there is still enough circumstantial evidence to associate him with the crime. It was clearly in his interest to see them gone, because so long as they lived he would never feel safe as king. Moreover, his opponents evidently presumed them dead, or they would not have backed the claims of Henry Tudor. Henry's own Act of Attainder passed against Richard in his first parliament contained the rather vague, but still significant charge of 'shedding infants' blood'. Interestingly, the chancellor of France, Guillaume de Rochefort, had gone very much further in a speech delivered to the Estates General a couple of years earlier in 1484, when he accused Richard of having murdered his nephews. If they had indeed been disposed of by the end of 1483, then it is possible that the skeletons later unearthed in the Tower of two children, one aged about twelve, the other about ten, could have been theirs.

The impression conveyed by the evidence is that Henry VII had no need consciously to blacken Richard's reputation because it was already tarnished in his lifetime. Richard's actions could be defended on the grounds that a royal minority would have led to instability and that he forestalled a Woodville coup; but there is no denying that his association with the disappearance of the princes and the unpopularity he incurred by his usurpation left him so bereft of support that it was open to so improbable a claimant as Henry Tudor to topple him.

C. Ross, *Richard III*, 2nd ed., New Haven and London, 1999; A. Pollard, *Richard III and the Princes in the Tower*, Stroud, 1991; J. Hughes, *The Religious Life of Richard III*, Stroud, 1997.

ROADS

After the collapse of Roman rule in the fifth century the road system which had once carried the legions to the furthest corners of Britain fell into decay. But it did not collapse entirely. Even where weeds were sprouting between the paving stones, the line of the road often survived the passage of time. Late in the eleventh century the law recognized the existence of four great highways on which travellers enjoyed the protection of the king's peace: Watling Street, Ermine Street, the Fosse Way and Icknield Way. These are still famous names today. And only the Icknield Way has sunk to the status of a country lane.

What mattered most to people in the eleventh century, however, was often not the high road which stretched from one end of the country to the other but the lane which led from the village to the local market town. In the course of the Saxon period towns grew up which became the hubs of local road systems serving the surrounding countryside. From Oxford and Northampton in the Midlands and Norwich in East Anglia roads radiated in all directions, just as they do today. The same considerations of economic development which contributed to an increase in the size and number of the towns also served to extend the network of routes connecting them. In fact, the road system which was to be portrayed on John Ogilby's map published in 1675 was essentially a creation of the Middle Ages. This can be appreciated when Ogilby's map is compared with the famous one in the Bodleian Library, Oxford, dating from the early fourteenth century and known from the name of a former owner as the Gough Map (plate 146). The Gough cartographer marked in five principal lines of travel:

1) London, Guildford, Farnham, Winchester, Salisbury, Shaftesbury, Exeter.
2) London to Bristol along the line of the modern A4.
3) London to S. Wales along the line of the present A40 as far as Gloucester, and then via Hereford and Brecon to St David's.
4) London to Carlisle, via St Albans, Coventry, Lichfield and Lancaster.
5) London to the north again, following the Great North Road for much of the route, but branching westwards across the Pennines so as to reach Carlisle rather than Berwick.

Then, as now, all the main roads in England radiated from the capital. Travelling north and south was easy. Travelling east and west was more difficult, although not impossible. Worcester was well served by roads. And over in East Anglia Cambridge and Norwich (q.v.) could be reached by turning off the Great North Road at Ware.

Medieval roads, of course, were very different in character from those before and after. A medieval road was not a physical entity – a thin strip of land with definite boundaries. Rather it was a right of way with both legal and customary status, leading from one place to another. Regular use turned it into a track. Some medieval roads were big. The main routes, particularly those stretching north to the border, had to be wide enough to allow the passage of armies and to take herds of sheep and cattle. Royal orders show that the king was anxious to lay down the width of a 'royal way', that is, a road always kept open. In 1118 Henry I (q.v.) laid down that two wagons should be able to pass each other, or sixteen knights be able to ride abreast. These were not narrow paths cut through the undergrowth; they were wide swathes marching across the countryside.

Most medieval roads would not have been surfaced. We have to imagine a well-trodden path lined by wide grass verges on each side. Only in towns, like Lincoln or Southampton, would the streets have been paved or, as at Winchester, given a flint surface. One of the few public highways to have been paved was the Strand, linking London (q.v.) and Westminster, but by 1353 even its condition had so deteriorated that property-holders along it were ordered to make a footpath seven feet wide on each side of the road. In the towns responsibility for upkeep rested with those whose property fronted onto the road. In the countryside the position was less clear. Sometimes responsibility rested with a local landowner, sometimes not. If the latter, a local benefactor might come to the rescue. In Wiltshire a pedlar woman called Maud Heath encountered so many potholes on the way to Chippenham that when she died in about 1474 she left money for the erection of a stone causeway 4½ miles long to facilitate passage over the marshy terrain of the Avon valley. Her causeway still remains. If a borough community wanted to undertake repairs or, more ambitiously, to lay down a stone surface, it could obtain permission from the king to impose a toll on travellers – a practice that was, of course, to become very popular in later times.

In the Middle Ages those who could afford it travelled on horseback and those who could not, on foot. Few added to the discomfort of a journey by using a carriage. Carriages and wagons would be reserved for the luggage. From the considerable body of evidence which has survived about the speed of travel in this period, it seems that under normal conditions about twenty or thirty miles could be covered in a day on horseback. Inns at regular intervals along the route offered overnight accommodation.

It is not altogether clear how people in the Middle Ages found their way. It seems that there were no signposts, although there may have been milestones. If a group of travellers were undertaking a hazardous or unfamiliar journey, they would probably have hired a guide. In a famous passage in *Piers Plowman*, Piers speaks up from the crowd and offers to show the Seven Deadly Sins the way to the Shrine of Truth. Langland's employment of this ruse to introduce his hero implies that he expected his readers to have no difficulty in recognizing a character like Piers who would come forward to offer his services to a party of travellers.

If the land route were circuitous or the conditions poor, it often made better sense to make the journey by water. Thus in 1319, when Edward II invited the scholars of King's Hall, Cambridge, to spend Christmas with him at York (q.v.), the older scholars did the journey on horseback in five days, and their younger colleagues by boat from Cambridge to Spalding, on horseback to Boston, and then the rest of the way by boat again. They arrived three days late. But they very likely had the easier journey.

B.P. Hindle, *Medieval Roads*, Princes Risborough, 1982; D. Harrison, *The Bridges of Medieval England: Transport and Society, 400–1800*, Oxford, 2004.

ROBIN HOOD

The first reference to England's most famous outlaw is found in the B-text of Langland's (q.v.) *Piers Plowman*. Sloth, the personification of negligent priesthood, says: 'I'd still not keep awake. I can't sing my Pater Noster properly, as a priest should sing it, but I know the rhymes of Robin Hood and Ranulph, earl of Chester.' It can be inferred from this reference that the Robin Hood ballads were circulating by no later than the 1370s. The oldest surviving manuscript text of any of the ballads, however, ('Robin Hood and the Monk') can be dated no earlier than the mid-fifteenth century. The fact that the manuscript texts are so late and generally so fragmentary makes it difficult to say how and when the Robin Hood cycle first entered circulation. The only evidence is the internal evidence of the ballads themselves. Of these the longest and most instructive is the poem known as the *Gest of Robyn Hode*, which brings together in a single epic cycle a number of separate stories about the outlaw hero.

The first theme of the *Gest* concerns Robin and the knight. Robin declares that he will not eat until he has a guest to join him for dinner. So Little John and his companions detain a knight who, it transpires, is on his way to St Mary's Abbey, York, to repay a debt which he has contracted. But the knight is penniless (his clothing is tatty), and he faces the prospect of losing all he possesses. Robin agrees to lend him the necessary £400, and accepts his word that he can offer no better pledge than his faith in the honour of Our Lady. Moreover, he lets Little John accompany him to York. By the time they arrive, the abbot and his friend the justice are looking forward to seizing the knight's lands. They are taken by surprise when he throws the bag of money down onto the table. The knight then takes leave of Little John, and returns to his home in Wyresdale to collect the money to repay Robin.

While the knight is away, the scene returns to the greenwood, where Robin is once again asking Little John to find him a guest for dinner. Little John chances on none other than the cellarer of St Mary's, York. After they have dined, Robin asks his unwilling guest how much money he has on him. The cellarer confesses to carrying only 20 marks, but on examination he is found to have no less than £800. Robin keeps the money and sends the monk packing. When the knight finally arrives to repay the outlaw, he is told that Our Lady has already paid the debt twice over.

The next main theme concerns Little John and the sheriff of Nottingham. The sheriff notices Little John's prowess as an archer and takes him into his service for a year. This is hardly to John's taste, and so he picks a quarrel with the sheriff's cook. The two come to blows, and the cook fights so well that John persuades him to come and join the outlaws in the forest. With them they take the sheriff's money and plate. A little later the sheriff is decoyed into the forest and forced to eat from his own silverware.

The *Gest* continues with the story of the king's arrival in Nottingham to deal with the outlaws. The king disguises himself and sets off on the road through the forest, where predictably he is captured and taken to eat with Robin. Eventually Robin guesses the true identity of his guest, and kneels to beg forgiveness. This the king grants on condition that he enters his service and comes to court. So Robin rides off to begin a new life afar. But he soon grows disenchanted. After little more than a year he returns to his old haunts. The *Gest* closes with a brief account of his death in Kirklees Priory through the treachery of the prioress and her co-conspirator, Sir Roger de Doncaster.

If more were known about how the Robin Hood ballads were composed and circulated, it would be easier to say something about by and for whom they were composed. As several writers have pointed out, Robin's exploits have much in common with those of other outlaws of medieval literature – Fulk Fitzwarin, Eustace the Monk and Gamelyn, for example. Gamelyn, whose career is usually associated with the fourteenth century, was the younger son of a knight who fled to the greenwood and became the head of an outlaw band. He ran into trouble with the sheriff and the justice, but finally, like Robin, was pardoned by the king. It is a case of ringing the changes on the same familiar themes. Familiar they might be, and hardly the stuff of which great literature is made, but their very repetitiveness is significant. It helps to explain their popularity. Common to all the ballads is the idealization of the outlaw (q.v. OUT-LAWRY). Technically, an outlaw was someone outside the normal protection of the law, who was forced to rob and steal to support himself. Why was someone in such a position regarded as a hero? The answer is found in the failings of the system of justice. The courts were so riddled with corruption that the conventional values of society were inverted. Sympathy was given to those who were the victims of the law not to those who enforced it. So who were the victims of the law? Who were the people whose cause Robin espoused?

In a famous passage in the *Gest* (stanzas 13–15) Robin tells his men whom they should harm and whom they should not:

> But loke ye do no husbonde harme
> That tylleth with his ploughe.
> No more ye shall no gode yeman
> That walketh by grene wode shawe;
> Ne no knyght ne no squyer
> That vol be a gode felawe
> These bisshoppes and these archebishoppes,
> Ye shall them bete and bynde;
> The hye sherif of Notyingham,
> Hym holde ye in your mynde.

Now this does not amount to a straightforward policy of robbing the rich to give to the poor. Certainly the husbandmen farmers are deemed deserving of assistance. But so too are the knights and esquires – the gentry. It is the mighty bishops and the sheriff who have to be beaten and bound. And interestingly it is an impoverished knight to whose rescue Robin comes in the *Gest*. This evidence suggests that the poet is thinking not so much of peasant grievances but of the economic problems faced by the knights in the thirteenth century. In most big abbey cartularies, records are encountered of the takeover of estates belonging to knights who were forced by the inflationary pressures of the day to turn to monastic mortgagees. On this basis it could be argued that the Robin Hood cycle is more an expression of gentry than of peasant discontent. Indeed, there is much in the cycle that points in this direction; and it is apparent from the Commons' petitions in parliament that the gentry were no happier than their inferiors with the collusion that occurred between sheriffs and wealthy landowners. But, when all is said and done, the extraordinary appeal of the legends can only be explained on the assumption that they had a near-universal appeal. Robin transcended 'class'. As Professor Holt has suggested, the stories may have started off in the hall, but they soon went below stairs. And the wider the audience became, the more numerous the versions of the story that were put into circulation. 'Robin Hood and the Potter' may be a product of the more popular turn that some of the ballads took.

One last question needs to be considered. Did a Robin Hood actually exist? Or was he a figment of the popular imagination? If he is to be found anywhere, it will have to be in northern England, though just where is open to dispute. The identification with Sherwood Forest in Nottinghamshire rests more on the appearance in the ballads of the notorious sheriff than any references to it by name in the earliest surviving texts. In fact, Sherwood is not mentioned at all in the *Gest*. The area that is mentioned in this poem is Barnsdale, Yorkshire, which lies between Doncaster and Pontefract. It was to 'the Sayles' in Barnsdale that Robin Hood despatched Little John to find him a guest for dinner. And significantly this spot is located on a stretch of the Great North Road where robberies are known to have occurred in the Middle Ages. But the problem with identifying a real-life Robin is that thanks to an excess of scholarly endeavour so many Robin Hoods have been traced in the records that it is hard to tell which, if any, provided the inspiration for the ballads.

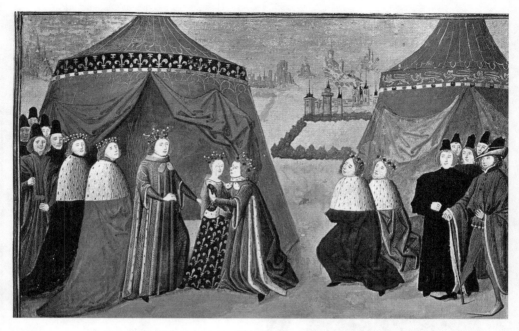

108 The meeting of **Richard II** and Isabella of France from Froissart's *Chronicles*. Richard married Isabella, his second wife, in 1396.

109 **Richard II**. The arrest of the duke of Gloucester in 1397, from Froissart's *Chronicles*.

Left: 110 **Agriculture**. Aerial photograph, Sulby, Northants, clearly showing traces of the strip division of fields in the medieval period.

Above: 111 **Anselm**'s seal as Archbishop of Canterbury.

Left: 112 **Architecture, Ecclesiastical**. Durham Cathedral: interior of the nave, 1099–1128.

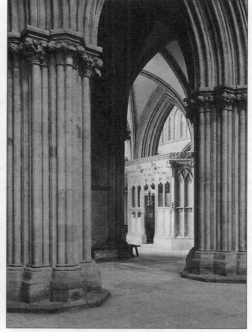

Above: 113 **Architecture, Ecclesiastical**.
Canterbury Cathedral: interior of the choir,
1175–84, designed by William of Sens and
completed by William the Englishman.

Above right: 114 **Architecture, Ecclesiastical**.
Wells Cathedral: south transept, looking into the
nave, *c.* 1175–80. Note the multi-shafted pillars.

Right: 115 **Architecture, Ecclesiastical**.
Westminster Abbey: the choir, 1245–60.

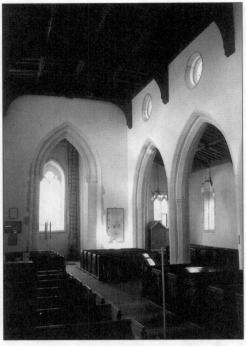

Above left: 116 **Architecture, Ecclesiastical**. Ely Cathedral: the West Tower with its tall perpendicular lantern, a rare late-medieval project in a 'great' church.

Above: 117 **Architecture, Ecclesiastical**. A parish church highly influenced by the friars' architecture, with high arcades and port holes in the clerestory, Chrishall (Essex).

Left: 118 **Architecture, Vernacular**. Cruck house, Ombersley (Worcs).

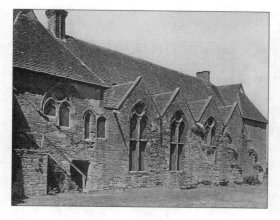

Clockwise from top:

119 **Architecture, Vernacular**. Stokesay Castle (Shropshire): the hall range, begun *c.*1285.

120 **Armour and Arms**. Late thirteenth-century effigy of a knight showing the surcoat and helm. Furness Abbey (Lancashire).

121 **Armour and Arms**. Brass of Reginald de Malyns and his two wives, 1385, Chinnor (Oxon).

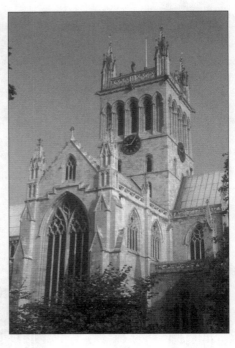

Clockwise from above left:

122 The martyrdom of St Thomas **Becket**, from a twelfth- or thirteenth–century Psalter. This is probably the earliest surviving representation of St Thomas's death.

123 Selby Abbey, one of the new houses established by the **Benedictine** Order after the Conquest.

124 **Brass** of Sir Thomas Brounflete, 1430, Wymington (Beds): London style 'D'.

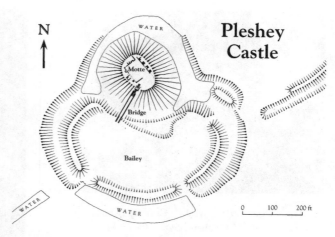

Pleshey Castle

Clockwise from left:

125 **Brass** of Robert Ingleton and his wives, 1472, Thornton (Bucks): London style 'D'.

126 Pleshey, Essex: a typical motte and bailey **castle**.

127 Conway Castle, built 1283–87, one of Edward I's chain of **castles** in North Wales.

128 The **castle** as status symbol: Cooling (Kent), built by John, Lord Cobham, *c.*1380. Note the heavy machicolations, coat of arms over the gate and inscription recording construction.

Above: 129 **Edward II**. The younger Hugh Despenser, from a window in the clerestory of Tewkesbury Abbey, *c.*1344.

Above left: 130 The **fine** as established in 1195, with a third copy – the 'foot of the fine' – to be filed in the treasury.

Left and below: 131 **Government**. A selection of royal seals. From the top: William I, Edward III, Edward IV.

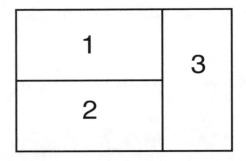

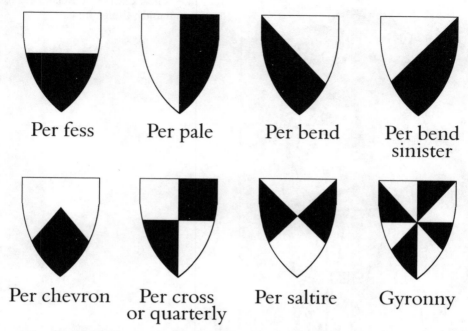

Per fess   Per pale   Per bend   Per bend
                                          sinister

Per chevron   Per cross   Per saltire   Gyronny
              or quarterly

132, 133 **Heraldry**. The earliest and most important heraldic devices, the 'divisions' (top), and the 'ordinaries' (bottom).

Chief   Fess   Pale   Bend   Bend sinister

Chevron   Cross   Saltire   Pile   Pall

134 Perkin Warbeck, who used **Ireland** as a base for his claim to the English throne.

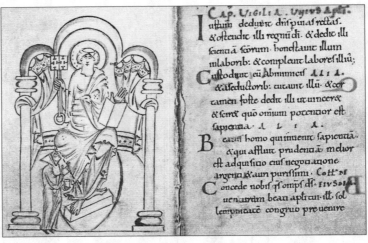

135 **Liturgy**. Prayers written for Aelfwin, abbot of New Minster, Winchester, *c.* 1012–20.

ehoc scrum ē indautonomo ñ ēt mandu
candū philsiolog' dicit dehoc q̃ tot' alb̄ ē.
ē nullam ptē habeint nigia.Cui urcior fimus.
curat caligine octox.Jtē matris regū inuenit
Siquis ante ēt inegnudine ostrure pbē cala
drii cognoscet si uiuet an moriet Si,tt.ē sfir
mitas hōint ad morte mox itt uidet sfirmū
ex moritur' ē:aūtt facie suam abeo.ē rccedit
Si aūtē infirmitas eī si pungit ad mortem

Clockwise from left:

136 Illustration from a twelfth-century Bestiary.
Such books inspired much of the fantastical
carving on **misericord** seats.

137 **Monasticism**. Malmesbury Abbey, Wiltshire,
a Benedictine house.

138 **Monasticism**. Ground plan of a typical
Benedictine monastery: Sherborne (Dorset).

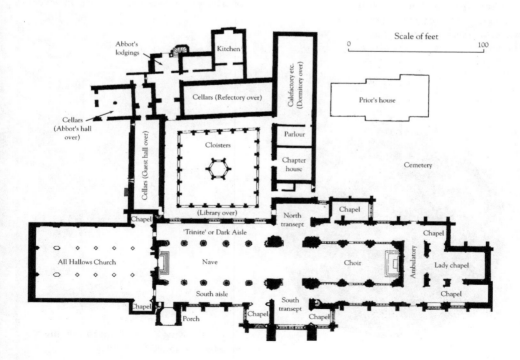

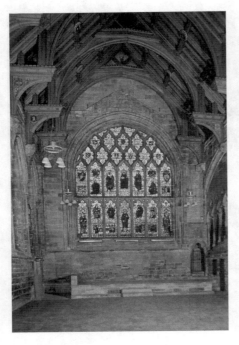

139 **Monasticism**. The chapter house, St Werburgh's Abbey, Chester, now Chester Cathedral, showing on the right the arcaded stair to the wall pulpit.

140 **Music**. Fifteenth-century Gradual, Florence.

141 Seal of the Kingmaker, **Richard Neville**, showing him mounted for combat.

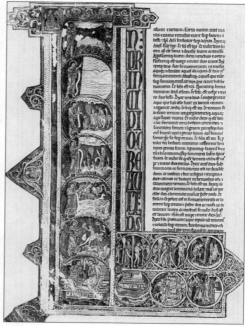

Clockwise from above:

142 **Painting**. The foundation charter of New Minster, Winchester, *c.*966–70.

143 **Painting**. Bible of Robert de Bello, abbot of St Augustine's Canterbury, 1224–53. Note the wide borders with medallions.

144 **Painting**. The 'Beatus' page of the *St Omer Psalter*, *c.*1330.

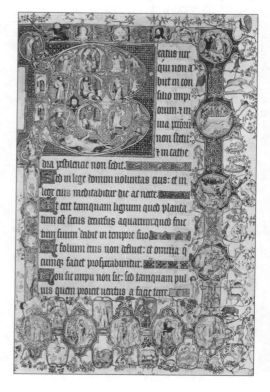

145 Self-portrait of **Matthew Paris** kneeling before the Virgin and child.

146 **Roads** on the Gough Map, *c.* 1360.

Above: 147 **The Wars of the Roses.** The Yorkist collar of suns and roses on the brass of Sir Anthony Grey, 1480, St Albans Abbey.

Right: 148 And so to **school**: brass of a schoolboy, *c.*1500, showing him with his penner and inkhorn, Little Ilford (Essex).

149 **William I**, in a window at St Mary's Hall, Coventry, late fifteenth-century.

Above: 150 **Sculpture**. The south door of Kilpeck church (Herefordshire). *c*.1140–5.

Below: 151 European **trade** routes in the 1470s.

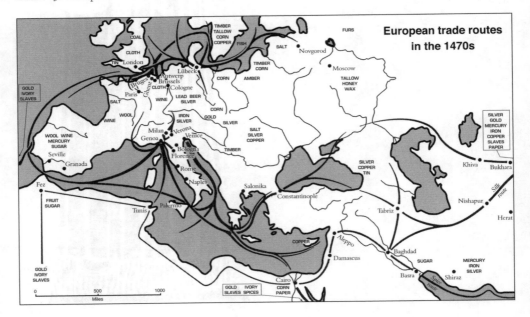

The candidate with the strongest claim to date is the Robin Hood described as a fugitive in a Yorkshire pipe roll of 1230. But the search for a real Robin, which has flourished in the past, will doubtless go on.

See also JUSTICE

R.B. Dobson and J. Taylor, *Rymes of Robyn Hood: An Introdction to the English Outlaw*, London, 1976; J.C. Holt, *Robin Hood*, London, 1982; A.J. Pollard, *Imagining Robin Hood*, London, 2004.

ROMANESQUE
See ARCHITECTURE, ECCLESIASTICAL

ROSES, WARS OF THE
The intermittent struggles lasting from the first battle of St Albans (1455) to the battle of Bosworth (1485) are known as the Wars of the Roses, a term coined by Sir Walter Scott in *Anne of Geierstein* (1829). The idea that the opposing sides adopted the red and the white roses as their respective emblems is a much older one. The idea is found in Shakespeare's *King Henry VI, Part I*, in the famous scene in the Temple Garden, in which York and his supporters pluck the white rose and Somerset and his allies the red one. Whether this scene is fact or fiction is hard to say. Certainly the Yorkists were identified with the white rose, but the principal mark of Lancastrian affiliation was the collar of SS, which had been awarded to the family's retainers ever since the days of John of Gaunt (q.v.), 'time-honoured Lancaster'.

Since the Wars of the Roses resulted in the replacement of one dynasty by another, Tudor historians tended to assume that their principal cause was a struggle for the throne going back to the deposition of Richard II. In fact the notion is doubtful, because the Yorkist lords were remarkably slow to take up arms against King Henry VI (q.v.). It is true that Henry of Lancaster's seizure of the throne had the unfortunate effect of making the succession an issue in English politics, but the successful kingship of his son Henry V (q.v.), placed the authority of the Lancastrian dynasty beyond question. What reopened the issue was the appalling kingship of his successor, Henry VI. By the late 1440s Richard, duke of York, had emerged as the principal critic of Queen Margaret and the clique that held sway at Henry's court. The duke had, as it happened, inherited a claim to the crown, and a good one: he was descended through the female line from Lionel, duke of Clarence, second surviving son of Edward III, whereas the Lancastrians were descended from John of Gaunt, the third son. But it was a claim which would never have been heard had the duke not found himself excluded from power by the queen. York's aim was to force his way back onto King Henry's council, and to do that he needed support. His main allies were his brother-in-law, Richard Neville, earl of Salisbury (d.1460) and the latter's son, Richard Neville, earl of Warwick (q.v.). The Nevilles were one of the leading families in the north. Their growing wealth made them rivals of that other northern lineage, the Percy earls of Northumberland. Once the Nevilles lined up behind York, it followed that the Percys would line up behind Queen Margaret and the court.

The first battle of the Wars of the Roses is usually considered to have been that at St Albans in 1455. Its significance is that it broke the bonds of restraint. York and his men had planned to intercept Henry VI and Somerset, who were going to Leicester to attend a council meeting packed with their supporters. After the failure of parleying, the battle broke out. The casualties included some of the greatest men in the land. St Albans, however, was quite a small-scale encounter, and was not immediately followed by further hostilities. Queen Margaret waited before making her next move. In September 1459 she launched a pre-emptive strike on her Yorkist enemies at Blore Heath. York and his men fled for their lives, and from their respective havens of exile (York himself had gone to Ireland, Warwick and Salisbury to Calais (q.v.)) decided that they should launch an invasion of England. In June 1460 Warwick and his party landed at Sandwich. They entered London, and in July marched north to Northampton, where they defeated the Lancastrians and captured the king.

On 10 October York returned to London, and to the embarrassment of his supporters laid claim to the throne. The reluctance of the nobility to recognize his title – for they were supposed to have been fighting the king's evil advisers and not the king himself – was shown by their equivocal reaction: they allowed Henry to reign for his lifetime, but diverted the succession to York and his heirs. Such a face-saving formula was hardly likely to satisfy Queen Margaret, who was rallying her forces in the north. In a change of fortune by no means unusual in these years she defeated and killed York at Wakefield (30 December 1460) and marched south, regaining possession of her husband at the second battle of St Albans (17 February 1461). But she frittered away the fruits of her victory. Her troops went on the rampage on the streets of St Albans and the Londoners took fright. On 27 February they opened their gates to the Yorkists. Queen Margaret thus had the king, and her opponents the capital. Without a king the Yorkist lords could do little. To legitimize their actions, they created a king of their own: they put the new duke of York on the throne as Edward IV (q.v.). On 29 March Edward gave reality to his title by crushing the Lancastrians at the battle of Towton.

Towton brought to an end the first phase of the wars. The Lancastrian partisans were dispersed and their leaders were in exile in Scotland. But the issue was reopened when Warwick and George of Clarence, the king's brother, rebelled in 1469, taking Edward prisoner and executing those Woodville relatives of his to whom they took exception. Complacent though Edward may have been in the past, he now fought back with determination. Warwick fled to France, where he renewed contact with Queen Margaret and the Lancastrian exiles. In perhaps the most astonishing volte-face in this period he formed an alliance with the Lancastrians to restore Henry VI. On 13 September 1470 he and Clarence landed near Dartmouth, and Edward was forced to flee. Henry VI was reinstated as king but Warwick's regime failed to inspire confidence. Edward returned in 1471 and defeated his adversaries at Barnet (14 April) and Tewkesbury (4 May).

Edward IV died peacefully in April 1483; but he had the misfortune to leave a thirteen-year-old son as his heir. The temptation which overcame his uncle Gloucester to seize the crown as King Richard III (q.v.) then undid all the good work that Edward had done in restoring political stability. Richard's usurpation precipitated the third and final phase of the wars. Henry Tudor, earl of Richmond, who claimed descent from the Beauforts, chanced his arm against the usurper and emerged victorious at Bosworth (q.v.) on 22 August 1485. He had won the crown, but his hold on power was not secured until after the battle of Stoke (16 June 1487), when John de la Pole, earl of Lincoln, the Yorkist pretender, was killed. Stoke has better claims than Bosworth to be regarded as the final battle of the Wars of the Roses.

The Wars of the Roses had far less impact on people's daily lives than, say, the wars of Stephen's reign (1135–54) or the Civil War of the 1640s. The towns escaped lightly. St Albans had the misfortune to witness two battles in its streets; on the other hand it was never besieged. This was a war pursued not by long-drawn-out sieges but by short pitched battles, and even these were largely confined to 1460–1 and 1469–71. The armies, moreover, were small, composed mostly of the great lords and their retainers. Yet the Wars of the Roses made a great impact on national consciousness. The fact that Shakespeare wrote an epic cycle about them indicates that his audiences, while fascinated, did not want to see a repeat of the experience.

See also BASTARD FEUDALISM

R.L. Storey, *The End of the House of Lancaster*, 2nd ed., Gloucester, 1986; A.J. Pollard, *The Wars of the Roses*, Basingstoke, 1988; C. Carpenter, *The Wars of the Roses: Politics and the Constitution in England,* c.*1437–1509*, Cambridge, 1998.

S

SCHOOLS

In the Middle Ages the Church was dependent on education and education on the Church. Without the clergy there would have been no schools and without the schools no clergy. It was the needs of organized Christianity which called into being a system of educational provision the size and extent of which can easily be underestimated.

At the lowest level in medieval England there were the 'reading' or 'song' schools, the medieval equivalent of modern primary schools, to which children were sent from about the age of seven. There they learned to read (probably aloud) and to sing. Elementary establishments of this sort were found not only in the towns, where they were fostered by the liturgical needs of the cathedrals and greater churches, but also in quite a number of country villages. Theobald of Etampes, who was teaching at Oxford in the twelfth century, says, admittedly in a polemical tone, that in the villages as well as in the towns there were as many schoolmasters as there were tax-collectors and royal officials. These men were not accomplished scholars; but they were practised enough in letters to be able to offer instruction to any youngsters who could be spared by their parents from labour in the fields.

At about the age of eleven or twelve the more fortunate or gifted of these children would have been sent to the 'grammar' school – so called because the study of grammar, that is Latin grammar, was the lynchpin of the medieval syllabus. These schools were largely a creation of the twelfth century, when the revival of learning extended the range of educational opportunities. As scholars have pointed out, the earliest and most important schools grew up around the cathedrals, and in particular around those served by secular canons as opposed to monks. In due course the schoolmaster became a member of the cathedral chapter and a person of some importance, so that as his duties accumulated he usually appointed a deputy to do the day-to-day teaching. Although the cathedral schools were the most important of their day, they were only the most notable of the many establishments called into being at this time.

The standard elementary textbook used to introduce young children to the study of Latin grammar was the *Ars Minor* of Aelius Donatus, a fourth-century writer who had been St Jerome's tutor. After they had mastered Donatus – not an exacting task as his book only extended to a dozen pages – the pupils moved onto the *Doctrinale* of Alexander de Ville Dieu (*c.*1200), a verse treatise of great popularity which ran through the parts of speech, syntax, metre and so on. At a higher level still, aimed at university students rather than schoolboys, were the books by Priscian, a scholar of Constantinople (c.500), whose lengthy and detailed studies of Latin left no stone unturned. In addition to textbooks the pupils needed dictionaries to enable them to pick up vocabulary. The work which did most to assist them here was the *Elementarium* of Papias, an Italian lexicographer who in 1053 hit on what was then the novel idea of composing a word list in order of initial letter. Obvious though the idea seems to us today, the concept of alphabetical order was one which took a long time to gain acceptance, not least in the archives of the English government which were practically useless without it.

In theory, an education should have cost nothing in the Middle Ages. The Lateran Council at Rome in 1179 ordained that each cathedral was to endow a schoolmaster adequately enough to enable him to teach the clerks of his cathedral and other poor scholars free of charge. Cathedrals, indeed, had long honoured their obligation to maintain a school, but it was the chancellor and not his deputy, the practising teacher, who was the beneficiary of the endowments. In a grammar school, therefore, the only pupils likely to be given a free education were the choristers; the others would have had to pay. That is not to imply that the expense was necessarily going to cripple their parents. For the grammar boys at Merton College, Oxford, in 1277 tuition fees were 4d a term or 1s a year; by the fifteenth century the going rate had risen to 8d a term. If the pupils were living away from home, they would also have had to pay for board and lodging, a bill likely to be far higher than that for tuition. At Merton scholars paid 8d a week for board in 1400, and at Winchester commoners 8d to 16d a week in the fifteenth century. As for books, it is known that a few pupils bought their own, though they hardly needed to in an age when teaching was for the most part done by reading aloud. More essential was the penner and inkhorn, the sheath-full of pens hung from the belt, which in 1526 could be purchased for as little as 4d.

If schooling were to be provided free, as the Lateran Council had envisaged, the schoolmaster would have to be given an adequate benefice to release him from dependence on fees. This the cathedrals rarely succeeded in doing. In the course of the late Middle Ages, therefore, it became increasingly common for benefactors to direct their charitable endeavours to establishing schools adequately endowed to provide free education for the needy and deserving. Sometimes, as at Ottery St Mary in 1338 or Cobham in 1389, these were essentially collegiate or chantry (q.v.) foundations, where the provision of schooling was secondary to the celebration of the divine office. In the 1380s, however, two schools were founded which were important for the novel emphasis which they placed on teaching above religious and devotional observances. The larger was Winchester, founded and endowed on a lavish scale by Bishop William of Wykeham (q.v.) in 1382 for the instruction of seventy scholars, who would spend four or five years there before qualifying for admission to the sister foundation at Oxford (q.v.) later known as New College. The other, perhaps more influential in the long run for being smaller and therefore more compatible with the means at most benefactors' disposal, was the 'House of Scholars' at Wotton-under-Edge (Glos) founded by Katherine Lady Berkeley in 1384. Like his colleagues at earlier collegiate foundations, the schoolmaster at Wotton had to sing masses for the souls of the foundress and her relatives, but his main duty was to give free instruction in grammar to the two poor scholars who received free board and lodging and to any others who might attend. From then until the Reformation many such endowed schools were to be founded with the aim of providing free schooling to the foundationers and even occasionally, as at Wotton, to all comers. Some of these schools were attached to chantries or hospitals, a few, as at Stratford-on-Avon, to guilds (q.v.). The schoolroom erected at Stratford in 1427 as part of the buildings of the Guild of the Holy Cross is still in use today.

What would life have been like for a schoolboy all those years ago? The implication of the low level of per capita tuition fees in the grammar schools is that a master hoping to gain a livelihood would have to teach large classes. In the case of the cathedral schools class size was probably in the order of forty or more. If classes were bigger than would be usual today, so too were hours longer. Judging by early Tudor regulations, the day would begin at six or seven in the morning and after lengthy breaks for breakfast and midday dinner would culminate in a long haul from one till five in the afternoon. Perhaps to keep his pupils on their toes, the medieval schoolmaster was free in his use of the cane. The schoolboy in Chaucer's *Prioress's Tale* promises to learn the song to the Virgin Mary.

Though they should scold me when I cannot say
My primer, though they beat me thrice an hour.*

Chaucer's schoolboy must have been one of many who looked forward to the start of the school holidays. For reasons which are unclear holidays were as long in the Middle Ages as they are today. In the ordinances which she laid down for her school at Wotton-under-Edge, Lady Berkeley said they were to last for 2½ weeks at Christmas, a fortnight at Easter, a week at Whitsun and six weeks in the summer.

As for the provision of urinals, to consider an irreverent but not unimportant aspect of

* Chaucer, *The Canterbury Tales*, ed. N. Coghill, Penguin Classics, 1951, p.189

school life, it seems that the boys were supposed to go outside to some recognized spot – too often, according to one Oxford schoolmaster who complained, 'As sone as I am com into the scole, this fellow goith to make water and he goyth oute to the comyn drafte.'

See also UNIVERSITIES; LANGUAGE AND LITERATURE

N. Orme, *English Schools in the Middle Ages*, London, 1973.

SCIENCE

If technology remained backward in the Middle Ages, that is not to say that advances in scientific thought were few. On the contrary, some of the theories of motion worked out by medieval scholars largely anticipated the theories which Galileo was to propose in his *Discourses* in the early seventeenth century. Nor did England herself have any reason to feel ashamed. Oxford could boast of Grosseteste (q.v.) and Bacon (q.v.) in the thirteenth century, and Bradwardine and the Merton mathematicians in the fourteenth. The scrutiny to which these men subjected Aristotle's view of the universe was to culminate in its eventual overthrow in the age of the Scientific Revolution.

In the central Middle Ages the Aristotelian view of the universe was the one which was broadly accepted by scholars. Aristotle's thinking had come to western Europe via the Arab world. One by one Aristotle's books had been translated into Latin by scholars like the Englishman Adelard of Bath who, in so doing, refined his cosmology and fitted it into a Christian framework. At the centre of the universe, according to Aristotle, lay an immobile Earth, composed of four elements – air, water, earth and fire. Around it rotated the moon, the sun, such planets as were then known and the stars. These were conceived as embedded in a series of concentric spheres, within which they made their orbital motions, preserved and continued by their love of God, who moved them indirectly as the object of that love. The spheres were hidden from the human eye because they were composed of an invisible substance called aether. Outside this universe, in Aristotle's opinion, no matter could exist.

Aristotle's Christian interpreters needed to postulate that it was 'love of God' that made the planets go round, because the master had assumed that anything capable of motion had to be moved by something else. This theory of motion opened up what was to prove one of the most fruitful avenues of scientific investigation in the Middle Ages, culminating at the end of the sixteenth century in the work of Galileo. Aristotle had argued that all terrestrial objects had a natural motion towards the centre of the earth, but that any other motion, contradicting as it would the ordinary tendency of a body to stay in what was regarded as its natural place, was dependent on the operation of a mover distinguishable from the body which it moved. His theory of motion, therefore, unlike the modern one, was a theory of inertia which assumed rest, and asserted that a body would come to rest as soon as the thing imparting motion to it was removed. Aristotle's explanation conformed remarkably well with what direct experience of the world suggested about the nature of motion, but nonetheless there were two phenomena that gave rise to misgivings. First, why did an arrow not fall to the ground the moment that it left the bow-string? Instead of stopping as soon as it lost contact with the bow which had given it motion, the arrow continues its motion for another hundred yards or so. Secondly, there was the problem of acceleration. Why did bodies falling to the ground move with an ever accelerating speed?

The answers which were given to these questions at Oxford and Paris in the thirteenth and fourteenth centuries, although adjusting Aristotle's theory in significant respects, were still rooted firmly in his system of physics. They entailed the introduction of the concept of internal resistance. Aristotle had held that in all mixed bodies one of the elements (earth, air, water and fire) would predominate and thus determine the motion of the body, in other words whether it would rise or fall. Not so, it was now argued. Rather, the total power of the light elements should be weighed against the total power of the heavy elements. If the light elements predominated, the body would move upwards, and if the heavy ones did, then it would move down. Consequently, in a falling body, heaviness would be regarded as the motive force and lightness as resistance; in a rising body, lightness would be the motive force and heaviness resistance. Expressed in the language of modern science, motion was therefore determined by the ratio of force to internal resistance. It was to be left to Galileo, in the sixteenth century, to make the vital breakthrough in this field. Galileo was almost certainly familiar with medieval writing on the subject of motion, but whether or not it influenced him in reaching his own conclusions is hard to say. For internal resistance he substituted what we now call specific weight. But for the final formulation of the modern law of inertia we have to wait a little longer, because it required an extra feat of imagination to conceive of that very un-medieval and un-Aristotelian concept, a void. The modern view says that in the absence of any other bodies or external resistance, a body will continue moving to infinity. That is not a conclusion which the medieval thinkers could have reached by direct experience alone.

Motion, naturally enough, led to considerations of velocity. It was in the study and analysis of this problem that the group of mathematicians associated with Merton College, Oxford, made their greatest contribution. As Dr Crombie has written, nearly every important English scientist of the fourteenth century was at some time in his career associated with Merton. Thomas Bradwardine, a distinguished theologian and later Archbishop of Canterbury, developed a form of algebra. His contemporaries, John of Dumbleton, William Heytesbury and Richard Swineshead were interested in how long it would take a body to travel a given distance assuming uniform acceleration. The rule which these men formulated, known as the mean speed theorem, has been described as the most outstanding single medieval contribution to the history of physics. It states that the distance traversed in a given time by a body uniformly accelerating from rest equals the total time of moving multiplied by the mean of the initial and final velocities ($S=\frac{1}{2} Vft$, where S=distance travelled, Vf=final velocity, and t=time of acceleration). This theory was given a geometric proof in about 1350 by the French mathematician, Nicholas Oresme, and was the precursor of the more detailed laws which Newton formulated several centuries later.

For all the intellectual ferment of the thirteenth and fourteenth centuries, medieval science nevertheless failed to break out of its Aristotelian straitjacket. It is doubtful if the dominance of the Church is to blame for this. Almost certainly the part played by the Church in obstructing scientific research has been exaggerated. For example, Copernicus, who proposed the heliocentric system in a book published in 1543, was a cleric himself and suffered no persecution. On the other hand, it has to be admitted that Copernicus did live a long way from Rome. Perhaps the most serious problem lay in the nature of medieval scholastic thought. Scholasticism became increasingly abstract and divorced from reality. A solution to a scientific problem was seen not as a contribution to the quest for physical reality but as a means of preserving the logical consistency of the Aristotelian system. What distinguishes Copernicus from his medieval forebears is that he saw his cosmol-

ogy not as an artificial construction necessitated by the requirements of logic but as a way of explaining the motions of the real, visible universe. That was a great step forward, but it did build on foundations laid in the Middle Ages. Sixteenth-century thinkers did not achieve this feat of intellectual emancipation without deriving inspiration from the past. This inspiration they found in what, to them, must have been the remarkable discovery that the great Aristotle had not in fact been without critics in earlier times. To take an example relating to the theories of motion already discussed: John Philoponus, a Greek commentator of the sixth century AD, denied that an external medium was always the cause of violent motion. In the 1130s a Spanish Arab, the Latinized form of whose name is Avempace, may have been influenced by Philoponus when he denied Aristotle's claim that the time it took a body to fall was directly proportional to the resistance of the external medium through which it passed. Avempace thought that what we observe as 'ordinary' motion was the difference between hypothetically unobstructed motion and the slowing down due to the medium. The potential of these admittedly still rather vague ideas was never realized in the Middle Ages, but men were groping towards the theory that natural motion could only occur in a hypothetical vacuum. It is that idea, as we have seen, that lies behind the modern law of inertia. In other words, it was not a failure to experiment or to observe the workings of the universe that held back medieval science but rather a failure to look at things in a new light.

That said, it is possible to identify a number of technical advances that took place in the Middle Ages. Large-scale building construction made heavy demands on the mathematical and engineering skills of the masons. The need to cover wide spans with stone vaults led to the adoption of the pointed arch, an eastern idea probably brought to the West by the crusaders in about 1100. Industries (q.v.), like glazing and cloth-making, also employed complex processes, and ones moreover that demanded some knowledge of chemistry. The introduction of cannons, rudimentary though these instruments were in their early days, represented an advance in the uses to which that knowledge could be put. But the breakthrough in medieval technology that did most to change everyday life was probably the invention of the mechanical clock. The combination of a falling weight which set in motion a series of geared wheels and an escapement mechanism which controlled the rate of motion gave medieval Europe an instrument which at last solved the problem of telling the time of day. The earliest such clock surviving in England is probably the one in Salisbury Cathedral thought to have been made in about 1386.

See also BUILDING; STAINED GLASS

A.C. Crombie, *Augustine to Galileo: the History of Science, A.D. 400–1650*, 2nd ed., Cambridge, 1961.

SCOTLAND

Among the non-English parts of the British Isles it was only in Scotland that a centralized polity emerged of the kind found in England.

In the seventh and eighth centuries the present Anglo-Scottish border did not exist. The Anglo-Saxon kingdom of Northumbria stretched from the Humber to the Lothians. The lands of the Picts and the Scots were confined to the present-day Highlands. In about 843, however, the powerful Pictish king Kenneth forced his own people and the Scots together to form a kingdom which, if not united in the modern sense of the word, was at least strong enough to throw the English onto the defensive. In 945 King Edmund ceded Strathclyde (probably including Cumbria) to the Scots, and thirty years later Edgar made over Lothian, bringing the bor-

der by the end of the Anglo-Saxon period to just south of Berwick on the east and somewhere by Rere Cross on Stainmore (Yorks) in the west.

The Scottish king at this time was Malcolm Canmore (1058–92), who had supplanted the infamous Macbeth. Malcolm's marriage to Margaret, sister of the English pretender, Edgar Athling, had resulted in a number of English refugees coming to the Scottish court. Margaret herself, who was later canonized, used all her considerable influence to undertake the kind of ecclesiastical reforms that Lanfranc (q.v.) was making in England so as to draw the Scottish Church into closer conformity with the new spirit prevailing on the continent. Malcolm's long reign ended, however, in a crisis. In 1092 William Rufus (q.v.) seized Carlisle and advanced the western border to the line of the Cheviots. Malcolm retaliated by marching south, but before he could achieve anything both he and his son were killed outside Alnwick. Under Donald Bane, Malcolm's brother and successor, there was a reaction against the anglicizing tendencies of the previous reign that lasted until the accession of Margaret's son Edgar (1097–1107). He was succeeded in turn by his two brothers, Alexander (1107–24) and David (1124–53).

David's reign was one of the most important in Scottish history. Though known in England chiefly for his defeat at the battle of the Standard (22 August 1138), he was in fact a successful king who did much to place the Scottish monarchy on a firmer footing. Certainly, the Standard put an end to his ambitions in England, but he managed to salvage something from the wreck. King Stephen (q.v.) was too preoccupied by the problems that beset him at home to follow up the victory won in his absence in the north. So when peace was made eight months later David acquired the English earldom of Northumberland for his son Henry. Coupled with his effective occupation of the city of

Carlisle, this agreement once more brought the Scottish border down to its limits in the time of Malcolm Canmore. David's involvement in English affairs was taken still further by his tenure of the honour of Huntingdon, which he acquired by his marriage to the daughter of the English earl Waltheof. He was not only a Scottish king but an English tenant-in-chief, and when civil war broke out in England in 1139 he lent his support to the Empress Matilda and her son Henry, the future Henry II (q.v.).

For all his eagerness to extend Scottish influence southwards, it is for his achievement in strengthening royal authority in Scotland itself that David deserves to be remembered. When a reforming influence had last been felt in Scottish affairs, in the reign of Malcolm Canmore, it had been one of English provenance. This time it was Anglo-Norman. With David's encouragement Anglo-Norman families came to settle in Scotland, and feudal tenure took the place of the old Celtic system of landholding. The newfangled titles of earl and baron made their appearance alongside the mormaers and toisechs of Celtic vocabulary. And in central and southern Scotland David began to establish the rudiments of a system of local administration: we hear of the office of sheriff for the first time in 1120.

David died in 1153 leaving an eleven-year-old grandson to succeed him as Malcolm IV. In the years that followed it became painfully apparent that the Scots stood little hope of clinging onto their gains in Northumbria once the English had closed ranks under the strong monarchy of Henry II. Malcolm handed back the northern counties in 1157. His policy was opposed by his brother and successor William the Lion (1165-1214), who took advantage of Henry's misfortunes in 1174 to intervene on the side of the rebels in return for the promise of Northumberland. But his ambitions were thwarted one misty morning when he was captured near Alnwick. He was released the following year on terms that were intended to clarify the relationship between the two kings. William became the vassal of Henry 'for Scotland and all his other lands', and he surrendered the castles of Edinburgh, Roxburgh, Berwick, Jedburgh and Stirling, the five strongest in his kingdom. At first Henry exercised his overlordship to the full, but in later years he relented a little. William's humiliation was finally obliterated in the reign of Henry's successor, Richard I (q.v.), who allowed him to redeem his country's independence for a payment of 10,000 marks.

The century that followed was one of the most tranquil in Scotland's history. Skirmishes and raids were still a fact of life along the border, but it gradually became clear that the Scottish kings would be unlikely ever again to push the frontier as far south as the Tees. Instead, they sought to extend their power northwards by subduing the rebellious lords of the Highlands. They even succeeded in making Moray, distant as it was, a shire within the governed area of the kingdom. All the same, this prospect of orderly progress was abruptly terminated one windy March night in 1286 when Alexander III was swept from his horse and killed. It was Scotland's misfortune that he should have died childless. His sole heiress was his three-year-old granddaughter Margaret of Norway. She set sail for Scotland in 1290, but died while making the passage. As no clearly recognized heir was left, Edward I (q.v.) of England was invited to arbitrate between the two principal claimants, Robert Bruce and John Balliol. He came down in favour of the latter. Once Balliol was installed on the Scottish throne, Edward seized every opportunity to insist on his rights as overlord. He went so far, in fact, that in 1295 the Scots rebelled and placed the government of their country in the hands of a council of twelve. Edward responded by invading in the following year.

These sad events ushered in the long period of Anglo-Scottish warfare that was to do so much to shape the respective political destinies of the two nations. Edward seems to have thought that he could subdue the Scots as easily as he had subdued the Welsh in the 1280s. But the experience of the next few years was to show that a victory in the field was not enough to conquer a country the size of Scotland, and that so far from crushing the spirit of the Scots his campaigns had the contrary effect of awakening Scottish nationalism. Worse still, when the Scots reached an agreement with Philip IV of France, he found himself fighting a war on two fronts. This was more than English political society could bear, and in 1297 discontent boiled over into open opposition to the king's exactions. The Scottish champion, William Wallace, took advantage of the crisis to sweep down from the Highlands and defeat the English at Stirling Bridge. By the following year Edward's position at home had recovered sufficiently to allow him to avenge this humiliation at the battle of Falkirk on 22 July. This crushing victory turned the tide of war in favour of the English: Wallace was driven into hiding and eventually captured and executed in 1305, and even magnates like Robert Bruce decided to lay down their arms. If Edward thought that was the end of the war, however, he was mistaken. In 1306 Bruce raised the standard of rebellion again and had himself crowned king at Scone. In the following year Edward I died while making his way north, and under his incompetent son Edward II (q.v.) the English conquests in Scotland were whittled away. But, feeble as he was, not even Edward was prepared totally to surrender. When news reached him in 1314 of a threat to English-held Stirling, he came to its relief with a large and impressive army. Bruce had no option but to fight and, taking advantage of his opponents' errors, he was able to reap one of the most decisive victories of the Middle Ages (q.v. BANNOCKBURN). Eventually in 1323 Edward decided to agree to a truce, but it took the regime of

Isabella and Mortimer, which supplanted his own, finally to recognize Scottish independence in the Treaty of Northampton, 1328.

Life in the border country in this period was difficult. Year after year crops were destroyed, and villages burned. Law and order suffered an irreparable breakdown. To protect their respective border marches, the English and Scottish kings relied on the services of local magnates, whose power in these disputed areas ultimately exceeded that of the kings they nominally served. Such magnates were the Douglases in Scotland, and the Percys and Nevilles in England. Moreover, the success in Scotland of Bruce and the nationalists created a sizeable party of 'disinherited' lords who had forfeited their lands for siding with Balliol and the English. These were the men who incited Edward III (q.v.) to reopen the war after Bruce died in 1329 leaving a five-year-old son, David II, as his heir. At Dupplin Moor in 1332 and at Halidon Hill the English succeeded in worsting the Scots and a puppet king, Edward Balliol, son of John, was put on the throne. As in the reign of Edward I, however, the Scottish War soon became caught up in the wider conflict with France. David II took refuge with Philip VI in Normandy, and so long as he stayed there it proved impossible for the negotiators to reach agreement on the other matters in dispute between England and France. Fearing that the French might land in England, Edward therefore invaded the Low Countries in 1338, in what proved to be the opening campaign of the Hundred Years War (q.v.). The diversion of the English forces to Flanders had the effect of relieving the pressure on Scotland, and in 1341 David returned to his native land.

Like his predecessors, David seized every opportunity to create havoc in England. In 1346, while the bulk of England's armed strength was encamped outside Calais (q.v.), he crossed the border, and was met by a hastily assembled army at Neville's Cross, where he was defeated and taken prisoner. For the second time in 200 years the English had a Scottish king in their custody. David was finally released in 1357 in return for a ransom of 100,000 marks, a vast sum for a country of only 400,000 people to have to collect. Nevertheless, David made a sincere attempt to honour the terms, and by the time payments ceased in 1383, some 45,000 marks had been handed over.

In the meantime David's unfortunate reign had drawn to a close. He died childless in 1371 and was succeeded by Robert the Steward, the founder of the line of 'Stewart' kings. Robert was the first king for nearly a century who did not have to worry about a threat from the south. The only serious outbreak of hostilities with the English in his reign resulted in a Scottish victory at Otterburn in 1388. But within the realm he was troubled by the increasing unruliness of magnates like the earls of Douglas and of March, on whom the monarchy relied for border defence. Moreover, the next king, Robert III (1390–1406), faced a serious rival in the duke of Albany, for fear of whom he sent his son and heir James to France for upbringing. Unfortunately, however, James was captured en route by the English a few weeks before his father died. Albany had no wish to see the young king back in Scotland and consequently took no measures to secure his release. Thus it was not until 1424 that James I returned from exile.

James proved to be an effective ruler – indeed, much too effective for the liking of some of the nobility who found their independence curbed. On the night of 20 February 1437 James was murdered, and the work which he had done in restoring order was undone during the minority of his son James II. By the time the new king was reaching maturity it was the turn of England to experience civil strife, and in the manner of his predecessors James took advantage of it to sally forth across the border. It was while he was besieging Roxburgh in 1460 that he had

the misfortune to be blown up by one of his own cannons.

The Scottish medieval monarchy was a very different sort of monarchy from the English. In style it was much more informal. The central bureaucracy was undeveloped and few written documents were used. In Scotland, political power was for the most part local power; so kings gave expression to their will by itinerating. By comparison with the English monarchy, the Scottish kings may appear weak. But appearances can deceive. The very flexibility of the Scottish monarchy contributed to its strength. The Scottish kings, when they needed to, could act decisively. In the 1450s James II destroyed the power of the turbulent Douglases at a stroke. This was a remarkable coup – and one unparalleled in England. The differences between the English and Scottish monarchies were chiefly ones of style rather than substance.

G.W.S. Barrow, *The Anglo-Norman Era in Scottish History*, Oxford, 1980; R. Nicholson, *Scotland: the Later Middle Ages*, London, 1974; A. Grant, *Independence and Nationhood, 1306-1469*, London, 1984.

SCULPTURE

Most of the medieval sculpture that has come down to us survives in our churches. It was intended both to decorate the buildings and to instruct the faithful. Despite the emphasis on instruction, however, surprisingly little of it is directly iconographic. In the thirteenth and fourteenth centuries on roof bosses, gargoyles and corbels masons gave free play to their imagination by combining Biblical exegesis with light comedy. It is the variety and vitality of medieval sculpture which makes it so enjoyable.

The Normans inherited from the Anglo-Saxons a vigorous sculptural tradition which had drawn on both the barbaric tastes of the North and Christian influences from the

Mediterranean to produce some striking works like the Romsey Abbey crucifixion. At first, the Normans had little to contribute to this tradition. They excelled at architecture (q.v.) rather than sculpture, and it is remarkable how little adornment there is on their major buildings. It is in small village churches that Norman carving is seen at its best, on fonts and tympana for example (the tympanum is the space between the door and the archway of an entrance). Here we meet dragons and strange beasts and ornamental patterns using the familiar dogtooth and billet-head forms. By the 1130s, however, there was a significant revival in sculpture. From around this time there survive the two stone panels at Chichester Cathedral, showing Christ at Bethany and the Raising of Lazarus. The Bethany scene, memorable for the haunting expression on the faces, has been described as one of the outstanding pieces of English medieval carving. The Chichester panels are matched in importance by the work which a school in Herefordshire was producing in the 1140s, in Stephen's reign. The Herefordshire school were a roving team of sculptors who displayed their skills most brilliantly at the churches of Shobdon, Kilpeck and Fownhope. On the south door at Kilpeck, Viking, Irish and French influences are drawn on to produce lively, sometimes demonic, carvings of dragons, snakes and long trails, in which vaguely human figures are engulfed (plate 149). The Herefordshire masons or their successors were responsible for two more masterpieces, the fonts at Castle Frome and Eardisley, which, if they are rightly dated to the 1160s, are among the last works of the school. In the Baptism of Christ at Castle Frome Romanesque sculpture attained an eerie intensity unsurpassed in the sculptural work of its day.

By the time the Herefordshire carvers were ceasing work, their style was being overtaken by the change in aesthetic from Romanesque to Gothic. This was a change just as significant for sculpture as it was for architecture. The wild, semi-abstract scenes that had fascinated the earlier age were rejected in favour of life-like figures of the saints portrayed as human beings with whom men and women could identify and sympathize. In northern France the entrance portals of the cathedrals of Chartres and Rheims were given figures of saints and angels which are among the most beautiful in Christian art. These idealized statues reflect a more optimistic view of the world – one that had shaken off the associations of the dark, pagan past. In England the nearest approximation to the sculpture galleries of France is the west front of Wells Cathedral (c.1230–50). Its 176 standing figures, 30 half-size angels and 49 narrative reliefs make up a vast iconographical scheme centred on the Coronation of the Virgin and supported on the south side by Old Testament and on the north side by New Testament scenes.

The assured quality with which the Wells west front was carried out was matched inside the cathedral, where stiff-leaf foliage, a characteristic motif of English thirteenth-century sculpture, was employed fully developed for the first time in the nave and transepts. Out of the transept capitals grow graceful sprigs of trefoil-shaped leaves. The foliage is not so much stiff as stylized, and it is brought to life by being used as a cover for the many delightful carvings for which Wells is famous – the man with toothache and the thieves in the orchard to name but two (plate 114).

By the time the Wells nave was nearing completion developments equally significant for the history of sculpture were taking place at Westminster. In 1245, under King Henry III's (q.v.) patronage, work commenced on rebuilding Edward the Confessor's abbey church. In sculpture no less than architectural conception the new abbey owed much to French ideas. For example, high up in the transepts are two sets of angels of undeniably French inspiration. They have a gentle smile reminiscent of the celebrated angels of Rheims, but the energetic treatment of the drapery marks them out as definitely English.

It is these Westminster figures which very likely provided the inspiration for the famous gallery of angels that fills the triforium of the rebuilt choir of Lincoln Cathedral, the so-called 'Angel Choir'. Less restrained than their forebears at Westminster, these angels – some playing musical instruments, and one carrying a hawk – were the work of local masons whose style was very different from that practised by the court school.

Another local school, based somewhere in the north, was responsible for the 'leaves of Southwell'. In the 1290s the chapter house of Southwell Minster was rebuilt, and its capitals decorated with foliage of unparalleled realism. Oak, maple, buttercup and hawthorn can all be recognized on the capitals round the walls. The canons of Southwell were fortunate not only in employing the sculptors they did, but in choosing to rebuild when they did: in the brief period of the 1290s English botanical sculpture attained a measure of realism never experienced before or since.

The vitality of the Southwell sculpture finds its counterpart in the gaiety and inventiveness of the architecture (q.v.) of the period. This was the heyday of English 'Decorated'. A favourite motif of the masons at this time was the undulating ogee curve, used to such good effect in the Ely Lady Chapel. Masons felt an irresistible urge to dissolve surfaces in a sea of decorative ornament. Niche mounted niche, canopy mounted canopy. The finest achievements of the period rank among the most daring of medieval creations. When we look at the Percy tomb at Beverley Minster and the tomb of Edward II at Gloucester, we find ourselves losing touch with reality as we are drawn heavenwards by the forest of pinnacles.

Such richness of detail was bound to provoke a reaction in favour of simplicity. It came with the arrival of the 'Perpendicular' style, which relied for its effect not on sculptural elaboration but on the simple definition of line. Consequently the later fourteenth and fifteenth centuries show relatively little sculpture to set beside the beautiful work of the thirteenth, and we have to wait for the work undertaken at Westminster Abbey in the early sixteenth to see the last flowering of the sculptor's art before the Reformation. The rows of prophets (c.1505–15) high in the triforium of Henry VII's Chapel are obviously the work of a highly accomplished portraitist who knew just which features of the human face needed stressing to bring out the idiosyncracies of personality.

Though the late Middle Ages can show little figure sculpture of distinction, the abilities of craftsmen found ample outlet in the production of tomb effigies. Many of these were carved in freestone, but an increasingly popular material was alabaster, a form of lime sulphate quarried in Nottinghamshire and Derbyshire. For the most lavish monumental commissions copper-gilt was used. The life-size copper effigy of Richard Beauchamp, earl of Warwick (d.1439) at St Mary's, Warwick, is one of the great achievements of the medieval sculptor.

Sculptors were also employed to satisfy the medieval appetite for heraldic display. Coats of arms and heraldic beasts were carved in profusion on the walls of both churches and manor houses. The show front of the gatehouse of Butley Priory (Suffolk) provides a good example. Shields of arms were popular both for their decorative effect and for their value in advertizing genealogical pride and family connections. The Tudor rose and Beaufort portcullis are two 'bastard feudal' (q.v.) devices that cannot escape the attention of the visitor to King's College Chapel, Cambridge, or any other building that the early Tudors had anything to do with.

See also TOMBS

L. Stone, *Sculpture in Britain: the Middle Ages*, 2nd ed., Harmondsworth, 1972; P. Williamson, *Gothic Sculpture, 1140-1300*, New Haven and London, 1995.

SEISIN

Seisin was a word commonly employed in the twelfth century to describe the possession as opposed to the ownership of land. In a later age, when conveyancing was effected by written instrument, the idea of 'livery of seisin' survived to describe the ceremony whereby a recipient was led into possession of a piece of land he had acquired. A man who held a free tenement was therefore said to be in seisin. If he was deprived of it, he was said to be disseised. In the 1160s and 1170s Henry II (q.v.) evolved a legal process, known as the Assize of Novel Disseisin, which enabled a person recently disseised of a tenement to recover it. The writ initiating the action instructed the sheriff (q.v.) to summon a jury whose duty it was to ascertain the facts of the case – only the facts, and not any questions of right or wrong that might complicate matters, for the essence of the procedure was its simplicity. In this, too, lay the secret of its success.

See also JUSTICE

SERMONS

Preaching was the principal medium through which the medieval Church communicated its message to the faithful. Most people could not read the Vulgate Bible for themselves as it was in Latin. However, they could hear its teaching expounded from the pulpit.

The sermons which have survived from the Middle Ages make an important contribution to our knowledge of the social, literary and ecclesiastical history of the period. Most of them date from the fourteenth and fifteenth centuries. But that does not necessarily mean that more sermons were preached in that period than before. Ever since the Council of Clovesho in 747 the English hierarchy had been encouraging their clergy to teach the Word of God. Yet, however hard they tried, they could do little to overcome either the reluctance or the inability of so many priests to mount their pulpits. In fact, it is far from clear whether churches actually had pulpits for much of the Middle Ages: the oldest surviving ones date from no earlier than the fourteenth century. For all the evidence that points to the rarity of a sermon in church in the eleventh or twelfth centuries, however, there are suggestions that those who thirsted for the word could hear it, and hear it from the lips of some very distinguished preachers indeed. Jocelin of Brakelond tells us, for example, that Abbot Samson of Bury St Edmunds, eloquent as he was in French and Latin, was quite happy to preach to the people in English, and even in the local dialect when he was in Norfolk, the county where he was born and bred. This information gives us a remarkable insight into the linguistic range expected of a twelfth-century preacher, who might find himself called upon to speak in Latin before clerics, French before the nobility and in the vernacular before more humble folk.

What must have led to an increase in the provision of preaching was the coming of the friars (q.v.) in the thirteenth century. The Dominicans (q.v.), or Black Friars, significantly were known to their contemporaries as the Friars Preachers. In the towns they built vast hall-like churches to accommodate the crowds that came to listen. Urban society suffered from no shortage of preaching in the late Middle Ages, because it was chiefly to the towns that the earliest mendicant missions had been directed. But it seems that in the rural parishes too there was an increase in the provision of preaching once the clergy became better educated. Writing in about 1450, the theologian Alexander Carpenter could say that 'now in many places there is greater abundance of preaching of the Word of God than was customary before our time'. A good many congregations could enjoy regular sermons. John Mirk's *Festial*, written in around 1400 for the benefit of a fellow clergyman, contains a cycle of seventy-four sermons – in other words, one for every Sunday of the year and for a good number of saints' days as well. One recent estimate is that something like sixty sermons a year would have been preached in some of the better-served parishes in England or France.

How did the medieval preacher set about his task? He had to present his message in terms that would be comprehensible to an audience whose education, if any, would rarely have extended beyond the elementary stage (q.v. SCHOOLS). This he did by abandoning generalities in favour of allegorical figures of speech and exempla, or moralized anecdotes. Robert Ripon's tale of the bailiff and the devil is a good example. A notoriously oppressive bailiff was riding to his village one day, when en route he met the devil. The bailiff said that he was travelling on his master's business. The devil then enquired if he would freely accept whatever was freely offered to him. The bailiff of course said yes, and likewise enquired of his companion. The devil replied that he would not take whatever men gave to him but only what they would gladly give with all their heart. 'Quite right', said the bailiff. As they made their way into the village, they met a ploughman angrily commending to the devil his uncooperative plough oxen which kept straying from their course. 'They are yours', said the bailiff. 'No, no', said the devil. 'That man does not give them with all his heart.' They went on, and next they saw a woman wishing her child to the devil because it would not stop crying. 'Now this one is yours', said the bailiff. 'No', replied the devil. 'The woman does not really want to lose her child.' Finally they came to the end of the village where they met a poor old woman whose only cow the bailiff had seized the day before. 'To the devil I commend you', she shrieked with all her heart as she saw the bailiff coming. 'To be sure, this one is mine', said the devil. And then he snatched the bailiff away to the perpetual fires of Hell.

That story of Ripon's illustrates how the preacher had to be a good raconteur. He made sure of retaining the attention of his audience by telling a good story and telling it well. To that end he might employ a number of devices and embellishments. Mirk, who was prior of Lilleshall (Salop), appealed to local tradition by writing homilies for the feasts of the local West Midlands saints Alkmund and Winifred. He also appealed to the legendary and the miraculous; his sermons contained lots of good yarns and lots of stories of miracles and shrines. To that extent he was ultra-traditional in his approach. Not all the pulpit oratory of the late Middle Ages was so good-humoured, however. Satire – often ruthless satire – poured from the lips of the preachers. In this respect the great Dominican John Bromyard stands in a class of his own. From his pulpit Bromyard lambasted the regular clergy for their wealth and avarice; he condemned the rich for their gluttony and extravagance; he attacked the nobility for their oppressiveness and the justices for their corruptibility; and just to be even-handed he complained as well about the slothfulness and idleness of the labouring classes. All that and more is contained within Bromyard's famous homiletic collection, the *Summa Predicantium*.

The richness and variety of medieval sermon literature was demonstrated over seventy years ago by G. R. Owst in his *Literature and Pulpit in Medieval England*. If a criticism has to be levelled against this book, which has become something of a classic, it must be that Owst took too static a view of his subject. He recognized that there was a movement towards greater realism in sermon literature, but failed to allow that the content and purpose of sermons might also have changed in the course of the Middle Ages. In the twelfth and thirteenth centuries preachers, for all the delight that they took in the use of satire, kept within the limits of an ecclesiological framework. In the fourteenth and fifteenth centuries, however, preachers were increasingly called on by kings and princes to place their services at the disposal of the state. A sermon would be given at the opening session of a parliament, setting forth the king's case for a grant of taxation. Sermons were often preached on occasions of national emergency. Bishop Orleton and others preached sermons in favour of the deposition of Edward II. Victories might be celebrated by sermons. Thomas Bradwardine, the theologian and future Archbishop of Canterbury, preached in celebration of Edward III's victories at Neville's Cross and Crécy (q.v.).

The use of the sermon as a medium of secular propaganda, couched in biblical terms but accommodated to current political needs, indicates a changed mentality towards interpretation of the Holy Scripture. At the same time, the appreciation by modern scholars that sermons may have been viewed differently as time went on indicates just how far sermon studies have advanced since Owst wrote his seminal studies in the 1920s and 1930s. One of Owst's favourite themes was the influence of sermons on the development of English literature. *Piers Plowman*, he claimed, was 'the quintessence of English medieval preaching gathered up into a single metrical piece of unusual charm and vivacity'. Nowadays it is appreciated that there is more to the poem than that. Certainly, Owst was right to say that satirist and allegorist alike were disciples of the pulpit. There are similarities in structure and modes of treatment. But at the same time it must be recognized that poet and preacher had differing purposes in mind. The latter placed the emphasis on explaining, on giving a straight, convincing answer to a question about the place of man in God's design for the world. The former, however, placed emphasis on artistry and explanation. To that extent, the dreamer in Langland's (q.v.) masterpiece is a long way indeed from the church pulpit.

G.R. Owst, *Preaching in Medieval England*, Cambridge, 1923; G.R. Owst, *Literature and Pulpit in Medieval England*, Cambridge, 1933; H.L. Spencer, *English Preaching in the Late Middle Ages*, Oxford, 1993.

SHERIFF

The office of sheriff (OE, *scir gerefa*, shire-reeve) can be traced back to the reign of Ethelred the Unready (978-1016) and by the time of the Conquest it was already the chief instrument of royal government in the shires. The medieval sheriff was the maid of all work, responsible for collecting the farm (the revenue due to the king from the boroughs and royal demesne lands in the shire), for presiding in the shire court, for making a twice-yearly tourn or visitation of the Hundred (q.v.) courts and, from the thirteenth century onwards, for proclaiming royal statutes at the principal towns in his bailiwick. Under the Norman kings the sheriff attained his greatest power and independence, but by the fourteenth century he was subjected to rigorous exchequer control and obliged to share his duties with new officials like the coroner (q.v.), the escheator (q.v.), the commissioners of array and the justices of the peace. All the same, if the sheriff became less independent, he did not become any less corrupt, to judge from the evil character accorded him in the Robin Hood (q.v.) legends.

It is evident from the dialogue between king and subjects in the thirteenth and fourteenth centuries that the king had one conception of the office of sheriff and his subjects quite another. The king, in an effort to maximize his revenues, wanted to appoint trusty royal servants as sheriffs and to keep them in office for as long as possible. His subjects, whose views were articulated by the Commons in parliament, demanded that only well-to-do local gentlemen should be appointed, rich enough not to be tempted by corruption, and that they should hold office for only one year. For a century or more the crown tried holding its position, but in 1371, on most points, it gave way. In later times the sheriff lost many of his duties to the lords lieutenant and the justices of the peace and although his office survives in England to this day it is largely honorific. The modern American sheriff has more in common with his medieval English forebears.

See also GOVERNMENT; JUSTICE

W.A. Morris, *The Medieval English Sheriff to 1300*, Manchester, 1927, repr. 1968.

SIGNET
See GOVERNMENT

SPORT

A number of modern pastimes were already known in England in the Middle Ages. On the other hand, several of the activities engaged in in this period were ones which are now either forgotten or disapproved of.

William FitzStephen, in a celebrated description of twelfth-century London, tells us how folk in the capital spent their leisure hours. Much of what he says will be familiar. He says that when Moorfields marsh was frozen over the young men would go skating and tobogganing. They would also go out into the fields to play ball games and at Smithfield they would engage in horse-racing. The pastimes which he mentions were ones long to remain popular. Skating and tobogganing on the frozen River Thames were to be depicted in seventeenth- and eighteenth-century genre paintings. It was ball games which were to have the rosiest future ahead of them. New varieties of games with balls caught on in the late Middle Ages. Tennis was evidently played by the early fifteenth century, to judge from the tennis-balls episode in Act I, Scene ii of Shakespeare's *Henry V*, which rests on good contemporary

authority. Indeed, there is a reference in Chaucer's *Troilus and Criseyde* to 'pleyen raket, to and fro'. Cricket is not actually mentioned until the sixteenth century, but it may have developed from an earlier game called 'club-ball' which was banned in a proclamation of 1365. At the foot of the east window in Gloucester Cathedral (*c*.1350) there is the tiny figure of a man hitting a ball with a club curved at the end. This man is usually described as a golfer, and golf was indeed known by the end of the Middle Ages, but he could equally well be playing hockey or club-ball.

These pursuits were ones which were all very popular. From the government's point of view, indeed, they were much too popular. In 1365 they were prohibited. Able-bodied men were told that instead they should practise archery: for the very practical reason that skill in archery was crucial to English success on the battlefields of France. The list of games prohibited in that year — and they were not all ball games — provides an index of what people liked doing in the fourteenth century. 'Hurling of stones, loggats and quoits, hand-ball, cock-fighting and other vain games of no value' were all mentioned.

The prohibition (or attempted prohibition) of cock-fighting affords a reminder that in the Middle Ages games involving animals provided idle amusement in a way that would be considered quite unacceptable today. Bear-baiting, for example, is one of the sports illustrated in the margin of a fourteenth-century manuscript of the *Romance of Alexander* (plate 7). William FitzStephen tells us that on winter mornings in London bears were set to fight each other, or were baited by dogs. And it goes without saying that hunting was the aristocratic sport *par excellence*. By the early thirteenth century vast tracts of countryside were set aside for the chase, and the deer and the boar within them were protected for the king's enjoyment by the savage code of regulations known as the forest laws. But it was not only the king who enjoyed hunting. So too did the peasantry, albeit for more practical reasons. And so too, according to Chaucer (q.v.), did the pilgrim monk,

> one of the finest sort
> Who rode the country; hunting was his sport.★

Hunting was a subject addressed in several treatises in the Middle Ages. One of the most popular of these was published in the *Boke of St Albans*, printed in 1485. This volume also contained a chapter on fishing, another popular rural pastime.

For the long, dark evenings there was a variety of pursuits. Since time immemorial men had been listening to minstrels singing heroic epics, ballads or popular songs. Every nobleman retained his company of minstrels and fools. But at the same time as listening to background music and singing, the lord and his friends might play chess, backgammon, cards or dice. All these games were known by the late Middle Ages. Gambling in particular seems to have been a pursuit to which noblemen were addicted. Between September 1413 and March 1414, for part of which time he was staying with Henry V at Eltham, the earl of March lost over £157 at cards, raffle and betting on cockfighting. The Black Prince is said to have lost as much as £100 on a single day's play with his father.

For the humbler folk there was always drinking. William FitzStephen in his account of London names 'the immoderate drinking of fools' as one of the two plagues from which the city then suffered (q.v. DIET). Most medieval towns (q.v.) were apparently as well supplied with taverns as they were with churches: which means very well indeed. The duty of controlling the quality and price of ale, and the hours at which it could be sold, lay with the local municipal

★ Chaucer, *The Canterbury Tales*, ed. N. Coghill, p.23

authorities, who then as now made great play of detailed regulations. By the 1530s the rule at Chester was that ale and wine were not to be sold after 9 p.m. on any day or during the hours of divine worship on Sundays. Doubtless medieval pubs like their modern counterparts had their 'regulars', and doubtless too there was more than ample drinking-up time.

A.C. Reeves, *Pleasures and Pastimes in Medieval England*, Stroud, 1995.

STAINED GLASS

Although only a small proportion of the stained glass created between the seventh century and the Reformation has come down to us, what remains is sufficient both to attest its high quality and to indicate the role which it played in the decorative schemes of both churches and domestic houses.

The earliest evidence for the glazing of a church in medieval England comes from the seventh century. In 675 Benedict Biscop, abbot of Monkwearmouth, sent to Gaul for glaziers to work in his churches, as there were none in England. Some of the glass which was made by these men has been excavated. It consists of small rectangles and triangles in blues of various hues, greens and yellows. Later in the Saxon period stained glass was manufactured in England. Fragments of English-made glass have been found at Brixworth, Repton and Winchester. English glass of this period appears chiefly to have been arranged in mosaic fashion. By the tenth century, however, figures and foliate patterns were shown.

The large-scale use of picture windows appears to have begun in the twelfth century. From *c*.1170 there survives a panel of a king from a Tree of Jesse at York Minster and from the 1180s the magnificent series of windows in Canterbury Cathedral. The general impression created by glass of this period is one of sombre and intense richness. The very colours that predominated – greens, purples and rubys – contributed to that atmosphere of mystery that must have pervaded the interior of a church in the age of Becket. To judge from the surviving glass at Canterbury, the subject matter of these windows included figures of saints, placed high in the clerestory so that they could be seen from below, and narrative sequences arranged in vertical tiers of medallions in the lancet windows in the aisles. In these aisle windows a separate stage of the story was told in each medallion. Another form of glazing occasionally found in this period is the pattern window, important for the fact that it fore-shadows the famous 'grisaille' or grey-patterned glass of the thirteenth century. The popularity of grisaille was probably a response to the desire for better lighting to illuminate the marble shafts and sculptured capitals that characterized early Gothic architecture. The windows were larger by this period, but that was not enough. The glass that filled them had to be lighter. Thus the deep colours of twelfth-century glass gave way to a shimmering grey-ish-green background on which was painted a foliate pattern that became steadily more naturalistic as time progressed. To appreciate on the grandest scale the kind of effect that could be created it is necessary to look at the 'Five Sisters' window in the north transept of York Minster, where five huge lancets, each 53ft high, were all filled with grisaille in the 1250s.

Grisaille glass continued to be used into the following century, but it was the earlier tradition of figures and narrative sequences that proved to be most compatible with the large, multi-opening windows of the 1300s. The characteristic window of this period contained a row of saints, as many as there were openings, or 'lights', to be filled, and each one surmounted by an elaborate canopy. Winged angels were usually placed in the small tracery lights. The subject-matter of a window was normally decided by the governing chapter of the abbey or cathedral church or by the donor

in consultation with the chapter, if the latter were not defraying the entire cost. As the Friar tells Lady Fee in *Piers Plowman*, 'We are having a stained glass window made for us, and it's proving rather expensive. If you would care to pay for the glazing yourself, and have your name engraved in the window, you need have no doubts of your eternal salvation.' As early as the 1290s at Merton College, Oxford, this attitude had led to the inclusion of kneeling portraits of the donor, Henry de Mamesfield, in a sequence of no fewer than a dozen windows: with a view no doubt to reminding the onlooker to pray for his soul. In seeking this lavish commemoration of himself in the College Chapel, de Mamesfield may well have been indulging his own sense of vanity; but he set an example that was to be taken up many times over by patrons and donors in the next two centuries.

As well as witnessing a major change in design, the fourteenth century saw a techno-logical breakthrough in glass painting. This was the discovery of 'silver stain', a method of combining white and yellow on the same piece of glass which was first used extensively in this country, it appears, on the 'heraldic widow' at York Minster (*c.*1310–20). This had the effect of both tilting the balance in favour of light over dark colours and of reducing the number of separately leaded panels that went to make up a window. Now that the design could be constructed without the need to cut so many pieces of glass, there was more scope for artistic excellence, and what these later windows lost in vividness they gained in architectural conception and originality of design. Some fifteenth-century windows were so vast that they afforded the chance to illustrate a full-length story, such as the life of a local saint, by narration in a series of panels beginning at the top left-hand corner and ending at the bottom right. How far the onlooker could make sense of what was happening in some of the largest of these windows is open to question, but the overall effect was certainly superb.

Contracts and other documentation help us to identify some of the men responsible for these beautiful windows. The largest of the windows in York Minster – the great east window – was executed by one of the most accomplished glaziers of the age, John Thornton of Coventry. John was given just three years (1405–8) by the chapter to complete this vast commission, the implication being that he was the head of a fairly large workshop. Although this major contract at York went to a Coventry workshop, York itself was an important centre of glazing, as can be seen from the many windows that have survived in the city churches. By the fifteenth century there were workshops in most major English towns, those at Norwich, Oxford and London being particularly worthy of mention. The workshop at Oxford produced some distinguished work in the later fourteenth century under Thomas Glazier. Examples of Thomas's output can be seen at New College, Oxford, and Winchester College.

A description of how medieval stained glass was made is given in a treatise, De Diversis Artibus, written in about 1100 by a monk called Theophilus. The first stage was for the master glazier to sketch a design for his window. This was usually a full-size drawing, executed in the twelfth century with charcoal on a whitewashed table-top and in the fifteenth on paper or parchment so that it could be preserved for later use. When the design was completed and a colour scheme arranged, the glazier took all the different coloured pieces of glass which he needed, laid them on the cartoon and cut them to shape. In the absence of diamond cutters, which were not introduced until the seventeenth century, this difficult operation was performed with the aid of a red-hot iron. The glass used by the glaziers was known in the trade as 'pot-metal', meaning that it had been coloured throughout by the addition of a metallic oxide of whatever hue was required – cobalt for blue, copper for red, manganese for violet and so on. When all the pieces of glass were in position, the glazier could begin to paint in the details, like faces and drapery folds, taking as his guide the design of the cartoon underneath. The earliest stained glass windows, like those in Canterbury Cathedral, were composed of a vast mosaic of tiny leaded pieces, resplendent in their vivid reds and violets. In the early fourteenth century, however, the art of glass painting was revolutionized, as we have seen, by the discovery of 'silver staining'. Someone had evidently noticed that a silver salt solution painted on a surface of white glass would turn yellow when fired. The significance of this breakthrough was that it enabled yellow and white areas to be depicted on the same piece of glass, thus reducing the number of separate leaded panes that needed to be used in making a window.

When the painter had finished his job, he could consider the glass ready for firing. This was the method by which the paint was fused onto the surface to prevent it from falling off with the passage of time. The pieces of glass were laid out on a tray covered with quicklime and fired in a kiln. Once the pieces had cooled, they were brought back to the table, where they were joined together by strips of lead. The window was then ready for delivery to the church.

The richest treasury of medieval stained glass in England is to be found in the Minster and city churches of York. Glass from the Norwich workshops, much of it of the highest quality, can be seen at East Harling (Norfolk), Long Melford (Suffolk) and in some of the city churches of Norwich itself. Other fine medieval windows survive at Tewkesbury Abbey, Great Malvern Priory, and the cathedrals of Wells, Exeter and Gloucester.

R. Marks, Stained Glass in England during the Middle Ages, London, 1993.

STEPHEN

In the reign of Stephen (1135–54) England was afflicted by a long civil war known as 'the Anarchy'. The Anglo-Saxon chronicler writing at Peterborough at this time reported that men said openly that Christ and his saints slept.

The war had its origins in a dispute over the succession. After the death of his only legitimate son, William, in the wreck of the White Ship in 1120, Henry I (q.v.) had made the barons swear to accept his daughter Matilda, wife of Geoffrey of Anjou, as his heir. The barons took the oath, but they hardly relished its implication: the prospect of an Angevin takeover. In 1135, when Henry died, they accordingly gave their support to a rival candidate – Stephen of Blois. Stephen, a younger brother of Theobald of Blois, was Henry I's nephew. He was one of the richest landowners in England and spent much time at his uncle's court.

In 1135 Stephen enjoyed the support of virtually all of the Anglo-Norman aristocracy. In late 1138, however, Robert, earl of Gloucester, and various others drifted away, and by September 1139 Matilda commanded enough support to make a bid for the throne. The event which triggered Matilda's bid was the arrest of three important courtier bishops at Oxford in June 1139 – Roger, bishop of Salisbury, the justiciar (q.v.), and his nephews, Nigel, bishop of Ely, and Alexander, bishop of Lincoln. These were the men on whom Henry I had relied for the administration of England. The bishops were rich – very rich. Stephen, however, was beginning to run short of money. He had had to meet a range of expenses, notably buying off rivals and paying for a war in the north. According to the author of the *Gesta Stephani*, Waleran, count of Meulan, urged the king to arrest the bishops and seize the money which they had pocketed at his expense. The move was a disastrous error. It alienated the former servants of Henry I who now felt increasingly insecure. Three months later, Matilda landed. The first to defect to her was her half-brother Robert of Gloucester, who disliked Count Waleran. Robert was followed by Miles of Gloucester and Brian FitzCount. Both of them were honouring the late king's memory by offering their services to his daughter.

Matilda attracted sufficient support to start a war, but insufficient to win it. The result was a long drawn-out struggle in which neither side held the advantage for long. At the beginning of 1141 Matilda seemed to be taking the lead: in February she captured Stephen at the battle of Lincoln. Four months later she entered the capital, but before she could be crowned the Londoners showed their hostility by driving her out. She fled south to Winchester, where in the second major battle of the year her half-brother Robert of Gloucester was captured. By November the two sides could do little but exchange prisoners: Stephen received his liberty in return for the release of Robert. The remaining years of the struggle saw no pitched battles of note, and the campaigns pursued by the two sides showed little coherence. With some justice, the chronicler Henry of Huntingdon observed that Stephen began many things vigorously but then pursued them slothfully. Much of the warfare was in fact defensive, based on the advantage which castles, erected in great number during the reign, conferred on the defender over the attacker. Stephen, for example, held an important castle at Malmesbury (Wilts), which found itself cut off from his main centres of support in the south-east by a rival fortification of Earl Robert's at Faringdon (Oxon). To counter the threat to his communications, Stephen needed to reduce Faringdon. Such was the importance of this castle that its fall and subsequent demolition in 1146 succeeded in tilting the balance of advantage strongly in his favour. In the next year Earl Robert died, and at the beginning of 1148 Matilda herself returned to Normandy.

Matilda's retreat from the fray did not mean that Stephen's problems were over. Stephen's great misfortune was to lose Normandy (q.v.). Many of the aristocratic families held lands on both sides of the Channel. By the 1140s, with Stephen controlling England and Geoffrey and Matilda Normandy, these families were faced with a divided allegiance: they could not recognize Stephen in England for fear of forfeiting their lands in Normandy, nor Matilda in Normandy for fear of forfeiting their lands in England. In the long term, their interests would best be served by promoting the succession of Matilda's son, Henry of Anjou. Henry crossed to England in 1153 and in August his army came face to face with Stephen's at Wallingford. The result was a prolonged stand-off. The barons, fearing the losses that would follow an outright victory by either side, urged compromise. A truce was arranged and in November a treaty was agreed at Winchester allowing Stephen to reign for his lifetime but recognizing Henry as his successor. The end of the reign came sooner than either side could have expected. Less than a year later, on 25 October 1154 King Stephen died. He was buried at Faversham Abbey in Kent, which he had founded.

Stephen, for all his faults, appears to have been a brave and chivalrous warrior. The Peterborough chronicler described him as a kindly man, of whom the nobles took advantage. On the other hand, William of Malmesbury, a hostile witness, said that he was changeable and untrustworthy. As king, he did not inspire confidence. His arrest of the bishops at Oxford was a major error. It seems that he was unsure in his judgements of either individuals or situations.

Just how extensive the devastation caused by the war was is hard to say. Even if the worst atrocity stories of castles filled with devils and evil men are discounted, it can hardly be supposed that rival armies spent season after season campaigning without leaving their mark on the landscape. In the Cambridgeshire Fens, where the notorious Geoffrey de Mandeville had his headquarters in the 1140s, life must have been close to intolerable. Indeed, the large number of monastic foundations, one of the most notable characteristics of the reign, may reflect the fears of barons and knights who wanted to lay up treasure in heaven to atone for their sins on earth.

R.H.C. Davis, *King Stephen*, 3rd ed., London, 1990; K.J. Stringer, *The Reign of Stephen*, London, 1993; D. Crouch, *The Reign of King Stephen, 1135-1154*, Harlow, 2000.

T

TAXATION

A system of public taxation was developed in medieval England in response to the king's need for money and his subjects' acknowledgement of their obligation to contribute to the preservation of the state.

At the beginning of the period, in the twelfth century, kings enjoyed three main forms of revenue. The first was the income of the royal demesne (q.v.) – in other words, the lands and revenues attached to the crown. The second was the incidents of feudalism (q.v.), principally scutage, relief and aid. And the third was the geld, the national land tax inherited from the pre-Conquest monarchy. The geld was potentially a highly lucrative tax, but its effectiveness was undermined by the many exemptions granted by Henry I (q.v.) as the price of making it a regular exaction. The geld was levied for the last time in 1162.

After the demise of the geld the Angevin kings became ever more dependent on the landed, feudal and judicial revenues at their command. It was these last two categories that proved the most lucrative to exploit. Richard I and John sought to meet the steep increases in their expenditure by using the right of feudal overlordship to exact unprecedented sums from their tenants in chief, who in 1215 reacted to the pressure by rebelling. Magna Carta (q.v.), the treaty settling the crisis, was concerned as much as anything to limit the king's right to name any figure he liked for wardships, reliefs, scutages and the other so-called 'incidents of feudalism' to which he was entitled.

The main drawback to feudal incidents as a form of taxation was that they hit the same group over and over again, in this case the tenants-in-chief. John (q.v.) appreciated this. For that reason, he began to look for a tax of broader incidence that would produce a yield big enough to meet the needs of government in war-time. He finally achieved his ambition in 1207 with the levy of one-thirteenth on moveable property which raised no less than £60,000. Although collected only once in John's reign because of the vehemence of the opposition, the levy on moveables proved to be the lifeline of the English monarchy for the rest of the Middle Ages, indeed into the sixteenth century. It served medieval governments much as income tax does their modern successors.

The levying of taxation in the Middle Ages generally involved the seeking of consent. In his capacity as feudal overlord the king could take reliefs and other 'incidents' from his tenants-in-chief as a consequence of their feudal relationship. But he could not impose a national tax like the moveables levy without showing due cause to his subjects. In medieval society there was general acceptance of the Roman law adage that 'what touches all must be approved by all'. The royal necessity for consent was thus inextricably linked to the summoning of representative assemblies. On several occasions in Henry III's reign the barons gave their consent to a tax in their capacity as the king's 'natural counsellors', but by the 1250s they were doubting whether they alone could speak for the entire community. In 1254 they told the king to summon four knights from each shire to consider a request for a levy on moveables. Eventually it became normal to summon the knights whenever a request for such a levy was considered. In the 1260s the burgesses from the towns (q.v.) were invited too. The knights and burgesses together were the constituent elements of the future House of Commons. The levying of taxation accordingly played a key role in the rise of parliament (q.v.) as a national assembly in which the needs of the king could be set against the grievances of his subjects.

The levying of taxation stimulated the growth of a local administrative infrastructure in the shires. By the mid-fourteenth century the levy on moveables was fixed by convention at the rate of one-fifteenth in the countryside and, in an effort to tap the greater urban wealth, one-tenth in the towns. Chief taxers were appointed in each county and, below them, sub-taxers, who were responsible for the assessment and collection of the tax in the villages. Up to and including 1332, individuals were assessed personally, but after 1334 the government opted to take a fixed global sum from each village or borough community. Apart from a reduction of £4,000 in the proceeds in 1433 to take account of the declining fortunes of towns like Lincoln, these sums held good for the next three centuries, despite significant shifts in the distribution of wealth. In theory people with moveable wealth worth less than 10s were exempt; but given the tendency to rapacity of medieval tax-collectors it is uncertain how far government guidelines were adhered to in practice.

Alongside the system of personal or direct taxation, there grew up a system of taxation of trade. The most important element in this was the taxation of wool exports. The history of these levies begins in 1202 when King John established customs duties amounting to one-fifteenth of goods imported or exported. These were probably abolished in 1206. However, they were revived by Edward I (q.v.) in 1275 in the form of the so-called Ancient Custom at the rate of half a mark (3s 4d) on each sack of wool (364lb) and 300 wool-fells and a mark on each last of hides. Edward went a stage further in 1294 when on top of this he imposed the 'maltolt' of £3 6s 8d on each sack of good wool and £2 on other wool, later standardized at £2 for both. The tax was so unpopular that it was abolished in 1297, but Edward II (q.v.) brought it back on alien merchants alone in 1303. In the course of the next forty years the maltolt became the subject of a bitter struggle between king and parliament, the eventual outcome of which was that the king retained it at the standard rate of 43s 4d but parliament won the right of granting it. As events were to show, 43s 4d was more than the traffic would bear, and the volume of wool exports fell from over 40,000 sacks in 1304–5 to less than 10,000 in the early sixteenth century. What was probably unknown to the government, however, was that the maltolt acted as a protective tariff behind which the domestic cloth industry could recover. Because it was only wool exports that were taxed, English cloth producers had access to their raw material cheaper than their Flemish or Italian competitors. And when, at the end of the manufacturing process, they exported their products, they had an edge over their foreign rivals because English broadcloths carried only a light duty of 14d each, equivalent to an *ad valorem* rate of about 3–5%.

With the wool export trade in decline and the moveables levy yielding less than it had, the government was well aware that the tax system needed reshaping. The poll taxes levied between 1377 and 1381 were one celebrated response to this need. In the light of these taxes' contribution to the outbreak of the Peasants Revolt (q.v.) the government was reluctant to tinker with the system again for some time. In the fifteenth century the exchequer experimented with a series of income taxes in 1404, 1411, 1431, 1435, 1450, 1472 and 1489, but these hit principally the landowners and evaded those like the clothiers and traders whose means were almost as great.

The government's failure to adjust the fiscal system after the mid-fourteenth century raises the question of whether Westminster had any clear idea of how wealth was distributed across society, either socially or geographically, or of how far wealth distribution had changed in the wake of the Black Death. One episode suggests that their understanding of these matters was fairly limited. In February 1371 parliament had granted a parishes tax. This novel subsidy of £50,000 was to be levied on each parish at an average rate of 22s 3d. But it was soon apparent that nothing like £50,000 was coming in, and in June a great council had to be summoned, to persuade the Commons to raise the rate to 116s per village. It had evidently been assumed that there were 40,000 parishes in England, whereas the returns showed that there were only 8,600.

In conclusion, a word needs to be said about taxation of the clergy. The clergy were in the unfortunate position of being subject to levies from both the king and the Pope. The increasing frequency of clerical taxation by one or other of these masters led to the emergence by the reign of Edward III of the twin convocations of York and Canterbury. Although usually summoned by the archbishops to meet simultaneously with parliament, the convocations were completely autonomous bodies within which the clergy of the two English provinces could decide how to respond to an appeal to their generosity. The valuation of benefices made in 1291, known as the Taxation of Pope Nicholas IV, remained the basis for clerical grants to the crown for the rest of the Middle Ages.

G.L. Harriss, *King, Parliament and Public Finance in Medieval England to 1369*, Oxford, 1975; J.R. Maddicott, *The English Peasantry and the Demands of the Crown, 1294–1341* (*Past and Present, Supplement I*, 1975).

TITHES

Since before the Norman Conquest the rector of a parish had been entitled to support himself by receiving the tenth part of the agricultural produce of his parishioners: hence the word tithe. In a wealthy parish the tithe could prove to be a valuable form of endowment. That was why in the twelfth and thirteenth centuries founders of monasteries had often chosen to provide income for their fledgling communities in the form of benefices rather than in the form of land. The new monastery would itself become the corporate rector, and would receive the tithes. Cure of souls would be entrusted to a vicar who would take what later came to be known as the lesser tithes. These might include milk, calves, eggs and young animals. The greater tithes taken by the monastery as corporate rector would include corn, hay and wood.

TOMBS

Tomb effigies and brasses (q.v.) represent a substantial part of England's medieval heritage. Not only are these objects often fine works of art; they also provide valuable evidence for contemporary armour (q.v.) and costume and for the aspirations of those they commemorated.

The idea of commemorating individuals by monuments was one which the medieval world took from the ancient. In the medieval period, however, memorials performed a very different function from that in antiquity. Antique memorials were for the most part concerned with terrestrial recognition – with the honouring of the deceased on earth. Medieval memorials, however, were concerned with negotiating the transition to the next world. The notion of celebrating the life and achievements of the deceased was never entirely lost; indeed, it staged a comeback in the late Middle Ages, when heraldry and other worldly insignia became more prominent. But the primary function of medieval monuments was always to elicit intercession. Monuments were *aides memoires* to prayer. They were placed to prompt the passer-by to pray for the deceased: to intercede with the Almighty for the safe passage of his soul. It is this function which explains the character and design of the memorial. The figure of the deceased was shown at prayer; the inscription opened with an appeal for prayer: '*Orate pro anima…*'

The earliest medieval memorials were very simple. Usually these took the form of coffin lids which were allowed to remain exposed on the church floor. Sometimes, however, they were upright grave markers – plain stone crosses, with or without an inscription. A good example of a grave marker is the stone to Ovin, Queen Etheldreda's steward, in Ely Cathedral, which dates from the eighth century. In the twelfth century monuments became richer and more elaborate. Increasingly, coffin lids were carved with symbols indicating the calling or profession of the deceased. An early example of this is the tomb of Bishop Luffa (d.1123) in Chichester Cathedral, which displays a mitre and crozier. Many slabs in the north of England are carved with symbols indicating the sex of the deceased, for example, a sword for a man and shears for a lady. In the thirteenth century Purbeck marble cross slabs became very popular. Examples of these are found in many

churches in southern England and South Wales. Usually they commemorated members of the clergy, but since few of them bear inscriptions identification is often uncertain: members of the laity may be commemorated too.

In the mid-twelfth century, effigial tomb sculpture entered the repertory. The earliest tomb effigies were carved in low relief – that is to say, they were formed by cutting away the slab around the figure. A good example of a low relief effigy is that of Bishop Roger (d.1139) in Salisbury Cathedral. Later, the relief became bolder and more three-dimensional. How quickly effigial art was developing at this time can be appreciated by comparing the two effigies at Salisbury of Bishop Roger and his successor, Bishop Jocelin de Bohun (d.1184). Bishop Jocelin's figure, though less than fifty years later, is a great advance on Roger's. The pioneers of effigial sculpture appear to have been the bishops and senior clergy. Fine series of episcopal effigies are found in the cathedrals at Salisbury and Worcester. By the thirteenth century, however, the well-to-do laity were seeking commemoration in the same fashion. In the Templar church in London there is a fine series of knightly effigies, including several to the Marshal earls of Pembroke.

A variety of materials were used for the making of tomb effigies. In southern England in the thirteenth and early fourteenth centuries the most popular material was Purbeck marble. Marble was not only a very durable material; it also provided an attractive finish when polished. But over time other materials were used too. From the middle of the fourteenth century alabaster was a very popular medium. Alabaster (or gypsum) was quarried in Derbyshire and was used for tombs, reredoses, devotional panels and other objects. An excellent example of an alabaster tomb is that of Ralph Greene and his wife at Lowick (Northants), 1420, for which Thomas Prentys and Robert Sutton of Chellaston (Derbs) were responsible. The contractors were paid £40 for their work. For the tombs of the royal family in Westminster Abbey, cast metal was normally employed. The effigies of Edward III and of Richard II and his queen are both of copper gilt, a mark of their prestige and importance. The effigy of Richard Beauchamp (d.1439) at St Mary's, Warwick, is of the same material. Beauchamp's tomb was another prestigious commission.

Tomb sculpture was a business carried on in a number of centres. There were well-established workshops at Bristol, London, Chellaston, York and elsewhere. Much the busiest of these were the workshops of London. Many of those engaged in the business were engaged in other alabaster- or stone-working activities too. Henry Yevele (q.v.), for example, the great fourteenth-century mason, ran a major conglomerate enterprise which involved him in architectural consultancy and the supply of building materials as well as the making of tombs. Yevele's primary employment was almost certainly as a master mason. Yet members of his workshop were responsible for the tomb chests of Richard II and Cardinal Langham in Westminster Abbey and of the Black Prince at Canterbury. Some of the grandest commissions of the Middle Ages are known to have been the work of several hands. This was the case with Beauchamp's effigy and tomb at Warwick. A painter called Clare was paid for 'painting the effigy' – probably for making a sketch of it. Next, a wooden model of the effigy was made by John Massingham. The effigy was then cast in bronze by William Austen, with Roger Webbe, a barber-surgeon, giving advice on anatomical details and Bartholomew Lambespring undertaking the gilding. The marble tomb chest was supplied by John Bourde of Corfe, and the latten epitaph by John Essex and Thomas Stevyns, both of them of London.

Most medieval monuments involved far fewer craftsmen than Beauchamp's. The majority of such monuments were produced in small-scale, even domestic, workshops. Yet in the busiest of these enterprises tomb production approximated as closely to mass-production as it was possible to get in the Middle Ages. Huge numbers of almost identikit marble coffin slabs or knightly effigies were produced between the thirteenth and the fifteenth centuries. A fourteenth-century manuscript illumination shows a patron inspecting tomb slabs in a workshop. This must have been how the business operated. In most workshops there were 'off-the-peg' effigies lying around for a client to order or carry away.

Given these circumstances, there was relatively little individuality in design. Portraiture was almost unknown in the Middle Ages. The first glimmerings of representational art are found on the late fourteenth-century effigies of Edward III (plate 59) and Richard II in Westminster Abbey. Individuality was found chiefly in inclusion of marks of status. Patrons attached high importance to the proper representation of status. This is apparent from the instructions which they gave in wills: patrons wanted their monuments in some sense to attest worldly honour. Attire, in consequence, normally corresponded to the 'three estates' conception of society. Knights and esquires were shown in armour, merchants in civilian attire and priests in copes or chasubles. Marks of affiliation could be included where appropriate: the SS collar for Lancastrian retainers, the sun in splendour for the Yorkists and so on. But most visible and striking was heraldic display. On many tomb chests there were magnificent galleries of arms. One of the grandest is on Thomas Chaucer's tomb at Ewelme (Oxon). Sometimes the place of shields was taken by weepers or angels. Individuality could sometimes find expression in the depiction of marks of piety.

Despite the high production levels of some of the workshops, the quality of craftsmanship in tomb-making was often high. Some magnificent monuments have come down to us from this period. One of the finest is that at

Ewelme (Oxon) of Alice de la Pole, duchess of Suffolk. This shows the commemorated in two poses – in grand estate on the top of the tomb chest and as a skeleton beneath: a reminder that mortality comes to even the most exalted in society. Also very fine are the series of monuments in Tewkesbury Abbey (Glos), chiefly to the Despensers and their kin. Unusually Edward, Lord Despenser (d.1375), is shown kneeling on the top of his chantry, under a tabernacle and facing the altar.

B. Kemp, *English Church Monuments*, London, 1980.

TOURNAMENTS

The nature of the tournament changed greatly in the course of the Middle Ages. From being a disorderly mêlée in the thirteenth century, the tournament evolved into the formalized joust of the later Middle Ages.

Tourneying appears to have had its origins in northern France in the early twelfth century. To the chronicler Ralph of Diss such combats were known as the *conflictus Gallicus* (the 'French fighting'). The roots of tourneying were to be found in the rise of cavalry warfare and in the young knights' need to secure proper training. The fighting at the earliest events was often disorderly, and in 1130 Pope Innocent II issued an edict banning them for their danger to life and limb. The edict was ignored, however, and the young tiros continued to meet. Often they fought in big teams, forty or fifty of them on each side, challenging each other from dawn till dusk. These contests gave the young enthusiasts ample opportunity to win wealth and renown. The *Histoire de Guillaume de Marechal* tells how William Marshal, a landless knight errant, was so successful on the tourneying circuit that he rose to be lord of Longueville and earl of Pembroke. On one occasion Marshal was offered as much as £500 a year each by the count of Flanders and the duke of Burgundy for his services. Tourneying found favour with kings and princes because it served to keep their knights in training for war. In 1194 Richard I (q.v.) legalized the tournament in England. He did this apparently because he believed that French knights were superior in arms to his own and that his own were in need of more practice. However, it seems likely that tournaments had been held in England for some time. What Richard did was simply try to make the practice more widespread.

Richard's enthusiasm for tournaments was not shared by his two successors on the throne, John and Henry III (q.v.). These kings actively discouraged the events, and not just because they resulted in so many violent deaths. Their concern was that tournaments were being used as a cover for political opposition. At the Dunstable tournament of 1244 the barons agreed on their plans for expelling the papal legate from England, and in 1312 feigned tournaments were used to conceal the rallying of troops to hunt down Edward II's unpopular favourite, Piers Gaveston, who had illicitly returned to England. In reigns when kingship was weak tournaments posed a threat to royal authority.

The attitude of the crown to tourneying began to change in the time of Edward I (1272-1307). In Edward's last, rather troubled, years tournaments were still occasionally banned on the grounds that they distracted knights from the real business of fighting the Scots. But Edward, unlike his father, actually enjoyed tournaments, and sometimes entered the lists himself. Edward's policy was to control and regulate tournaments rather than ban them altogether. In the past, what had contributed to disorder was the behaviour of the esquires who attended on the knights. Thus at the Rochester tournament of 1251 the esquires had hammered the fleeing knights with sticks and clubs. Accordingly in 1292 Edward decided to embody in statute form a code of rules that had first been drawn up in 1267. Knights were limited to just three esquires each, and participants were to use only the blunted broad sword for tourneying, not a pointed sword or knife. A committee was set up to enforce these regulations.

In the fourteenth century the nature of the tournament underwent further change. The influence of chivalric literature, in particular of Arthurian romances (q.v.), led to a formalization of the combat. What had once been a conflict between massed 'armies' now became a single combat between two champions. Separated by a barrier or tilt, the knights would charge towards each other with a blunted lance watched by the heralds (q.v.) and by a large crowd of onlookers, ladies included. The tournament had become respectable; it was reinvented as a form of entertainment. Nothing demonstrated the change more clearly than the so-called 'Round Tables', in which the actual jousting was just one part, probably only an incidental part, of a much wider round of social engagements spread over several days. Edward III (q.v.), the chivalric king *par excellence*, appreciated the lustre which this kind of event could confer on his kingship. In 1343 he spent as much as £317 a day on the festivities accompanying a tournament at Dunstable. Tourneying and chivalric culture generally became mainstays of his kingship. The king often entered the lists himself; sometimes, as at Dunstable in 1342 and London in 1359 he appeared incognito. By regularly meeting his nobility in the lists, he forged closer ties with them. A process of bonding occurred, the relationship between him and them becoming almost physical.

In the fifteenth century the older form of tournament fought *à outrance* (using pointed weapons) became less common. The characteristic later medieval encounter was the joust *à plaisance* (with blunted weapons) for polite entertainment. Kings and princes jousted in the lists less often than they once had.

Richard II, for example, used the tournament lists chiefly as a setting for hierarchical display. Rather than engaging in the joust himself, he kept his distance, looking on from a high stand. A stronger emphasis in the late Middle Ages was placed on ceremony. The grander tournaments were often preceded by processions. At the Smithfield tournament of October 1390 each of the participating knights was led 'with cheynes of gold' by a lady of the sorority of the Garter. Women assumed a much more prominent role in tournaments. Sometimes women were given the task of judging and awarding the prizes.

In the late Middle Ages tournaments were sometimes accorded a role in international diplomacy. At the big Smithfield event of 1390, for example, one of the guests was a Low Countries prince, William, count of Ostrevant, whom Richard and his ministers were trying to draw into an alliance. Froissart describes the count's cordial reception, the brilliance of the jousts and the balls and banquets which followed them, and finally the count's investiture with the Garter at Windsor. The showy aspect of diplomacy which found full expression at the Field of Cloth of Gold in 1520 had its origins in developments a century or two earlier.

J.R.V. Barker, *The Tournament in England, 1100–1400*, Woodbridge, 1986.

TOWNS

Although the bulk of England's population lived in the countryside, the towns were vital to the rural economy as centres of exchange and markets for the disposal of produce. By modern standards medieval towns were small. London, with a population before the Black Death (q.v.) of around 80,000, was the only one that could compare with the great cities of the continent like Ghent and Florence. The larger provincial centres, such as York, Norwich or Bristol, would have mustered between 5,000 and 10,000 each, and the smaller towns, which were plentiful in central and southern England only 1,000 each or fewer.

The small size of medieval towns raises a definitional problem which has much troubled modern historians: just what was the difference between a town and a village? Size and population can hardly be considered a sure guide. For that reason, legal criteria have normally been invoked, and the essential characteristic distinguishing an urban settlement has been identified as burgage tenure – in other words, the right to hold land freely for a money rent. There is much to be said for this view, but what really mattered to townsmen was not so much technicalities of tenure as the desire to have themselves recognized as self-governing communities independent of the surrounding shire. It is the movement towards separateness which formed a major theme in the urban history of the Middle Ages and which gave the towns their own institutions of government.

When English society was feudalized after the Norman Conquest, the king made sure that he held most of the towns himself 'in chief' (q.v. FEUDALISM). This meant that he was entitled to the profits collected for him in each town by the official known as the reeve. Before long, however, the townsfolk wanted to have a greater say in the running of their own affairs, and at London and Lincoln in 1130 they took the first steps in this direction by winning from Henry I (q.v.) the right of electing the reeve and of themselves collecting and paying over to the king the fixed sum known as the 'farm'. Although this gave them a measure of self-government, the leading citizens still felt that they needed an institution which could represent their interests. They eventually found this in the body generally known as the 'guild merchant'. Unlike the more familiar craft guilds of the later Middle Ages, the guild merchant embraced most if not all of a town's burgesses, whatever their

trade. It was the community of burgesses under another name: the guise they assumed to press the demand for self-government. How successful the burgesses were in pressing their demands can be measured in the flood of municipal charters issued by Richard I and John (q.v.). Provided the townsmen would pay, the kings were prepared to let them have what they wanted. Constitutionally the result was often anomalous. Towns which had already spawned a 'shadow' government in the shape of the guild merchant now acquired a second and official one in the shape of an elected council with executive officers. These councillors were known interchangeably as jurats, portmen (*port* = trading centre) or aldermen – borrowing a term used by the guilds (q.v.) – and the executive officers as bailiffs or mayors – borrowing a French word which has survived to this day. Borough community and guild merchant in fact overlapped, and often shared the same officers. They were different houses lived in by the same occupants.

Once the townsfolk had obtained self-government, the guild merchant had served its purpose and faded away. The burgesses had obtained all they wanted from the king. Now they could concentrate on enjoying the higher standard of living which a rising volume of trade brought their way. At the same time, many peasants flocked into the towns in search of better conditions than those they knew in the countryside. As the towns became more populous, and potentially more difficult to control, so the leading citizens reacted by drawing the reins of power ever more tightly into their hands. In other words, despite the vague provision in the early charters for officials to be elected, urban government fell into the grip of a charmed elite. By the thirteenth century full citizenship was no longer extended automatically to all those who held by burgage tenure. In London in 1274 the decision was taken to restrict it to those who could obtain it by any of three ways – patrimony, for those born in the city; apprenticeship, which normally lasted three years; and redemption for those with the money to pay.

Not surprisingly, these restrictive tendencies produced a reaction, and in many towns, notably London, the later fourteenth century saw fierce struggles between the oligarchies on the one hand and popular movements led by the craft guilds on the other. It was to give the townsmen a greater opportunity to express their views that 'common councils' were grafted onto urban constitutions in the fifteenth century. The way in which this came about can be illustrated from the history of Norwich (q.v.). In 1417 the old council, which consisted of twenty-four members, was reconstituted as a committee of aldermen and a new council of sixty, chosen by the four wards of the city, was set up to represent the commons, the lesser folk. 'Outer' or common councils of this kind were established in many towns in the late Middle Ages in an attempt to satisfy the aspirations of those who had hitherto been denied any say in the affairs of the town. But before long the familiar oligarchical tendencies set in once more. Co-option replaced election, admissions to the freedom were controlled and manipulated, and governing bodies became self-perpetuating elites. In other words, the late Middle Ages saw the emergence of the notorious 'close corporations' which ran so many of the English towns till their abolition in 1835.

Whether there was any connection between the drift to oligarchy and the economic difficulties facing the towns in the fifteenth century is hard to say. It is possible that in some cases elitist government drove business out. But in many others business and employment had already begun to move elsewhere. Generally, urban policies appear to have been reactive to decline.

At the same time a parallel process was going on which may well seem more significant to us today than it did to contemporaries. This was the movement towards muncipal incorporation. All that securing incorporation did was give the towns the standing at law of corporate personalities. The first such charter of incorporation was granted to Coventry in 1345, and by the end of the Middle Ages most other towns had acquired them too. What lay behind this enthusiasm for corporate status was the growing acquisition of property by the towns. Of course, urban communities had long owned municipal or semi-municipal buildings like guildhalls. But now they were also staking a claim to land that fell vacant within the walls and after 1348, when many properties were deprived of their owners by the plague, that could add up to quite an acreage. So the towns became property owners; as they did so, they needed protection at law, which they obtained by seeking incorporation.

In truth, many late medieval councils needed all the rental income they could secure because the decline in population after the Black Death (q.v.) left them smaller and less prosperous than before. The crowded conditions in the towns enabled the plague to spread quickly, causing a massive drop in numbers. How soon population recovered varied from place to place. At Norwich there was apparently a fairly rapid recovery but elsewhere later plague visitations kept numbers down. As if this were not enough, many of the traditional centres of population, like Winchester and Lincoln, were faced in the late medieval period by a prolonged depression in their staple industry – textiles. To explain this we have to go back a long way, to the twelfth century. The English textile industry (q.v.) had long been run by great merchant employers who treated the weavers and fullers as little better than employees. These two groups sought to improve their position by forming themselves into guilds, through which they could control entry into the trade and regulate hours and conditions. Faced by this upward pressure on wages at the very time when stiff competition was coming from Flemish products, the merchants retaliated by moving the industry into the countryside where there was already a long tradition of making cloth. Some of the towns, like Lincoln and Beverley, staged a partial recovery in the fourteenth century but others were less successful and by 1500 the geographical pattern of textile manufacture looked very different from what it had three centuries before. The industry had shifted from the old-established towns to areas like East Anglia and the western Cotswolds, where swiftly moving streams could turn the wheels of the fulling-mills. The prosperity which textiles brought to the English countryside in the fifteenth and sixteenth centuries is manifested today by the noble parish churches of Lavenham and Long Melford in Suffolk and Cirencester in Gloucestershire.

Today it is the parish churches that do most to evoke the atmosphere of a medieval town. The division and subdivision of urban parishes in the eleventh and twelfth centuries had left many English towns with a church on almost every street corner. Norwich and Winchester each had as many as fifty-six churches at the height of the Middle Ages. Norwich, as James Campbell so aptly puts it, 'was always an overchurched city', and even after demolitions and amalgamations there are still thirty-one today. But then in medieval London there were over a hundred.

It needs to be remembered that in the Middle Ages parish churches were not places that were visited only on Sundays. They were social centres, meeting places, objects of civic esteem. After the citizens of Ipswich had obtained their charter from King John in 1200, it was in the churchyard of St Mary Tower that they met to elect the bailiffs and coroners (q.v.), and again a few months later to hear what these officials had decided. Later on, in the fifteenth century, parish churches became the focus of local loyalties in another way when the religious fraternities under which the guilds (q.v.) so often masqueraded founded chantries and altars in them. Many of these fraternities were modest affairs which could only afford to pay for a candle to burn daily during the celebration of mass. Others, however, were rich enough to pay for the building of a side chapel dedicated to the patron saint of the guild. Sometimes the connection between a church and a particular guild became so close that the church became identified with that guild, as St Helen's in York was with the glass-painters.

The more substantial guilds and companies had the money not only to endow altars but also to erect halls, like the Merchant Venturers' Hall at York. These of course would be the very grandest civic buildings, and it must not be supposed that all urban architecture was on that scale. On the other hand, it would be equally wrong to jump to the opposite conclusion, that every medieval town was squalid and overcrowded. Some perhaps were. Old Sarum (Wilts) affords a good example. Here, castle and cathedral were awkward neighbours on a windswept hilltop. For this reason Bishop Poore abandoned the place in 1221 in favour of a more spacious site a few miles to the south in the Avon valley. His remarkable idea of transplanting a town from one site to another was imitated three-quarters of a century later by Edward I, who moved the port of Winchelsea from its exposed coastal position to its present location facing Rye. Edward I, of all our kings, was the keenest to promote urban development, not just in England but also in Wales (q.v.) and in the English possessions in France. He was following the example of private lords who had sought to increase their revenues from trade by founding market towns. In all these new settlements the streets were laid out on a straightforward grid plan that says much for medieval town planning. Often, as well, the plots – burgage tenements as they were called – were quite wide, allowing double-fronted houses to be built. In the course of time these tenements became sub-divided, so that tall, jettied houses became the rule, forming such familiar street scenes as the Shambles at York (q.v.). Most town houses were apparently of timber-framed construction, but the evidence suggests that stone, which obviously carried advantages from the point of view of fire prevention, became a more common material in the thirteenth century for those who could afford it.

Something needs to be said about the poor and their experience of life. It is reasonable to suppose that by the early fourteenth century, when population (q.v.) reached its height, the poor were living in very crowded surroundings. But after the Black Death there was room for everyone to breathe. There is evidence that in the late Middle Ages hygiene and sanitation gradually got better. We know that from the late thirteenth century tolls were being levied to pay for the paving of streets. One such street, now metal-surfaced but otherwise little changed, is Brasenose Lane in Oxford. Its surface slopes from each side down to the middle, where a gulley carries away the water. It made good sense wherever possible, if these gulleys were not to be open sewers, to run streets vertically up a hillside. It is this thinking which explains why some medieval towns have such very steep main streets. The aptly named Steep Hill at Lincoln is a good example.

Around the bigger and more important towns there would have been lengthy circuits of walls, like those which survive at York and Chester. Just as pavage was levied to pay for improving the streets, so murage was levied to pay for building these fortifications. The walls at Norwich were substantially complete by the 1340s, after half a century's labour, but at King's Lynn the circuit proved too much for the citizens and was left unfinished. Thanks to the blessing of internal peace, walls were rarely needed for the primary purpose of defence except in those parts of England along the south coast exposed to the danger of French attacks: Rye, Winchelsea and Southampton come to mind here. Elsewhere, they were valued as a kind of customs barrier which allowed tolls to be collected with the minimum of evasion. Often, the building of walls was prompted by civic pride. Walls symbolized that separation of town from country for which the merchant guilds had struggled back in the twelfth century.

C. Platt, *The English Medieval Town*, London, 1976; *The Medieval Town: a Reader in English Urban History, 1200–1540*, ed. R. Holt and G. Rosser, London, 1990; R. Britnell, *The Commercialisation of English Society, 1000–1500*, Cambridge, 1993.

TRADE
The map at plate 151 shows England's position in the European trading network.
See also AGRICULTURE; INDUSTRY; TOWNS

TROYES, TREATY OF
See HUNDRED YEARS WAR

UNIVERSITIES

The idea of a community of masters licensed to teach at the highest level – a university – is one which has its origins in the Middle Ages.

In the eleventh century there was a revival of learning in Europe which manifested itself in the establishment of schools attached to monasteries or cathedrals. Most of these schools derived their importance from the presence in their midst of a great teacher, like Lanfranc (q.v.) at Bec. In other words, it was the teacher who made the school. This informality was tolerable for as long as the students wanted only a simple grounding in the arts. But if they wanted to pursue a lengthier course in what were to become the higher faculties of theology and law, then it was necessary for them to belong to a more formal and permanent institution that could satisfy the growing professionalization of knowledge of the twelfth century. So the monasteries and cathedral schools were overshadowed as centres of learning by the new schools of Bologna for law and Paris for theology, which were the prototypes of the later universities.

In England, just as on the continent, the intellectual renaissance of the twelfth century witnessed the opening of schools – for example those at Exeter, Oxford and Northampton. With the benefit of hindsight we know that Oxford (q.v.) was to surpass the others in importance, but its early history was not without its crises and difficulties. The inevitable rivalries between town and gown led to periodic confrontations, and one of these in the reign of King John ended in the departure of a group of scholars to Cambridge (q.v.). The scholars stayed in the Fenland town, and the sister university was born. The rise of Oxford and Cambridge did not immediately lead to the elimination of the other schools, but it was certainly the aim of Oxford, and perhaps Cambridge too, to prevent any rivals from awarding degrees and conferring the licence to teach. In 1264 Oxford used the influence of its alumni on Simon de Montfort's administration to suppress the incipient splinter university at Northampton and seventy years later in August 1334 it used similar tactics to thwart a group of secessionist masters at Stamford (Lincs). It was by means of such string-pulling that the 'ancient' universities acquired the joint monopoly of higher education in England which they kept until modern times.

Education in the Middle Ages was necessarily a clerical monopoly, its purpose being to train men for a career in the Church. So it needs to be remembered that when undergraduates came up to university at fourteen or fifteen, they were young clerks in the making. The Liberal Arts course which formed the basis of what today would be called the undergraduate curriculum was divided according to ancient usage into the 'trivium' (grammar, rhetoric and logic) lasting three years and the 'quadrivium' (arithmetic, geometry, astronomy and music) lasting another four. By his seventh year a candidate was eligible to supplicate for the degree of Master of Arts for which, as for all degrees, he was examined orally. Today at Oxford and Cambridge, although the exercises and residence requirements it once entailed have long gone, the MA is still taken seven years after matriculation. The more ambitious scholar was then free to begin the exercises leading after another five years to the degree of Bachelor of Theology and after two more to the doctorate. Although this period of study was long, it was shorter than at contemporary Paris. In the thirteenth century, in response to the growing demand for well-trained lawyers, Oxford and Cambridge developed two more graduate faculties, namely civil law, involving four year's study for those who had taken their MA, and canon law, calling for three.

Teaching at medieval Oxford and Cambridge was by a combination of lecturing and disputation. In the schools or lecture rooms the young scholars received a grilling in the works of prescribed authors like Aristotle and Boethius. Once they had familiarized themselves with the texts, and very likely learned them by heart, they were expected to sharpen their wits in that characteristically medieval exercise known as the disputation where a master or senior pupil would argue a thesis and maintain it against his pupils. Although the exercises were apt to be pettyfogging, they encouraged precision of thought and clarity of expression.

Then, as now, lectures provided by the University were supplemented by instruction given in the colleges and halls. In Oxford and Cambridge today it is the colleges which dominate the scene. However, this was not the case in the Middle Ages. The majority of undergraduates lived not in the colleges but in lodging houses known in Oxford as halls and in Cambridge as hostels. These were ordinary properties leased on a year-to-year basis by a principal who took in student lodgers and gave them tuition. St Edmund Hall, Oxford, is the one such establishment to have survived to the present day (though in 1957 it became a college). Having most likely passed their undergraduate years in one of these halls, the clerks who wanted to read for a doctorate then faced the daunting prospect of finding the money to finance the long years of residence that lay ahead. It was to provide them with the means to do this that the earliest colleges were founded in the thirteenth century. These were corporate institutions endowed with sufficient property to support a community of fellows and graduates. The first colleges in Oxford were Merton, Balliol and University, and in Cambridge, Peterhouse, Michaelhouse and King's Hall, the last two later absorbed into Trinity. The first college to admit undergraduates was Exeter, but then only in the third year of their BA course and without any provision for teaching. It was William of Wykeham's (q.v.) New College, founded in 1379, which broke new ground in this area. According to Wykeham's statutes, the younger members of the College, all of them drawn from the sister foundation at Winchester, were to receive tuition from the older Fellows for a period of three years. It is in this novel arrangement that the origins of the Oxbridge tutorial system are traditionally sought: although it is fair to add that the originality of the founder's intentions are still subject to argument (plate 41).

Palatial though the buildings of the colleges often were, they housed far fewer students than the halls. In early fifteenth-century Oxford the seventy or so halls were matched by a dozen and a half colleges at most. For the majority of the undergraduates living accommodation in the halls was likely to be neither spacious nor luxurious. A largish hall would have been occupied by between fifteen and twenty students, three or four of them to each room. Apart from the principal only a well-to-do student, or perhaps a master, would have had a chamber to himself. On the basis of these figures, which admittedly involve a fair amount of conjecture, we can guess that there were something like 1,500 scholars at Oxford in the fifteenth century and rather fewer at contemporary Cambridge.

To say that medieval undergraduates enjoyed few of the comforts of life is simply another way of saying that the cost of living was very low. At a time when a single chamber in a college or hall would have fetched 8s or 10s a year in rent, it made good sense for a group of friends to spread the cost by sharing a room or even a bed. There are a few figures in the accounts which show just how cheap-ly this could work out. For John Wood, a student at an Oxford hall in 1424, board and lodging came to 4s 8½d, or less than 4½d a week. John Russell, another student in the same hall, paid as little as 3s 4d for seven weeks. These scholars would have needed some spare cash to spend in the alehouse or in one or two of the bookshops that then lined Catte Street. But, by and large, life for the undergraduate in medieval Oxford would have been inexpensive. It was the length and cost of study in the higher faculties that moved benefactors like Walter de Merton to found the colleges.

See also SCHOOLS

A.B. Cobban, *The Medieval English Universities. Oxford and Cambridge to c.1500*, Cambridge, 1988.

VILLEINAGE

The origins of villeinage may be traced to the Anglo-Saxon period, when peasants were drawn into greater dependence on their lord by accepting from him the gift of a home and some land. Typically, they would be required to till his demesne (q.v.) for several days a week. In the twelfth century, when the king's justices were often asked by lords to determine the legal condition of their tenants, liability to perform labour services was one of the tests they applied. A tenant who did 'week-work' on the demesne was a villein, and one who did not was free. In its heyday in the thirteenth century villeinage was a hereditary condition of personal character. It was not the same as slavery, but it did place severe limitations on freedom. A villein could not leave his village; he had to perform labour services; and he was liable for such payments as merchet (q.v.) and heriot (q.v.). Someone who was born into villein condition would always be a villein, and his children after him. However, if he married someone of free blood, or acquired land previously held by a free man, his status would inevitably be more difficult to determine. Practical considerations of this sort probably led to a weakening of villeinage in real life. But what did most to bring about its decline was the decline in population (q.v.) after 1348, which strengthened the bargaining position of the labouring classes *vis-à-vis* the lords. In the Great Revolt of 1381 the peasants made the abolition of villeinage one of their forefront demands. Although charters of manumission were issued to them, these were quickly repealed, and in the long run it was the laws of supply and demand which did most to help their cause.

R.H. Hilton, *The Decline of Serfdom in Medieval England*, London, 1969.

WALES

Medieval Wales, like Metternich's Italy, was a geographical expression. The people of Wales, united by language, were divided by geography. If the mountain ranges served to protect the Welsh from the English, they also served to prevent the Welsh themselves from coming together.

At the end of the eleventh century Wales was divided into three main principalities – Deheubarth in the south and west, Powys in the centre and Gwynedd (or Snowdonia) in the north – and as often as not their rulers would be engaged in either fighting one another or fighting the English. In the eighth century Offa had striven to keep out the Welsh in the same way that Hadrian had the Scots by building a great rampart from one side of the country to the other. Impressive though this was, the Dyke did not prove a lasting solution to the problem of the border and for as long as the Welsh retained their independence that wide and ill-defined no-man's land west of the Severn known as the March of Wales retained something of the character of the Wild West.

William the Conqueror (q.v.) proposed to defend his newly won kingdom against the Welsh by appointing three powerful earls along the border, Hugh d'Avranches at Chester, Roger de Montgomery at Shrewsbury and William FitzOsbern at Hereford: rough and determined men whose early experiences on the marches of Normandy (q.v.) and Anjou had instructed them in the arts of border warfare. Defence, as so often, however, turned into offence. Before the 1080s were out, Earl Hugh was across the border, fighting at first successfully to bring north Wales under Norman rule. However, a major rebellion in 1094 put paid to his hopes, and the initiative was taken up instead in the south. Robert Fitzhamon, lord of Tewkesbury, advanced into Glamorgan, establishing a castle at Cardiff. After his death in 1107 his successor, Robert, earl of Gloucester, a bastard son of Henry I (q.v.) continued the offensive, and extended Anglo-Norman lordship into what is now Pembrokeshire. The spur to the endeavours of these early *conquistadores* was the same combination of motives that had inspired their fathers to follow Duke William in 1066: greed, energy and ambition. It should not be forgotten that the Norman conquest and colonization of South Wales was a private enterprise affair, in contrast to Edward I's conquest of Snowdonia in the 1280s, which was state-directed. And it was accomplished remarkably quickly. Geography had much to do with this. The Glamorgan coastal plain fell to the Normans because it was the kind of flat landscape in which they could practise the tactics of mounted warfare they excelled at.

Gwynedd, on the other hand, remained independent for much longer because its hilly and impenetrable terrain kept out the knights.

Welsh society was very different in character from that of contemporary England. In the first place, it was predominantly a society of freemen. Unfree tenants were to be found, but only in the lowland plains, where the manorial system had been imposed, did they form a majority. The mountains were peopled almost entirely by free tenants. Another peculiarity of Welsh society lay in the nature of the seigneurial dues that were imposed. Welsh freemen discharged their obligations by offering a communal render of food and livestock which was less a rent for land than an acknowledgement of lordship – a sort of tribute. The third distinctive characteristic of Welsh society was its rejection of primogeniture in favour of partible inheritance, i.e. division between coheirs. Inevitably in a country where land was in short supply the result was fragmentation of the open fields. Although the Act of Union brought the English law of primogeniture to Wales in 1536, commentators writing nearly a hundred years later could still notice the effect that partibility had on the pattern of landholding in the principality.

These, then, were some of the characteristics that gave medieval Welsh society an identity of its own despite the all too apparent political disunity. Every so often, however, that disunity would be overcome by the appearance of a leader sufficiently powerful to command the loyalty of all the Welsh peoples. Rhys ap Gruffydd in the later twelfth century was one such prince; Llewellyn the Great of Gwynedd in the early thirteenth was another. Llewellyn was an impressive figure. Taking advantage of the civil war in England at the end of John's reign, he succeeded in extending his rule throughout central and southern Wales. But his success, like that of earlier rulers, proved ephemeral. After his death in 1240 Welsh unity crumbled, and with the Treaty of Montgomery in 1247 the

English recovered the district between the Dee and the Conway known as the Four Cantrefs. But not for long. In 1256 the people of the Four Cantrefs rebelled and appealed to Llewellyn's successor as ruler of Gwynedd, Llewellyn ap Gruffydd, who was already striving to restore the dominion exercised by his forebear. Like earlier princes he was able to take advantage of civil war in England, this time between 1258 and 1265, but after the accession of Edward I (q.v.) in 1272 he had to face a masterful king determined to enforce his overlordship in North Wales. Edward was provided with an excuse for intervention when Llewellyn's brother Dafydd took shelter in England following an unsuccessful bid for power in the principality. In 1277 what is known as the First Welsh War broke out, and Edward recovered two of the Four Cantrefs. Five years later with the Second Welsh War he ended Welsh independence altogether. When next there was a prince of Wales, in 1301, it was not a native princeling but the heir to the English throne.

The conquest of Gwynedd was very different, as we have seen, from the conquest of Glamorgan. It was an act of state. The castles built in the south were privately held. The castles built to encircle Snowdonia were the king's. On the other hand, the techniques used to perpetuate and entrench English rule were much the same. Colonists were established on lands forfeited by the Welsh and new towns were founded. In Wales towns were in fact largely, though not wholly, Anglo-Norman creations. Back in the reign of Henry I the native population had been expelled from Pembroke to make way for Flemish settlers. Again, in the reign of Edward I plantation boroughs were established regardless of the disruption caused to any existing community, be it a Welsh town as at Beaumaris or an abbey as at Conway. At Beaumaris Edward even went so far as to fine a doctor and more than thirty others for unreasonable delay in getting out.

Although there is considerable evidence for what has been termed easy collaboration between English and Welsh in the fourteenth century, the ruthlessness with which the Edwardian settlement was carried out contributed to an undercurrent of anti-English sentiment. The racial distinction between English and Welsh was one of the striking characteristics of late medieval Wales. The new administration recruited most of its senior officials from people of English descent. The lower ranks were staffed by Welshmen; but a Welsh gentleman observing that between 1284 and 1343 not one of the justiciars or chamberlains of North Wales was of his own nationality would be right to conclude that the channels of promotion were effectively blocked. If there was little outward expression of discontent, apart from some attacks on English officials and burgesses in the 1340s, it seems likely that hostility towards English domination was the mainspring of Glyn Dwr's rebellion in the early fifteenth century.

Owain Glyn Dwr (q.v.) was a well-to-do squire whose estates in north-east Wales lay close to those of Reginald Lord Grey of Ruthin. In 1400 a bitter dispute broke out between the two men, with Glyn Dwr accusing Grey of seizing some of his lands. Within a year or two this local feud had developed into a full-scale national uprising which it was to take Henry IV's government the best part of a decade to suppress. Feelings evidently ran deep, but time was a great healer. Wales was to cause no more problems for English kings in the fifteenth century.

J.E. Lloyd, *History of Wales from the Earliest Times to the Edwardian Conquest*, 2 vols, London, 1911; R.R. Davies, *Lordship and Society in the March of Wales, 1282-1400*, Oxford, 1978; R.R. Davies, *Conquest, Coexistence and Change. Wales, 1063-1415*, Oxford, 1987.

WARDROBE
See GOVERNMENT

WARDSHIP
If a feudal tenant died leaving an heir under age, custody of the heir and of his inheritance passed to the lord of whom the lands were held. The lord possessed rights of 'wardship' which lasted until the heir came of age (twenty-one for a man, fourteen for a married and sixteen an unmarried girl). Wardship was one of the most valuable of all feudal perquisites because it gave a lord temporary possession of an inheritance which he could then either exploit directly or sell to the highest bidder for the duration of the minority. Abuse of the right of wardship in the reign of William II (q.v.) led Henry I (q.v.) to promise that, if granted away, wardships should be given to the widow or next-of-kin of the deceased tenant. Even so both the king and his barons continued to exploit wardships that came into their hands to the full, until the development in the fourteenth century of the form of trust known as the 'enfeoffment to us' provided a legal means whereby this unfortunate consequence of a minority could be avoided.

See also FEUDALISM

WARWICK 'THE KINGMAKER'
See NEVILLE, RICHARD

WHITTINGTON, RICHARD
The legend of Dick Whittington and his cat has just enough grounding in fact to give it a ring of truth. According to the nursery story, Dick left home to make his fortune in London. He found employment as a kitchen scullion in the house of a merchant whose ships plied the route between England and the Barbary coast. On one occasion, the merchant asked his servants if they would each

like to contribute some object or possession that would bring good luck to the ship on its passage. Dick gave his cat. When the ship arrived at its destination, the sultan took particular delight in the cat, because it would rid his palace of its mice and vermin. He showed his gratitude by giving more for it than for anything else on board, and Dick was set on the road to prosperity.

As James Tait showed, the story of a cat bringing its owner a fortune is a familiar one. It need not be supposed that the Whittington yarn has any more truth in it than the others, but the notion of a poor lad made good is not so far from the truth. Dick's father was Sir William Whittington of Pauntley (Glos). Being a younger son, the boy stood little chance of inheriting the family estates. He accordingly went to London (q.v.), where he accumulated a fortune in the mercery trade. Once rich enough, he started lending, principally, it seems, to the king. Lending to the crown was a risky business because a creditor could never be sure of recovering his money, and in financial terms there was little to gain, since loans to the crown did not carry interest. What made such lending worthwhile was the access that it brought to the corridors of power, and this can be seen in Whittington's case by his appointment to Henry IV's council in 1400. Whittington's links with the court actually went further back, to Richard II's reign, when the high regard in which he was held carried him to the mayoralty for the first time: Adam Bamme, the mayor of 1397, had died during his term of office and the king appointed Whittington to take his place until the next election. As it happened, he was then elected for the following year. Whittington served as mayor twice more, in 1406-7 and 1419-20, and as an MP in 1416.

While the public career of this successful mercer can be traced in some detail, his character and personality remain elusive. Whittington's will is an enigmatic document. Wills can often be long and informative, but Whittington's is not. In a sense, what is omitted is of more interest than what is included. Whittington made no bequests to any of his relatives, friends or servants. His elder brother Robert, by now lord of Pauntley, was still alive, but he was given nothing. Richard was in touch with Robert from time to time, but his relationship with the family in Gloucestershire was not close. Richard had become a Londoner even to the extent, unusual for a merchant, of keeping his fortune in liquid capital rather than choosing to invest it in a country estate. A possible reason for this was his lack of children by his marriage to Alice, daughter of Sir Ivo Fitzwaryn. Alice died before 1414, and Richard did not marry again. He used much of his fortune to found a college of priests at the church of St Michael, Paternoster Royal, and almshouses for thirteen poor men and women. He died in 1423, and was buried in St Michael's.

C. Barron, 'Richard Whittington: the Man behind the Myth', in *Studies in London History presented to P. E. Jones*, ed. A.E.J. Hollaender and W. Kellaway, London, 1969.

WILLIAM I

The twin disadvantages of illegitimate birth and the early loss of his father condemned William to an uncertain and unpromising start in life. Yet, despite the difficulties that lay in his path, he made himself one of the most powerful rulers in the Europe of his day.

William was born at Falaise, probably in 1028, the bastard son of Robert I, duke of Normandy, and Herleve, a tanner's daughter. Though illegitimate, he was allowed to succeed to the duchy in 1035, after his father had died on the way back from the Holy Land. In the Middle Ages royal minorities were often accompanied by a collapse in public order, and this one was no exception. Normandy (q.v.) lapsed into a civil war that was to last the better part of ten years. The chaos ended in 1047 when William's feudal overlord, King Henry I of France, intervened on his behalf and defeated the rebels at the battle of Val-es-Dunes. But if the French king did not want Normandy to descend into anarchy, neither did he want it to become a state which would overshadow his own. So, once William's authority was restored, he switched his support to Geoffrey, count of Anjou, whom he joined in an attack on Normandy that ended humiliatingly in their joint defeat at Mortemer in February 1054. William was at last free from danger, both internal and external. Indeed, nine years later, after Henry and Geoffrey had passed from the scene, he was able to carry the war into the enemy camp by occupying Maine, the buffer state which separated Normandy from Anjou. The security which this gave him on his southern border was important in allowing him to depart for England in 1066.

The nature of William's claim to the English throne is a subject which has given rise to much debate. According to Norman sources, in 1051 he was given a promise of the succession by the childless King Edward the Confessor, whose action seems to have provoked his over-mighty subjects, the Godwin family, into open rebellion. Godwin, earl of Wessex, and his sons, Harold among them, fled from England, but their triumphant return in the following year made Edward's promise to William worthless. Matters rested thus until about 1064, when Harold made the visit to Normandy depicted on the Bayeux Tapestry (q.v.). Just why Harold crossed the Channel – if he did so at all – will never be known. The Tapestry simply tells us that he was shipwrecked on the coast of Ponthieu, and that he was transferred to the keeping of Duke William, whose vassal he became in the course of their expedition against the count of Brittany. After returning to Normandy, Harold swore an oath of allegiance to William, which may have included some obligation to uphold the latter's interests at the English court. But after King Edward's death on 5 January 1066 Harold seized the throne, and was crowned the following day. William decided to challenge Harold's possession of the throne and having obtained papal support he assembled a fleet on the Norman coast. He was prevented from sailing as planned in September by the same northerly winds that brought the other claimant, Harold Hardrada, king of Norway, from Scandinavia to the Yorkshire coast. It was in fact while Harold was in the north, defeating the Norwegians at Stamford Bridge (25 September) that William landed on the Sussex coast at Pevensey (28 September). Harold marched south again, pausing only at London before he advanced to meet the Normans on a hill on the edge of the Weald, some six miles north of Hastings (q.v.). In the battle that followed (14 October) William emerged as king of England. He was crowned on Christmas Day in Westminster Abbey.

The new king's immediate task was to turn the victory at Hastings into the conquest and settlement of England. Here William was fortunate in the support which he received from a tightly knit, if aggressive, Norman nobility whom he amply rewarded with estates in England, granted in return for the performance of military service. This was the system generally known as feudalism (q.v.). The knights whom his tenants-in-chief provided were in constant demand, both in England to crush rebellions in 1068, 1069 and 1070 and across the Channel to recover the city of Le Mans, which had rebelled against Norman rule in 1069. Nor was William ever to be entirely free from the fear that another attack might be launched on England from Scandinavia. Cnut of Denmark was planning just such an attempt in 1086 before he was assassinated.

While William was in England, his wife Matilda carried on the government of Normandy, and discharged her duties ably. William, however, was to be disappointed by his sons. In his final years William was troubled by rebellions led by his eldest son, Robert, which were the more dangerous for bringing together the discontented Norman barons in alliance with Philip I, king of France. It was to cope with the threat from France that William embarked on a campaign in August 1087 which was to be his last. He was thrown from his horse in the town of Mantes, sustaining injuries from which he died at Rouen on 9 September. His body was interred in the abbey of St Stephen which he had founded at Caen.

William I was one of the outstanding rulers of his age. His reign coincided with the most creative and expansionist period in Norman history, when Norman ambitions found expression not only in the conquest of England but also in the foundation of the kingdom of Sicily. The battle of Hastings (q.v.) changed the course of English history because it brought about the formation of a cross-Channel dominion over which William ruled as king-duke. The link between England and Normandy was only to be ended for good in 1204.

D.C. Douglas, *William the Conqueror*, 2nd ed., New Haven and London, 1999; D. Bates, *William the Conqueror*, 2nd ed., London, 2003.

WILLIAM II

The second of the Norman kings, known to history as 'Rufus' from his ruddy complexion, was a man criticized by the English chroniclers for his oppressiveness, but regarded more highly by the Anglo-Norman knightly class whom he rewarded well.

Rufus, his father's second son, succeeded the Conqueror in England on his death in September 1087, while his elder brother Robert succeeded him in Normandy. In his youth the new king had been taught by the great Lanfranc (q.v.), later Archbishop of Canterbury. Rufus turned out to be no friend

of ecclesiastical privilege, however. After Lanfranc died in 1089, he kept the see of Canterbury (q.v.) vacant for four years until 1093 when he lay ill, on the point of death as he thought, and fear compelled him to agree to the appointment of the saintly Anselm (q.v.). He recovered, and probably regretted his decision. He and Anselm soon quarrelled. In November 1097 the latter went abroad, where he remained till the accession of Henry I in 1100. The voluntary exile of his archbishop was a hindrance for Rufus from the public relations standpoint, but no more, since it provided him with the chance to seize the revenues of Canterbury for the rest of his reign.

The reason for his need for money was the need to pay for military activity both at home and in Normandy. The division of the Conqueror's dominions had satisfied none of the sons. William wanted to recover Normandy and Robert, rather more half-heartedly, to win England. Thus there was bound to be conflict between the two. Within a year of his accession Rufus was faced with the first rebellion mounted by those who supported Duke Robert's cause in England. The prime mover of the revolt was Odo, bishop of Bayeux and earl of Kent, a shifty character who operated more in his own interests than in those of any nominal superior. The rebellion, though failing to win much support from Robert himself, detained Rufus in sieges at Pevensey, Tonbridge and finally Rochester, where Odo gave himself up. The next rising came in 1095, when Robert de Mowbray, earl of Northumberland, and his supporters tried to replace the king. Once again they failed. This was to be the last rebellion which Rufus faced in England. Although such disaffection was inconvenient, it did not prevent him from taking the conflict into the enemy camp. In 1091 he crossed the Channel, and support for Robert melted away, forcing the latter to make a settlement granting his brother considerable lands in the duchy.

Ironically, when Rufus did finally reunite Normandy with England, this outcome came not by force of arms but by purchase. In 1096 Robert decided to join the First Crusade (q.v.). To equip his army he needed money, and he therefore pawned the duchy to his brother for 10,000 marks of silver. By 1097 Normandy was in Rufus's hands.

William Rufus is today less famous for his achievements in his lifetime than for the manner of his death. On 2 August 1100 he was hit by an arrow while engaging in his favourite pursuit – hunting – in the New Forest. It is unclear whether his death was an accident or an act of assassination. On hearing the news, his younger brother Henry (q.v.) immediately rushed to Winchester to be acclaimed king.

Rufus, it is said, was mourned only by his mercenaries. His body was dumped on a cart and carried to Winchester, where it was buried without ceremony under the central tower of the cathedral. Seven years later the tower collapsed, and the monks interpreted the event as God's judgement on them for accepting so notorious an enemy of Christ and his Church; in fact, the cathedral's faulty foundations were more likely to blame. Rufus's court certainly had an unsavoury reputation. Rufus never married and, unlike his younger brother Henry, he sired no bastards – shreds of evidence that suggest he may have been homosexual. He was not a bad king, however, in the sense of being ineffective. His subjects must have thought him all too effective. His rule was predatory. He took much in taxation, particularly from the Church. It was for this reason that he was regarded unfavourably by the chroniclers. With his knights and courtiers he was highly popular.

The tomb in Winchester Cathedral which used to be thought his is now considered to be that of Bishop Henry de Blois.

F. Barlow, *William Rufus*, 2nd ed., New Haven and London, 2000.

WINDSOR

Windsor Castle is one of the oldest royal residences in England. Before 1066 the Saxon kings had had a hunting lodge on a low-lying site at Old Windsor nearby, but William the Conqueror chose to construct a new fortification on a hilltop site to the west: present-day New Windsor. The Conqueror's layout, which governs the plan of the thirteen-acre castle, was a variant of the motte and bailey scheme. In the centre was a motte crowned by a shell keep but instead of the usual single bailey there were two, the present Upper and Lower Wards. For the next two centuries there was little to distinguish Windsor from any other royal castle periodically visited by the king. The process of converting it into a much grander fabric was begun by Henry II. Henry rebuilt the Round Tower on the motte and replaced the wooden walls of the Upper Ward with stone (c.1165–7). His grandson Henry III substantially rebuilt the Lower Ward apartments. The real turning-point in the castle's history, however, came with Edward III's foundation of the Order of the Garter in c.1348, in connection with which the chapel in the Lower Ward was rebuilt and rededicated to St George, the patron saint of the new order. Edward III not only inaugurated the long connection between Windsor and the nation's oldest order of chivalry; he also turned the castle into one of the most luxurious palaces of its day, commissioning a fine set of state apartments in the Upper Ward. St George's Chapel in its present form is primarily a work of the later fifteenth and early sixteenth centuries. The rebuilding process was initiated by Edward IV, who envisaged the chapel as a Yorkist mausoleum, but work was completed under Henry VII by Sir Reginald Bray KG, whose badge, the 'hemptray', is much in evidence in the nave. The master masons, or architects, employed on the chapel were Henry Janyns and William Vertue. Edward IV himself was the first king to be buried there.

See also CASTLES

WORCESTER, WILLIAM

Worcester was the effective founder of the distinguished English tradition of local antiquarian and topographical study. He was born at Bristol in the 1420s and was educated at Oxford, probably residing at Hart Hall, now Hertford College. By 1438 he had passed into the service of the elderly and by now irascible Norfolk knight Sir John Fastolf (q.v.) of Caister Castle. After Fastolf's death in 1459 he complained that he had spent ten years of his life ministering night and day to his invalid master and was yet ill-rewarded for his service. No provision was made for Worcester in Fastolf's will, despite the fact that he had a wife and family to support. Although Worcester was quick to criticize his late master, he worked hard after his death to ensure that the terms of the will were carried out when they were challenged by the duke of Norfolk. Only with reluctance did he agree to abandon the struggle in 1470 when he accepted a settlement of the debts still owing to him in return for allowing the Archbishop of Canterbury to transfer administration of the estate to Bishop Wainfleet of Winchester.

During his years in Fastolf's service Worcester made many journeys around England on his employer's behalf in the course of which he was able to pursue his topographical interests. Subsequently, in retirement he embarked on a long trip to St Michael's Mount which he had meant to undertake for some years. As usual he took his notebook with him and jotted down details about the places he passed through and the churches he looked at. He may have intended eventually to write the notes up in a finished version; but when he died in 1482 it was only the notes that he left. Though he is remembered today chiefly for his topographical collections, Worcester was a man of wide interests, and astronomy, heraldry and natural history were just some of the subjects that engaged him.

See also PASTON LETTERS

K.B. McFarlane, 'William Worcester: A Preliminary Survey', in his *England in the Fifteenth Century*, London, 1981; *The Itineraries of William Worcestre*, ed. J.H. Harvey, London, 1969.

WYCLIFFE, JOHN

An academic turned controversialist, Wycliffe was the man from whom the Lollard (q.v.) movement derived its philosophy and inspiration.

Wycliffe was probably born in Yorkshire around 1330 but the first we hear of him is at Oxford (q.v.), where he became a Fellow of Merton in 1356. Four years later, in 1361, he was elected Master of Balliol. In the medieval period, academic appointments of this sort were valued mainly as stepping stones to ecclesiastical preferment, and when the Balliol living of Fillingham (Lincs) came up in 1361, Wycliffe took it. It was not his intention, however, to leave Oxford for good. Within two years he had returned, taking lodgings at Queen's, a college which had accommodation to spare. His benefice at Fillingham, which was a valuable one worth £20 a year, gave him the means to live on at the university. Cash-flow problems, however, forced him to exchange it for the less lucrative living of Ludgershall (Bucks) in 1368; by this time he had also acquired a valuable prebend in the collegiate church of Westbury-on-Trym (Glos). As various of his critics have pointed out, Wycliffe, like many other medieval scholars, was an absentee pluralist. Absenteeism was the inevitable price which the Church had to pay if its clergy were to be given the opportunity to study at university. Nonetheless, it does seem hypocritical of Wycliffe to practise the very abuses he was so ready to criticize in others; to judge from his writings, however, he seems never to have been conscious of the inconsistency.

By the 1370s Wycliffe's intellectual distinction and polemical skills had brought him to the attention of the king's government, which at the time was seeking to launch an attack on the 'possessioners', the great property-holders in the Church. Since the reopening of the war with France in 1369, the English had been on the defensive, and the absence of any victories in the field made the Commons in parliament (q.v.) reluctant to make grants of taxation (q.v.). If further wealth were to be tapped to pay for the war effort, the Church was the obvious target. In the closing years of Edward III's reign, therefore, the anticlerical party at court, led by John of Gaunt, duke of Lancaster (q.v.), made use of Wycliffe's pen to launch an attack on papal supremacy and clerical immunity from taxation.

Wycliffe proved a willing ally of the government because the latter's policy accorded with his own views. He was specifically asked to justify releasing the secular state from any subordination to the authority of the Church. This he did by a consideration of the related questions of dominion and grace. It was generally agreed that 'dominion' or lordship had been instituted over society by God, but beyond that opinions differed. According to the extreme papal theorists, like Giles of Rome, lordship was bestowed by God on secular rulers through the mediation of the Church. But others disputed this. According to the Franciscans, the exercise of lordship was dependent upon being in a state of grace, a quality which the Church could never attain until it had divested itself of its worldly wealth. Wycliffe was fully in agreement with such reasoning; and he went on to claim that an anointed king had a divine mandate to undertake the reform of the Church within his own realm. These arguments were precisely what John of Gaunt wanted to hear, and predictably they drew a counterattack from the Church. Wycliffe was summoned to appear before William Courtenay, bishop of London, in St Paul's on 19 February 1377, but the meeting broke up in disorder before his teaching could be condemned.

Had Wycliffe contented himself with scourging the possessioners and attacking papal supremacy, he would have been regarded as an inconvenient polemicist but no more. After 1379, however, he started to question some of the most fundamental assumptions of the Catholic Church. In the generation before his own the synthesis of reason and faith so painstakingly effected by Aquinas had come under attack from William of Ockham (q.v.), a distinguished Oxford philosopher. Ockham and the nominalists argued that men's knowledge was confined to what they could understand by direct experience. Men could not therefore know God's will and the workings of grace; they were free agents to a greater extent than Catholic theology had previously allowed. So radical a departure provoked a strong reply from Thomas Bradwardine, who took the predestinarian position of St Augustine as his point of departure. God, he said, has the capacity of foreknowing everything. Wycliffe went further still: God alone knows who are the elect. He then drew the conclusion that the Church was composed only of the elect, who might or might not include the priests. In that case there was little point in trusting the clergy, least of all his former allies, the friars. These arguments supported his own largely instinctive belief that the doctrine of transubstantiation was a trick, perpetrated by the Church, and devoid of support in the Gospels. The sole authority for the Christian religion was the Bible, which he accordingly thought should be made available to all in English.

In the last years of his life religious tracts poured forth from his pen in abundance. Wycliffe was past bothering what the consequences of his writings would be. In the spring of 1381 he appears to have left Oxford for the obscurity of the rectory of Lutterworth, to which he had been presented back in 1374. There he remained until his death on 31 December 1384. Partly because of the exalted patronage he had enjoyed in the past, and partly because the beginning of the Great Schism in 1378 had weakened the power of the Church, he escaped excommunication in his lifetime. But Courtenay, who was promoted to Canterbury in 1382, lost no time in eradicating the unsound ideas which had grown up in the University of Oxford. Wycliffe's ideas were condemned (though his own name was never mentioned) at a meeting at Blackfriars, London, in May 1382, known from the event which marked its last day as the Earthquake Council. In November 1382 Courtenay took the dramatic step of holding the next meeting of the Canterbury Convocation at Oxford to enforce the Blackfriars decrees and root out the heretics. Henceforth the Lollards, as Wycliffe's followers were known, were drawn mainly from the humbler ranks of the clergy and not, as they had been, from the lecture schools of Oxford.

Wycliffe himself was an intellectual, and a dogmatist at that; and though he was interested in politics, he was no politician. He got carried along by the force of his own eloquence, far beyond the limits to which his patrons would back him. Yet he never troubled to institutionalize himself. So consistent was he in his opposition to sects that he did little to encourage the one that grew up to propagate his own doctrines.

K.B. McFarlane, *John Wycliffe and the Beginnings of English Nonconformity*, London, 1952; A. Kenny, *Wyclif*, Oxford, 1985.

WYKEHAM, WILLIAM OF

Wykeham was one of medieval England's most important bishops and a generous educational benefactor.

Wykeham took his name from the village of Wickham (Hants), where he was born. He was of humble, although not necessarily unfree, extraction and through the generosity of a local knight was given an education in Winchester which enabled him to enter the service of the crown. At the instance, it appears, of Bishop Edington of Winchester, the chancellor, he was given charge of the king's works at Windsor Castle (q.v.). This appointment gave him responsibility for the building operations at a time when Edward III (q.v.) was transforming the castle into the 'Versailles of its day'. The efficiency with which Wykeham discharged his duties marked him out for rapid promotion; in 1364 he was made keeper of the privy seal and in 1367, chancellor. 'Everything was done through him, and without him was nothing done', as Froissart put it. In the year that he became chancellor he was rewarded with promotion to the wealthy diocese of Winchester.

Wykeham's experience in government planted in his mind the idea of founding a series of educational establishments which would provide skilled clergy to serve Church and state. The establishments were to be Winchester College, a school for seventy pupils, and New College, Oxford, which was to support the same number of students recruited from Winchester. Wykeham's plan for a college in Oxford (q.v.) owed much to founders and benefactors before him, notably Walter de Merton, but in linking the college with a school in Winchester, he was setting an example which King Henry VI (q.v.) was to follow in the next century when he endowed Eton and King's College, Cambridge.

It took well over a decade for Wykeham's plans for New College to come to fruition. One reason for the lengthy delay was the difficulties that his political career ran into. In 1371 complaints about the predominance of churchmen among the king's ministers led to his dismissal from office and replacement by a lay chancellor, Sir Robert Thorp. But Thorp and his associates could do no more than Wykeham to halt the slow erosion of Edward III's conquests in France, and at the Good

Parliament of 1376 they in their turn were dismissed, and Wykeham recalled to office. This was hardly to the liking of John of Gaunt (q.v.), who distrusted the clerical party, and once parliament was dissolved he sought to humiliate Wykeham by bringing charges of corruption against him. The timely death of Edward III in June 1377 brought the bishop's sufferings to an end, and in the reign of Edward's grandson and successor Richard II he was able to resume unhindered his work on the two colleges.

From 1389 till 1391 Wykeham once again held the great seal, but in his closing years he retired from active politics to pick up the task, begun by his predecessor, of rebuilding the nave of Winchester Cathedral. His master mason was the ever faithful William Wynford (q.v.), whom he had engaged to design his colleges. Wykeham died on 27 September 1404. He was buried at Winchester in the chantry chapel on the south side of the nave which he refers to in his will as 'lately built by me'. At the foot of his effigy are three mischievous-looking clerks kneeling at prayer – one of the most attractive touches in English medieval sculpture.

See also SCHOOLS; UNIVERSITIES

G.H. Moberley, *Life of William of Wykeham*, 2nd ed., London, 1893.

WYNFORD, WILLIAM

Wynford was one of a distinguished generation of 'master masons', or architects, in the later fourteenth century,. He was probably born at Winford (Somerset). By 1360 he was employed at Windsor Castle (q.v.) on Edward III's ambitious programme of rebuilding there. Since he is referred to by this time as a 'master' (i.e. master mason), he may be credited with conceiving the novel layout of rooms there: he placed the chapel and hall end-to-end so as to fill up an entire range, an idea he was to use again at Winchester and New College. It was at Windsor that he first worked with William of Wykeham (q.v.), later bishop of Winchester, who was to be his principal patron and employer for the rest of his life. The educational foundations which Wykeham conceived at Winchester and at Oxford offered exciting opportunities for a mason like Wynford, then at the height of his powers. The two colleges were in process of construction simultaneously and show many similarities, but the plan of Winchester, based as it is on two quadrangles not one, represents an improvement on New College. In the east window of Winchester College Chapel, Wynford is shown kneeling at prayer alongside Hugh Herland (q.v.), the carpenter, and Simon de Membury, the clerk of the works, both of whom he would have known.

Before these commissions were completed, Wykeham asked Wynford to undertake the remodelling of the nave of Winchester Cathedral. Rather than demolish the old Norman structure, Wynford chose to preserve it, reshaping the pillars in the latest style and crowning them with a stone vault that seems to leap upwards into the sky. This composition begs comparison with the contemporary nave at Canterbury (q.v.), attributed to Henry Yevele (q.v.), and it is hard to judge between them. Each in its own way is a masterpiece, and utterly characteristic of its creator. Wynford died in about 1403, only a few years after Yevele.

See also ARCHITECTURE, ECCLESIASTICAL

J.H. Harvey, *English Medieval Architects. A Biographical Dictionary down to 1550*, 2nd ed., Gloucester, 1984.

YEVELE, HENRY

Henry Yevele was the most talented, and probably the most widely employed, master mason of later medieval England. Among his outstanding works were the naves of Canterbury Cathedral and Westminster Abbey.

Yevele was probably the son of one Roger de Yevele of Uttoxeter (Staffs). The Yevele family may have been involved in the masonry business, as Uttoxeter is very close to the alabaster-quarrying districts of Tutbury and Chellaston. By 1353 Henry had moved to London. On 3 December that year he was admitted to the freedom of the City of London and within two years was among the leaders of his craft in the capital. In 1357 he was probably appointed chief mason to the Black Prince (q.v.), for whom he agreed to undertake works at Kennington manor. In June 1360 he was appointed disposer of the king's works of masonry at the Palace of Westminster and the Tower of London. This appointment gave him a general responsibility for the king's works in the south of England, and it is likely that he was responsible for designing the remarkable new circular castle at Queenborough, Kent, which dates from this time. By the 1370s he was advising a wide range of clients on building and design matters. In 1371 Sir Walter Mauny engaged him to design the cells and cloister of the new London Charterhouse. Later in the same decade he became consultant mason to Westminster Abbey, where he was charged with designing a new nave. Around 1380 he was given a variety of commissions by John, Lord Cobham – notably the provision of a set of furnishings for Cobham church and the building of Cobham College and Cooling Castle. A year or two later he was involved in the building of the West Gate at Canterbury. In the 1390s, the final decade of his life, he was engaged on the two largest and most prestigious projects of his career – the nave of Canterbury Cathedral, and the new Westminster Hall, for which his carpenter associate, Hugh Herland (q.v.) provided the great hammer-beam roof.

Yevele died on 21 August 1400, aged around eighty. He left his property to his wife Katherine; presumably he had no son.

For the last twenty years of his life Yevele presided over a very extensive business empire. Not only was he engaged in the design of buildings and the supply of materials to sites; he was also producing tombs, screens (notably the Neville screen at Durham) and other church fittings. In his will Yevele made passing mention of all his 'marble and latten goods and tools' – a phrase which suggests that he was also engraving brasses. The question has been raised whether Yevele could possibly have designed all the buildings with which he has been associated. A.D. McLees has suggested that he was more of an entrepreneur than an architect – someone whose main responsibility was supervising labourers and contracting for materials – and adds that Yevele was only retained as a consultant at Canterbury in 1398, some nineteen years after work on the nave had commenced. McLees's sceptical observations are probably without foundation. There can be no doubting Yevele's responsibility for the nave of Westminster, because payments to him are recorded in the abbey accounts, and the Canterbury nave must also be his work because the moulding profiles throughout are almost identical to those at Westminster. Yevele's buildings, besides, exhibit a common aesthetic and style. Yevele had a liking for plain ashlar surfaces relieved with the minimum of ornament. He veered to the lean, elegant and economical. Yet he had a sense of the sublime. The Canterbury nave exhibits his style to perfection: it is tall, spacious and ethereal. Without doubt, Yevele was one of the great masons of the age.

See also ARCHITECTURE, ECCLESIASTICAL; BRASSES; TOMBS; WYNFORD, WILLIAM

J.H. Harvey, *English Medieval Architects. A Biographical Dictionary down to 1550*, 2nd ed., Gloucester, 1984; A.D. McLees, 'Henry Yevele: Disposer of the King's Works of Masonry', *Journal of the British Archaeological Assoc.*, 3rd series, 36 (1973).

YORK

In the narrow, winding streets of York the appearance of a late medieval town can be recaptured better than anywhere else in England. The survival of this remarkable fabric is due largely to the post-medieval decline of the city, which left it without the means for ambitious rebuilding until the coming of the railway in the nineteenth century.

The physical character of the medieval city is best savoured in The Shambles, once the centre of the meat trade, where one irregular storey overhangs another until the two sides of the street almost meet each other at roof level. York is fortunate, too, in that like Chester it retains its circuit of walls. From the stretch south of the river, by the railway station, an excellent prospect can be gained over the city skyline. The view is dominated today, as it was in the Middle Ages, by the towers of the Minster; the city churches, never as lofty or ambitious as those of Norwich, hardly manage to peep above the uneven rooftops. Like the Minster, however, they have been fortunate in retaining a large collection of medieval stained glass (q.v.) windows, those at All Saints, North Street, being the best.

The architectural importance of York is matched by the wealth of its historical associations. In the late ninth century York became the centre of a Danish kingdom in the north. To the Danes it was Jorvik, from which the present name is derived. Even after this separate kingdom was extinguished in 954, the city remained the unacknowledged capital of the north for the rest of the Middle Ages and beyond, and when Edward III reopened the war against the Scots in the 1330s he made it the seat of his government.

York was also of course the seat of the northern primate of the Church in England. Its archbishops figure less prominently in history, perhaps, than the Archbishops of Canterbury, but all the same they were great public figures who often found themselves drawn away from their province by the demands of government business. The men who were responsible for the day-to-day running of the Minster were the dean and canons. It was they who had to organize, and raise money for, the long programme of rebuilding between 1220 and 1472 which was to make the Minster the largest medieval church in England. Its spaciousness and its splendid collection of glass make it one of the great churches of the world.

The Noble City of York, ed. A. Stacpoole, York, 1972; *A History of York Minster*, ed. G.E. Aylmer and R. Cant, Oxford, 1977.

APPENDIX I

KINGS OF ENGLAND

1066–1485

William I	1066–1087
William II	1087–1100
Henry I	1100–1135
Stephen	1135–1154
Henry II	1154–1189
Richard I	1189–1199
John	1199–1216
Henry III	1216–1272
Edward I	1272–1307
Edward II	1307–1327
Edward III	1327–1377
Richard II	1377–1399
Henry IV	1399–1413
Henry V	1413–1422
Henry VI	1422–1461, 1470–1471
Edward IV	1461–1483
Edward V	April–June 1483
Richard III	1483–1485

APPENDIX II

ARCHBISHOPS OF CANTERBURY

1070–1500

The first date given is the year of consecration, not of appointment.

Lanfranc	1070–1089	Simon Meopham	1328–1333
Anselm	1093–1109	John Stratford	1333–1348
Ralph d'Escures	1114–1122	Thomas Bradwardine	1348
William of Corbeil	1123–1136	Simon Islip	1349–1366
Theobald of Bec	1139–1161	Simon Langham	1366–1368
Thomas Becket	1162–1170	William Whittlesey	1368–1374
Richard of Dover	1174–1184	Simon Sudbury	1375–1381
Baldwin	1184–1190	William Courtenay	1381–1396
Hubert Walter	1193–1205	Thomas Arundel	1396–1397
Stephen Langton	1207–1228	Roger Walden	1397–1399
Richard Grant	1229–1231	Thomas Arundel	1399–1414
Edmund Rich	1234–1240	Henry Chichele	1414–1443
Boniface of Savoy	1245–1270	John Stafford	1443–1452
Robert Kilwardby	1273–1278	John Kemp	1452–1454
John Pecham	1279–1292	Thomas Bourchier	1454–1486
Robert Winchelsey	1294–1313	John Morton	1486–1500
Walter Reynolds	1313–1327		

APPENDIX III

THE ENGLISH ROYAL LINE

WILLIAM I–RICHARD III

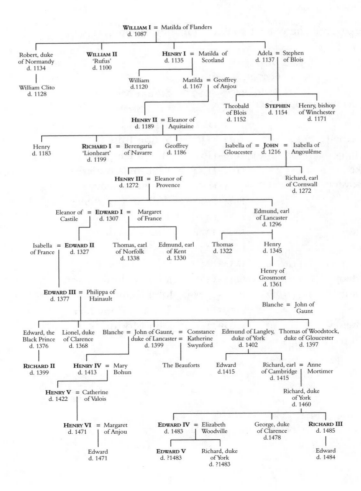

LIST OF ILLUSTRATIONS

TEMPUS REVEALING HISTORY

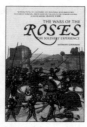

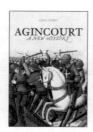

The Wars of the Roses
The Soldiers' Experience
ANTHONY GOODMAN
'Sheds light on the lot of the common soldier as never before' *Alison Weir*
£25
0 7524 1784 3

The Vikings
MAGNUS MAGUNSSON
'Serious, engaging history'
BBC History Magazine
£9.99
0 7524 2699 0

William the Conqueror
DAVID BATES
'As expertly woven as the Bayeux Tapestry'
BBC History Magazine
£12.99
0 7524 2960 4

Agincourt: A New History
ANNE CURRY
'Overturns a host of assumptions about this most famous of English victories... *the* book on the battle' *Richard Holmes*
£25
0 7524 2828 4

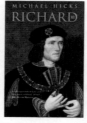

Hereward The Last Englishman
PETER REX
'An enthralling work of historical detection'
Robert Lacey
£17.99
0 7524 3318 0

Richard III
MICHAEL HICKS
'A most important book by the greatest living expert on Richard' *Desmond Seward*
£9.99
0 7524 2589 7

The English Resistance
The Underground War Against the Normans
PETER REX
'An invaluable rehabilitation of an ignored resistance movement' **The Sunday Times**
£17.99
0 7524 2827 6

The Peasants Revolt
England's Failed Revolution of 1381
ALASTAIR DUNN
'A stunningly good book... totally absorbing'
Melvyn Bragg
£9.99
0 7524 2965 5

If you are interested in purchasing other books published by Tempus, or in case you have difficulty finding any Tempus books in your local bookshop, you can also place orders directly through our website

www.tempus–publishing.com